35 YEARS ON THE JOB

Also by Patrick Campbell

AN IRISHMAN'S DIARY
A LONG DRINK OF COLD WATER
A SHORT TROT WITH A CULTURED MIND
LIFE IN THIN SLICES
PATRICK CAMPBELL'S OMNIBUS
COME HERE TILL I TELL YOU
CONSTANTLY IN PURSUIT
BREWING UP IN THE BASEMENT
HOW TO BECOME A SCRATCH GOLFER
ROUGH HUSBANDRY
ALL WAYS ON SUNDAYS
MY LIFE AND EASY TIMES (Autobiography)
A BUNCH OF NEW ROSES
THE COARSE OF EVENTS
GULLIBLE TRAVELS
THE HIGH SPEED GAS WORKS
WAVING ALL EXCUSES
PATRICK CAMPBELL'S GOLFING BOOK
FAT TUESDAY TAILS

35 YEARS ON THE JOB

The Best of Patrick Campbell
1937–1973

PATRICK CAMPBELL

BLOND & BRIGGS

For my three private furies
Vivienne, Irene and Desmond

First published 1973 by Blond & Briggs Ltd.
56 Doughty Street, London WC1

Printed in Great Britain by
The Anchor Press Ltd.,
and bound by Wm Brendon & Son Ltd.,
both of Tiptree, Essex.

SBN *85634 020 0*

Contents

Each section is devoted to various aspects of Patrick Campbell's life; within each section, the essays have been arranged, as far as possible, in chronological order.

Introduction

This year, to my surprise, I find I've been working away at keeping alive for no less than sixty years and—equally astonishingly—that for thirty-five of them I have been writing for newspapers, magazines and, if the price was right, for anyone else who wanted a bit, like film companies, television producers, distilleries and the Irish Tourist Board.

For thirty-five years, in fact, I've lived almost exactly the kind of life that I wanted, unsupported by any diploma, degree or other professional qualification, mostly by keeping well away from the many organisations that have employed me.

I have always maintained that it is vital for a writer who is a kind of journalist, or a journalist who is a sort of writer, to preserve a wide physical gap between himself and the editor for whom he is working, on the grounds that if the editor catches so much as a glimpse of him it starts off a chain reaction which almost always results in the hatchet.

Once they see you, in person, quite possibly not entirely sober after lunch, it starts them wondering if this thing here is all they've got for £70 a week and secondly—the dangerous Phase II—is this, for £70 a week, all that he does?

Next week you've got a desk and they start giving you ideas and you part, for ever, at the end of the month.

For a long, long time now I've been writing a column for one newspaper or another, fifty-two weeks in the year. (Once I asked Charles Eade, the late editor of the *Sunday Despatch,* if I could have a holiday. "A holiday," Charles said, "from what?")

Fifty-two times per year I put my column into a large, clean white envelope, mark it clearly in the top left-hand corner: COPY : URGENT, and send it off by express post. As a column its most powerful asset is the fact that it is always exactly the right length.

This diffidence about actually going to the place of work stems from my early days on the *Irish Times* in Dublin, when I was scarcely ever out of it. I began by writing short paragraphs for the Diary column, then the fourth leader as well, until one fearful day I found I was the Literary Editor also, in addition to being the film critic and, three days a week, trapped in the press gallery of Dail Eireann writing the parliamentary sketch. For this I drew down £2 17s. 6d. per week until, after endless bleatings at him in the Pearl Bar, the Editor, Bertie Smyllie, raised it to £4, advising me sternly, at the same time, about the evils of drink.

As silently as a snake sloughing off its skin, I got rid of all these jobs and finished up as the sole author of the daily column, *An Irishman's Diary,* to the rage of the other reporters who up till then having been making 10s. 6d. a time by contributing short, illiterate paragraphs to it. I myself received £6 a week for 1000 words every day except Saturday and—the most important thing of all—my own room, an attic at the top of the back stairs, furnished with one table and two hard chairs.

So far as the *Irish Times* was concerned I might just as well have been working at home, since I only appeared at six o'clock every evening to hand in my copy and run, before anyone wanted something different.

Alan Montgomery, the Chief Reporter, would receive it sadly. From time to time he would say, "But, God, it isn't a column at all—there's no names in it, no news, nothing."

One day, however, having been more or less badgered into it by Frank O'Connor, I got my first exclusive scoop—Frank's battle with the Irish Censorship Board. I was the only newspaperman in Dublin to get the full text of the correspondence. That slashing, provocative column, written in 1945, begins this book. In 1945, it caused no stir whatever. Next day I did a piece about an old man who rented barrel organs in the Coombe.

I had to wait another ten years or so for my next exclusive. It concerned the romance between Princess Margaret and Peter Townsend, both besieged in Clarence House by newspapermen from all over the world. The battle had been on for about a week when, on television, I saw a youngish man called Peter Townsend, interpreter to the stars of the Chinese National Theatre, who had just arrived in town.

Next day I went to interview him at his hotel, with some fairly carefully formulated questions on the lines of, "If the curtain goes up on this show, how do you think the public will take it?"

He gave enthusiastic answers to the first four questions, all beautifully quotable, until something seemed to warn him that all was not well, and he dried up cold, leaving me, however, with quite an amusing column for the *Sunday Dispatch,* my then employers, written of course as though I'd been talking to Group

Captain Townsend himself, and explaining only in the last paragraph about the Chinese National Theatre.

The *Dispatch* gave it the full treatment:

PATRICK CAMPBELL TALKS TO PETER TOWNSEND EXCLUSIVE! I shot a quick look at the last paragraph. Someone had removed it in its entirety!

Panic-stricken, I rang Dick Malins, the news editor, at his home. I'd scarcely announced my name before he cried, "That you, Pat? Great stuff. We all knew you'd get in there somehow. Great story—"

"Who took off the last bloody paragraph?" I enquired.

"I did," Dick said. "I thought it didn't really work." For all the difference it made to Princess Margaret or anyone else I need never, in fact, have written it at all. Next Sunday I was back on the problems attendant upon travelling only with a trunk, with one broken handle.

After thirty-five years of this sort of thing I must have written several million words, never really knowing what it was going to be about until I started, and certainly continuing in total ignorance of what the end would be until I got to it.

This book presents what are probably the easiest pieces to read of all this vast, disordered output. To get it together Desmond Briggs, a good man, read some 800,000 words, hacking away at the basic slag until he reduced it to about 100,000, and left immediately for a health farm.

Perhaps I should have joined him.

But then, if you're suddenly sixty years of age, it's probably too late.

South of the Border

THE INVISIBLE MIDNIGHT COURT

Greeted by the literary men with a hoarse cheering, and showers of manuscript flung in the air like confetti, the Censorship of Publications Appeal Board came into existence in the spring-time of this present happy year.

The idea was that the Appeal Board would hear the appeals of authors whose work had been banned by the Censorship Board.

The first appeal has now been made. The book involved is *The Midnight Court,* newly translated by Frank O'Connor from the Irish of Bryan Merryman. It is published in Dublin by Maurice Fridberg.

I shall now, with extreme accuracy, trace the course of this appeal from its hopeful beginning to its singularly abrupt conclusion.

It began with a letter addressed to "The Secretary, Censorship of Publications Appeal Board, 5 Ely Place, Dublin." The letter was dated June 25th, 1946. This is how it read :—

"Dear Sir,

"We have been consulted by Mr. Maurice Fridberg, of 27/28 Clare St., Dublin, in connection with the publication by him of a book entitled 'The Midnight Court,' described as a Rhythmical Bacchanalia from the Irish of Bryan Merryman, and translated by Frank O'Connor.

"We understand from our client that this book has now been placed on the list of banned books, and our client now desires to appeal against the decision of the Censorship of Publications Board in prohibiting the sale and distribution of this said publication.

"We enclose herewith cheque for £5, being the necessary deposit, 'together with six copies of the publication,' in compliance with the provisions of the Censorship of Publications Act, 1946. We shall be glad if you will acknowledge receipt of this letter and enclosures, and state that this letter will be treated as formal notice of appeal."

The letter was signed by Mr. Herman Good, solicitor.

It was despatched to Ely Place, and the appealing parties sat down to wait for an answer.

There was no delay. An answer came back by return of post, a swift, but somewhat peculiar-looking document.

It was written in longhand, in sky-blue ink. At the top of the page a number of erasures had been made—the printed words, "Censorship of Publications Board," in Irish and English, being crossed out heavily, and the words substituted, in longhand : "Censorship of Publications Appeal Board." The Appeal Board seemed to be short of official notepaper.

This is how the letter read : "I am to acknowledge receipt of your appeal (HW/PH, of 25th instant) on behalf of the publisher, Mr. Maurice Fridberg, of 27/28 Clare Street, Dublin, against the prohibition order at present in force against the translation by Frank O'Connor of the book, 'The Midnight Court,' by Bryan Merryman, together with 6 (six) copies of the aforesaid publication, and the statutory appeal deposit of £5 (five pounds) per your cheque, and to inform you that the matter will have the early attention of the Appeal Board.

"Pending the publication for sale of the official appeal form, the Board has decided to accept informal applications of the type of your communication."

This letter was signed, in black ink and a different hand-writing, "B. MacMahon, Runaidhe."

In view of the sky-blue ink, and black ink, and the longhand, and the erasures, it would seem that the Board's own communications were of a fairly informal nature, too. One was also left with the hope that the man who wrote the letter had the strength left, again in longhand, to make a copy of it.

After this the appealing parties heard no more of the matter for nearly a fortnight. They filled in the time with the preparation of their case, in consultation with senior counsel.

Then a letter arrived dated July 10th, 1946. It was on the same notepaper as before, but this time only the English version, "Censorship of Publications Board" had been crossed out and "Censorship of Publications Appeal Board" substituted in ink in its place. The Irish version remained undisturbed.

This letter, however, was typewritten—the Appeal Board apparently having been able to borrow a machine in the interval. This is what it said :—

"I am directed by the Minister for Justice"—then, "Minister for

Justice" was crossed out, and the word "Board," written in above it—"to inform you that, at a meeting held on the 9th instant, your appeal, lodged on behalf of your client, Mr. Maurice Fridberg, of 27/28 Clare Street, Dublin, publisher of the book, 'The Midnight Court,' as translated from the Irish of Bryan Merriman by Frank O'Connor, from the Prohibition Order in force against the said publication, was dismissed.

"The Board, however, directed the refund of the deposit lodged by you on behalf of your client, and, accordingly, I enclose herewith a pay order, made out in your favour, to the amount of £5 (five pounds), as provided by Section 12(e) of the Censorship of Publications Act, 1946."

This letter was signed, as before, "B. MacMahon." A pay order for £5 (five pounds) was enclosed.

It would be no exaggeration to say that the appealing parties were taken aback by this communication.

It surprised them to learn that their appeal had been heard already. They wondered who spoke on their behalf and what he said and if he was defending the right book.

They felt they would like to know how many members of the Appeal Board were present while the matter was under discussion and if they all paid attention to the argument.

They felt, too, that it would be nice to know whether a vote was taken at the end and who voted for what and why. And, when they came later to examine this aspect of the situation, they wondered what they were doing with a solicitor, Senior Counsel and a case of their own when they never even got as far as the halldoor of No. 5 Ely Place.

I cannot see what they are complaining about. The processes of the law are known to be exceptionally expensive and tedious for those involved in them. This new system, however, as inaugurated by the Censorship of Publications Appeal Board, effects an enormous saving in time, money and nervous strain.

You merely wait in the cells while your case is going on and then the warder comes in and tells you what happened. "Sorry, pal," he says, "you weren't too good in the box—ten years."

Always provided, of course, that the warder remembers you're there and still interested.

THE LORD AND FAMILY

My mother said to me on the telephone from Dublin, "I don't want to talk too loudly because I think he can hear me, but you'd better come over. He had a bad night and he's very feeble."

I said I'd come at once.

I found I was neither shocked nor sad, but only excited. My father, Lord Glenavy, was going to die. It would be an event of some importance in Dublin and I, as the inheritor of the title, would be playing a leading part in it.

For fifteen years or so my father and mother had lived in Rockbrook, a large house in the Dublin mountains. If the weather was very clear you could see the whole city laid out beneath you, and the shadow of the Mountains of Mourne eighty miles away to the north.

A brown mountain stream ran through the grounds in a series of natural waterfalls. My father had planted hundreds of trees and shrubs around the swimming pool, which he'd had blasted out of solid rock that sparked with quartz. On a summer's day it was a magic place, a thousand miles away from the uproar of cities and people. But in the winter, when the wind and the rain howled down from the ruins of the Hell Fire Club above, it was peculiarly lonely and desolate, and full of dying.

Two favourite dogs had died there and a few miles farther up in the mountains was the Military Road with its lonely crosses, marking the places where men had been shot during the Civil War. In the winter it was too far from Dublin, and to close to death. My father sold it and bought this much smaller house, called Rockall, on the sea road to Sandycove, on the outskirts of Dun Laoghaire.

There was a tiny croquet court at the back, overlooked by terraced houses, but in the front only the garden and the sea road separated it from Dublin Bay.

My mother's taste and highly developed capacity for home-making had, at least, made it comfortable and original inside, even if the back of the house was the only part that got the sun.

The sun was shining now. The door was open and the house seemed to be empty. I called out several times, "Anyone there?" but there was no reply.

I was sure that my father had had another of his miraculous recoveries and that he and my mother had gone out for a drive in the sunshine. Just to make sure I went upstairs to my father's room and opened the door and saw the most frightening thing I've ever seen.

A shrivelled little old man was propped up against a lot of pillows in my father's bed. The face was yellow, and the bones were protruding through it. The right forearm was resting on top of the head in the position of someone trying to think of something, when the thought won't come. The figure was motionless, as still as death.

I was staring at it, paralysed, when a pretty little blonde girl in a white coat came round the end of the bed. I saw she must be the nurse, and that she was as startled as I had been.

I said, "I'm Mr. Paddy—his son." She said, confusedly, "I knew you would be." Then I found myself sitting on the chair beside him. I took his hand. It was very small and bony and cold. I said, not knowing what I was saying, "You're a great man. You're a great man."

His eyes were opaque, completely unseeing.

The little nurse bent down and spoke clearly and precisely into his ear. "It's Mr. Paddy. It's your son."

My father stayed absolutely motionless. He seemed not even to be breathing. "It's me," I said. "Paddy. How are you?"

The little nurse spoke to him again. "Just squeeze his hand," she said. "Tell him you know he's here."

The cold, bony little hand lay lifelessly in mine.

"I think he knows," the nurse said to me. Then she spoke to him again. "Just move your finger," she said. "Tell him."

I believe I felt the faintest little flutter.

The little nurse looked down at him with a gentleness which seemed to come from more than just a familiarity with death. "He knows you're here," she said. Then she said suddenly, "He was a lovely man. We had the grandest laughs."

I realised then for the first time that I'd never talk to my father again. "He *was* a lovely man." Very soon now he would be wholly dead.

I said, "I'd better go." I didn't have the courage to wait to see it happening. I said to the nurse, "Is my mother in?" She said she thought she was in the garden.

She was sitting on a bench, very composedly looking out at the sea, waiting for it to happen, as she'd been waiting for nearly a year.

"Hello," I said, "it's me."

"Darling," she said, "it's lovely to see you."

I said, "I thought you'd gone out for a drive and then I went up to his room. It's awful."

Both of us struggled for a moment with tears and then she said, cheerfully, "He was grand last night. Dr. Werner, of the Eye and Ear Hospital, came out to see him and he brought a bottle of champagne. Werner didn't know how ill he was. I think the Lord was delighted that someone from the Eye and Ear had turned up at last. I think he thought they'd forgotten all about him."

(My father had been chairman of the hospital for years.)

"They had a long talk all about racing," my mother said, "and the Lord had a glass of champagne. I don't think it was very good for him. He had a bad night and now—"

We struggled with tears again. Then I said, tritely, "It's a good way for him to go, having a glass of champagne and talking about racing with that pretty little nurse looking after him."

"I used to hear peals of laughter coming from the room," my mother said. Neither of us looked up at the curtained window.

"She told me they had the grandest laughs," I said. "He was a great man."

"I've just remembered," my mother said, "we got married fifty years ago tomorrow. When we knelt down at the altar everyone saw that Gordon had a huge hole in the sole of his shoe. Malcolm came to the wedding in a top-hat, with a tennis racquet." (Malcolm was her brother.)

After a while my mother said, "It was very queer, but every time I sat with him he used to ask, 'Where's Nurse?' As if I was a stranger. I just felt so glad that there were people like the nurse that he wanted."

We talked for a while about this curious feature of the Lord—the gloom at home and his care-free abandon when he got away from it—and all at once the nurse was standing in the door. After a moment, possibly wondering how to put it, she said, "I'm afraid his Lordship's gone."

My mother and I both stood up. The nurse said, "Would you like to see him?" We followed her upstairs. The nurse had put the arm under the bedclothes that had rested on his head, otherwise he looked exactly the same as when I'd seen him an hour before. In turn my mother and I kissed the top of the curiously bristly skull, and that was that.

We were sitting silently beside the fire when we heard a small bump on the floor upstairs. It could not be ignored. My mother said, as if it was a small joke, "I wonder what she's doing to him."

I shook my head quickly, to tell her—without saying it—that we didn't have to pay any attention to the practicalities of death.

Suddenly, then, I said, "I don't feel he's dead at all. He's all around everywhere. He's pottering about in the garden or playing croquet or watching the yachts. I'm sure that death really isn't anything."

But it wasn't true. I did feel that his spirit, the essence of him, and the memory of him, were indestructible, but the true reality was that a huge, empty hole had suddenly opened up in my life for the first time—a hole that would never be filled again.

"I know what you mean," my mother said. "But it's extraordinary, I just feel relieved that it's all over. It's been such a long time and it's marvellous to know that he won't suffer any more."

I had that aching in the jaws, almost like rheumatics, that comes from trying to hold back tears, and I could see my mother had it too. And yet she was profoundly happy because the man with whom she had lived for fifty years was now out of pain for ever, and had died comforted by the presence of a little nurse from Dublin. The fact that he had seemed to feel no need for her in his last days gave her no feeling of rancour, no feeling that her life might have been wasted. She regarded it, rather as an emotional phenomenon, a fascinating quirk in human nature to be discussed objectively, to be respected for itself.

I remembered, when my sister had been killed, in the war, that an elderly cook we had at the time had complained to me, "Her Ladyship doesn't suffer right." The cook had been looking forward, with Catholic fervour, to my sister's portrait being draped in black, the blinds in the house drawn, the whole family convulsed in solitary grief. Yet everyone was sitting out in summer clothes in the patio at the back of the house, and there was even laughter, at small things.

My mother had said to me, with complete simplicity, "The worst thing that can happen to anybody is to lose a child," and then she had begun to talk about Biddy playing in goal for the Irish lacrosse team "with a queer thing like a fencing mask all over her face". A moment later she said, "I was sure the poor child was going to be killed." We both laughed, because it was so very much the wrong thing to say. But the memory of the fencing mask, and the emotions it had created, were too strong to be censored.

In fact, I could never remember anything being censored in our family. There was always an atmosphere of lively discussion, of absorbed curiosity in the motives of others, usually led by my mother, with her favourite introduction, "I thought it was terribly interesting when—"

And yet the Lord was always a little apart from these free-for-alls. There was never any question of a stern, Victorian father-figure, yet I always felt that the things that my mother and Biddy and I found "terribly interesting" seemed to him to be merely frivolous and self-evident. He had read Spengler, Nietzsche and Schopenhauer and seemed to have found much in common with these sombre philosophers.

My mother, almost certainly not having read him, was a stern anti-Spengler woman. "All that about the decline of the West," she would say. "It's nonsense. The world's getting better all the time."

Neither my mother nor the Lord ever seemed to be parents in the way that I'd seen other mothers and fathers being parental. There was never any feeling of discipline. Rather, there were things you could do that were anti-social, that caused annoyance or inconvenience to others, and there was a kind of unspoken indication that it would be better if you didn't do them again. But here again, the Lord was different. He left what little discipline there was to my mother, seeming to have a set of principles of his own that were too lofty and too austere, even to him, to be applicable to ordinary human beings.

Suddenly, my mother, sitting by the fire, said, "I never really knew what sort of man he was."

She, too, had been remembering the past, looking back over many more years with the Lord than I had known.

The noises from the room upstairs had ceased. It seemed to be the right time for this kind of examination, almost a formal board meeting to consider the evidence and to come to conclusions, the old, insatiable curiosity over again.

"Neither did I," I said. "What did he do, for instance, when he went to the Bank?"

She gave a small, rather helpless laugh. "I could never imagine," she said.

Hundreds of people all over Ireland—businessmen, farmers, trades union officials, cattle dealers, industrialists, politicians—all of them certainly knew more about my father's commercial capabilities than I did.

All that I knew of his working life had been what I'd read in my mother's voluminous scrap books, cuttings of every kind which she'd kept since the first war.

I knew that he'd been a barrister in London before 1914, and during it had worked under Churchill in the Ministry of Munitions. I knew, like his father, who'd become Lord Chancellor of Ireland and later Chairman of the first Irish Senate, that he could have had what is always called a brilliant career at the English Bar, but that he'd given it up and come home to Ireland to do what he could to assist the first Irish Government, under President Cosgrave. In this he became Parliamentary Secretary to the Ministry of Industry and Commerce, a job he held until Cosgrave lost the election to de Valera.

This return to Ireland had always seemed to me to be a strange sacrifice for a man who liked being successful and who had enjoyed in the literary life of London the serious, cultivated kind of discussion that he never really found in sufficient measure in Dublin.

In fact, he frequently railed against "the cretinous slobs who pass for people of intelligence in Ireland". Once, when I asked him, "Why did you come back here, then?" he shook his head—an instinctive gesture that said the question was out of order.

The truth was, of course, that he'd come back to Ireland because he loved Ireland, and loved the idea of taking part in the formation of what he thought of, romantically, as being a new and ideal Free State. One of the first tastes he got of the new and ideal State was when the I.R.A. burnt down our house on Christmas Eve, 1922, and it seemed for a long half hour that they were going to execute him on his own front lawn.

I never knew how he made the transition from politics to business. I must have been at school in England when it happened, or at Oxford or in Germany, but when I came home again the Lord was a director of the Bank of Ireland, Chairman of the Great Northern Railway and of the Royal Hibernian Insurance Company, and on the board of a number of other companies he never mentioned.

I formed the idea—and literally formed it, almost out of nothing, because I had to have one—that he was a kind of financial mystic or seer, the kind of genius who can be shown the balance sheet of an unknown company and can diagnose its ills an hour later.

Mysterious figures from the world of international finance would occasionally come to the house on Sunday evenings. Large, weighty Swedes or silent Englishmen with big foreheads. More often than not my mother, by her own passionate enthusiasm, would draw them into some discussion of painting or the theatre in which everyone except the Lord would join.

With increasing frequency he'd sit by himself at the window, looking bored and more and more resentful of what he'd come to describe as "women's kitchen gossip". Soon, we were able to identify "kitchen gossip" as any form of emotional communication, any expression of subjective opinion that was not based upon knowledge or reasoned thought.

Once, trying to compensate the Lord for a particularly bitter and silent evening, I asked him, "Why do all these experts from the World Bank or whatever it is come all the way to Dublin to see you?" He gave the self-deprecating grin that wasn't deprecatory at all and said, "They come to get straightened out."

Probably much of his time in the Bank of Ireland was spent in wondering whether to allow a farmer in Mullingar to increase his overdraft by another £1,000 or in trying to talk the bank clerks' leaders out of another strike, but I do believe he had a visionary sense of money. It was his form of art, a desire to see money irrigating the affairs of individuals or companies to the best possible effect. In exchange for this service, however, he never seemed to receive very much of it for himself.

For as long as I can remember the family lived in considerable comfort—on the very edge of bankruptcy. An unnecessary shovelful of coal on the fire, or a stove left on in an empty bedroom, would bring on the Lord's grim look and the statement, "You people simply don't understand the value of money." My mother often said, "The Lord's always telling me I'll be scrubbing floors in the workhouse but I wouldn't mind at all. I've been scrubbing floors all my life."

This refusal to be depressed by the constant threats of bankruptcy seemed to the Lord to be the essence of feeble-mindedness and irresponsibility, and then he'd go to the races or buy a new, if modest, car.

We never knew where we were, and the Lord's certainty that we were incapable of understanding the fearful position we were in meant that he never took the trouble to explain it in any realistic detail.

In this he was abetted by Archie Robinson, who'd been the family solicitor for as long as anyone could remember. But Archie was more than a solicitor. He was the silent, dedicated guardian of the lifeblood of the family. It always seemed to me that the whole of his working day, every day, must have been concerned exclusively with our affairs, whatever they might be. In this, he and the Lord were one, and particularly in the belief that there was no point in inviting interest or understanding on the part of the rest of us.

The only other person I knew of who had the Lord's confidence in matters of money was Willy Ganly, despite the fact that Willy was at least twenty years younger.

He was one of a huge family of Ganlys, most of whom were in the cattle business in Dublin. He'd first come into the Lord's life as a friend of mine and particularly as a friend of my sister, Biddy.

Willy was direct and forceful and a very astute businessman. Like my father, he loved fishing and any kind of outdoor life. He was also incorruptibly honest, a quality that the Lord admired, in business, above all others. Before long, he took Willy into the Bank of Ireland as the youngest director the Bank had ever had. In one day Willy said of my father, "He's the only completely incorruptible banker I've ever known," and my father said of Willy, "You could trust him with your very last shilling."

Though Willy and I were close friends I never learnt anything from him about the hidden, commercial side of my father's life. It was as though he had complete respect for the Lord's certainty that his wife and children were incurable imbeciles where money was concerned. And I have no doubt that this unquestioning respect, as much as Willy's outstanding qualities, went a long way to warm the Lord towards him. Unquestioning respect was not one of the things he enjoyed in his own household.

The little nurse came into the room, dressed in her outdoor clothes. After hesitating for a moment, she said, "Everything's arranged, so I'd better catch the bus."

My mother thanked her for all she had done, and the nurse said again, "He was a lovely man." When she saw what this did to us she left the room at once. We heard the front door close.

My mother said, "I think I'll go upstairs and lie down for a bit." I helped her to her feet—she was very tired—and I said, very quickly and as simply as I could, "Don't go and look again."

She said, "I won't," and thanked me with a little smile.

Alone in the sitting-room, I sat in the Lord's chair by the window, looking out at Dublin Bay. His race glasses—I think they'd belonged to his father—were on a stool beside the chair. I picked them up and tried to focus on a small collier steaming out of the Liffey past the Poolbeg Lighthouse, but the image was blurred.

Suddenly, I got into a state of desperation. Everything was slipping away. The feeling that I'd known nothing about his business life became unbearable. It was idle, ungrateful, unforgivable. And now all the memories of him were becoming shadowy and confused. I had to arrange them, file them away, before it was too late.

I got up and went out of the house, through the front garden and to the sea road and down to the rocks at the Forty Foot, a roughly concreted enclosure that had been a bathing place for Gentlemen Only for many years. The Lord had sometimes bathed here before breakfast in the very early morning, loving the feeling of solitude, the sun coming up over the Hill of Howth and the clean, new sea.

He said, "I lurched into the Forty Foot the other morning and when I came out I found I'd begun to grow a whole new crop of hair."

It was true. In the last year of his life—perhaps it was some manifestation of the disease that killed him—grey and bristly hair had begun to sprout all over the top of his scalp. He was proud of it, and massaged it constantly while he was reading.

I tried to remember some of the other, human things, to make up for my lack of knowledge of what he'd done for a living.

Years ago, he'd written a play called *A Treaty With the Barbarians*. It was produced at the Abbey Theatre one Sunday night. I had a vague memory of having read it. It had a flavour of Shaw, but without Shaw's vitality. My mother said, but not in his hearing, "There seemed to be an awful lot of talk."

A few years before he died he astonished me by sending to me, in London, written on thick, lined paper in his beautful handwriting, "six television plays for Charlie Drake". In a rare burst of enthusiasm he'd spoken of Charlie Drake as "more imaginative, more of an all-round comic character than Chaplin".

The plays were written under the pen-name of Carl Hendry, though he'd taken the name of Richard Erroll for *A Treaty With the Barbarians*. They were beyond hope. Some of them might have played for ten minutes, others for about twenty. In the majority of them it was impossible to tell which was the role intended for Charlie Drake. The style in places was reminiscent of the stage Irishry of Donn Byrne, in others it was no more than an attempt to imitate the comic business in a pre-war music-hall sketch. In a covering note he said I was sure to know someone in the BBC who'd be interested.

I thought first of all of sending them back, with some convincing words of praise, but qualified by reminding him of the tight time-factor in television. Then it seemed to be unfair not to give an airing to something on which he'd worked so hard, so I sent them to Eric Maschwitz, who was then Head of Light

Entertainment at Television Centre. In a letter, I explained the unusual circumstances.

Eric was very good. He sent them back with a note that said, "While your friend Carl Hendry shows very considerable promise as a writer of comedy for television, he still has something to learn about the technical matter of length. I should be delighted to see any revisions he might care to make."

I posted the six plays back to Dublin, with Eric's letter, and heard no more about them for a year or more. Then, talking about something I'd written for television, the Lord said to me, "I still think my stuff would have worked." He didn't like to be beaten by anything.

But this wasn't the kind of thing I wanted to remember, standing on the rocks at the Forty Foot, looking out at Dublin Bay where we'd sailed every Saturday afternoon before the war, racing in an old 21-foot cutter called the *Garavogue*. The Lord would never give up, even long after the evening breeze had died away into a flat calm and the ebb had begun to carry us south past Dalkey Island, getting farther and farther away every minute from the finishing line in Dun Laoghaire Harbour. "We'll just hang on a bit longer," he'd always say. "There'll be a puff of wind sooner or later."

My sister and I, with a party to go to in Dublin, would beg him to let us get the sweeps out and row ourselves back into the harbour, and the Lord would put on his grim and injured look. Once again we were being irresponsible and feeble-minded.

He loved sailing and was for ever inventing methods of marking the sheets with coloured thread so that, after we'd won a race, almost entirely by luck, we'd be able to reproduce the same winning trim again.

He had a passion for games of every kind and, failing the proper equipment, he would improvise a completely new one out of an old biscuit tin, a piece of wood and a tennis ball and play it with a fanatical regard for the rules which we invented as we went along.

He could read three detective stories in an evening with such complete absorption that he might have been under a general anaesthetic and when he'd finished them he could give you neither a glimmering of the plots nor the name of a single character. He relied on the girls in Switzers Library to give him one he hadn't read before and when they slipped up he'd read as many as twenty pages before realising what had happened.

He adored the company of pretty women, without going too

far out of his way to look for it. He had a teasing, flirtatious way with them that often reduced the less resilient to tears. Their failure to appreciate that this teasing was a form of love-making left him feeling injured and depressed, so much so that he would sometimes, during the weekends, retire to bed with his detective story as early as four o'clock in the afternoon.

Once, he astonished me by saying, "When it comes to kissing the Campbells run away." In his case it was almost certainly true.

Or perhaps it wasn't.

I never really knew him at all.

I never even knew whether he was disappointed to find that neither my brother Michael nor I had any capacity for business or banking. Michael did make an attempt at a professional career by being called to the Irish Bar, after studying law in Trinity, but he never practised. Like myself, he was eased into a job on the *Irish Times* by the Lord, who was an old friend of the editor, Robert Smyllie. Indeed, if it hadn't been for the *Irish Times,* it's difficult to tell what would have become of either of his sons.

Yet the Lord's disappointment—if disappointed he was—never took the conventional, demanding form. He did say to me once that he should perhaps have been fiercer with me, making me train for a profession, and with Michael, compelling him to go on with the law. But being fierce with people was never his way. I think he laid out in his mind an ideal course of behaviour for everyone he knew and cared about and felt personally injured when they failed to live up to it. And to get them back on the rails he used persuasion so oblique and delicate, and with such concern for their *amour propre,* that it was often difficult to perceive that the process was going on at all.

I suddenly remembered an old gardener who'd got into an incomprehensible tangle with a seed merchant, ordering enough bulbs to fill the whole of Phoenix Park. My father straightened out the mess in a couple of minutes. The old gardener paid him a tribute straight from his heart.

"His Lordship," he told me with love, "could mind mice at a crossroads."

The sun was going down behind the Dublin Mountains. The sea, washing round the rocks of the Forty Foot, was turning grey and cold. I began to walk back to the house.

I met my mother outside the Lord's room the following morning.

"Did you—go and look at him—during the night?" she asked me.

"No."

"Neither did I."

We went downstairs to breakfast.

Archie and Willy arrived about an hour before the hearse. They were calm and efficient, hiding their own private grief. I couldn't even guess at the amount of work that Archie had done, in arranging the funeral. I tried to thank him, for everything. He said, "That's all right."

When the hearse arrived, backing into the short drive in front of the house, they went upstairs with the undertaker. My mother and I sat in front of the fire in the living-room. I talked about London, trying to distract her attention from the noise above. After rather a long time we heard the bumping of the coffin being carried down the narrow stairs, and then the sound of feet on the gravel outside.

After a few more minutes Archie came into the living-room, with Willie behind him. They were both very quiet, keeping a tight control on themselves. Willie's face was ghastly. I could almost imagine what he'd gone through upstairs.

Archie said, "The hearse is just leaving."

My mother said, "I don't think I want to see it."

I said, "Come on. We'd better."

My mother stood up. "You're quite right," she said. "One should always see everything."

The hearse was brilliantly black in the narrow drive, and seemed to be almost completely covered with flowers.

My mother said, "Look at all the flowers. Where did they all come from?"

The back doors of the hearse were still open. The coffin, inside, was very shiny, in some light wood, like oak. The whole equipage seemed to be much too highly polished, for the Lord.

Very clearly, in my own mind, I said to my father, "Get up out of that silly thing and come and play croquet."

Then the undertaker closed the doors and the hearse drove away, along the shore of Dublin Bay, to the church in Dun Laoghaire.

My mother went straight upstairs to my father's room, pulled the curtains back and opened all the windows. Then she pulled the bed away from the wall, turned it round and put it with its head against the one opposite.

In the living-room I gave her an inch of brandy, with a little soda. She sat in her usual place by the fire. She sipped her drink. Suddenly, she said, "He just got tired of wearing that old overcoat."

I was surprised. It didn't sound like her. She smiled apologetically. "That nice young clergyman, Mr. Day, said it last night." Then she made one of her positive judgements. "I think it's rather good."

After a moment I said, "That's what it was. Just tired of wearing his old overcoat. That's all that happened."

About an hour before my father's funeral service my mother said, "Perhaps I can't go to the church looking like this."

Her hat and coat were lying on the arm of the chair. Two shades of beige. Her dress was of the same oatmeal colour. I'd once referred to her exceedingly modest wardrobe as "variations on the theme of porridge". She'd thought the description exact, and felt not at all wounded. For years her only interest in clothes had been that they should be comfortable and anonymous.

"I never go out anywhere," was her contention, "so I don't really need them."

In fact, she did go out quite often, to lunch parties, art exhibitions or the theatre, but on these occasions she could have worn an old dressing-gown without anyone noticing. Her own burning interest in what was going on, her hungry curiosity, her passionate concern with the world outside herself meant that it didn't matter in the least what she wore.

She was telling me once about an opening at the Royal Hibernian Academy and said, "There was poor Maureen, wearing a hat looking like a beehive spattered with custard and thinking everyone was looking at her when just behind her on the wall was a hideous but terribly interesting picture by Louis le Brocquy."

But now, probably for the first time for as long as she could remember, she felt the pressure of convention.

"But I never had anything black in my life," she said and thought for a moment. "I'd look a fool dressed up in black," she decided, "so I'll wear this. Anyway, I'm not a widow—I'm a bride."

I remembered that she and my father had got married fifty years ago on the previous day.

"You'll do grand like that," I said. Then I remembered something else. "I haven't got a black tie," I said. "I'd better go out and buy one."

My mother said, immediately, "The Lord's got dozens of them up in his room. He was always going to funerals."

After a moment, I said, "I think I'd better go out and buy a new one."

I walked up Ballygehin Avenue to the bus route, to the small haberdasher's on the corner, thinking that this was the way the Lord had come every weekday morning, on his way in to the Bank.

He'd travelled to the Bank by bus for years, sharing it—at 10 o'clock in the morning—with housewives going shopping with yelling babies, the essence of discomfort. But he always found it more agreeable than driving a car in Dublin traffic, and he had this strange affinity with very young children.

When they were living at Rockbrook he used to drive the seven or eight miles down to the bus terminus in Terenure. He told me once, with great pleasure, "Two little boys outside Doyle's cottage on the corner have it in for me. Every time they see the car coming they yell, 'Dere's Dord Dendavy—t'row de mud.' And they do."

His normally gloomy face shone for a moment with pure delight.

And this, now, was the small suburban road he'd walked up every morning, with the whizzer probably already beginning to do its work.

It used to take him the best part of a couple of hours to have breakfast in bed, get up and shave and have a bath. It was the time he did his thinking, about the farmer in Mullingar or about the approach of yet another weighty Swede. And suddenly, then, he'd find it was later than he thought and he'd come hurrying downstairs in a state of disorder, his hands full of papers and telephone messages and the gardener's wages and for several minutes he'd deliver a stream of instructions to anyone who happened to be present, the right forefinger bent and stabbing the air for emphasis.

Most of the things he wanted done had been done already, or were things that only he could do. Everyone waited patiently for the storm to subside, while making gentle and meaningless sounds of assent.

The Lord would then shoot a desperate look at the big clock in the hall. It was always kept twenty minutes ahead of the real time, but it never got him out of the house before ten. Then, wearing his strange, grey Homburg hat—the only Homburg I'd ever seen that was turned down in the front—he'd stride into the dining-room and, still with the hat on his head, dive into the drink cupboard in the corner.

In the recesses of this cupboard he'd pour himself a large glass of gin, throw in a splash of lime juice and lower the whole lot in a single gulp. He never drank very much but this "whizzer", as he called it, a little defensively, was as much a part of his morning routine as the brushing of his teeth.

That strange, grey Homburg hat. I'd always felt he'd invented his own clothes. They had an odd, home-made look about them. The white bawneen trousers he'd bought in Galway that were like two large and solid cylinders from ankle to waist. The heavy, practical shoes that his feet twisted into their own unique shape within a week. And the suit.

One evening the Lord came home from the Bank looking, for once, almost elegant in a dark-blue suit—a sharp change from his usual, shapeless grey. No one had seen him leave the house in the morning, so that for a moment I thought he must have bought it in Dublin. But there was something odd about it. It didn't look new.

He sat in his usual chair by the window and settled down to the extreme pleasure of analysing the racing results in the *Evening Herald*.

After a moment he gave one of those convulsive sneezes which were his speciality, and reached for the handkerchief in his breast pocket, while continuing to read the paper. He couldn't find the handkerchief.

My mother and I had both been watching him, but she was the one who was brave enough to speak.

"Your handkerchief's on the other side," she said.

Slowly, the Lord looked up over the top of his paper with the look of puzzlement, and of indignation, which was normal to him when interrupted in his reading. He looked at my mother, as though trying to work out in his own mind whether or not she was speaking English.

"Your handkerchief," she explained. "It's in your breast pocket—on the other side."

The Lord reached for the handkerchief, as if he'd known where it was all along, blew his nose and resumed his study of the paper.

It was not a thing that my mother could let go. Her curiosity, as usual, was too great to allow her to be diplomatic.

"I thought men's breast pockets were always on the left," she said. "Why is yours on the right?"

The Lord put down his paper. He addressed us with board-room solemnity. "I had Paddy's suit turned," he said, and sat there fully armoured against whatever might happen next.

I was so surprised that I, too, forgot to be careful.

"Where did you find it?" I asked him.

"It was wrapped up in a parcel in the hall."

"But I was going to give it to Mrs. Donovan, for her husband," my mother said. "I thought she'd taken it. He's out of work."

"There's plenty of good wear in it still," said the Lord, and went back to the *Evening Herald*.

In his honour, in the little haberdasher's shop, I bought a horrible, shiny, string-like black tie for 5s. 11d. It was the only one they'd got. Rather than wear such a thing himself—he hated all synthetic fabrics—he would probably have tried to make one out of some piece of black cloth, sewing enormous irregular stitches in the privacy of his bedroom and throwing it away, with a sense of injury, when he found it didn't work.

Back at the house Willy and Archie had once again arrived, bringing with them, as usual, the comforting sense that all the details of the funeral had been attended to. Now all that my mother and I had to do was to endure it.

Archie had one brief, troubled look at my mother's oatmeal ensemble, but he said nothing.

We got into the chief mourners' car, a shiny black Cadillac of endless length dating from the years when they still had the giant tail-fins. We drove slowly and in silence along the coast road, to the church in Dun Laoghaire.

There seemed to be a lot of people, mostly men, standing about outside the church in their best clothes. At the gate, talking to one another confidentially, were two high-ranking officers of the Irish Army—possibly Colonels by the red flashes on their collars.

My mother and I got out of the huge car and stood uncertainly for a moment on the pavement. The Colonels approached us. One of them saluted gravely.

"I represent the President, my Lady," he said. "He wishes me to present his deepest sympathy."

The other Colonel also bowed. "Mr. Sean Lemass," he said, "and the other members of the Government wish me to add their condolences to those of the President."

I was overwhelmed to find that my father had been recognised by the President and by the Prime Minister of the Irish Republic, although of course I should have expected it. But it seemed to take him away from us, to turn him into some kind of monument.

For as long as I could remember the Lord had been corrosively scathing about de Valera and his Fianna Fail party, talking about "the utter hopelessness of trying to get a bunch of ex-gunmen to understand even the rudimentary basis of economics", and here now de Valera and Sean Lemass were presenting their sympathy on his death.

It made him into the public figure that he'd been for many years, the public figure we'd never really appreciated or understood.

I took my mother's arm and we walked slowly into the church. The first thing I saw was the shiny, pale coffin, with its head pointing towards the altar. I looked away instinctively, knowing that the Lord wouldn't like to feel that his family were watching him, giving so public a performance, and then I saw that the church was full, right into the gloom of the last row of pews. I saw a few familiar faces, but most of them were strange to me. They were the faces of the businessmen, the farmers, the trades union officials, the cattle dealers, the industrialists and the politicians—all the men who'd known the value of his public life so much better than I.

My mother and I knelt for a moment in the front pew and then we sat back, unable to take our eyes off the coffin, now that it stood so squarely in front of us.

I became aware of organ music and looked to see where it was coming from. There was a small organ on the left of the altar. Above it I could just see the small, polished bald head of my mother's cousin, Jack Elvery. He was playing a strange kind of preoccupied, thoughtful lament that rose at times to a note of strident but controlled protest, before resuming its grumbling theme. The music went on and on, showing no sign of approaching a finale.

I whispered to my mother, "What's Jack playing?"

She whispered back, "He's making it up."

"It sounds exactly like the Lord talking."

She nodded, and we both struggled with tears. But even through the tears I was thinking with pleasure of the Lord's astonishment, if he could have heard what Jack was doing for him.

Ever since I'd been a child Jack had been in charge of the Elverys' shop in Nassau Street, a sports outfitters that sold everything from trout rods to remarkably dowdy cardigans for elderly ladies. There was another branch in O'Connell Street which was looked after, to even less effect, by Jack's brother, Fred.

The Lord moved in on the business, to try to resurrect it, for the good and sufficient reason that my mother, as an Elvery, held a substantial proportion of the shares. If the dividends could be increased by better business methods it would be another small insurance against the bankruptcy that seemed to threaten us every day. And yet in this, as in all his commercial enterprises, the Lord was not seeking only personal profit. He was also thinking of all the other Elvery sisters and brothers and cousins, all over the world, who needed even more urgently a boost in their incomes.

He ran head on into Jack Elvery. For centuries, it seemed, Jack had been sitting behind the huge, littered desk in the back part of the shop in Nassau Street, getting in the way of better business methods, and insisting on the continued employment of ancient assistants who should have been pensioned off years ago. "They know where the stuff is," Jack would say, indicating the mass of broken cardboard boxes that littered every shelf in the place.

"I went in there the other day," the Lord told me once, "wanting to buy a couple of golf-balls, and there was Jack behind the desk scratching away in a mound of papers, looking for something that didn't matter a damn to anyone. I asked him for a couple of Dunlops and he went on rootling through his papers. Then he looked up and said, absolutely cheerfully, 'Dunlops? My dear chap, we haven't seen a Dunlop for weeks. Same thing with Silver King. Simply can't get 'em. Tell you what you do, though. Just nip round the corner to Hely's. They've got boxes and boxes of them there. Dunlops *and* Silver Kings'."

Hely's were then Elverys' only competitors in the sports goods trade in Dublin.

Jack was equally provocative at board meetings, into which the Lord had inserted two capable directors of his own choice. "We'd at long last," he said, "got something straightened out, some practical proposal agreed to, and then we'd ask Jack for his opinion. He only had one. 'I'm not satisfied,' he'd say. 'I'm not satisfied at all.' Utterly hopeless," the Lord would say, with gloomy but profound relish. And then he'd go on to add, with even deeper satisfaction, "Jack also turned down the Irish agency for the Yo-Yo. He said no one would want to buy a fiddlefaw like that."

But here now was Jack Elvery, who was never satisfied, who never had any golf-balls and who had turned down the Yo-Yo, playing a lament for the Lord on the organ, a lament that sounded exactly like the Lord's own voice.

I could just see his small, pale face below the polished, bald head. Jack must have been nearly eighty years of age but he was composing and playing his music with fire and passion, all the emotions of a young man.

The Lord, I thought, would have been well satisfied. One of his many ineffective methods of attacking kitchen gossip was suddenly to shout, in a lull, "You lot—either tell me a thing I didn't know before, or didn't think you were capable of saying!"

Almost certainly, he never would have thought that Jack was capable of saying what he was saying now.

Mr. Day, my mother's "nice young clergyman", began to recite the funeral service, and all at once I found there was a new aspect of my father to be considered.

I hadn't been inside a church since compulsory attendance at school. I'd forgotten about, or ceased to be consciously aware of, the faith that insists that we are all children of God.

It was extraordinary to hear my father referred to as—"Gordon Glenavy, Thy son". I'd never thought of him as being anyone's son, not even the Old Lord's. But on the other hand I was very much his. However little I might have known about his public life, at home he was my father beyond any possible doubt. Though we might laugh at turned suits and incomprehensible instructions, he always had the fundamental dignity and authority of a father, and a father's generosity in the dispensation of gifts to his children.

I must have been nearly fifty when I'd last played golf with him, yet he'd come out of the pro-'s shop with a couple of new golf balls for me.

"Better put those in your bag," he said, with the diffidence that afflicted him when he was giving us any kind of present. Then he added, even further to reduce the importance of the gesture, "They might come in useful."

In the bar afterwards he insisted on buying both rounds of drinks. "And," he told the barman, "you'd better give my son another large one. There's a lot of him."

As the words of the funeral service unfolded I began to get a frightened feeling—or it was nearly fear—that the Lord and I had missed something, had deprived ourselves of something that might have nourished us a very great deal, by standing away from religion. It might have warmed both our natures, where warmth was not an outstanding ingredient.

It was too late for me now. The habit of irony was too deeply ingrained. But the sense of living with a missing limb persisted.

The educated, Protestant voice of Mr. Day filled the church :

"I know that my Redeemer liveth, and that he shall stand at the latter day upon the earth. And though after my skin worms destroy this body, yet in my flesh shall I see God : whom I shall see for myself, and mine eyes shall behold, and not another."

It didn't sound like a belief that the Lord, with his objective intellectualism and high capacity for amusing self-mockery, could have held. That self-mockery of his didn't come from humility, but from what always looked like a pretty solid conviction that he was invulnerable to criticism and was therefore in a position to provide entertainment by criticising himself, in flights of fancy that bore less and less relation to the truth, with advancing years.

The moment passed. My heart closed up again. Wherever the Lord was now, I thought, and whatever might be the nature of the inquisition he was facing, he was dealing with it in his thoughtful, calm and rational way which, for all its calm and rationality, still contained an emotional element of injury—almost injured innocence—as though only people of malicious disposition could find a motive for questioning him.

But it still wasn't much consolation for something which I knew—and would always know from now on—that we'd both missed.

Suddenly, Monk Gibbon was standing at the lectern, looking strangely smart in a dark suit, his vigorous, grey-white hair unusually neatly brushed.

He began to read, in an emphatic, powerful, actor-like voice. "Remember now thy Creator in the days of thy youth, while the evil days come not, nor the years draw nigh, when thou shalt say, I have no pleasure in them—"

After my parents had moved to Sandycove, Monk, who lived round the corner, had become an indispensable part of my mother's life.

As a writer, he kept her in touch with the world of books, pouring out his opinions in a non-stop, bounding flood. Even before he became ill, the Lord had been a somewhat morose companion. Monk provided my mother with the vitality, the running commentary on the life of Dublin, even the kitchen gossip, that she loved.

"And the splendid thing about Monk," she told me, "is he's completely uninsultable."

Monk's uninsultability was fairly frequently put to the test. At times my mother, whose delight it was to keep open house for everyone, would suddenly feel that she was being put upon, being used by people who weren't properly appreciative.

"You," she told Monk, in one of these unexpected flare-ups, "you and your enormous family only use this house for eating and drinking, and some of you don't even speak while you're doing it."

That broadside caused Monk to disappear for a week. Then he came bounding round the following Sunday evening, with news too vital to be kept to himself.

A woman's body had been found in the sea near the Forty Foot a couple of nights before, with her stocking tied round her throat.

"Beattie," Monk boomed from the door, his eyes alight with joy, "I don't want a drink and my family aren't coming to dinner, but we've all just been interrogated for hours by the police."

"I know," said my mother, in a satisfied voice. "They came here first and I sent them round to you."

The two friends were friends once more.

Monk's great voice echoed round the church.

"Or ever the silver cord be loosed, or the golden bowl be broken, or the pitcher be broken at the fountain, or the wheel broken at the cistern. Then shall the dust return to the earth as it was, and the spirit shall return unto God who gave it."

Once again the feeling came to me that my father had been taken over by other people, that his death had made him public property.

If, for instance, the Lord had been alive I don't think Monk would have got very much further with his reading from Ecclesiastes.

The Lord, who was probably envious of Monk's inexhaustible vitality and equally inexhaustible good nature, treated him openly, as a small and noisy boy, to be tolerated only when he was silent and even then only for short periods of time.

If Monk had been reckless enough to begin reading aloud in his presence, the Lord would certainly have watched him for a moment over the top of his detective story, softening up the victim, and then have said, in the gentle voice that reduced the pretty women to tears—the gentle voice that contained so much more malice than he really intended—"Monk, why don't you go and do that in the garden? In your own garden, I mean."

"The preacher sought to find out acceptable words: and that which was written was upright, even words of truth. The words of the wise are as goads, and as nails fastened by the masters of assemblies, which are given from one shepherd."

The choice of this chapter of Ecclesiastes had been made by Monk and my mother. It was as exactly right as Jack's music.

It seemed to me that all the people who'd been wary of the Lord, and specially wary of his tongue, had in fact loved and understood him, and it was sad that he had to be dead before they could tell him so.

Once again, these convoluted admonitions sounded so like my father talking.

"The words of the wise are as goads, and as nails fastened by the masters of assemblies, which are given from one shepherd."

I didn't know what it meant, but it was the Lord all right. He was certainly the master of the assembly that was gathered every Christmas Day around the remnants of the lunch table. The assembly consisted of my brother and myself, and it was convened by the Lord in his usual diffident and conspiratorial fashion.

Before lunch he'd say to me, very privately, something like, "We'd better have a bit of a chat about money, after lunch. If you could get Michael to stay. . . ."

Like myself, Michael would not have missed these occasions for anything.

The subject under review was the avoidance of death duties and the imperative need for the Lord to hand over to Michael and myself the monies held in the Glenavy Trust. The Lord always called them "the monies", probably with the intention of giving them the sacrosanct and untouchable quality of the Crown Jewels.

He would begin, every Christmas Day, by reviewing the history of the Trust, Michael and I having another brandy and the Lord pouring himself a second bottle of stout.

The opening theme was always the hopeless situation that had been created by the Old Lord's will. So far as Michael and I could make out, the Old Lord, in the last years of his life, had lost a great deal of money on the Stock Exchange, but had taken no account of this in his will. In fact, he hadn't left sufficient "monies" to cover his numerous bequests.

At this point Michael would sometimes say, in a carefully casual manner, "How much did he leave?"—and the Lord would reply that he'd come to that in a moment.

The next and equally appalling facet of the situation was the clause in the Old Lord's will that said that "the monies" in the Trust should go to the holder of the title of Lord Glenavy.

"This," said the Lord, with evident satisfaction, "has given Archie and myself some fearful headaches. Legally, you see, Paddy, I can't give it to you until you're Lord Glenavy and—" the bent forefinger would come out, gently stabbing the air—"you won't be Lord Glenavy until I've passed on."

He would look at both of us intently, to see if we had any glimmering of understanding of this abstruse and complex point.

Michael and I would nod, our brows furrowed in concentration, trying not to meet one another's eye.

"But, you see," the Lord would go on, "if I—pass—on before—doing something about it, you and Michael are going to be absolutely bankrupted by the appalling death duties."

"They'd be pretty big?" I'd suggest.

"Yes. So Archie and I have been working night and day to try to find some way out of the mess. I must say, Archie's been marvellous, but it's killing him. He's not looking at all well. At this rate he'll go before I do and then we'll all be finally ruined."

At this point Michael and I knew we would be safe in sitting back and abandoning for another year all hope of discovering anything about our financial prospects. The Lord had worked himself into his favourite morass, buried so deeply in a pit of troubles that he could see no gleam of hope anywhere, and determined to make it impossible for either of us to do anything else except join him.

For the next half hour he would give us a review of the prohibitive cost of running the house. "Beattie's got to have a car and the cook's wages have gone up and the fence has fallen down in the lower field. . . ." From these domestic burdens he would pass to more serious matters. They were always centred around his certainty that in the next couple of months he would be stripped of all his directorships. "They don't like Protestants, you see, and they can't wait to get me out." In this welter of approaching disaster, however, he was prepared to give us one piece of good news. "I suppose the Bank would probably keep me on, as I'm the only person that knows anything about it." But it was instantly neutralised by the threat of a greater catastrophe than any we'd been faced with yet—the threat not merely of personal bankruptcy, but of bankruptcy on a national scale.

"This present Government," the Lord would say, savouring every word, "simply hasn't got the faintest idea what it's doing. Lemass is all right but the rest of them couldn't run a village shop in—in Ballyslumgullion. The trade figures are appalling. They're recklessly importing every kind of trivial foreign luxury at prohibitive cost and all they can do in exchange is send a few flea-bitten cows to England. Within the next couple of months you'll see the biggest economic crash here since the American Depression and then God knows what will become of Beattie—"

Michael and I always knew that the prospect of Beattie scrubbing floors in abject penury was an indication that the Lord was feeling better and that the talk had almost come to an end. This would be confirmed when he'd suddenly say, "Anyway, you and Michael don't have to worry. There's plenty of money there."

In some curious way this reassurance seemed to be the logical outcome of all that had gone before. Then the Lord would say, reaching for the brandy, "Give me a swash of that stuff there." He'd pour himself half a glassful, throw it straight down, and say, "I suppose we'd better try a bit of croquet before the rain."

Another assembly had come to an end, leaving Michael and myself as totally ignorant of the financial situation and of what, if anything, was going to be done about it, as before.

Then an extraordinary thing happened. One day, in the bar of the Grange Golf Club, the Lord suddenly said to me, out of the blue, "Well, it seems that the Campbells are solvent at last."

I could only imagine that the news was so good that for once he was unable to keep it to himself, or to turn it into his usual recital of despair.

I said, "What's happened?"

"It's these marvellous stockbrokers. They've been making some pretty useful investments."

"How much have we got?"

But the question was too direct. Like a flat-fish, menaced by the approach of some predator, the Lord began to scuffle himself into the sand.

"Very difficult to say. You see, these appalling death duties. It's a very difficult situation. I'll probably have to go and live in England or Tahiti or somewhere. Archie and I are working at it night and day."

"Have one on me, anyway, to celebrate our solvency."

"No, no," said the Lord, taken by surprise and suddenly concerned. "I'll do this. You keep your money. You'll probably need it."

"Let us hear the conclusion of the whole matter," Monk read in his powerful voice. "Fear God and keep His commandments: for this is the whole duty of man. For God shall bring every work into judgement, with every secret thing whether it be good, or whether it be evil."

He stood at the lectern for a moment, looking down at the big Bible. Then he closed it. It was the last thing he could do for Gordon Campbell. I guessed he was sorry he'd been unable to do more.

I can't remember the rest of the service. Perhaps it came to an end then. But all at once I was holding my mother's elbow as we walked out of the church behind the coffin.

It seemed almost unnecessary to disturb the Lord again, after his peaceful and solitary night in the church. It was as though we'd buried him there, with Jack's music and the funeral service and Monk's requiem, but the coffin had still to be put into the ground in Glasnevin, where soon there would be a headstone with my mother's beautiful lettering saying that the second Lord Glenavy was now lying here beside the first.

Very shortly there would be only a grave, and memory, and nothing else. It was impossible for us to restrain our tears.

My mother got into the back of the car. The door was still open when Eric Mieville, almost running, came out of the churchyard. He seized my mother's hand. He was unable to speak. The tears were running down his face.

My mother pressed his hand. She, too, could say nothing. Then Eric shut the door and the long, black car moved off.

Eric Mieville was one of the few people for whom the Lord had expressed unqualified admiration and affection. The fact that they met infrequently no doubt assisted their relationship a good deal.

Eric was all the things that the Lord wasn't and would probably have liked to be, if he hadn't been himself.

"He's the perfect Renaissance man," the Lord said to me. "The complete all-rounder."

Before the Hitler war Eric had been a major in the French Foreign Legion, and still retained the uniform for special public occasions in Dublin. During the war he'd been one of those mysterious, lone-handed adventurers that every war throws up. In his maddeningly evasive and mock-modest way he'd tell us of his part in the kidnapping of Otto Scorzeny from his prison in the Italian Alps and then go on, as though it were part of the same story, to sketch in a gun-running deal with an Arab state that was never precisely named.

The Lord would listen to him in silent glee, with a look almost of pride on his face. He very much liked Eric's laconic, allusive way of telling a story of heroism and dangerous adventure. It was the way he would have told it himself, if he'd ever become involved in such escapades.

Eric seemed to have known every beautiful woman in Europe. He spoke every European language and could talk art, literature, religion and philosophy as profoundly as the Lord himself.

He'd come to Ireland at the end of the war to create, at Ballykeane, a stud-farm of incredible elegance and efficiency, drilling his yard-boys and farm-hands into a condition of Swiss cleanliness and precision that was unique in a country with no great partiality for either of these virtues.

The Lord had a passion for rough gardening, breaking up old rockeries or tearing out patches of brambles. The result was never quite perfect, but it made him happy to know that he'd done it all by himself. Eric's capacity to give orders to Irish labourers and to see them achieve a result almost beyond perfection was always a source of wonder and pleasure to the Lord.

"I swear to you," he said to me, "the gravel in front of Eric's house must be raked three times a day by men on hands and knees, with hair-combs. I don't know how he gets them to do it."

He probably didn't realise that his own gardeners and casual labourers were just as devoted to him, and might have achieved the same kind of result if he'd been as stern with them as Eric was with his. But that wasn't the Lord's way. He could only give an order by roundabout suggestion, making it seem, if possible, that it was the man's own idea. And, always, the whole enterprise would be so wrapped in humorous fantasy that no one could be quite sure if he meant it or not.

"In the end," he would say, "we'll probably have to borrow a couple of pile-drivers from the Great Northern Railway, but you have a go at it with your shovel first."

They'd touch their caps, laughing delightedly, and then hold anxious deliberations among themselves after he'd gone.

My mother and I were walking along a path in Mt. Jerome cemetery towards an untidy pile of earth and planks that looked very like one of the Lord's major reconstructions. The grass on either side of the path was long and ragged. It would have given him the greatest pleasure in the world to bring it to order, strewing the scene with all manner of lawn-mowers, shears and scissors, working away on his own on a summer evening, long after the sun had gone down, and long after he'd been summoned to dinner.

In the sunshine, and amid the litter left by the grave-diggers, the burial service was quick and seemed unnecessary. The young clergyman in his white surplice looked altogether out of place in this rough and ready garden, the symbolism of the sprinkling of the earth altogether too perfunctory.

My mother and I just wanted the whole thing to be over now, and grass growing on whatever was left in the coffin. I took her back to the car before the grave-diggers began to fill in the earth. I think it was the most desolate moment that either of us had yet endured.

Back home again she took her usual place on the sofa by the fire, and I gave her her inch of brandy and soda. After a moment I saw that she was smiling. When she saw me looking at her she said, "I was just thinking—Dev must have had a terrible job to find two Protestant Colonels in the Irish Army."

It meant that the time had come to begin again, that the tears were over and that we now had to try to find out what the house would be like, what life would be like, now that the Lord had left it for ever.

Archie and Willy again appeared, Archie with the keys of the small safe which had sat for years in the ground-floor room which my mother used as a studio.

Archie said, "I don't suppose there'll be anything in it. Your father and I went through all the papers that were of any importance some time ago. Oh, by the way, you'd better sign this."

It was a death certificate. It said that my father had died of cancer, of the stomach and liver. It was impossible to imagine how he'd kept himself alive for so long.

Willy, as one of the Trustees, followed me into my mother's studio. Archie opened the safe. There were a number of sheets of lined foolscap paper, covered with my father's beautiful handwriting. They looked quite like the six television plays he'd sent me for Charlie Drake.

Archie glanced through them.

At the back of the safe I found a small ring with a cheap stone in it, almost the kind of thing a young girl might buy for herself in Woolworths. There was nothing else. I put the ring back in the safe. It didn't matter any more.

Archie said, "These are only some notes your father made about the question of death duties. They don't apply any longer."

He tore up the sheets of foolscap.

There was nothing left of my father's private life.

Still looking for something I went upstairs to my father's room. I opened the two top drawers of his dressing-table. One of them was empty. The other contained a couple of pipe cleaners, a device for sharpening razor blades and a member's badge for Leopardstown race course.

There was nothing else. No personal jewellery, no passport, no letters, no keepsakes, no photographs—no mementoes of any kind.

Perhaps he'd never needed the things by which other people set such store.

Perhaps because he was a truly great man.

A GOSS ON THE POTTED MEAT

There was no doubt that Mr. Jotuni Jaakkala's English was outrageously good.

He seemed to be a lecturer in his native Finnish at Cambridge. "An unhurried existence," as he put it, "seeing that the number of those *in statu pupillari* who wish to study our language and culture is sharply limited by the widespread, but nevertheless groundless, suspicion that we are domiciled in igloos, and live on boiled reindeer's feet."

You could hear the commas tinkling as he shovelled it out.

In the general laughter which followed this ornate revelation, someone, complimenting Mr. Jaakkala on his English, said that he must have lived in England all his life. He looked about thirty.

"I have lived in England since 1947," said Mr. Jaakkala, with charming modesty, "but from the pleasure it has given me you might well say that it has been all my life."

Excited protests followed to the effect that Mr. Jaakkala could not possibly have contrived so perfect an accent, so rich and flexible a vocabulary, in a mere five years.

Mr. Jaakkala smiled with even greater modesty than before, and lit a straight-grain pipe.

I felt compelled to intervene. I didn't like the look of his tweed suit either. For a youthful, *English* don it was exactly right.

"Oh, I don't know," I said, "if you've any ear for music, and it's necessary to learn a language to earn a living, it should be a matter of two or——"

Mr. Jaakkala opened his mouth.

"It should be a matter *only* of two or three years," I said quickly, "before one becomes entirely fluent."

Mr. Jaakkala smiled again. He knew he'd nearly nipped me. "I believe," he said, "you worked with a German electrical firm in Berlin for some time."

It was a direct invitation to reveal my ear for music.

"Have another glass of sherry before supper?" I said.

Mr. Jaakkala gracefully and confidently declined.

During supper he skimmed up and down and round about the English language with such mastery that gradually everyone else fell silent. To join with him in discussion would have been like accompanying Caruso on a jew's-harp.

After supper it looked as though we might settle down to listen to Mr. Jaakkala for the rest of the night. He had reached Sibelius, and was carving him up with swift, dexterous strokes. I intervened on, "the egregious dramaturgy of the avalanche, translated into terms of the contra-bassoon."

"What about a game of croquet," I said. "Let's go roll those balls."

Mr. Jaakkala, flexible as ever, showed immediate delight.

"Croquet?" he exclaimed. "But indeed yes."

"Don't tell me you play croquet in Finland," I said, surprised. "Surely the reindeer would get in the way?"

"They do," said Mr. Jaakkala generously. "But not on the immemorial Cambridge sward."

As we walked down to the court, I came to the conclusion that it was even better if he knew something about croquet. The shock, when it came, would be all the greater.

It was decided that I should play with Mr. Jaakkala, against my father, and an elderly economist called Lowther. We seemed to be equally matched, in view of the fact that Lowther, while a fast man with a fiduciary issue, was incapable of getting his back leg out of the way of the mallet, and had never been known to hit the ball more than a few feet.

"It's golf croquet," I told Mr. Jaakkala briefly. "First through the loop wins it for his side, and then all on to the next."

"You mean the hoop?" suggested Mr. Jaakkala.

"No, I don't," I said. I looked at him, puzzled, not getting his meaning. He gripped his mallet uneasily, and looked away. Fractionally, I'd already got him on the run.

"You start," I said, "with the blue. Far side of the loop, coming up."

He played quite a reasonable shot, but hit it too hard. It rolled over the edge of the grass. He stood back.

"Well," I said, after a pause. "The courtesy *remplacement*."

Mr. Jaakkala's brow furrowed. "The put in," my father said. *"Pour la politesse."* I was glad to see that he was abiding by the traditions of the game.

Mr. Jaakkala seemed to get it. He walked after his ball, picked it up, and placed it on the boundary.

As was usual with the first hoop no one succeeded in hitting another ball, and by the end of the first turn we were all lined up at varying intervals along the boundary line. It was Mr. Jaakkala's shot.

I examined the position. "It seems to me," I said, "that after a little Roedeanery off the yellow you should be able to *faire* direct *pénétration."*

Mr. Jaakkala shaped up to his ball, and then a slight cloud came over his face. "How—" he said—"exactly, do you mean? Could you, perhaps, explain——"

"Explain what?" I asked him.

My father intervened. "He means play a gentle shot off the yellow, which will leave you in posish. Then penetrate the loop."

"Excuse me," said Mr. Jaakkala. "I should like to understand the terms your son has used. This Roedeanery——"

"A lady-like shot off the yellow," I explained. "Followed by position. *Et la loopage.*"

Mr. Jaakkala looked at me malevolently. His shoulders hunched. He surveyed the other balls without hope, and suddenly lashed out in the direction of the hoop. He missed it by several feet.

"Which robs," my father said. Mr. Jaakkala walked after his ball, saying something, probably in Finnish, to himself.

Lowther, under my father's direction—two Roedeans, a bumble-over, followed by *pénétration* with a Kurdistan oblique—astonishingly enough made the first hoop, and we all surged down to join Mr. Jaakkala, waiting in silence by the second.

"Well, now," I said, "let's see how she shapes up. We're one down. We don't want to fruddle."

"I do not intend," said Mr. Jaakkala, "to fruddle." He smiled, in a ghastly way. "I presume fruddle to be an onomatopœic derivative, with the sense of making a mistake."

"It's near enough," I said. "How are you on the Kurdistan oblique?"

"Kindly tell me, please—what is it I am to do?" said Mr. Jaakkala. I knew then that I'd got him, because there, very faintly, like, perhaps, the opening bars of *Finlandia,* was the first sign of the lilting Finnish accent.

"My wife," I said, "born in India, finds it easier to *faire loopage* from an angle of 45 degrees. The Kurdistan oblique. Perhaps we'd better centralise. Take a Roedean on the black."

With the utmost care, Mr. Jaakkala rolled his ball along to hit the black. "Which strikes!" I cried. "Now—stac on the yellow!"

"Pleece?" begged Mr. Jaakkala.

I felt almost sorry for him. "Staccato blow on the yellow," I explained. "It's an in case."

Mr. Jaakkala peered about him like a man who'd lost his glasses.

"*Faire removage* of the yellow!" I cried, urging him on, "in case you fail on *pénétration* of the loop!"

I let him get his mallet about half-way back when I flung my own on the ground in front of him. I shouted, "STOP!" Mr. Jaakkala started convulsively and then shot me a glance in which fear and rebellion were mixed in equal parts.

"Total change of plan!" I cried. "Do a goss on the potted meat!"

This time it was Mr. Jaakkala who flung his mallet on the ground. "Aie goss!" he cried wildly. "How do I know what is aie goss——?"

Lowther intervened. He probably thought that violence was

going to be done. "A gossamer, or glancing blow," he said hurriedly—"on the potted meat."

"Vaat iss potted mitt?" roared Mr. Jaakkala.

Lowther seemed stunned. We'd been calling it the potted meat so long that he was incapable of providing a translation.

"The red," said my father.

"The paint's coming off it," I explained. "It looks like potted meat. Chicken and ham."

"Awwwh!" said Mr. Jaakkala. It was a kind of groan. He took a pace back, and then with a low, sideways sweep he flogged out at the blue. It struck the yellow about half-way up, and crushed it into the jaws of the hoop. The blue ball sped on and disappeared, at the height of several feet, through the back netting.

"That's done it," I said. "You've gone and played an onomatopœic derivative."

"The total fruddle," my father said.

"You've gone and yawssed the jellow ball."

"What? Pleece? I do not know——?" Mr. Jaakkala was miles out at sea.

"You've jawsed the yellow," I said. "A former Swedish Consul in Dublin, a regular player here, always referred to it as a yawssing of the jellow. His accent," I added, "was not impeccable."

"I yawss the jellow," said Jaakkala wonderingly. "I yawss the jellow." He tried it again. "Is it good, yes?" He was like a small child with a new toy.

I clapped him bravely on the back. "It's a beezer, boy," I said. "*Faire remplacement!* Take your goss on the potted meat!"

He did as he was told. He finished up with as fine a Kurdistan bouncer as we had ever seen, the blue ball leaping over the jellow in the yawss, to *faire* a tremendous *loopage*.

After the game, which we won easily, was over, Mr. Jaakkala drank a pint of whisky with echoing cries of "Skoal!" Before he left he delivered an address in Finnish, and then had to be helped down the steps.

I only hope he pulled himself together before his lectures began again next term.

BACK-SEAT DRIVERS

I now know that when a married woman says, "Do come along —*he* certainly won't mind," it's time for third parties to take to the woods.

This is knowledge, however, to be gained only in the hard school of life. It had not yet come my way when Suzanne Talbot suggested that they should put me up for the night.

There was no denying that some small emotional feeling had arisen between us during the Hunt Ball, warmed, no doubt, on Suzanne's part by the fact that her husband, Herbert, had spent the whole evening cementing a deal in cattle with three heavy men from Ballinasloe.

"But what," I said, "will the dashing rancher feel about it?"

"He," said Suzanne, with the faintest, contemptuous emphasis, "certainly won't mind."

I guessed she was telling me that Herbert's life was bounded on all sides by cows, leaving him no time to consider the fact that his wife was only thirty-seven.

"It would save me," I admitted, "a long drive home." She was a pretty little thing, somewhat crushed by the rigours of Irish country life. "We might," I said, "have some further conversation about art, music, and letters."

"You don't know what it's like," she said with sudden passion, "not to have to talk about hairball, footrot, and hookworm." She dropped my hand. Herbert was on his way across the room.

"You ready, Annie?" he said. He nodded uncomfortably towards me. "Hello, Mick——" he said. Herbert was certainly short on social graces. We had already been introduced. He might have tried to get a little closer to it than Mick.

"I'll get my things," Suzanne said. "I'll meet you in the hall."

Herbert and I looked at the floor. I thought it would be unwise to tell him I was coming back for the night. Suzanne could do that in the car.

"Well, cheers," said Herbert—"look after yourself." He slouched away.

I followed them home at a safe distance. Herbert, rigid in a boiled shirt, looked to me like a man who was ready for bed, but nonetheless I wanted to give him plenty of time to get tucked away.

He was waiting for me at the front door as I drove up. It was raining, but he came out on to the avenue in his shirt sleeves. "Here," he said, "what sort of a game is this? Annie says you're staying the night." His powerful face was knotted. A proposition had been made to him which passed his comprehension. "You're a Dublin fella, aren't you?" said Herbert. "What's stopping you going home?"

"Herbie!" cried Suzanne, "whatever will Mr. Campbell think of our manners?" She opened the door of my car. "Do come in," she said—"have a drink—it's not so late——"

"Well," I said—"I'll just have one——"

Herbert crowded me enough to make it embarrassing to get out of the car. "Here——" he said, protestingly, and then followed me, right on my heels, into the house.

There was no doubt that the situation had undergone a change. As a man who didn't mind Herbert was under false colours. And it no longer seemed important for me to brighten the life of his wife.

Suzanne threw open the sitting room door. "You have your friends," she told Herbert angrily, "I don't see why I shouldn't have mine. Sit down and have a drink—darling," she added, "and I'll get your bed ready."

She was merely being defiant. It was probably the first time in her life she had turned on him. But Herbert, a simple man, took the words at their face value.

"By God," said Herbert, "there'll be none of that!" Resolutely, he walked across the room and picked up a shotgun, which was leaning, surprisingly enough, against the desk.

I felt for the handle of the door. "There is no need for us to behave like savages," I said.

Herbert pulled out the top drawer of the desk, and broke open the gun. I knew he couldn't possibly be going to shoot, but still—if he loaded the thing—it might go off in his hand——

"Good night all," I said, "and thank you for a wonderful time." I was in the car a moment later, driving hard down the avenue, waiting for the shots to crash round my ears.

What did crash round my ears, three miles farther on, was a soft little sigh, followed by a sort of plopping noise. I swung round in sudden terror. The back seat was occupied in its entirety by a large black dog—a labrador, by the look of it, waking from a deep sleep!

I stopped the car. I opened the back door. The dog looked at me heavily. It was not yet fully conscious. I examined the label round its neck.

ROGO

My first instinct was to put Rogo out into the night, and leave him to find his own way home. But Rogo looked much too large to walk three miles, even if he did happen to know the way. I decided to take him back to Herbert's gate, and leave the rest to his own good sense.

I coasted up to the gate, with the engine switched off, and left the car a little beyond it, under the shelter of a tree. I didn't know if the Talbots had gone to bed, but I did know that I had no further desire to meet them personally.

I lifted Rogo out of the back seat. He felt exactly like a fat woman in a fur coat. "Good boy," I said, "go home." It was still raining. Rogo shivered and slowly climbed back into the car again. I tried to stop him, seizing him round his large waist, but he snarled so fiercely I had to let him go.

I got the starting-handle from the boot and tried to prod him out on to the road. The handle sank horribly into his large and yielding flank, but Rogo refused to move.

I started to bark softly, waving my hands about in the dim light of the dashboard lamp, I thought the disturbance might cause the dog to rise to his feet, and then I could suddenly push him out while he was off-balance.

I was absolutely astonished to see the face of the policeman looking in through the open door.

"Well, hello," I said, after a moment, "I was trying to get this damn dog out of the car." Then, I said. "You're out very late. Are you looking for murderers?" I wanted to remind him that he probably had some more important job to do.

He came round to my side, a young policeman like a bullock, probably a native Irish speaker if given a chance to gather his wits.

He looked at me cautiously. "It's not in me powers," he said, "to acquaint the civilian population with the nature of me duties. Is this your dog?"

"Well, no," I said, "it belongs to Mr. Talbot, up at the house. I'm trying to get him to go home."

"And what," he said, "is the animal doin' out of the owner's jurisdiction at this hour of the night?"

"I drove it away, by mistake," I said. "It got into the back of the car by itself and now I can't get it out."

There was a long, baffled silence.

"I'll have to ask you," said the young policeman, "to proceed up to the premises. You'll be drivin' the vehicle," he added. He was not going to take the risk of being shot in the back.

We drove slowly up the avenue. The policeman seemed to occupy three-quarters of the front seat. Rogo took up the whole of the back. I had fled lightly from the Talbots. I was returning to them laden down to the scuppers.

The policeman got out. "As a matter of a precaution," he said to me, "I'll have to ask you to dismount." I joined him on the doorstep. He seized the knocker. A thunderous sound rang through the darkened house.

"Bad old class of a night," said the policeman, in a conversational tone. I told him I'd never known worse. Then the door opened and Herbert, in a dressing-gown, stood on the threshold. The policeman must have been accustomed to rousing people from their beds. He paid no attention to Herbert's suffused face.

"It's me duty, sir," he said, "to make official enquiries into the ownership of an animal found in this gintleman's motor vehicle. The gintleman is making allegations that the animal belongs to you."

Herbert saw me for the first time. He took a pace forward. "You've taken my *dog*!" he exclaimed. He meant that I'd settled for his dog, having failed to take his wife.

"It got into the back of the car," I snapped. "I didn't want any part of it."

Herbert looked. "Where is it?" he said.

The back seat was empty. Rogo had gone back to bed, no doubt sensing that he was home again, after an inexplicable interruption.

"Holy fly," said the policeman, "an' wasn't it only lookin' at me a minit ago."

"A black overgrown thing," I said crossly. The policeman seemed to think a miracle had happened. "It was called Rogo. It was there all right."

"That's my dog," said Herbert. "I wouldn't lose that dog for a fortune." Suddenly he wanted to get hold of one concrete fact. "I'm going to see if that dog's in his kennel," he announced, "and if he isn't——" He made a wild gesture. He didn't know what would happen after that.

We followed him round to the yard. Rogo was at home, fast asleep in a kennel the size of a block of flats.

"Well," I said, "are you satisfied now?"

Herbert looked round heavily. "With what?" he said.

I'd had enough. "Officer," I said. "We're going home. You can issue the summonses in the morning." It really didn't matter what anyone was talking about any more.

I drove him into the village and left him outside the police station. He seemed surprised I wouldn't come in. "I've all me reports to do about the occurrence," he complained. "The sergeant is the divil an' all for writin' . . ."

I drove off abruptly without saying good-bye. I must have gone less than a mile when a voice said, "Guess who's here." It was a subdued and wary voice, and it came from the back seat.

I had no difficulty in identifying it as the voice of Suzanne, the lovely wife of Herbert Talbot, cattle dealer, of Grange House, Westmeath.

I stopped the car. With a weary sense of repetition I went round to get the starting-handle out of the boot.

CUCKOO IN THE NEST

Once, while I was in the Irish Marine Service, I saw a woman going aboard a Greek freighter late at night wearing a fur coat. I got on to my bicycle at once, and hurried back to headquarters.

Coogan, the duty officer, was lying face downwards on his bed, one hand trailing on the floor. I shook him by the shoulder.

He struggled in his sleep, and opened one eye.

"Whassamatta, dear?" he said.

I gave him time to come round. "Sir," I said, "a woman has just gone aboard the *Katerina* at the deep-water berth wearing a fur coat and carrying a suitcase. Do you want me to turn her off?"

He sprang up. "What's that?" he shouted. "What? Where?"

I tried to calm him. "She looks respectable, sir," I said. "She may have a special pass. I was wondering if you happened to know anything about her."

"Get back there at once!" he cried. He was half out of bed. "That bag is full of bombs!"

He started pulling on his trousers. Nothing much ever happened in our part of the docks, so that when it did everyone blew up at once. We had a special fear about women going on board ships with bombs in their handbags. The possibility had been invented by the army authorities, and we paid it close attention.

Coogan had his tunic on by now. "Are you coming too, sir?" I asked him, glad of the assistance.

"Me?" said Coogan, surprised. "No, I'm going to get a cup of cha."

I saluted. "I'll report back, sir," I said.

It was still raining. I pedalled down to the *Katerina* in my oilskins, sea-boots, and sou'wester, nearly a mile along the cobblestones into a headwind.

The ship was in darkness, save for a light on the bulkhead just below the bridge. The woman in the fur coat might have been anywhere by now, and, with a crew of twenty-eight Greeks, Egyptians, and Swedes, doing almost anything.

I decided to explain the situation to Captain Demetrius, hoping that for once he might make some effort to understand English.

I knocked on the door of his cabin. It was nearly four o'clock in the morning.

There was a pause of several seconds, and then suddenly the door was wrenched open from the inside. I'd been holding the handle on my side, and there was no time to let go. I was whipped right into the cabin, and right into Captain Demetrius himself.

"Ah, frand," said Captain Demetrius. He was about nine feet high, with a heavy black moustache, and a face the colour of tomato soup.

I stepped back and pushed up my sou'wester, which had been crushed over my face. "Excuse me, sir," I said. "I have information that a woman has been seen on board your ship. This is a controlled area. No unauthorised person is allowed in here without a pass."

I had little hope that any of this would come through to the Captain, but I thought he might be impressed by its official tone.

Demetrius nodded resignedly. "All right," he said. "You weesh sheep's peppers." He stepped aside to let me in.

The woman in the fur coat was lying on his bunk! She'd taken off the coat, and was wearing a purple dress with a halter of sequins round the shoulders.

"Oh gosh," I exclaimed. "That's her!"

An enormous smile spread across the Captain's face.

"You lof her?" he asked. Then he added, with pride, "My weef."

The lady feeling herself become the centre of attention, sat up and settled her hair. It was dead black, arranged in tight curls all over her head. She smiled, showing four front teeth bordered with gold.

"She's your *wife*?" I said, nonplussed. The Captain seemed to have laid me a stymie.

"We to marry up," said the Captain. He laid a knotted, affectionate hand on the lady's thigh.

I couldn't make out if he meant they were married or were going to be married.

"Has your wife a pass?" I said, clearly and distinctly.

"Noh! Noh!" cried Captain Demetrius. "She iss Grik! Like me —Grik!"

I waited for a moment and began again.

"Has she a pass," I said, "—a permission—a letter saying it's all right?"

"Iss peppers?" said the Captain, peering at me closely, trying to help. He opened a drawer in the table, and pulled out a bundle of documents.

"Iss rats peppers, cargo peppers, crew-men peppers, steward smoke peppers?" he said, showing them to me one by one.

I gave them back. "No," I said. "I've seen all those. It's your wife. Has she a *pass*?"

It was very hot in the cabin. There was a smell of foreign cooking and cigars.

"Pass—pass?" said Captain Demetrius. "Wot is pass?" He shook his head ponderously. A new idea occurred to him. He threw an arm like a tree-trunk round the lady's shoulders.

"No pass," he said. He smiled proudly. "We are make up bebe," he announced.

I thought I'd better get out. "I shall have to report this matter to the duty officer, Captain," I said. "I may be back."

Demetrius waved his hand. "You come up for bebe," he said. "Iss vino. Drinkeng to frands."

I had no idea what he could possibly mean. As I shut the door the lady lay down again on the bunk.

Coogan was again fast asleep when I got back to the billet. This time, when I tried to wake him, he seized my hand.

"C'm here, love," he muttered, "—c'm over here."

I shook him off. I was getting too much involved in other people's private lives.

Coogan sat up. "What the hell's the matter with you?" he said. "It's the middle of the night."

"Sir," I said, "there's a very difficult situation on the *Katerina*. Captain Demetrius says the lady is his wife. I think she's going to have a baby."

"You're a damn fool," shouted Coogan. "Of course he says she's his wife. *Go and get her off!* If the C/O hears about this you're for the glasshouse."

I tried to reason with him. "She's going to have a baby, sir. It's pouring rain . . ."

"You'll have a baby if you don't get to hell out of this," cried Coogan. "Get back aboard that ship and do your job."

I got on to my bicycle again. There was a faint trace of dawn in the wild black sky.

This time there was no answer when I knocked on Demetrius's door. I beat harder. Suddenly it flew open.

"What the holy Gott you want?" said Captain Demetrius. He was breathing hard and wearing a thick woollen vest.

I decided to be ruthless. "The lady has got to go ashore, Captain," I said.

Demetrius shook his head desperately. "I am telling," he said. "Iss not a shore. Iss weef. Iss *weef*!"

I pushed past him. "That's quite enough of that," I said crisply.

The lady was lying on the bunk scarcely concealed by an emerald and gold kimono.

I spun round and faced the wall. "Tell her to get dressed, Captain," I said. "And be quick about it."

Demetrius shrugged his shoulders. So far as he was concerned the world had gone mad.

He shook the lady roughly, and said something to her in Greek. I heard her expostulating, and then Demetrius trying to soothe her. There was a sudden silence. When I looked round they were clenched in a long embrace. They showed no signs of stopping. In the end I had to tap Demetrius on the shoulder, and show him my watch.

The lady got dressed. She put on her fur coat and picked up the suitcase.

Demetrius suddenly gripped me by the arm. "Iss not damage," he said threateningly. "Not make up bebe. Iss now honeymorn."

I said, "That's quite all right, Captain. I'm sure she'll be able to find a taxi." I couldn't make head or tail of what he was trying to say.

I escorted the lady off the ship, and as far as the dock gates. I was surprised to find her trying to hold my hand, but thought she was probably afraid of falling into the water.

I freed myself outside the gates. "Not go back," I told her. "Must get pass. Comprenez?"

I pedalled away. She gave a cry of what might have been dismay, but I didn't look round. I'd done enough.

I went off duty at eight that morning. When I got back next day there was an urgent message for me to see Lieutenant Coogan.

He wasted no words. "What the flaming hell do you think you were doing the other night?" he said.

"What other night, sir?" I asked him.

"Tuesday," he cried. "The *Katerina*. There's about a yard and half of complaints here from the agents. They say you insulted Captain Demetrius's wife, and insisted on her coming with you. Demetrius seemed to think you thought you'd first claim, or something, although God knows how *that* happened. At any rate there's hell to pay all round."

"But, sir," I said—"sir, I told you she was his wife."

"I couldn't make out what you were trying to tell me," said Coogan crossly. He bit into a pencil. "I knew from the beginning you weren't up to this job."

He removed a sliver of wood from his teeth, looking worried. "God knows," he said, "it only needs a little tact."

MOTHER—I'M BACK!

What we're liable to get for Christmas this year is a tiny tartan bag containing three pencils in the form of miniature golf-clubs, another one, and a net made of string to be hung between two chairs, on which woollies can be dried without losing their shape.

What we want for Christmas is a new parlour game, and I've got it—a divertissement so richly satisfying that I can't imagine how I came to invent it with such ease, round about two o'clock on the morning of Boxing Day last year.

We'd just passed through the unspeakable degradation of charades, the last one, presented by an aunt of mine and two helpless victims called Burke, being a true collector's piece in the field of dramatic paralysis.

My aunt, a slow-change artiste of infinite jest, whom Fate had tricked out of going on the boards professionally in 1902, came in with a look of profound solemnity, wearing a deer-stalker with the flaps down and one of my shirts, overhanging a pair of dress trousers tucked into red and white hooped football stockings, an ensemble which could only have been based on the Eton Wall Game, though I was certain she'd never heard of it.

She was followed by Mrs. Burke, a rather smart but tense little woman with the bright, staring eyes of a bush-baby, now hopelessly unbalanced by a man's tweed cap, pulled low down to her eyebrows, with the peak standing out sideways over one ear. She might just conceivably have represented Jackie Coogan wearing a black net cocktail dress, a swoop into transvestism too beastly to invite analysis.

Behind her, after a long interval, came her husband, a deeply serious and thoughtful lecturer on economics. On his head he wore a pith helmet with a single paper rose protruding from one of the ventilation holes in the crown.

They arranged themselves in a line in front of us, my aunt struggling unsuccessfully to restrain her laughter at the inspired humour of her disguise, while the Burkes looked like the victims of a firing squad composed of maniacs, who'd compelled them to don fancy dress, in which to meet their end.

We gave them a scatter of applause.

My aunt took a pace forward. "First syllable," she announced with extreme solemnity, indicating that she had momentarily stepped out of character, and that we were not to assume that this was part of the show.

She rejoined her familiars. "Now," she said, in a hoarse whisper. Slowly, she raised her right hand in the V-sign. With the other she removed an imaginary cigar from the general area of her face, which she'd inflated into global form. The Burkes did likewise, Mrs. Burke, through nervousness, using the V-sign to remove her cigar, an effective economy which, I was surprised to find, had not occurred to me as a *modus operandi* before.

My mother, having given the demonstration insufficient thought, called out, "Churchill!" Mr. Burke seized swiftly and thankfully on this release. "That's it," he said, and immediately removed his pith helmet.

But it wasn't, as we learnt from my aunt, without further delay. It wasn't Churchill at all, despite the powerful supporting evidence. It turned out, in a long and peevish altercation between the players, that what they were really doing was "hat", the first step on a colourful programme leading to a grand finale in a modiste's, where clues were to have been laid that would have led us to "hat-box", if our wits had been razor keen.

"We were only doing Churchill," my aunt cried, "to throw you off the scent!" The fury of her indignation was in no way impaired by the insanity of her dress. "Churchill wears funny *hats,* doesn't he?"

No one seemed to find this explanation fully satisfying, specially my mother, a long-time admirer of Sir Winston's. "What's the idea, then," she asked truculently, "of the football socks? And Sir Winston never had his shirt hanging out in his life."

Victor Burke ventured a thought. "Possibly," he said, "a black coat and striped trousers would have been more in character." The memory of that rose-tipped pith helmet was going to come between him and the laws of supply and demand for a long time to come. Mrs. Burke was encouraged by the firmness of his stand. "Honestly," she said, "I'm quite sure Sir Winston doesn't wear caps and if he did they'd be straight." Her Coogan image must suddenly have given her another stab. "It's impossible," she snapped, "to act properly if you're wearing the wrong clothes. . . ."

It was at that moment I invented the new parlour game. It sprang into my mind, round and complete, the perfect antidote to the squalid incompetence of charades. "That's it!" I cried. "You've got it, duchess! There's no proper acting in charades. We're just clowning around, numb with incompetence and embarrassment, trying feverishly to be funny—an endeavour which has brought trained, professional comedians, skilled in every artifice of timing and technique, with a routine worked out to the last detail and someone to write their jokes. . . ." At this moment a bottle of cherry brandy which I happened to be holding started to play "The Bluebells of Scotland". I put it down quickly, stopping its nonsense before some fool started laughing. "An endeavour which has brought trained comedians to bankruptcy, alcoholism and an early grave. If we want to act—and who doesn't at two o'clock in the morning—let us turn our talents to the exposition of tragedy, an infinitely easier ride."

After a pause of a couple of seconds a young man called Tom something or other—living, I calculated, on borrowed time at someone else's family Christmas—suggested a game of Murder. "Is that sad enough for you?" he said.

I put a stop to that. "If you can stand being cross-questioned by a detective who keeps telling you he can't think of any more questions to ask, I can't," I said. "We'll try this. Each of us is going to go out of the room in turn, have a short period of meditation outside and then come in again, and with every crumb of heart, soul, spirit and imagination we can summon to our aid deliver just one line, and mean it. Let's see if we can really act, and not just muck about with pith helmets."

They couldn't see it, though my aunt was eager to have a crack at anything that was going. "How do you mean?" she said. "What do we say?"

It burst, unbidden and unconsidered, upon my mind.

"Mother—I'm back!"

Although I say it myself it was, even without rehearsal, a beautiful rendition. There was deep pathos in it. There was love and homesickness and humility and contrition, and a melting sadness for the futility of all the wasted years. It got even the man who wanted to play Murder. "Where have you been?" he asked respectfully.

"Imagine that for yourselves," I told them. "Twenty-five years in the Siberian salt-mines, or for the ladies a similar spell as the plaything, in mid-Sahara, of a licentious Arab sheik. The important thing is that you're back. You steal into the old familiar room and there is Mother, older and frailer now, but still bowed over her favourite spinning-wheel, just as she used to be. She doesn't see you. Her back is to the door. You approach her, and from the depth of your being you say, 'Mother—I'm back!' "

Suddenly, they all wanted to do it at the same time, and I had to steady them down. It had occurred to me that we wanted a real mother, a bowed figure at the writing-desk, failing a spinning-wheel, who would turn in tremulous wonder as the long-lost child appeared, and give us something solid to play against. Unfortunately, as soon as my aunt saw that a slow turn and tremulous wonder were on the agenda she insisted on playing the mother herself, and disappeared for twenty minutes, to return with a black shawl over her head and burnt-cork lines on the face, a piece of up-staging so powerful that I decided to have first stab at the prodigal, to get the thing off the ground.

Outside the door I made the interesting psychological discovery that I was incapable of projecting myself with complete sincerity into the role of a middle-aged son returning to the old manse after —the scenario was sketchy even in my own mind—twenty years beachcombing in Tahiti. I felt merely like myself, about to try to justify a passing flight of fancy before some not entirely sober friends and relations who, judging by the roar of conversation coming from within, had already forgotten completely the modest entertainment promised by him without.

But that, I reasoned, was the actor's craft, to induce attention for a fiction in persons nine-tenths occupied with their own reality. Assuming an expression of melancholy—brow furrowed, mouth turned deeply down—I opened the door . . . and immediately went into a comic routine that would have disgraced a stand-in Widow Twankey at a Wednesday pantomime matinée in Pontypridd.

I got my finger stuck in the keyhole. I allowed myself to be assaulted, indelicately, by the door-handle. When the time came for me to deliver my line I seemed to be chewing gum. "Mother," I said, in a slow, Texas drawl, "Ah'm Buck."

It was nearly the end of the new game. Most of them believed it was a hoax, aimed at providing me with a solo comedy spot. I'd the greatest difficulty in persuading them to let me do it again. "You've no idea," I said, "how difficult it is to project yourself with sincerity. And there's audience pressure, as well, and door-handling, composition of the features, the remembrance of things past. . . . It's fascinating. Watch this."

Next time I got my melancholy going much better and quite unexpectedly added a piece of business that everyone later said was extraordinarily interesting—a defensive raising of the right hand, on the delivery of the line—"suggesting," as someone said, "you suspected that Mother's welcome home would be accompanied by the throwing of decayed fruit."

After that they all wanted to do it, and they did it three or four times, each time revealing a new and more fascinating neurosis.

Little Mrs. Burke, on her first couple of runs, which were severely diluted by nervousness, merely chirped, "Mother—I'm back," as though she'd been round the corner for half a pound of streaky bacon. At the third attempt, however, she suddenly spat out, "Mother—I'm back!" with such vicious resentment that Mother at the writing-table reared back in genuine fear.

The solid Victor Burke, on the other hand, produced his line practically in baby talk, suggesting that his image of the reunion was Mummy's enfolding arms, fortified with hot milk and rusks in front of the nursery fire, while the youth Tom, an operator of apparently draught-proof self-assurance, not only fell on his knees upon entering the room but also failed to get further than the word, "Mother . . ." before being seized by a racking sob which, we were all agreed, owed nothing to artifice.

We carried on until five o'clock or so in the morning, all adding or subtracting minute nuances from our performances until they represented the final and definitive statement of the ego, and then we did it twice more each, to set the mould.

I can recommend "Mother—I'm back!" for Christmas this year, in place of charades, but with one word of warning. Be careful to select for the part of Mother a friend or relative who, through diffidence or lack of ambition in the dramatic art, is content to confine her performance to a slow turn and tremulous wonder, or difficulties will ensue.

I myself was just coming in on Take Nine, ready for the charged pause after closing the door noiselessly behind me, when my aunt, who'd been getting fidgety over her admittedly modest responsibilities, suddenly swung round from the writing-table, flung her arms wide and cried in a voice sonorous with emotion, "Rupert, my boy—you've returned!"

It would have taken Sir Larry himself, on a good night, to carry on from there.

A BOY'S BEST BODYGUARD

When a fellow is faced by armed men it's my honest opinion that he should have his mother around, if the situation is not to descend into flurry and confusion.

Three times I have looked down the muzzle of a gun. On the first two occasions my mother was present, and an orderly conclusion was achieved. In her absence, the third time, I handled the business so maladroitly that even the police got it back to front. The lesson is plain.

My mother and I first started gun-slinging, as it were, in 1922. The Irish Civil War was in progress and one of its victims—or very likely to be if he didn't look slippy—was my father, then a member of the Cosgrave Government. He had returned once to our house outside Dublin with three perceptible bullet holes in the back door of his car, in no mood to share my mother's opinion, aimed at restoring his confidence, that the IRA had probably mistaken him for someone else. The shots had, apparently, been fired near Portobello Bridge. So sure was my father of their intended destination that he covered the three miles home in three minutes, and went straight to bed.

When, therefore, the thunderous banging came on the back door a few nights later it had the effect of freezing him to his armchair, in which he'd been reading the evening paper. It was my mother who went to the top of the kitchen stairs, to see what was afoot. I joined her almost immediately, a pale lad of nine, having been roused from my sleep by the noise. I'd been sleeping badly of recent weeks because it was nearly Christmas, and my whole soul was crying out to take possession of my first Hornby train.

"It's all right," my mother said, taking her customarily steady view, "it's only some men."

We heard the bolts being shot on the back door, and then the voice of the cook raised in indignant surprise. She was a loyal retainer, who'd been with the family for some years. "It's youse lot, is it?" she said. "Janey, I thought yez wasn't comin' till half-eleven." It was, in fact, only ten-fifteen.

A male voice said peevishly, "Ah, don't be shoutin' . . ." and then the first of the raiders came running up the stairs. I had a brief glimpse of a gun, then a face masked with a cap and a handkerchief. My mother stopped him dead. "If there's going to be any murder," she said, "you can get back out of that and go home."

More masked faces and caps appeared at the bottom of the stairs. Querulous voices arose. "What's the matther, Mick?" "Get on with it, can't ya?" But Mick was explaining the matter to my mother.

"Nobody's gettin' shot, mum. You needn't take on. We've orders to burn down the house, that's all." He sounded injured by the false impression.

"You're sure of that?" my mother asked him, wishing to have the matter absolutely clear for the benefit of my father, in the event that he was still able to receive messages, in the next room.

"There'll be nobody shot," said another raider impatiently. "Now will you stand back owa that an' let's get on with it. We haven't all night."

My mother remained firm. With the first matter on the agenda settled to her satisfaction, she passed to others, now of equal importance. "What about all my lovely books?" she said. "First editions, signed by Lawrence and Katherine Mansfield and Middleton Murry. And the pictures—Orpens, Gertlers, the little drawings by John . . ."

The raiders, jammed on the stairs, were getting hot and angry. An exposed youth, still stuck in the passage, was being berated by the cook. He appeared to be a cousin of hers, and was refusing to carry her trunk out into the garden.

"All right, all *right* . . ." said the first raider. The protracted conversation was causing the handkerchief to slip off his face. "Take out annything you want, but for God's love hurry up about it." He turned to the men behind. "Who's got the pethrol an' the matches?" he wanted to know.

At this point my father appeared in the hall, unobtrusively, and still unsure of his welcome. The raiders appealed to him. "Ask your missus to give us a chance, sir, will ya? Sure, we're only actin' under ordhers. . . ."

He took command, in a voice slightly higher than normal, advising me to wake my sister, still peacefully asleep, and to put on some warm clothes. He then suggested to my mother that they should both try to save a few personal mementoes before we all withdrew to safety in the garden.

"And leave," my mother cried passionately, "all the children's Christmas toys behind? Certainly not!"

The possible outcome of the night struck home to me for the first time. "Me train!" I cried. "Don't let them burn me train!"

"Of course they won't," said my mother. She rounded on two of the men. "You," she said, "go to the cupboard in the bedroom and bring out all the parcels you can find. And look out for the doll's house. It's fragile."

They shuffled their feet, deeply embarrassed. Several other men were throwing petrol around the hall. "Well, go on!" my mother shouted at them. "And leave your silly guns on the table. Nobody'll touch them."

By the time the first whoosh of petrol flame poured out of the windows she had five of the men working for her, running out with armfuls of books and pictures, ornaments, and our Christmas toys. They'd become so deeply concerned on her behalf that they frequently paused to ask what should be salvaged next. "Is the bit of a picture in the passage anny good, mum?" "Is there ere a chance of gettin' the legs offa the pianna, the way we could dhrag it out . . .?"

When they disappeared into the night they left my mother, bathed in the light of the flames, standing guard over a great heap of treasures in the middle of the lawn, with Orpen's picture under one arm and the little drawings by John under the other—a clear winner on points.

Next time it was the IRA again. My unfortunate father was now officially on the run—an appalling situation for a peaceful and dignified man—while the rest of us, being homeless, were staying with my mother's parents in Foxrock, a base that at first sight could not have been more neutral. But then, in the middle of the night, the caps and the handkerchiefs appeared again, and it turned out that we were sitting on a miniature arsenal, not, admittedly, of the first calibre, but undoubtedly containing weapons of war.

Once again it was probably the domestic staff who provided the link between the beleaguered fortress and its attackers, but—as is common in the uncertain art of espionage—they'd considerably exaggerated their report, in the interests of making it seem worth while.

After twenty minutes in the house the IRA were dissatisfied to find themselves in possession of two assegais, a knobkerry, a Gurkha knife, a 1914 bayonet and a pith helmet from the Boer War, trophies brought home from foreign service by my mother's numerous brothers. All these warriors, however, were now somewhere else, so that the depleted garrison put up no great struggle as the IRA ranged through the house, throwing open cupboards and peering under beds in search of the machine-guns and Mills bombs promised them by the cook.

While all this was going on I was standing on the rug beside my bed with a pillow between my knees, placed there by my mother. The burning of our house, followed by close proximity to my grandmother, who was a fast hand with a ruler, had brought my nerves to a low state. From the first crash on the back door my knees had been knocking together so rapidly that they were now severely bruised on the inside, making each new percussion an agony. The pillow, however, eased things considerably. I was holding it in position, fore and aft, when the raider burst into the room, waving a huge Service revolver, but I dropped it immediately when he shouted, "Hands up!" The knees started rattling again, like castanets.

My mother went into immediate action. "How can he put his hands up?" she shouted at the raider. "Look at his little knees!" She slotted the pillow home again into position, and returned to the attack.

"How dare you frighten the life out of a little child!" she cried. At the age of nine I was nearly six feet tall, but the principle was right. "Give him your gun! Let him see it isn't loaded!"

As usual, the speed and directness of her assault bouleversed the enemy. He was a lumpish youth in the regulation cap and trench-coat, with a handkerchief over his face which looked as if it had recently been used for cleaning floors. He became placatory. "I wouldn't frighten the little fella, mum. A'course it's not loaded. Amn't I only afther findin' it down below? . . ."

My mother pounced upon this new intelligence. "That's Malcolm's revolver," she cried. "Put it back where you found it! Didn't he risk his life with it, defending you and all the other hooligans like you from the Germans?"

"Put it back, mum?" The proposition staggered him. "I can't do that, mum. Sure, the commandant'll kill me. . . ."

At this point my mother snatched the gun out of his hand. "Let him hold it, anyway," she cried. "I'm not going to have any child of mine having nightmares over a filthy, silly revolver." She thrust it into my hand.

I didn't want it at all. I only wanted to hold on to my pillow. I dropped it on the floor, with the pillow on top of it, and tried to put my hands between my knees.

In the midst of this confusion there was a hoarse shout from downstairs: "Christy, come on owa that, willya! There's nothin' more here. . . ."

Christy made a move towards the gun. My mother put her foot on it. They faced one another for a moment, with a thin, obbligato sobbing from myself. "You'll be hearin' more of this," said Christy unconvincingly. Then he turned and ran.

My mother put me back to bed, then she picked up the revolver by the muzzle and threw it into the bottom of the cupboard. "I'll put it in the bank in the morning," she said. "Filthy, silly things. Don't you ever have anything to do with them."

Down Mulberry Lane

THE DEFENCE OF MON REPOS

This was a weapon that had not been used before—a guided missile, by comparison with their previous light grenades.

In this battle I had held them for months by lobbing back everything they sent over, with the addition of some homemade grapeshot of my own. Such persistent give and take seemed to guarantee a state of deadlock so obviously permanent that I was sure they would break off the engagement, and go after some less resolute garrison.

Then this other thing arrived, smack home on the target, discharged from miles behind the lines, a *billet-doux* from the Special Commissioners of Income Tax—the top brass. Here was no local collector, sniping from a makeshift position with the fire-power of two middle-aged spinsters and a tea-boy. This, in fact, was it. The Special Commissioners had dropped The Bomb, and now wished to settle the terms of the armistice on their own ground—in Turnstile House, 94–9 High Holborn, London, WC1. I noted that the Solicitor of Inland Revenue would represent the Crown.

It seemed that the end had come. Dazed by the blast, and hopelessly short of *matériel,* I saw no prospect of further resistance.

Then I suddenly remembered the American officer, surrounded at Bastogne, who replied: "Nuts!" to the German surrender demand. And no sooner had I remembered him than I remembered an equally resolute friend of mine called Broth. The Broth used to drive about the outskirts of Dublin in an open Morris Cowley letting fly at street lights with a shotgun, while steering the car with his knees.

With the Broth by my side, I mused, and the spirit of Bastogne in our hearts, defeat might even now be turned into victory.

I was doing this musing in the kitchen, having just received the Special Commissioners' guided missile, from the postman, through the window. Looking down the narrow drive it struck me all at once that my house, by reason of its special topography, could probably be held for quite a time against an attacking force. I'd been thinking in military terms all along, otherwise the idea might not have occurred to me.

Slowly I poured myself another cup of tea. How would it be, I wondered, if I answered the Special Commissioners with "Nuts. . . ."

The Broth and I spent the first morning nailing up the shutters on the downstairs windows, cutting loopholes to give us a field of fire down the drive. I'd explained the position. The summons to appear before the Commissioners, my refusal, the reissuing of their invitation, my second refusal, the summons to appear before the High Court, my third refusal, and now, what must amount to the show-down.

"You're only doing," said the Broth, "what's right. Sure whose money is it, anyway?" I'd always known he would grasp the essentials.

When we'd made all secure downstairs I told my wife to fill the bath and as many saucepans as she could find. "Even if they do cut off the water," I explained, "we can hold out for several weeks, if we ration it."

She was pale, obviously nervous, as the Broth and I strengthened the bedroom defences. But I knew she had the right stuff in her when she said: "We've four tins of herrings in tomato sauce, two tins of Australian sausages, a carton of cake-mix—"

"Speed to the grocer. Load up. Don't forget the pemmican. If they're here before you get back just fight your way through."

We covered her down the avenue—the Broth with his shotgun—I with my Daisy air-pistol. There was still no sign of the enemy.

"It can't be much longer now," I said. "I was supposed to appear in court this morning—10.30. We'll be seeing the Tipstaff soon."

"Is he a class of racing man?"

"He's the official who comes to get you if you don't appear in answer to a summons. He carries a rod."

"Begob," said Broth, "they've some hairy institutions over here."

The Tipstaff still hadn't appeared by the time my wife got back with the supply train. She'd done well. "Just get all that into a cool place," I told her, "and while you have the chance better run up some grub. We don't know when we'll be able to eat once the shooting starts."

The Broth and I settled down again, our ears and trigger fingers alert.

When the Tipstaff arrived at the gate he clearly had no idea that he was covered. He plodded up the drive, a heavy, tank-like man in a bowler hat, carrying a rod, but he stopped dead when I called out : "Ho—Tipstaff ! What is your business?"

"Excuse me, sir—I've a warrant here for your arrest." He licked his lips. I knew he was yellow.

"Get out," I said simply.

He hesitated, one eye on his line of retreat. "I advise you, sir—"

"Poom !" There was a ringing blast in my ear. I struck up Broth's gun. "Hothead !" I barked. He looked at me mutinously.

"You've shown them your fire-power." The Tipstaff, nicked, was in full flight down the drive. "Lookka here, you," said Broth, "I'm only in this for the fun of shooting a couple of policemen. I'm a freelance."

Our eyes clashed, for a long moment. It was Broth who broke. "Okay," he said—"skipper". I knew that from then on the lives of our small party were in my sole command.

The Mem-sahib appeared with the chow. Baked beans and a fried egg apiece. I tried to keep my temper. "We'll have to have them poached," I said. "We can't afford to waste the lard. We'll need it for rolling rush tapers when they cut off the light."

She said, "The house is full of candles."

I gave a short laugh. "We'll be eating those, ere long."

She threw me a startled look. Perhaps it had been foolhardy of me to put the position so bluntly. Then I knew she'd have to face up to it sooner or later. "Get your jodhpurs on," I said. "That dress will get in the way when you're reloading the carbines."

She had grit, all right. "Aye, aye, sir," she said, and withdrew.

Nevertheless, I was worried. "Better keep an eye on her," I told Broth. "Women, under siege, always have a tendency to rush out, shouting, 'No more bloodshed—no more bloodshed !' "

"You mean—" said Broth. That itching finger of his touched the trigger of his Purdey.

"No, no, y'fool," I said, "just stun her with the butt."

He nodded. He was loyal, right through.

I'd scarcely finished my beans and egg when a low, warning whistle from Broth called me to the window. The Tipstaff, and Constable Blower, were peering over the gate.

With care I lined up Blower in the sights of my air-pistol and drilled him through the helmet. Broth looked put out. "Blower's not very bright," I explained. "You've got to speak to him sharply."

Blower and the Tipstaff had by now disappeared from sight

behind the hedge, but we could hear their voices raised in altercation. The Tipstaff was shouting something about Scotland Yard, and Blower was doing his best to pacify him. I guessed the nature of Blower's trouble. He'd probably lost his handcuffs, and the station was untidy. The last people he wanted down were the Yard. Nothing upsets the branch manager more than a visit from head office. I decided to put the two of them finally, for the last time, in the picture.

"Hey, you!" I called. "Do something for me, will you?"

Their faces reappeared. Blower had removed his helmet, no doubt to avoid getting it punctured again.

"Go and tell the Special Commissioners of Inland Revenue," I shouted, "that I no longer regard myself as being under their jurisdiction. I'm signing off. I've paid enough. I'm free, white, independent, and harmless if left alone, and that's the way I propose to stay. Goodbye."

"Good man yourself," came the low response from Broth.

Blower and the Tipstaff exchanged a glance, and hurried off down the road. They were almost certainly going to obtain reinforcements. They returned, in fact, with the fire brigade. I should have remembered that the police, faced with a knotty problem like a kitten up a tree, or a child with its head stuck in the railings, always send for the fire brigade even before they begin to take people's names and addresses. It's a reflex action.

We could see the firemen, laden to the scuppers with respirators, electric torches, hatchets, and hip-length waders striding about trying to get some sense out of Blower and the Tipstaff. Then they shot the escape ladder up above the trees, with a fireman holding on to it. He peered briefly down, and then suddently let go a great cascade of water. Broth was too quick for me. He drilled the hose with a right and left, so that the fireman seemed to disappear into a haze of miniature but violent fountains. They lowered him, leaping about on the ladder, and then all was silent again.

"You shouldn't have done that," I said. "We've got to conserve our ammo."

"He was shootin' the wather at us, wasn't he?" Broth looked aggrieved.

"They always soak everything the moment they arrive," I explained. "It's Rule I in the instruction manual. I should think you've probably done it now all right. Attacking fire brigades and bursting their hoses is sacrilege. They may have to rush off next and save a lot of children or hospital nurses from a burning building, and then we'll really be for it, if the hose doesn't work."

"Begob," said Broth, "they're a soft-hearted lot on this side."

My worst fears were quickly realised. The sun was just beginning to set when I heard the first rumble of tanks on the road. There they were, twelve of them, with pennants flying and the younger sons of Gloucestershire landed gentry standing in the turrets with ginger cavalry moustaches, and spotted scarves to add a touch of gallantry to the uniform. And following them was a large, olive-green scout car. In the back seat was a familiar, sharp-visaged figure, wearing a black beret, with two badges side by side.

"Good Lord," I said—"they've put Monty on the job!"

We watched them narrowly, but as yet they seemed to have no aggressive intent. Small fires sprang up on the road, and bivouac tents. We heard the clink of spades, and the small domestic sounds of a soup kitchen.

"He's digging in," I told Broth. "He always likes to get everything organised up to the hilt before he makes a move. Those tanks have probably come all the way from Camberley. He'll want to get them repainted and cleaned up and, of course, the chaps'll have to get their feet inspected. You can turn in for a couple of hours. I'll take the first spell."

It was a long night. Both Broth and I were in poor shape as the staff officer, under a white flag, came down the drive. It was just before dawn.

The emissary stopped outside the kitchen window, and looked up. "I say, you chaps," he called, "do pack it in. You're being a frightful nuisance."

I leant out of the bedroom window. "Nuts!" I said.

"Well, dash it," said the officer, "we'll have to winkle you out." He looked pained. "Mummy used to live near here before she married Daddy. Hate to see the place pasted about."

It was clear that they were going to paste us about. One of the tanks nosed into the gateway. The muzzle of the gun raised itself to the bedroom window. "Begob," said Broth, "if they let that lot off they won't find the soles of our boots."

I gave him a short, whimsical grin. "You've underestimated the quality of your C.O.," I said. I opened the window wide. "Hey," I called, "tell Bernard I want a word with him."

There was a stirring among the tanks, and the black beret separated itself from the tin hats. I noted that his trousers were as sharply creased as ever.

"Listen, F.M.," I said, "you can't possibly go knocking this place about. Seventeen-twentieths of it belong to the Abbey National Building Society. Shell it, and they'll sue you to the back teeth."

He looked up at me for a long moment, and then shrugged. "He'll play ball," I told Broth. "Generals have to be both politically and sociologically minded these days."

The road by now was so cluttered with fire-engines, fire escapes, tanks, Bren-gun carriers, tents, soup-kitchens and bivvies that the big black Humber, when it arrived, could scarcely force its way through. Churchill, when he got out, didn't seem to be in the best of tempers.

"Is that the man himself?" Broth asked.

"That's him. He always attends these private sieges. The last chance he got was in Sidney Street. He'll sum it all up now, you'll see, and work out his logistics.'

I'll say this for the Old Man, he puts his finger on the nub of the thing at once. He saw there was only one path of attack, down the drive. Daisy Air-Pistol Alley, I'd come to call it in my own mind. There was no chance of taking us from the other three sides. Private property, owned by three yeomen of England, staunch—up till then—Conservative supporters.

"He's shrewd," I told Broth. "He'll parley. He only slashes at the soft under-belly in time of war."

Parley he did. The first meeting, in the neutralised tent on the lawn, was set for midday. "I'll be back in six months," I told Broth, as I got my documents and briefcase together. "Remember Panmunjong. I'll fill in till the new year with an agenda to discuss the agenda—"

I came to with a start to find my wife standing beside the kitchen table in her dressing-gown. "Get back to your post!" I cried, involuntarily.

She seemed surprised by my vehemence. "Has it come?" she said.

I realized what she meant. "There was only one letter," I said—"for me." I lit a cigarette. "Thing from the Special Commissioners of Inland Revenue. They'd like to see me at 10.30 this morning."

"Are you going?"

"Oh, well," I told her, "I may as well drop in and talk it over. I don't see that it can do any harm."

A COOL FIGURE IN WHITE

I was making, being unemployed at the time, a tour of the English shires, carrying all my possessions in a cabin trunk, and had put in a fortnight of adequate eating with a harmless young couple called Gossett. Paul and Primula their names were, and you had to talk to them slowly even about the weather.

The three of us lived a quiet life, because Primula, in about a month's time, was going to have a baby.

The Gossetts existed in a sort of daze; while I filled in the long spring evenings with old copies of the *Sporting and Dramatic.*

But, suddenly, one night, Primula put down her knitting.

"Paul," she said. "I think—I'm . . ." She fell back in her chair, her face white.

Gossett shot up from the sofa.

"No!" he cried—"you're not! You can't . . .!"

I looked at Primula with some concern. If she really was going to have the child now it was me for the open road. But I had thirty shillings and a cabin trunk. Any move would have to be cautiously organised, with motor transport, and a certain destination at the other end.

"Perhaps," I said, "it's only indigestion."

Paul swung round. Even in this extremity he was polite.

"It may be," he said. "It's quite possible. But we must be careful. Do you mind ringing the nurse?"

This had been arranged for some time. A maternity nurse lived in the town. She was to move in at once as soon as the crisis began.

I rang her up. An indifferent and apparently idiot voice replied that Nurse Fletcher was down with the shingles.

For a moment I thought the Shingles must be some family nearby.

"Get her back," I cried. "Tell her to come here at once!"

"It's spots," said the voice. "She carn."

There was a pause.

"You could 'ave Nurse Foley," said the voice. "She's 'olidyin'."

I couldn't make out what Nurse Foley was doing.

"Send her along immediately," I said. "Tell her to take a taxi."

"Ar," said the voice, and the line went dead.

An hour later there was a knock on the door. I'd been tramping up and down the sitting-room, waiting anxiously for any sound from upstairs. I rushed out into the hall.

A large woman stood on the door-step, wearing horn-rimmed glasses, a pot hat and a green tweed suit. She carried a suitcase, and there was a stub of a cigarette in the corner of her mouth.

She stepped over the threshold.

"Well," she said, "talk about luck. Here's me takin' a week off from me labours, and lo and behold doesn't Fletcher go an' get herself stretched, an' before I can turn round an' ask meself the time isn't there another young one yellin' to be brought into the world, an' here's me at your service day an' night, never in the mornin'."

I took a pace back.

"Are you," I said, "Nurse Foley?"

She stubbed out the remnants of her cigarette in a flower pot.

"That's me," she said. "Foley, from Tralee. I've all me certy-fikates, so don't you be botherin' your barney. Sure, we'll have the young one before morning,' an' be pourin' out the flowin' bowl with the rest of them."

I looked at Nurse Foley. I tried to picture the effect she was going to have on the Gossetts.

"I'm not," I said, "actually the father. Mr. Gossett is upstairs with his wife. Perhaps you'd better go up and see them."

"Ye gods an' little fishes," said Nurse Foley, "look at me puttin' me big feet in it again."

She leant forward confidentially. "Tell us," she said, "what class of a pair are they? To tell you the truth I was sweatin' comin' up the drive. I'm not used to this class of a place at all. Done all me work in Tralee. Are they havin' anny of them specialist fellas in? Sure, it'd put the heart across me if there was one of them Hartley Street fellas lookin' over me an' me doin' me work . . ."

Paul Gosset appeared at the head of the stairs.

"Paul," I said, "this is Nurse Foley. Nurse Fletcher is ill . . ."

Foley put down her bag.

"Come on down owa that, you," she said, "an' get yourself a drink. Me an' McNab'll have a bit of a chat, an' sure your troubles is only little ones."

Paul's hand went up to his small moustache.

"McNab . . .?" he said, faintly.

"I think she means Primula," I said.

"Primula!" exclaimed Nurse Foley. "There's a name for you—up the banks and down the braes!"

She stumped up the stairs, pushed past Paul, and vanished into Primula's room.

Paul and I went into the sitting-room.

After a moment he said, "Do you—er—think she's all right?"

I didn't see why I had to accept responsibility for Foley, even if we did share the same nationality.

"I'm sure she knows what she's doing," I said. "And, in any case, you can always get someone else tomorrow."

Nurse Foley walked into the room.

"Be the look of it," she said, "we're here for the duration. If that one comes off before the new moon I'm a Dutchman."

Paul, polite as ever, stood up. "The new moon?" he said anxiously.

"A fortnight," replied Nurse Foley. "But, sure, what's the harm in waitin'? All the better when he comes. Put a bit of hair on his chest."

Paul winced.

Nurse Foley looked round vaguely. "Any chance," she said, "of unpackin' me traps? I've a few bits I'd like to wash before me dinner."

When I went into the bathroom some time later three pairs of grey woollen stockings were hanging on the pipes. There was also a sky-blue thing, with elastic, from which I quickly looked away.

Primula came down to lunch the following day. It was a difficult meal, because Nurse Foley was clearly unaccustomed even to the modest succession of dishes provided by the Gossett home. She toyed suspiciously with a leg of chicken, and said she always was partial to a bit of steamed fish. When lunch was over she asked for a cup of tea.

This was provided—the Gossetts always had coffee—and then the four of us settled down for the afternoon. It was raining. There didn't seem to be anything else to do.

By 4.30 p.m. Nurse Foley had been talking for two hours and twenty minutes. She sat squarely in the middle of the sofa in her tight tweed skirt, making it abundantly clear that she had completed the laundering of the sky-blue part, at least, of her traps, and she talked and talked and talked.

By tea time the Gossetts and I were nearly mad. Nurse Foley smoked incessantly—"Fletcher says they're nails in me coffin, but sure what harm is it?—a short life and a merry one an' the divil take the hindmost . . ." She gave us the most appalling details about her previous cases, and included a long anecdote about two people who'd had twins, a certain Mr. and Mrs. Donald Norman.

"Donnie and Duckie they called each other," said Nurse Foley. "Upstairs and downstairs. Donnie this and Duckie that. I declare to God you'd think it was Clark Garrymore on the pictures."

I took a quick look at the Gossetts. I'd heard them, privately, address one another as Primmy and Polly, but hoped they would be so confused by Clark Garrymore that they wouldn't take Donnie and Duckie to heart.

They got it at once, and it didn't make it any better when Nurse Foley told us that Donnie had walked out three weeks after Duckie had been delivered. "An uncertain class of a man," said Nurse Foley, "with an eye swivellin' round all the time for the mots."

Primula looked so distressed that I broke in to explain that "mots" was an Irish word for a girl. A rather common sort of girl, I tried to explain, making it clear to Primula that there was no danger of her losing Paul to this sort of competition.

"Common," said Nurse Foley, "as mud, but sure the fellas is all the same. I'd a butcher once in Tralee was thinkin' serious of puttin' a ring to me finger, but I up an' sent him off with a flea in his ear. Mind you," said Nurse Foley, "a fella's all right as a friend, but I'd never put up with that other class of caper."

Primula, looking faint, said she thought she'd go to bed.

"D'you know what I'm goin' to tell you?" said Nurse Foley, after Primula had gone, "that young one's not too hearty. We'll want to keep an eye on her, or the Lord knows what larks we'll be upta."

Paul jumped up.

Nurse Foley laughed. "God love you," she said, "you'd think you were the first ever brought one into the world. Go on up, now, an' give her a bit of kissin' and cuddlin'."

Paul, bright red in the face, walked out of the room.

Nurse Foley lit another cigarette. "That's a weedy lookin' little fella," she said indifferently. "We'll have him on the flat of his back the next."

That night, Paul and Primula had something on a tray in their room. Nurse Foley and I dined downstairs. She had a couple of glasses of sherry and—in the absence of the Gossetts—let herself go on the subject of complications.

By midnight I was ready to kill her, or to tell the Gossetts that I'd caught her taking drugs. And worst of all was the thought that this was going to go on day after day. I knew that she was probably right, in some awful psychic way, in believing that Primula would not come off—I was even *talking* like Nurse Foley now—before the full moon. I was in for Duckie, Donnie, and all the rest of it, for another fourteen days!

I wasn't. That night, just as I was about to go to bed, Paul Gossett came into my room. He was fully dressed, and his small dog-like face was grim.

"Look here, Campbell," he said, "I went to speak to you."

He'd never called me Campbell before. I didn't like the sound of it.

"I must ask you *and* Nurse Foley," said Paul Gossett, "to

leave this house tomorrow morning. You're turning the place into a—a shillelagh."

I looked at him without comprehension.

Gossett made an impatient gesture.

"A bear-garden," he said. "A shambles, or whatever you call it in Ireland. It's very bad for Primula. A car will be here at nine o'clock."

He turned on his heel and walked out of the room.

Nurse Foley and I left immediately after breakfast.

We'd almost reached the outskirts of the town before Nurse Foley spoke.

"Ah, well," she said, "come day, go day, God send pay day. Sure, wasn't I only tryin' to do me best."

She turned to me suddenly.

"Do you know what I'm goin' to tell you?"

After a moment I shook my head.

"When the fella told us to hop it," said Nurse Foley, "didn't I go an' have a good blub in the lav."

At the station I left her without saying good-bye.

CURZON STREET ON THAMES

It's a romantic old riverside coaching inn, and its name and situation are as firmly welded together as smoked salmon and fillet steak.

It's called the Old Bell at Bulford. It can also be called the Old Bull at Belford, but whichever it is it's as much as your status is worth to drop one name without the other.

The very sound of the Old Bell at Bulford creates its own brand image. (If there is a place called Bulford which contains an Old Bell I'm talking about the Old Bull at Belford, and vice versa.)

The brand image is based upon "driving out of Town for lunch" or "popping in for a bite after the races". It's a place to be travelled to in cars costing more than £2,000. (If it was the Old Bell *tout nu* it's the pub on the corner, which is approached on foot or by bicycle.)

The frontage of the Old Bell at Bulford is gleaming white plaster with shining black beams, and the only indication that it isn't a property dealer's private retreat from the rigours of Park Lane is a single sign of impeccably heraldic taste, designed and executed for 300 guineas by the art department of a distinguished advertising agency.

Chiffon, looped and draped in old English cottage style, veil the upper windows, where every bedroom contains hot and cold water and persons of wealth and breeding outwitting private detective agencies.

The entrance is at the side, affording a breathtaking glimpse of an old English garden, as lovesome and trim as anything at the Ideal Home Exhibition. But step inside, me Lord, and you're done.

Outside, the sun has not yet set upon the long spring evening. The last slanting rays lend a strange, exciting radiance to the tulips, the lawns and the river. But here, inside the Old Bull or Bell or Hell, we're damn nearly in pitch darkness, as though it were the middle of the night in a flash shebeen in Curzon Street.

Everything is, indeed, precisely similar to Curzon Street. Peach lighting behind the bar, carpets to the armpits, Grik *maître d'hôtel,* Italian beach-boys in white coats making like waiters until the American matron rough-shooting season breaks out in Portofino.

Six and sixpence for a doubtfully large gin and tonic while the Grik *maître d'hôtel,* hefting as best he can a two-foot-square menu, tries a soft-sell on the Sole Normande. "I tail you, sir, I have something vairy special, just for you. . . ." At the other end of the bar the victor in a take-over battle pats the leg of an outwardly—and probably inwardly—bored piece of shorthand from the office. "They do me very well here," he tells her, having just fallen for the Sole Normande, ten days frozen and seventy miles from the sea.

Outside, the sun is going down in rare splendour behind the column of poplars, marching by the bend in the river. A white cabin-cruiser drifts by, looking for a "No mooring" sign at which it can tie up for the night. The birds are singing their evening song.

But inside, me Lord, you're being shown to a table in an alabaster-white, brocade-curtained dining-room, each table with its own red-shaded, electric candle, and the river could be as far away as the sea. No bird sings, only the hushed rasping of heavy business men clinching deals, the strained chatter of family parties rendered nervous by the thought of Dad's bill for this foolish treat and, loudest of all, the silence of the couples, out-witting the detective agencies, from whom all sense of pleasurable adventure has been beaten by this thick, rich, concealed-lighting, urban, Curzon Street gloom.

That's what goes on, at prohibitive cost, inside the Old Bull at Belford, that romantic old coaching inn which looks so captivating from the outside. And that's why, with increasing despair on my beat up and down the Thames Valley, I continue to look for the riverside joint which will do the river the kindness of allowing that the river is there.

If the joint be beside the river we do not want a peach-lit bar buried among the stables at the back. We want a bar with one long window and a balcony overhanging the river. We want dramatic floodlighting on the weeping willows and the dark, mysterious water, so that, with benefit to our souls, we can look out instead of in. And the same thing goes for the dining-room, however architecturally impossible it might be. A riverside joint should seem to float, like a ship, with windows that disappear, because it isn't as cold as all that in England all the time.

Let no landlord trumpet that he has this very thing before assuring himself that his bar *and* his dining-room overlook the river, and all his dining-tables too—not just the four in the window reserved for the friends of the Grik *maître d'hôtel.*

If it were ever to come about I'd abandon all status-creating patronage of the Old Bell at Bulford and travel joyously, even by bicycle, to the Riverama Rooms.

THE IMPORTANCE OF BEING STARKERS

My dear—I simply cannot tell you. But absolutely shattering. Simply Endsville. You won't believe a word of it, but I swear to you it's true.

You know this ghastly charity thing we have for the village? It used to have something to do with the harvest, or something like that, except that no one's harvested anything round here for years, except a fortune for selling their land to people like us, but anyway this ghastly Amateur Dramatic Society does a bit every year at about this time. Usually *The Ghost Train* because we all know it and can swan through without much bother.

But then this new young couple arrived—rather swish with a foreign sports car and apparently wads of money. They seemed to know all about the theatre and television and that kind of thing so it was really rather a relief to let them take over the Dramatic Society, even if they wanted us to do *The Importance of Being Earnest.*

Actually, we'd read it once at a kind of rehearsal, but the plot was so muddly no one could really understand it, so we did *The Ghost Train* again, that year.

I must say, though, these young people, Tarquin and Fenella Brackett, were quite clever at it and explained it was a kind of satire on society or something, and most of us got a fairly good hang of our parts. After all, that bossy Mrs. Dickson-Drayne only had to be herself as Lady Bracknell and the Vicar simply chewed up Canon Chasuble. Tarquin and Fenella, of course, played Algernon and Gwendolen and I was Miss Prism, which as it turned out was lucky because I didn't come on until the beginning of Act Two.

Well, my dear—let me tell you what happened. I know you won't believe it, but it's true-true-true.

It started all right with all that rather boring talk between Jack and Algernon about cucumber sandwiches. Actually I helped it along a bit by standing at the back of the audience and laughing at fairly regular intervals, encouraging the rustics to do likewise. Funnily enough, some of them laughed when I didn't, but they were probably only trying to please.

Then, just as Jack and Algernon began talking about that difficult Bunbury business, I became aware of what I can only describe as a disturbance in the wings. I could hear a lot of smothered giggling from Fenella Brackett—that girl's always giggling at something, one never quite knows what. And, at the same time, I could hear the hoarse voice of Sybil Dickson-Drayne whispering in a kind of frightened way, "No, no—certainly not!"

I simply couldn't imagine what was going on. I mean, the Dickson-Drayne woman hasn't been frightened of anything for absolutely years. It sounded as if Fenella was trying to make her do something she didn't want to do—and then a second later as if she'd decided to do it. Anyway, I heard her give the most extraordinary kind of laugh—more of a sort of a fat chuckle really. And then they came on. My dear—STARK NAKED! And Mrs. Dickson-Drayne said, "Good afternoon, dear Algernon. I hope you are behaving very well."

There wasn't a single sound from the audience. They just sat there, paralysed, until Tarquin—absolutely coolly—said to Fenella, who was wearing only a pair of court shoes, "Dear me, you are smart." Then some horrible boy in the audience let out a piercing whistle, so no one could hear the rest of the play until Fenella said, with a positive leer, "Oh, I do hope I'm not quite perfect. It would leave no room for developments, and I intend to develop in many directions."

With that, she sort of bulged, practically all over the stage.

My dear, pandemonium. Some of the nastier old women holding their sides, and the dirty old men clapping like mad and all those horrible boys whistling their heads off. You couldn't hear a word until suddenly the Dickson-Drayne said, "I'm sure the programme will be delightful, after a few expurgations," and rose to leave the stage.

I cannot tell you! I must! Before she could get off the Vicar, as Canon Chasuble, came bounding on, wearing only a figleaf and nothing at all behind. Of course, this was absolutely unfair because really he wasn't on until after me in the next act, and some sort of madness seized me and I rushed right through the audience tearing off all my things and I was only wearing my bra when I reached the stage and the Vicar unhooked it for me, saying, "Allow me, madam," which was rotten of him because it wasn't in the play at all. But then none of the rest of it was either.

Something very queer seems to be happening to the Theatre these days.

THE STEAMY LIFE OF THE SHIRES

"I wish to God Dick would get here, if he's coming!" the Major cried, a little turbulent after a couple of glasses of champagne at 11.30 on a Sunday morning.

"You're churning up the air," I said. "Be calm. I'm not accustomed to the luxury life of the Shires. I'd like to enjoy it at my leisure, with perhaps another glass of that excellent—"

"It's Mrs. Barnes I'm worrying about," the Major continued. "She's given notice twice this month already. By the time we get back from Norman's the sirloin will be like an old boot and she'll go for good."

He thought for a brief second. "Of course, if only I'd asked Dick to lunch I could have left a note telling him we'd be back by one, after Norman's, but I forgot."

He was stamping up and down in front of the fire, agitating my breakfast. "You forgot what?" I asked him.

"I forgot to ask Dick to lunch and now we can't possibly tell Mrs. Barnes there'll be one extra because of her strawberry shortcake."

I was about to say I'd never seen a man in such a mess when I heard the front door crash open and suddenly the drawing-room was full of a huge, reddish person in a gingery check suit.

"My damn chap got a puncture," he announced. "Give me a drink. What's for lunch?"

The Major counter-attacked like lightning. You could see how he'd won his M.C. "You weren't asked to lunch," he snapped. "Anyway we're all lunching with Norman."

"With Norman? Funny thing he didn't ask me." For a moment I thought he was going to continue the theme, but he didn't. He pulled a sheaf of papers from his side pocket instead and said, "Got all the figures here. We'll go into the shop."

He strode out of the room. The Major paused to address us from the door. "You people go on," he said loudly. "I'll see you there."

In the car on the way to Norman's no one spoke. To break the silence I eventually enquired, "What's the shop?"

The Major's wife explained, vaguely. "The study. They'll be in there for hours. It's something about the beater's wages." I knew what she was really thinking about. The sirloin, turning into an old boot. And before that happened the succulent smell of it filling a house in which lunch would not, ostensibly, be taken.

Norman was waiting for us on the steps of his house, unmistakably tart in manner. "You're late," he said. "I'll give you one drink and you can go." Then he added, explaining everything, "Beale's dumplings are nearly ready." At the same moment, though without apparent connection, the Major's wife said, "Oh, Lord! Peggy!"

We sorted it out in Norman's drawing-room. We explained about Dick. Then the Major's wife explained about Peggy. Peggy, the other guest, would shortly be arriving at the Major's house, to apologise for being late for lunch, and she would certainly do so in the presence of Dick. The Major's wife had forgotten about her and so, she was sure, had the Major.

Our discussion about what to do next was interrupted by the arrival of a man-servant who glared at us from the door, before going away again.

Beale, with his dumplings done to a turn. Norman, alarmed, wanted us to leave without further delay, but allowed me to ring the Major in case he turned up in—as it were—mid-dumpling, after we'd left, having come by the other road.

The Major's news was mixed, being both good and bad. Peggy had been secretly intercepted, and sent on to us, and Dick had gone. Unfortunately, however, only to have lunch in the pub next door, having left his car and chauffeur in the drive. It would be necessary, therefore, for the Major to follow Peggy, not only to satisfy the chauffeur but also Dick himself, who appeared to be keeping a suspicious eye on the traffic from the saloon bar window. The Major was leaving now, by the conservatory, to avoid Mrs. Barnes.

Peggy arrived, and then the Major, and we all sat it out in Norman's drawing-room until the pub shut at two. Beale made several appearances, during this time, each more outraged than the last.

We got back to the Major's round about 2.20, to find the coast clear save for a brace of pheasants on the doorstep, with a note from Dick saying they were a present he'd forgotten to deliver.

The Major had a wild plan about asking Mrs. Barnes to cook them for lunch, but we had the sirloin instead.

Peckish as we were, we had to agree that it was more than slightly overdone. As, no doubt, were Beale's dumplings.

LOOKING OVER EDEN

As I came round the corner and started to drive down the hill into the little valley I was as deeply moved as ever to see that the Universal Provider was maintaining his reputation on his small portion of the opposite slope.

So far as I could see he was pricking out his lettuces, crawling along on hands and knees an inch at a time, totally absorbed in the delicacy of his task.

I was further delighted to see that his plot had prospered far beyond even our expectations. Row after row of fresh and blooming young vegetables marched down the slope in perfect military order. His new fruit trees were in full, rich leaf, and all round the borders of his plot there was a profusion of flowers amid the rose bushes, with every rose bush—as I well knew—hygienically cleansed of green fly, black fly and every other kind of blight.

The Universal Provider, with his large wife and equally large son and daughter, had moved into their derelict cottage three years ago, and he had set to the following morning to remake it, working single-handed. The son and daughter seemed to have jobs in the market town a few miles away, because they left early every morning on their bicycles.

Six months later the cottage was transformed. The roof was newly thatched, the walls gleamed with pure white paint. Then the Provider started on his half-acre patch of thistles, nettles and brambles. After burning off the scrub he began to dig the half-acre inch by inch, picking out every weed and every stone, however small. The weeds went on the compost heap, the stones became the foundation of paths, later to be concreted by the Provider himself.

All these staggering activities were held under constant surveillance, often with the aid of fieldglasses, by my friend Arthur, and his wife, from the terrace of their house on the other side of the valley. In the winter they watched through the large windows of the living-room, by the hour, because Arthur was retired and whatever the weather was like the Provider always found some useful job to do.

I followed his activities with equal delight myself, whenever I came down to Arthur's for the week-end, and had been responsible, indeed, for naming him the Universal Provider.

It had been, I remember, one of those rare golden evenings in England, when old walls and lawns and trees still give back the heat of the day. It was, indeed, still so warm that we had continuously to replenish the ice in our glasses, as we watched the small, lean figure trudging up and down the opposite slope with a fully laden wheelbarrow.

"We believe," Arthur said on that occasion, "he used to work for a seed merchant in Reading, but now he's set up on his own. We are rather looking forward," he went on, with the enthusiasm of a fat man contemplating food, "to sharing in the fruits of his labours. And at competitive prices. After all, direct sales from producer to consumer are going to save him all the worry and trouble of distribution, haulage, price fixing and all that. Fresh young peas," Arthur said, with his eyes closed, "crisp lettuces, nutty little beets, beautiful crunchy onions. And," he added, opening his eyes again, "I don't have to touch a spade myself."

"And," his wife said, "all those beautiful little plants and things for our herbaceous borders."

"The Universal Provider," I said, and the name had stuck.

The front door was open, as it always was in the summer, so I went straight in through the house and out to the terrace at the back. Arthur and his wife were in their usual viewing position, looking out across the valley at the Provider, who was now spraying his roses with a large copper canister on his back. Yet there was something slightly strange about them. They were slumped in their chairs. There seemed to be something lacklustre about the attention they were giving to the Provider's work.

Then Arthur suddenly spoke, with surprising malevolence. "Step back, you little rat," he snarled. "'Stand on your own blasted beetroot."

"Well," I said, taken aback, "we seem to have changed our attitude a little towards our good neighbour."

They greeted me perfunctorily, Arthur breaking off to shout an injunction across the valley. "Pump some of that sulphate into your own ear-hole!" he cried, but fortunately the Provider was too far away to hear. Then Arthur turned on me. "We met him in the post office," he said with fury, "the day before yesterday and asked him, perfectly civilly, when he would be prepared to begin selling us some vegetables, and he said they were not for sale, that all his produce was for the exclusive benefit of himself and his family. The greedy, slavering hound," Arthur said, choosing the words with care.

After the second round of drinks I said, "You could leave a ten-gallon oildrum outside his gate, with a note saying, 'For your vegetable soup'."

Arthur brightened momentarily, and then slumped back again into savage watchfulness.

The view from the terrace was not the same.

SHERLOCK ON THE LAWN

"Do be a honey bun," called Cynthia Tinkle, from what was probably her bedroom window, "and drag the new chairs in before it starts to rain."

She flapped a hand to encompass the lawn in front of the house and was about to withdraw when a new thought occurred to her.

"We were just going to get ready," she said, "when Timmy and Tilly arrived and we had to talk to them and now we're all behind."

She inspected the sky again. "It's going to do it now," she said, and waggled her fingers in the direction of the litter on the lawn. "You'd better hurry," she encouraged me, and disappeared.

A nice business. Driving all the way out into the country for dinner at the urban hour of 8.30, and now owing to the intervention of two unknown ciphers called Timmy and Tilly they were all behind. And, furthermore, the new chairs had to be dragged in before it started to rain. A warm welcome indeed.

I approached the lawn through the pergola and for the first time saw it in its entirety. I set to work with what speed and efficiency I could muster.

Half an hour later I was lying, spent, on the sofa in the living-room, when the Tinkles came down, freshly bathed and ready for the pleasures of the evening.

"I've been a honey bun," I said, "and put the deck chairs in the porch, and everything else where I could find appropriate places for them. There was a good deal of guesswork, of course."

"Angel," said Cynthia vaguely, and then became more positive. "I'm dying for a drink," she said.

"Thanks to the clement weather," I said, "you had a busy day out there on the lawn. Breakfast in the sunshine round about nine?"

"That's right," said Tinkle, surprised. "How did you know?"

"There were two dining-room chairs, approximately at right angles to one another, facing east. Beside one of them, inside out, was a copy of the *Daily Mail,* lying on the grass and weighted down with a hair-brush and a tin of lacquer. You washed your hair before breakfast?" I asked Cynthia. "And subsequently dried it in the sun?"

"I wanted it to look nice for this evening," Cynthia said.

"While all this hair-dressing was going on," I said to Tinkle, "you moved into the shade to finish *The Times,* and to listen to Housewives' Choice. You were still in pyjamas at the time. I found *The Times* neatly folded under a transistor radio, and your bedroom slippers beside it. You sat in one of the deck chairs during this period, with a cushion behind your head, but found it was uncomfortable for reading so you put the cushion on the grass beside you. It was still there."

"Yes," said Tinkle, mildly interested. "You're probably right."

"Right about eleven," I said to Cynthia, "you topped and tailed some French beans, in the sun in the middle of the lawn, leaving the tops and tails in a plastic bowl. I judge it was round about eleven," I explained, "because there were two slices of lemon lying beside the bowl. The first gins and tonics of the day and Tinkle, here, too lazy to go into the house and wash the glasses for the bottle of wine you had for lunch in the shade of the willow. A cork, lying on the grass. But before that you had some larking about with a hose. The hose was still there and Tinkle's bathing-shorts were hanging on the rose-bush, beside your shower-cap. You were protecting your hair."

"I simply don't know how you guessed," said Cynthia.

"It must have been very hot during the after-lunch siesta, too hot—at any rate—for deck chairs. You lay on a towel," I told Cynthia, "while Tinkle nicked the Li-Lo. He also broke the drinking habits of a lifetime by providing himself with a jug of iced orangeade. There was no glass so he drank it out of the jug. You wouldn't do a thing like that," I told Cynthia, "so it must have been him."

"He was noisy about it, too," she said.

"Then the respectable Timmy and Tilly arrived unexpectedly

and you," I told Cynthia, "ran into the house to put on a dress, leaving your sandals beside the towel. After they'd gone you took off your best white shoes and put them under the Li-Lo for safety."

"Do you mean to tell me," said Tinkle, "that all that stuff was lying out there?"

"It always is," I said, "after a hot day in an English garden. But there was one thing that puzzled me. What was the purpose of the rubber boot filled with gravel?"

"That," said Tinkle, "was my idea. I was going to stick the handle of my golf umbrella into it, to give me some shade while I was asleep, but it didn't work. I should have put the umbrella in first and then the gravel, but I was too tired to tip it out and begin again."

"I've done it for you," I said. "The gravel is back on the drive."

And then the rain came down, making an end of the problems of al fresco living probably for another month.

Crippled by Christmas

A CHRISTMAS PARTY

I enjoyed, the other Christmas, a hot bath of nearly an hour's duration—a pleasure which even in an abbreviated form seldom comes my way.

The bath, when I need it, normally contains a wife, a child, sodden woollen clothing, lukewarm water or a spider of such extraordinary size and helplessness that I settle for a rinsing of the extremities in the basin.

When I went downstairs I discovered I'd been upstairs just about an hour too long. Madame was sitting beside the telephone with that look of secret, sparkling triumph which means that an enterprise has been successfully launched which would not have been allowed to occur had I been there, with slow, measured argument, to prevent it.

"Oh," she said, "there you are—I've asked twenty-seven already."

The sense of langour created by the bath vanished, a chill, pimply anxiety taking its place.

"You've asked twenty-seven what to what?" I asked, creating an appearance of bewilderment, in the hope of avoiding future responsibility.

"Twenty-seven people to our party," she said. She consulted a list written on the back of, I noted, a specially large laundry bill. "And there are twenty-three more I haven't got hold of yet."

"Why are we having this party?" I asked. "Why are we having such an enormous party? I don't *know* fifty people. Fifty people can't get into this room. Who's going to pay for drink for fifty people? Why are we——"

"Don't get hysterical," she said, putting her finger on what was happening. "I was just sitting here, I'd finished my book. I'd nothing to do, so I just rang a few people up. Do you think they'd like cold turkey?"

"They're not going to eat, too?" I cried. The telephone rang. She picked up the receiver immediately. I forgot about the cold turkey faced with a new anxiety.

She was speaking in a low, purring voice, one I had never heard before. "M'm—I *knew* it would be you. You can? Your wife's in Dundee. M'm—of *course*. 'Bye."

"Who was that?" I said, jauntily, after a moment. It seemed to be high time that I began giving this party too.

"Just a person," she murmured, "who's coming." She suddenly turned round, considerate, generous, and kind. "Please don't worry, I'll fix everything."

She ticked off a name on her list, presumably that of the person whose wife would be in Dundee. "Of course," she said, "if there was anyone you'd like to ask——"

"No, no, please," I hastened to reassure her. "No, really. It's your party. Don't bother about me."

During the next week practically every delivery van in the county called two or three times a day, with redfaced, sweating men carrying in crates of commodities, stacking them in mountains here and there—or so, at least, it seemed to me, standing pallidly in the hall trying to keep out of their way.

The party began at midday, with the arrival of two total strangers and a small child. The hostess at this moment was upstairs putting the final touches to her appearance.

Finding the strangers viewing me with hostility I introduced myself and gave them a drink. Then there was another peal on the doorbell and another and another, and we were off.

At 11.45 p.m. I urged the last of them to leave. They went reluctantly, two men and a girl with a fringe. They believed my name to be Jim.

Now, two days later, I think I've discovered the reason for the whole thing. There was a woman's magazine beside the bed, and an article that said: "Keep him interested by leading a life of your own."

"Interested" is a lame word to describe the vigilant, unceasing, almost cloyingly affectionate attention which will be my portion from now on.

...TO ALL OUR READERS

Once upon a Christmastide five wise persons set off south from the bitter winds of London, from the bursting Christmas car-parks, from the plastic holly leaves of Oxford Street—south to the sleeping Riviera, where nearly everything is sensibly shut for the season of peace and goodwill.

These five wise persons were two ladies and two gentlemen and a Spare, though the Spare belied his name. As they all drove south no one could have been more rotund and rubicund and jolly than he. The sleeping burgesses of Avignon were aroused, indeed, at seven o'clock in the morning by a merry Christmas carol sung fortissimo, and a week too soon.

The hamlet to which these five wise persons came lay in the foothills of the white-capped Alpes Maritimes. Snow also lay upon the ripe, golden oranges growing upon the orange tree in the garden of the villa, providing fresh orange juice straight from Mother Nature's fridge and conditions somewhat nippy for the Côte d'Azur. But these five wise persons were in a delirium of delight to be away from it all, from the jostling people, the roaring buses and the snarling multiple stores.

They set to with a will to make all snug for the festival, chopping wood for the fire and laying in crates of Christmas cheer at 2s. 3d. a bottle, with the sun glittering through the laden olive trees and gift hampers and Christmas cards and paper-hats and Oxford Street a thousand merciful miles away.

As the busy, rural days wore on towards Christmas four of the wise persons continued to be in a delirium of delight, but a change seemed to be coming over the Spare. He, in fact, had fallen into preoccupied, not to say sombre mood, spending much time staring sightlessly out of windows at the sparkling sunshine of the Christmas Côte d'Azur, the brow deeply furrowed and the lips moving silently in some private incantation, a man suddenly severed from all connection with Christmas cheer.

In the end one of the four wise persons was moved to ask him what had thus cast so deep a shadow—a shadow, she said, which had not only darkened *his* Christmas cheer but was now threatening to envelop everyone else's as well. If, she said, this aforesaid shadow were to darken even the merest trace further it might well endanger, in her opinion, the celebration of the festival throughout every kilometre of the area lying between Menton and Marseille. She requested an alleviation of same.

The Spare spoke, for the first time for nearly two days. "It's all very well for you lot!" he cried passionately. "All fine and lovely for you! But I've got to compose a New Year message for a million readers and we haven't even had Christmas yet!" He struggled for further expression. "If things go on at this rate I'll be writing about the Men's Singles at Wimbledon before we've had the Grand National!"

They asked him—pleased that he was, at least, speaking to them—to clarify his predicament.

"I've got to post a New Year's message from here," he roared, "two days before Christmas, if it's going to get to London before Easter, and I haven't even bought all my Christmas presents yet!" He held his clenched fists high in the air. "Blithering Christmas," he bawled, "bunging up the mails, bringing everything to a paralytic halt!"

They were sobered immediately. "But surely," one of them said after long thought, "you could send your New Year's message by telephone, perhaps on Saturday morning, when you've got Christmas out of the way."

"Ho, yes!" he cried. "There's a brilliant idea. A great newspaper, probably going to press with the Berlin Wall opening and the Minister of Transport being burnt in effigy in a Christmas car-park and all the rest of it—they'd surely be prepared to set aside an hour in which to take a New Year's message from me."

No one did much on the Saturday or the Sunday. They sat around in a silent group, trying to think of ideas, while the fertile columnist glared at them from the warmest chair by the fire. In quick, contemptuous succession he rejected New Year resolutions, the wonder of snow on ripe oranges, the sleeping, shuttered Christmas Riviera and even the possibility of rehashing last year's piece.

On the Monday before Christmas all the taps in the villa suddenly became alive with electricity. "There you are," they cried, "you've got it now." His scorn was corrosive. "What does it mean," he asked them in the jargon of his profession, "New Year-wise?"

It happened at 6.15 on the morning of Christmas Eve. The sudden rattle of a typewriter, the fertile columnist rushing round the villa rousing people from their sleep to show them what he had written:

A HAPPY NEW YEAR TO EVERYONE EVERYWHERE!

After that he settled down to enjoy Christmas with a vigour which suggested that he might not survive to enjoy the new year to which he had given so felicitous a welcome.

PLENTY, AT THE INN

"Ah," she said, with menacing vigour, "there you are. I've got something for you that you're simply going to adore."

I prepared for flight—a quick jink through the group of people behind me, round the back of the piano and out into the night. Christmas presents from people I don't know make me very nervous, and sad, too, and—if it comes to that—angry at the necessity for generating gratitude. Before I could move, however, she was right up against the buttons of my jacket, locked into the No. 1 boring position.

"You're simply going to love it," she said, "because I feel it's so exactly *you*."

Some "amusing little nonsense, no doubt, dreamed up on the basis that it's so much more the thought than the gift. A toothbrush transporter in the form of a golfbag, with a cowl, in plastic? A personalised packet of razor blades for a razor I hadn't got?

"You really shouldn't," I said.

"No, wait," the lady went on urgently. "Listen till I tell you. My small Christopher goes to school with this dear little boy called Robin."

Worse than I could have imagined! Robin and Christopher—hideous concatenation—had run up between them something grubby for me in felt, perhaps with paper ears. Just a little something for my desk.

"So naturally," the lady swept on, "we've got to know Robin's parents. They're very nice, really. Specially Bill."

"It's nice," I said, trying to choke the flow, "that he's nice."

The lady laughed in silvery fashion, "Don't be silly," she said. "Bill's Roger's wife."

The lady went on talking while I repeated to myself the meaningless sentence, "Bill's Roger's wife", until I found I was inducing actual unconsciousness. I came out of it hurriedly to hear the lady saying, "And then this terrible blow fell. The games mistress told poor little Robin that after all she thought he'd be much better as the Innkeeper. And after," said the lady dramatically, "Bill had gone to all the trouble to make him this super costume as one of the Wise Men."

I began to list my assets. On the credit side was the welcome fact that no Christmas present was going to emerge from the Robin-Christopher—(I didn't dare invert it)—bloc. On the other hand, the stark debit had to be faced that the next fifteen minutes of my life would be spent in listening to a funny, yet deeply touching, story of a small boy, unknown to me, and his school Nativity Play. I dug in, for the duration.

"Anyway," said the lady, "Bill told me that little Robin was very good about it. He's very grown-up, you know, for his age. He just said, in his manly little way, 'Of course, it is a disappointment. I'll just have to think about it, that's all.' "

I could just hear manly little Robin saying it, too, the manly little fraud.

"Anyway," went on the lady, a thought repetitively, "a couple of days later Robin came to Bill and said, 'About the Nativity play, Mummy. It's all right, really. I mean, I know what I'm going to do.' Bill, of course, was delighted, and said, 'That's lovely, darling. I'm sure you're going to be a super Innkeeper.' 'I think I am, too,' said little Robin. 'You see, Mummy, I know what I'm going to do.' "

All at once, I became aware of a pleasurable sense of anticipation. Suddenly, I was certain that Robin, this manly little operator, was going to brighten my Christmas beyond measure.

"Go on," I said confidently.

"Well," said the lady, "suddenly Bill got a bit nervous. I mean, Robin saying twice, like that, 'I know what I'm going to do.' So she asked him 'What are you going to do, darling?' And Robin said, 'Well, you know, Mummy, when Mary and Joseph come to the inn and ask if there's any room—well, I'm going to say, 'Plenty'."

THE MINUTIAE OF LUNCH

Rather unexpectedly we had seven people to lunch two days after Christmas—four adults and three small children. So, while Madame prepared a ton of spaghetti and a ten-gallon drum of sauce, I went down into the cellar, bent double on the back stairs, and came up again with the collapsible card-table, so that the juveniles could munch theirs at a discreet distance from the adults.

I set up the table, brought three chairs down from upstairs and then spread out nine large knives, nine small knives, nine forks, nine side-plates, nine large plates, nine napkins and that sort of thing, so that with two salt cellars and two pepper-pots I had, personally, handled fifty-four pieces of eating equipment. Before, I'd pulled the corks of six wine bottles, and put parsley on three butter dishes with butter in them.

Well, we had that lot, including Christmas cake—one knife, one cake-plate—and then Madame Tarragoni came in after lunch and washed up seventy-three things, while I put the three chairs back upstairs and the card-table back in the cellar and Madame G. poured six coffees—six coffee spoons, six saucers, one sugarbowl, six liqueurs. Coincidentally, by six o'clock that evening the guests had gone and everything was back to normal.

I said this lunch party was rather unexpected. It was, in fact, a last-minute arrangement, because next day we were having a long-planned lunch—for fourteen.

We started early, because this lunch was going to take place in the garden-house, which is fifty-three yards away from the main one. First, we moved two sofas out of it and then carried three tables and fourteen chairs in. Eight of these were metal garden chairs, so I put thirty-two felt pads on the feet of each to prevent them squeaking on the tiles.

After that we carried out fourteen large knives, fourteen small knives, fourteen forks, fourteen side-plates and that kind of thing, so that by the time we'd finished we had handled eighty-one separate items, including paper napkins, ashtrays, etc.

Madame then applied herself to putting the finishing touches to 1486 freshly baked beans, with three slices of fat bacon on top. I began to carve the ham, which she'd baked the day before, and thirty-five minutes later judged that I had carved enough for fourteen people.

In three instalments she carried out one hot-plate, fourteen coffee cups, fourteen coffee saucers, fourteen coffee spoons, two sugar bowls and two coffee-making machines, covering fifty-three yards there, fifty-three yards back, making a total in mileage alone of 318 yards.

In two instalments I carried out twelve bottles of wine, and pulled the corks of ten of them. Two instalments were not, of course, enough, so in two more I carried out one bottle of Calvados, one bottle of Marc, one bottle of crème de menthe, one bottle of Cointreau, one bottle of Benedictine, one bottle of Remy Martin and fourteen liqueur glasses. Then I went back for two ice-buckets and, once again, the card table in the cellar. Things were becoming crowded in the garden house so we'd decided to put the bar outside, on the card-table.

On this I arranged one decanter of rum, one of whisky, one of vodka, one of gin and one of pastis, together with twelve bottles of tonic, a jug of water, a small plate with a lemon on it and a knife to cut it with, two large bottles of Perrier water and a litre of beer.

When the guests arrived one lady asked if she could possibly have just one small glass of sherry, so I walked fifty-three yards back to the house, bent double down the backstairs, found the sherry and walked fifty-three yards back again, carrying it on a small tray.

The last guests from the lunch party left at 7.35 p.m. Madame and I began by carrying the three tables out of the garden house and the two sofas back in. We then carried the three tables back into the main house, together with the six dining-room chairs and the eight metal garden chairs and then I got a huge basket and into it we threw 497 knives and forks, 2563 large plates and small plates and 3945 wine glasses and liqueur glasses and Madame Tarragoni was there at the receiving end again and by ten o'clock that night you wouldn't have known that anything had happened, just like the previous day but rather later.

All this jollity has enabled us to form the most beautiful New Year's Resolution. We are resolved to pass the next three days in a luxury hotel in Switzerland, pressing bells, shouting orders, demanding newspapers, insisting upon service—and let the Swiss get on with it.

After all, they like running hotels.

The Eternal Combustion Engine

LITTLE SPRINGS AND RATCHETS

It was a time for iron self-control, a time for cool, rational thinking, a time to begin cleaning the windows or polishing shoes, a time to smash the screwdriver into two or more pieces with the hammer. In particular, it was a time not to read the news story again.

I read it again.

An investigation has been ordered by the British Motor Corporation into the safety of door handles used in their mini-car range. This follows complaints and reports of serious accidents in which the door handles figured.

The eye skittered down the column, towards the forbidden paragraph at the end :

. . . a million mini-cars have been fitted with forward-pointing handles . . . there is no particular reason why the door handles were designed in this way . . . our design experts are carrying out tests . . .

And then the final paragraph, the forbidden one, the bottle of whisky lurking in the cupboard that croons to the reformed alcoholic. It read :

One Birmingham driver who has already made the modification on his own car said last night : "The operation takes only two or three minutes and involves removing two screws. It makes it easier to open the door and if anything improves the appearance."

What a filthy thing to say. What a foul revelation to make. What a disgusting temptation to spread in the path of the innocent. On a level with disseminating erotic postcards in the kindergarten, encouraging Boy Scouts to examine advertising material in the vestibules of night clubs.

The operation takes only two or three minutes and involves removing two screws.

The original siren song, sweet and simple, the irresistible lure to disaster.

"Don't listen to it, dear," I said to myself. "Clean the windows, polish our shoes, dismantle the screwdriver. Do not touch pitch."

"But listen, dear," the other half said, "it's a perfectly simple operation. The man says so. It's only a matter of removing two screws, reversing the handle and there you are."

"You listen to me, my friend," I said. "*Think.* You know about door handles. When you depress a door handle, to open a door, you compress a spring and the tongue of the lock goes in. When you release the door handle the tongue protrudes again automatically. It's the way doors work—"

"Oh, Lord," I said, "everyone knows that. Let's just nip down and have a look at the car. See if the two screws are on the inside. We wouldn't have to bring the screwdriver—"

"Will you never learn?" I said. "Does experience mean nothing to you? Do you not recall the last time you dismantled the lock on the bathroom door? If you remember, it wasn't engaging properly so, proceeding with the greatest care, we removed the screw that held the door knob on the axle, and then gently pulled out the axle and then with infinite precision we unscrewed the four screws from the plate on the inside of the door and with extreme delicacy eased off the plate and suddenly there was an explosion and the bathroom was filled with little ratchets and springs and levers in such profusion that we could scarcely imagine where they'd all come from—"

"But probably," I said, "the lock on the car door is much simpler—"

"And then," I said, "for hours and hours we tried to put all the little springs and ratchets and levers back again, telling ourselves over and over again that it was a perfectly simple piece of mechanism that a half-way competent child could instantly perceive how it worked—"

"We could just," I said, "have a little rootle at the door on the passenger side. That's the easy one—"

"And hours and hours later," I said, "we decided we'd have to leave out the spring and we reassembled the lock without it and we put the plate back on again and we inserted the axle and screwed on the door knob and then we shut the door from the inside and hours and hours after that a kindly person broke the door down to let us out again—"

"Anyway," I said, "let's just go down and have a look at it. Think of the rather special distinction of having a Mini with the handles facing backwards . . ."

It was irresistible. I went down, taking the screwdriver with me, just in case, and there was the man next door, with a screwdriver, doing something to the handle of his Mini. He looked hot, and tormented. When he saw me he got into his car, with an appearance of nonchalance, and slammed the door. It failed to shut.

I went straight back upstairs again, gleaming with virtue.

A CAR WAS CLEANED TODAY

There was an aura of instability about the lady. I could see only the back of her head through the rear window of her car, but even her hair looked uneasy, as though it had been subjected to some experimental cutting that hadn't quite worked.

Also, she was busy, in a quietly desperate way, trying to fix one of the huge new residents' parking confusions to the windscreen.

As the next customer disappeared into the maelstrom of the car-wash emporium I gave her a little toot on the horn, inviting her to move up in the queue.

It had a bad effect. The parking thing fell off the windscreen, the lady shot a terrified glance at her driving mirror, found it was out of alignment, threw up a hand to adjust it and dropped what was probably her handbag on the floor. At any rate, she disappeared downwards, from sight.

The man behind me gave an impatient blast on his horn, so I gave the lady another little tootle on mine. The difficult looking hair suddenly appeared again, jerking from one side to the other as the lady looked for the starter, which had evidently moved since she'd last seen it.

The man behind me gave me two blasts, I gave him a couple of digits in reverse, the lady's car, in a series of short, compact leaps entered the maw of the car-wash place and halted just in time in front of the two enormous, woolly rollers.

As usual, the laundry staff had altered completely since the previous week. In place of the three cheerful Africans there were now a couple of indolent white natives, round about seventeen years of age. One of them, in rubber boots, pressed the button and the rollers began to whirl, flinging out sheets of water. The lady sat there, in her car, without moving, terrified of the spray.

The lad in the boots switched off the machinery. "Come on in, missus," he bawled, waving his arms. He switched on again. The lady, blinded by the water, drove straight into one of the rollers, instead of between them, stalled her engine and came to a halt. She became invisible in the heart of the cascade, with her radiator jammed up against the whirling roller.

The booted boy switched off again. In a frenzy of indignation he pounded the windscreen of the lady's car, once again waving his arms. She opened her window, and they held a short conversation. At the end of it the boy pushed the car back, away from the roller, lined it up straight through the window, switched on again and then let out a great cry of, "MISSUS!" The lady, edging forward into the spray, almost had time to shut her window but not quite. It must have caught her in the ear, because I saw her shoot up a protective hand before she disappeared into the Niagara.

When the boy switched off again I saw that the lady had got through to the other side, and was trying to make adjustments to her sodden hair, in the driving mirror. The lad, on the other hand, was leaning against the wall, holding his stomach in an agony of laughter. After a while, he recovered, and both lads soaped down the lady's car. While I passed through the rollers she survived another deluge of water, this time apparently without damage, and moved on into the drying tunnel.

I had a clear view of what happened next. The lady, probably seeking instruction, opened her window again and got, straight into her affected ear, the full blast of the hurricane generated by the machine. Among the other things in the car that rose into the air and whirled around like demented birds was her residents' parking placard, which fastened itself grimly to the back of her neck.

Both lads leant against the wall, this time, sobbing with laughter, their knees visibly giving way.

The lady got her window closed. She sat at the wheel, her head bowed over it, her very soul soaked in water and shredded by the recent typhoon. After nearly a minute she recovered enough to put the car into gear. It leaped forward out of the tunnel, took another buck-jump into the forecourt of the garage and stopped stone-dead, the engine once again stalled. The lady made gestures indicating that she was unable to re-start it. The two lads, holding on to one another, staggered forward and gave her a push. The engine started with a roar. The booted lad, already weakened, fell down. The lady, perhaps with the intention of thanking them, threw open her door. It struck the fallen lad on the head.

The lady drove away, disorientated beyond recall. That evening, her husband probably said brightly, "I see you had the car cleaned today."

THE DELICATE, AWFUL ANGELS

This is certainly going to provoke another revolution.

This is the absolute end.

They'll simply have to think again. It's a wise statesman who, seeing that he has made an unpardonable blob, apologises handsomely to the nation and quietly erases it. So get on with it, M. Chalandon, *de suite*.

Let me explain, if this sudden dryness in my throat will permit it.

M. Chalandon is the new Minister for Equipment and Housing in the Pompidou Government—and I don't know what sort of Equipment he looks after either but that doesn't matter because this M. Chalandon has just forbidden the sale of alcohol on all the autoroutes in France.

This also doesn't really matter because it seems that there are only five bars in the whole autoroute network, so to make tolerable the endless kilometres ahead nearly all French drivers have filled themselves to the brim before starting out, just in case one of these five bars doesn't lie somewhere ahead, but the really unpardonable thing that M. Chalandon has done is to issue 120,000 breathalysers to the police.

Breathalysers, in France, to be used by the police against hard-working French—and other—citizens who have merely been using their inalienable privilege to take three hours off for lunch with, naturally, *quelques apéritifs*, followed by a litre or two of the good *rouge maison*, topped up with as many fortified coffees as may be necessary to ward off sleep so that we may hit the road again in racing condition.

Breathalysers, in France!

Incredible.

As yet, M. Chalandon has not fixed the permissible level of alcohol in the blood, but even if it's four times the British allowance it will still prove a crushing burden upon the *liberté* of the French motorist, to say nothing of the hundreds of thousands of auberges, cafés, bistros, estaminets, restaurants and bars who keep him going.

The breathalysers—they are called "alcootest"—will provide the police with the equivalent of the nuclear bomb, as if they weren't sufficiently heavily armed already.

In France the motor-cycle cops, who will presumably be empowered to use the bomb, are known as the Angels of the Road—*les Anges des Routes*. Even in the good old days, before the *alcootest,* it was a joke that made Frenchmen—and others—smile between tightly clenched teeth, because the Angels give the impression of being as angelic as barbed wire.

They always travel in pairs, on huge black German motor-bikes. They wear white crash helmets and jet-black sunglasses, even in the middle of winter. They have blue shirts, black riding-breeches and black boots and they're slung around with white Sam Browne belts with an enormous revolver in a white holster convenient to their right hand. To see them in the rear mirror makes the heart stop beating altogether. Even a glimpse of them, dismounted and chatting amiably together, causes people to drive into walls.

They have a method of nicking you that deprives you of the power of speech. While the second one waves you in to the side the first one goes on ahead, in case you're mad enough to make a break for it, and stops some way down the road.

Then the second one takes exactly nine minutes to get off his bike. He's precisely ten yards ahead of you, and throughout the performance he keeps his back turned. A booted leg is swung over the saddle, the bike is carefully elevated on to its stand. Then we have the glove removal business, one finger pulled slowly and deliberately at a time, until both gloves are ready to be laid side by side on the petrol tank, and adjusted for alignment. Then we have the hitching of the belt and the easing of the revolver holster and then—and only then—does he turn and come walking back purposefully towards you. Nor are the bloodcurdling preliminaries yet over.

He stands beside the window and then very slowly touches his hand to his crash helmet. "M'sieu," he says.

At this point I've seen grown men bury their faces in the steeering wheel and sob like terrified little children.

Now we are to have the *alcootest* on top of this conglomeration of horror, shoving Liberté, Egalité and Fraternité right down the pipe.

There's another bitter blow. The Chief of Police in Paris is M. Perrier. The tormented motorist might like to think that he's a member of that distinguished mineral water family but he certainly won't be allowed to say it.

KLAXONNEZ ET CLIGNOTEZ

At a time in France when the *autoroutes,* the *routes à grande circulation,* the *routes secondaires,* all the *agglomérations* and even the *pistes* are jampacked with cars with camping equipment on the roof or rubber dinghies, or others towing caravans or whole yachts, or cycling clubs travelling at 40 m.p.h., and all of them hounded not only by the police but also by the Army, I feel that the time is coming for me to take a French driving test.

It's a wise decision prompted by hysterical terror. The fact is that I've got quite a little nasty on my British driving licence and I don't want to have to spell it out in French to a motor cycle cop wearing a white crash helmet, black glasses and a huge gun.

In France the amber section of the traffic lights is almost beyond question operated in some secret fashion by the police themselves, in that the green always changes the moment one is passing through at more than 15 m.p.h., and is red a split second later. My belief that these lights are controlled by the police is buttressed by the fact that one of them is always concealed behind a stationary car and blows his whistle piercingly as one trundles helplessly through against the *Rouge*.

The fine, payable on the spot, is usually about £2 10s., enough in all conscience, but it's the filling out of the charge sheet that kills. It includes your mother's maiden name and takes about twenty minutes to complete and you're always in a hurry to get to the airport while it's being done.

It's not the time to have quite a little nasty even on a British driving licence, so that I have come to the wise, terrified decision to obtain a nice clean French one.

Seeing that I have been driving a car with only some minor bing-bongs and buffets for nearly forty years it would seem that I should have no difficulty in passing the French test. I actually like driving and, though I say it myself, I am neat, quick and efficient and give the minimum amount of offence to other users of the road. I am also about eighty-nine road signs short of receiving a French permission to conduct, or a *permis de conduire*.

There are indeed eighty-nine of them and when you look at them, illustrated in glaring primary colours in the driving school handbook, you can hear—as surely as though it were actually happening—the scream of brakes, the crash of glass and the shrilling whistles of the police. There's one picture of four cars and two huge lorries with trailers boiling along in different directions on an autoroute that makes me lose my balance even when I'm sitting down.

Part of the trouble is, of course, the language. I think of *l'agglomération* as "the agglomeration", instead of the simple "built-up area". The agglomeration sounds like a boiling cauldron of traffic hemmed in to bursting point by endless barricades of one-way streets, and I never want to be in one as long as I live.

To blow the horn is to *klaxonner* and conjures up an instant vision of a mad motorist with an enormous moustache and his cap turned back to front thundering down upon you while he pumps the long cast-iron lever of a screeching Klaxon horn.

To put out the direction indicator, in English, is admittedly a somewhat cumbersome and elongated phrase, but it's blessedly calm in comparison with the French *clignoter,* which sounds like an absolutely desperate emergency, full of sharp spikes. The thought of being on a *route à grande circulation* when some lunatic suddenly shoots out of a *route secondaire,* ignoring *le Stop,* and you've got to *klaxonner* and *clignoter* all at the same time makes me want to stay in bed.

Level-crossings, which seem to be everywhere, are another source of panic. There's the level-crossing armed with barriers and looked after by a custodian. There's another one armed with a luminous, automatic, sonorous signalling with automatic half barriers where a red light begins to *clignoter* like crazy only 20 seconds before the arrival of the train. There is also another kind. It's without barriers and without automatic signalling and the handbook advises you not to get on to the iron way until you're sure that the train will not be there at the same time.

In case, when if ever I take the test, the worst comes to the worse, I have armoured myself against disappointment with a small jest.

An English girl, an expert driver, failed hers the other day. The examiner told her, in English, "Your driveeng ees magnifique but your Code ees terribul."

If the same thing happens to me I propose to say, "I dough. I'b had id for weegs."

And walk home.

P.S. The French Government has just announced that the possession of a British driving licence entitles one to apply for a French one, without enduring the trials of a test.

They would.

A CARLOAD OF PAINT AND PORN

A couple of hundred yards ahead, on the left-hand side of the road, the sudden heart-stopping spectacle of police activity presented itself.

Five or six policemen, three or four cars and some curious looking equipment. Perhaps lifting gear, after some appalling mass accident.

As is normal for the motorist under these circumstances I began to make a number of swift modifications in behaviour. Having been bowling along happily in the middle of the road at some 50 m.p.h. I slowed rapidly to 30, drawing in towards my own side. I threw away a cigarette, removed my elbow from the window and placed my hands on the wheel in the ten-to-two position as advised and practised by the constabulary themselves.

When there are five or six policemen ahead with some curious looking equipment it is wise for the motorist to behave in a manner so unobtrusive as to be almost invisible.

The immediate effect of all these precautions was to let hell loose behind and then immediately beside me.

A horn screamed and suddenly a vulgarly red sports car drew level with me on the outside. The swine driving it made filthy gestures at me and shouted dreadful words. I judged that he had been frightened, probably having been about to pass me on the inside, by my slowing down fairly abruptly and drawing over into that lane, and was taking his revenge in the only way he knew.

In normal circumstances, of course, I would have rebuked his bad manners with an answering blast on *my* horn, various fingers in the air and the headlights blazing into his driving mirror, but this time I let the vulgarian go in peace, being more concerned about the Heat ahead.

It turned out that they were engaged in an innocent and even kindly enterprise, beneath a large notice which said that they were prepared to give any motorist who dropped in a free test of all his lighting equipment, while at the same time passing an eye over his windscreen wiper and tyres.

For a single split-second I thought I'd been successfully wooed. It seemed to be such a nice thing to do—drawing into the lay-by, giving a friendly greeting to the police and then thanking them in advance for offering—free of charge—all these generous services. So different from the normal cowering terror. Mercifully, a moment later I came to my senses and drove past the testing station with averted eyes and both hands on the wheel at ten-to-two, just like they do it themselves.

The fact of the matter is that I don't want anyone to take a close look at my car—and least of all the police—because I can scarcely bear to look at it myself.

It's in good running order—a great little goer—but it has gathered to itself, both inside and out, a number of curiosities that would be difficult to explain to someone else.

For a start, the outside is almost completely covered with the paw marks of the cat Griselda, who has taken to sleeping on the roof-rack. She sleeps there, disdainfully, because the other cat, Pompom, is pregnant again and she herself can't have any, but I wouldn't care to have to explain all that to the police who, if they got the chance, might like to warn me of the danger of driving with a windscreen almost opaque with cat's pads.

There's no point in cleaning it because Griselda just tramples all over it again that night and the windscreen washer doesn't work because the plastic bag that holds the water for it is full of white paint.

This great little goer has the engine at the back so that the boot, with the plastic bag in it, is at the front. Some time ago I bought a huge 2-gallon can of white paint, for some home decoration, and when I got it there Madame said it was too yellowy so I threw it back into the boot in a fury and the lid came off and the windscreen washer hasn't since.

There's a shelf behind the back seat which is covered with paper-back books with pornographic covers in full colour which were lent to us by a friend who has moved. I don't like to bring them into the house, so there they remain for ever. A saucepan of pea soup fell off the kitchen windowsill and filled the louvres of the engine cover and I don't have the strength to remove it either. What's under the back seat I do not wish to know, but the lighting equipment is quite good.

Or, at least, good enough for me.

TOO HIGH IN A BARE SKY

Instead of turning south in Turin we carried straight on in the direction of a town called Susa.

I'd had enough of the endless tunnels on the autostrada that runs along the coast behind Genoa, Savona and so on, particularly as there always seemed to be at least two cars that had run into one another—police, documents, gesticulations—at the end of every tunnel, so that our own personal buffeting must surely be on the way, probably by a fifty-ton lorry, with a trailer to execute the *coup de grâce*.

Perfectly simple route on the map. Susa, then Sestrière, crossing the border into France at Clavière and then all down-hill into Briançon for a dinner gastronomic and an early night.

After Susa Madame became totally absorbed in the map, paying no attention of any kind to the scenery, as we swirled upwards round a long, long series of hairpin bends.

"After you've looked at it," I said, "you might care to describe the scenery as majestic."

She looked at me instead, and spoke gloomily. "We're on the wrong road."

I hauled the car round two more hairpins, following the colossal lorry ahead and trying to keep away from the even bigger one behind. In the brief interval before the next bend I said, "There's nothing I can do about it."

"In that case," she said, "I give up." Glasses off, map put away, arms folded—perfect posture for the infallible map-reading wife led into the wilderness by the wilful idiocy and blindness of the car-driving husband.

Hours later, still sandwiched between the giant lorries, we came out on a flat bit, and the Customs post. I stopped and looked at the map myself. An error had indeed been made. A right instead of a left turn in Susa. And before us, inescapably, the pass of Mont Cenis—6000 feet above sea level and going due north towards Switzerland.

I started off and instantly got the two giant lorries glued on fore and aft, as before. The three vehicles ground upwards into the clouds, and then all three of us swirled down the other side of the mountain, still irrevocably glued together. At the end of the second hour I said, "On the map, just after a place called Modane, there's a squiggly little yellow road that turns south."

She said, "At this hour of the evening I am not turning south on any squiggly little yellow road. I am staying the night in Modane, even if it hasn't got an hotel."

It had an hotel, quite a nice little one, even if it was in eternal danger of having the awful mountains fall upon it. We went for a walk and saw a train leaving the station. There were four cars full of people on the flat trucks behind the engine. They were all peering ahead through their windscreens as the engine plunged into the bowels of an alp. We held on to one another. We were far, far too high in the thin, bare sky.

By ten o'clock the following morning we were even higher. On the map the squiggly little yellow road for some reason looked as if it was all downhill, but it wasn't. It climbed and climbed, squirming, doubling on itself, redoubling, resquirming, until it straightened out for a moment at the very top of the Col du Galibier. There was a house there, a kind of restaurant and souvenir shop. There was a man outside it sitting on a bench and reading a newspaper. *We were all nearly 8000 feet up in the air.*

I said, "Like—brandy?"

Her eyes were closed. She said, "Just get me down."

We began to descend. Suddenly, she cried in a low, urgent voice, "No! No—it's not! *Stop* it!"

"What?"

"Aeroplane. *Underneath* . . ."

Flying, apparently very slowly, up the valley below us was a light aeroplane. Creeping along the edge of the cliff, in the car, we could look down upon it. She said, very thinly, "We've only got—wheels." The plane banked, turned and flew off down the valley again. I wrenched the wheel to the left to stop myself taking off from the road and following it. When we saw the sea again late that afternoon it looked like terra firma.

By now, of course, these revolting, vertiginous Alps are covered with screaming slippery snow. And people are sliding about all over them, 8000 feet in the sky, and actually enjoying themselves.

I like it here, under the bed, holding on to the floor.

Troubles with the Others

A MILKER IN THE MAIL

Riffling through my souvenirs in search of a prescription for vertigo, I came upon a short paragraph roughly hacked from an American magazine.

It's an extract from Ripley—"Believe It or Not"—and it announces a new wonder of the world.

John L. Lunnon, of Well End Farm, Buckinghamshire, sent a live cow to market by post.

Even after an interval of some years, the cutting causes me a thin smile. John L. Lunnon sent it, did he? You might as well say that Enid Blyton wrote *Look Back in Anger,* that *Lolita* was the brain-child of Wilhelmina Stitch.

I was the poster of that cow, the first man in the history of the world to do so, and I want to say that there was nothing to it. It was a down-hill trot, nearly all the way.

Let's marshal the facts.

The business was started by Mr. Ernest Marples, at that time the Assistant Postmaster-General, during the course of a speech to some gathering whose identity I forget. Mr. Marples, always a buoyant publicist for his own department, said that the Post Office was ready to post anything anywhere. Even, he added—probably at random—a cow.

I have to admit that the report whipped me up into no great lather. It seemed to be no more than routine, after-luncheon jollity, and I passed on to some more interesting matter on the next page. It wasn't, in fact, until the following day that I saw its real potential, in the course of a conversation with my employer, Mr. Charles Eade, who was then editing the *Sunday Dispatch.* I retain a clear recollection of the dialogue.

"Good morning. Got any ideas?"

"No, sir. Not yet."

"I see that Marples says you can post a cow."

"Yes, sir. I saw that."

"Well, then—go and post one."

"Yes, sir."

I didn't like the look of it at all. The project was beset with difficulties, not the least of which was to find a postable cow. Then I took heart. A single telephone call to any post office would surely reveal that Mr. Marples, in the heat of oratory, had gone too far. I might even get a column on the familiar theme of bureaucratic confusion, with the workers struggling to keep up with the impractical boastings of the boss.

I suddenly remembered that my village post office was also called the Parade Dairy—an ideal branch in which to fail to post a cow. I called upon the sub-postmaster, a brisk young man called Browne, with whom I'd already had some amusing chats about arrears of National Health stamps (self-employed).

"Afternoon, Mr. Brown. I want to post a cow."

"To post a cow, sir?" He was polite and unsmiling, wary—I thought—of some ham-handed practical joke.

"Mr. Marples says you can post cows. I just wanted to put it to the test."

"I see, sir. Do you mind waiting a moment while I check with head office in Maidenhead?"

I followed him into the inner part of the shop, to listen to the telephone call.

"Hello—Bourne End sub-post office here. I have a gentleman who wishes to post a cow." Short pause. "Thank you very much." Mr. Browne put down the receiver. "That will be perfectly all right, sir. The animal can be dispatched where and when you wish." Not a trace of a smile. The head slightly on one side, waiting for my further pleasure.

"Thank you, Mr. Browne. I'll be back. I just have to get in touch with a cow——"

I guessed what had happened. As soon as Marples shot off his neck the GPO must have got in touch with every post office in the land, warning them to stand by for cow-posters. One up—again—to the Establishment.

The position was serious. Cow-posting was on, Mr. Eade desired it, but I hadn't got a cow. Then I remembered that the field over my boundary fence was infested with cows belonging to John Lunnon, with whom I'd already had some tart conversations about the injuries that might be sustained by cows struck in vital places by golf balls.

I approached him with caution.

"John, would you like to post one of your cows?"

"Post it—where to?"

It was an aspect of the matter I hadn't yet contemplated.

"Well, anywhere you'd like one of your cows to go."

He thought for a moment. "There's a market at Bracknell this week."

"The very place. Nice and handy."

"On the other hand, it's not a good time to sell. I'd get more later."

It was no time for cheeseparing. "The *Sunday Dispatch* will make up the difference."

He considered the matter again.

"Do they actually put a stamp on them?"

I saw he was hooked. "I'm sure they do—right on the rump."

He suddenly rubbed his hands. "Let's post a cow."

Unbelievably, the whole thing had fallen sweetly into place. I rang Charles Eade.

"Sir—the cow-posting's all sewn up! I've got a cow to post and a post office to post it from! We're ready to go!"

"Oh, that," he said. "Well, just make sure it doesn't get slaughtered. A lot of our animal-loving readers wouldn't like to think we'd taken a cow out of a field, and posted it to its death."

"No, sir. Of course not."

"Good-bye."

I didn't mention the matter of Bessie's possible fate as John and I closed in on her the following morning, in a corner of the field. I already had a clear picture—captioned—in my mind of a rubicund old farmer who, overjoyed to find himself the owner of the world's first posted cow, put her out to grass in a special paddock for the rest of her life, with a notice on the gate underlining her distinction.

The Post Office van, when it arrived to take delivery of the parcel, was a set-back. It wasn't red and it didn't carry the royal insignia. It was, in fact, just an ordinary lorry with a ramp, chartered from a private haulier. But in attendance there was a representative from the GPO—an apprehensive telegraph boy on a motor-cycle, wearing uniform, a crash helmet and goggles. He looked about thirteen. Probably the older and wiser lads at Maidenhead head office had stuck him with the job by general consent.

He regarded us warily. "Orders," he said in the end, "to collect an item for delivery——"

"It's in there," I said. "Breathing."

It was clear that Bessie didn't know she was making history, because it took the four of us to post her up the ramp and into the lorry. For the record, she was a thin, brown-and-white cow with a curiously prim disposition. I was sorry we hadn't got a cow that entered more into the spirit of the thing.

The telegraph boy didn't like her either. Post office regulations, it seemed, compelled him to accompany her from the point of dispatch to the place of delivery. He abandoned his motor-bike with obvious regret and climbed into the front seat of the lorry beside the driver, still wearing his crash helmet and goggles. When I suggested that he should, strictly speaking be in the back, with Bessie, he said, "Do me a favour, willya?"

No extra sparkle was provided by our first call, at the Parade Dairy sub-post office. John and I were reversing Bessie with the intention of pushing her, for stamping, as far into the shop as she would go, when Mr. Browne appeared with a small buff form. It was only necessary, it seemed, for me to sign it, and to pay the parcel post charges, and then Bessie could be on her way.

A small crowd had gathered, seeing a cow being pushed into the post office. A lady with shopping basket was kind enough to stick a $2\frac{1}{2}$*d.* stamp on Bessie's forehead, and to wish us luck, but there was no further public demonstration. We beat Bessie back into the lorry again, and started for Bracknell.

Here, things were rather livelier. Word of the enterprise had clearly preceded us, because there was quite a posse of press photographers, mostly from local newspapers. The telegraph boy and I, with Bessie in the middle, posed for a number of pictures on the ramp, until a representative of the auctioneer appeared to say that we were holding up the business of the market, and would we kindly get the lorry out of that.

Somewhat cast down by the increasingly chilly reception being accorded to our glorious, posted cow, John and I went into the pub next door, having discovered that Bessie would come up for auction at about two o'clock.

We emerged at 1.45, to find that Bessie had already been sold for £40, which was about right.

On second thoughts, now that I've marshalled the facts, I don't mind so much about Ripley giving all the credit to John L. Lunnon for posting a live cow.

Viewed in the round, it seems a pretty filthy thing to do.

THE HOME OF THE MOLE WRENCH

"And now," he said passionately, "now do you know what They've gone and done to me?"

The capital "T" was unmistakably there, indicating that he could be speaking only of the Government.

"They," he said, "have sent me this."

He held up, between finger and thumb, the familiar brown envelope. Through its transparent window gleamed the thin red line of the Final Demand.

"Pay it quickly," I advised him. "After March nineteen they'll be slapping you into a concentration camp on the Isle of Man if you're five minutes in arrears."

He made an impatient gesture. "Never mind that," he said. "Just look at it."

I took the envelope from him, also employing finger and thumb. "You never know where these things have been," I said.

"That," he said with conviction, "has been somewhere indescribably beastly. Just look."

I looked. Stamped on the envelope, just below On Her Majesty's Service, was the injunction, "Ship through Newport (Mon) the Home of the Mole Wrench."

"You're right," I said in a low voice. "It's absolutely filthy."

"But what are they trying to do to me?" he cried. "Even if I do pay the thing, do I really have to ship it to them through Newport Mon—"

"The Home of the Mole Wrench," we said together.

"I see it," he said after a moment, "as an obscenely Welsh secret ceremony, carried out at dead of night on the far side of some bestial slag heap—"

"The word has been passed around all day," I suggested, "from Dai to Dai—"

"We're wrenching tonight, boy bach. Same time, same place, whateffer."

"And then Dai and Dai and Trefor Whateffor—"

"Just a moment," he said. "I'm handling this. At midnight—exceedingly heavy rain, of course—the whole male population of Newport (Mon) is gathered behind the slag heap—"

"And then there's about an hour of choral work—Land of Our Fathers—that sort of thing—"

"Possibly," he said impatiently. "Very possibly. And then the lads begin to get a bit restive. Some hothead calls out, 'Well, then, whateffer—are we wrenching or not, boy bachs?' "

"It's a pity we're so short on Welsh dialect," I said, "whateffer."

"But, of course," he went on quickly, "they're waiting for Mordreth, the Queen of the Bardic Druids, Newport (Mon) Branch, who is bringing the Mole. She arrives. The lads form a circle around her, let lash with Land of Our Fathers again, then Mordreth holds the Mole high in the air, there's a great cry of 'Wrench—Wrench!' "

"Whateffer!"

"And Mordreth wrenches, doing the poor little animal in."

"That," I said, "is the Mole Wrench."

I couldn't get this ludicrous business out of my head for several days afterwards, and indeed went so far as to look up Inland Revenue in the telephone book, without finding the courage, however, actually to ring them. Well, you know what they're like. Once they've got you out in the open they'll have you, for sure.

Suddenly, then, I could stand it no longer, slotted in a couple of purple hearts, waited for the buzz, and then rang.

"Good morning, I want to make an enquiry."

"Yes, sir. In connection with—?"

"Well, this friend of mine got a final demand and stamped on the envelope was the order, 'Ship through Newport (Mon) the Home of the Mole Wrench'. We were wondering what a Mole Wrench was."

Absolute silence, and then the nervous female voice saying, "I'll put you through to the Press Office."

The Press Officer cleared the matter in a flash. He himself had been using a mole wrench for years—a device which can be clamped on to a pipe and screwed tight—and it must have been the Post Office who had stamped the envelope because the Revenue *never* did that kind of thing.

I thanked him, soberly, regretting the loss of a dream.

A HORRIBLE OLD WIDOWER

As I entered the room the lady said, "Actually, I've just started a new one. A disgusting old widower with cultural interests. I'm signing myself Charlene Mary Sears. It sounds quite American, don't you think? And of course he's going mad with excitement over the Sears bit. He thinks I'm mixed up with Sears Roebuck."

She stopped. She turned to me and said, "Hello, how nice to see you. I haven't seen you for ages. How are you?"

"Abandon instantly," I said, "these tiny politenesses, and tell me about the disgusting old widower with cultural interests. And, furthermore, why you're signing yourself Charlene Mary Sears."

George said, with some pride, "She's on the Personal Column trail again, handing out punishment for potential sin."

"I've had flu for ages," the lady said, "but I'm feeling much better now so I thought I'd start a new one."

"She answers advertisements in the Personal Column," George explained.

"*The Times* is best," the lady said, "but *The New Statesman* is quite good too. Of course, I only do it if I think they deserve it. I forget where I found this horrible old widower. We've been at it now for nearly a month. I've had three from him and he's had two from me. I'll probably keep him waiting until the end of next week before I write to him again. It doesn't do to be too forward, you know."

"Would you mind," I said, "explaining your technique in absolutely precise detail, omitting nothing?"

"It's just that some of them annoy me," the lady said. "This horrible old widower said he was interested in water-colours and sought the companionship of a lady with private means and of similar bent."

"How does that make him horrible?"

"Well," said the lady vaguely, "he was obviously going to bore her to tears going on and on about water-colours and with her private means she'd be paying for all the little lunches and dinners. I just thought he ought to be punished. And specially for using the word 'bent'."

"What was the nature of your first communication?"

"In the beginning," the lady said, with the seriousness of an expert explaining a technical point, "it's very important to build up their confidence. It's like fishing. You want to strike firmly but not too hard. I just told him I was a widow on vacation from Chicago and that I'd taken up water-colour painting quite recently, to fill in the time."

"And signed it Charlene Mary Sears."

"I thought that Charlene would make him think I was quite young and gay," the lady explained. "It did, too. He wrote back by return of post asking for a photograph."

"Surely," I said, startled, "you didn't send him one?"

"O, yes," said the lady. "Rather a nice one of my sister. I've got a lot of family albums," she explained. "They come in useful."

"Does your sister know about this?"

"Oh, no," said the lady complacently. "It would make her nervous if she did."

"And what address do you give?"

"My own. After all, I'm not Charlene Mary Sears and if he

ever turns up in person I can only tell him that someone's been giving him a wrong address."

I digested this information for quite a while. Then I said, "And how will all this end?"

"I don't really know," said the lady indifferently. 'I'll think of something. I once ended a correspondence with a young man who wanted one more to make up a caravan holiday, sharing expenses, at Clacton, by revealing, after a lot of letters, that I was a novice monk who had to wear a truss and it rather showed while I was bathing. That time I was called Sylvester Mackenzie."

"My God."

And I've been thinking about it ever since. I mean, knowing that this lady is lying in wait gives the Personal Columns in *The Times* and the *Statesman* an interest for me that, frankly, they never had before. Until Charlene and Sylvester Mackenzie cropped up I'd never really believed that anyone answered these advertisements. They always seemed to be too dotty, too remote, to arouse anyone's interest. Now I know better. And there's another thing. What about biting the biter?

What about spending Easter quietly devising an advertisement that would once again flush Sylvester Mackenzie from his lair?

Young theologian interested in skin-diving wishes to meet . . .

MR. EGG AND THE LONG AMERICAN LEGS

Madame came out into the garden round about 7.30 in the morning and said, "Mr. Egg has just been on the phone. He sounds agitated. He's coming round at once."

It seemed unilke Mr. Egg—a cool and elegant man of about fifty. He lives alone in a charming old farmhouse back in the mountains, and has never been agitated about anything, as long as we've known him. He even likes being called Mr. Egg, or M'sieu Oeuf, the closest his French neighbours care to get to his rightful christian name of Hugh. We are very fond of Mr. Egg. He's extremely good on sub-tropical gardening and the preparation of new plaster for painting and the making of fish soup and many other social graces of that kind.

When he arrived, half an hour later, he brought with him a bottle of chilled champagne and a jug of fresh orange juice—a combination known in these parts as a mimosa. As he poured he said, "A little early, but then the situation is tense."

We toasted one another silently. Then Mr. Egg said, "I've just been to New York. There I met a lady called Amanda. Divorced, thirty-nine, two first-class, long American legs, beautiful Park Avenue penthouse, well read, extremely chic and absolutely childless. We saw a lot of one another."

That's another thing we like about Mr. Egg. When serving he does it quickly, neatly and in just the right amount.

"Four days ago," Mr. Egg went on, "she phoned me from London, where she had arrived unexpectedly. I asked her to come down here and stay with me."

After a moment Madame said, "Why not?" It was a way of telling Mr. Egg that that part of the business, at least, was quite rational.

"The following morning," said Mr. Egg, "at 11.35, when she got up, I found she couldn't drive a car. She could not conduct," he said, choosing the words with care, "an automobile. A chic, long-legged American woman, well read, childless, who could not drive a car, never had and did not propose to begin now. I found out," he said, "she couldn't drive a car because she wanted to have her hair done in Nice, at 11.35, at an address given to her by a friend in New York."

Mr. Egg diluted this vision of hell with a little more mimosa. "I explained," he went on, "that the establishment would be closed from midday until 3 p.m., that it would be fully booked out because the new French travel allowance has deposited the whole of the haut monde of Paris on the Côte d'Azur and that in any case I couldn't possibly drive her there because I had been waiting for three weeks for the arrival of the plumber, Jean-Claude, and that if I left the house even for ten minutes he would certainly appear and then go away again for ever."

Mr. Egg paused, with bowed head and closed eyes. "I offered," he said, "to ring the hairdressing establishment and, if an appointment were available, to get her a taxi that would leave her at the door. She refused this offer," he said, "on the grounds that she didn't want to be alone in a taxi with a French taxi driver for the reason that she could not speak French, never had been able to—"

"And did not propose to begin now," the three of us said in unison.

"Instead," Mr. Egg said, "she wanted a dry Martini made with gin. Of course I had no gin so she had the last of my last bottle of whisky instead. At lunch she couldn't drink the economical wine I've been drinking for years and had three brandy and Perrier in its place. After lunch she wanted to go down to Cannes, to the beach. I explained again about the congestion of the coast in August and that in my case, during the heat of the day, many of us like to lie down with the shutters closed. She didn't want to do that either."

Mr. Egg sighed. "Before dinner," he said, "we walked down to the Bar Napoléon in the village, looking for a bottle of gin. They didn't have one but Jean-Claude was there with his brother, so we had a pastis or two but she just sat there, tapping her fingers on her knee. She said the place was dirty. As of course," Mr. Egg said generously, "it is, but it's the only one we have. After dinner," he said gravely, "she wanted to go night-clubbing. It was nine-thirty p.m. I could hardly keep my eyes open. She sat up for hours after I'd gone to bed, trying to get Radio Luxembourg on my little transistor, but apparently there was only a lot of yelling in Italian."

He thought for a moment. "She's asleep now," he said, "but what am I going to do when she gets up?"

"Nothing," Madame said, coming to one of her well-known, firm decisions.

That's what he must have done, because he drove past here yesterday alone save for a large sack of fertiliser on the seat beside him.

He tootled the horn and gave us the thumbs-up sign. It had all come right in the end.

MISS DEVLIN MISLAID

To:
Miss Bernadette Devlin
No. 1A The Barricades
Belfast
N. Ireland

Dear Miss Devlin,

You don't know me and I don't know you but nonetheless I feel compelled to inform you of certain events that took place down here in the South of France on the night of Thursday, September 25th, in the hope that you will be able to take steps to ensure that nothing of a similar nature occurs again.

On the night in question my wife and I—you don't know her, either, nor does she know you—my wife and I had retired to bed at the comparatively early hour of 5.30 p.m. We were suffering from exhaustion. Since the beginning of February, starting with

Rowena, Kenneth and Pearl, we have given board and lodging to 32 guests, in such rapid succession that the spare beds have scarcely had time to cool before receiving their next occupants.

Thursday, September 25th, was in fact our first day off for seven months. Brigid and Peter had left the previous day and Robin and Jonquil weren't arriving until the following one, so we had these cups of Bovril in bed and were sound asleep by 6.10 p.m. approx.

The next thing we knew was that someone was pounding fiercely on the front door and it was 11.15 p.m. exactly.

I pulled myself together as best I could, went downstairs and saw our next-door neighbour, M. André Barbier, standing outside the french windows in bright moonlight. I let him in. He informed me that two men were prowling about the place looking for me, and annoying him. Feeling a trembling in the knees I asked him if they were English. He said he believed them to be French. Holding on to the wall for support I asked him if they looked like coppers. He said they could be. Just before I fell down there came another thunderous knocking on the front door. I opened it, mostly to cause my heart to start beating again, and saw a pale, very tired young man standing on the mat.

Speaking in French, he said, "I regret to derange you, but I am from Radio Luxembourg. I have just arrived from Belfast and I believe that Mademoiselle Bernadette Devlin is staying here."

Well, Miss Devlin, you can imagine my surprise. I mean, after Rowena, Kenneth and Pearl and Fritz and Kappie and Jacqui and Martin and Tim and Colin and Barbara and Desmond it was quite a bit of a shock to me to learn that you might be staying here too.

Playing for time and also because it was a matter of some interest, I asked him how he had found my address, this remote part of the Alpes Maritimes being some considerable distance removed from the Falls Road.

He said that a Miss MacCafferty in Belfast had given it to him.

Now, Miss Devlin, I don't know anyone called MacCafferty and my wife doesn't either. Nor, perhaps, do you know her. Under these circumstances I thought the best thing to do was to ignore the MacCafferty angle and to concentrate on you.

Not only, I told him, were you not staying here but also, if you happened to be on your way, you'd be out of luck, as all the spare sheets were hanging on the line. Furthermore, if you arrived tomorrow, you'd be even further out of luck because Robin and Jonquil would be occupying the only two spare beds, apart from the one in my study and it would be a bit awkward to have you in there in case I wanted to do some work.

In the end he went away, reluctantly. From the kitchen window I saw him rejoin his colleague, who was assembling recording equipment on the bonnet of their car. After a long discussion they got into it and drove away.

Next morning, at 8 a.m., we were once again shocked into unwanted consciousness, this time by the telephone. It was the same young man again. He seemed to have got sacked from Radio Luxembourg during the night because he now said he was working for a newspaper (unspecified). Furthermore, this newspaper had reliable information that you were staying here and that he and his colleague could be with us in half an hour if you would be good enough to grant them the favour of an interview.

Seeing that he'd been in Belfast, I lapsed into English, shouting, "Bernadette Devlin isn't here and hasn't got a hope in hell of getting in anyway!" To this he replied, "Yes," apparently his only word of the language, so that even if you had been here it would have been a thin interview.

No more of this, please, Miss Devlin. It's really too irritating for words.

Yours, etc.

BRÜNNHILDE IS WOTAN'S UNCLE

I was listening the other day to some rather good talk about opera.

They were discussing the melodic line of the Italian school, and appeared to be in general agreement about Verdi's skill in ensemble work, when, without warning, someone suggested that the phrase, *O patria mia! mai piu ti reverdo,* could only be assessed as derivative, in the light of the famous *Non ti scordar* from the "Miserere" in *Trovatore.*

This, to my surprise, threw the others into a ferment, and the discussion descended precipitously into accusation, and personal abuse.

On this level I attempted to join in. I shouted, "Well, in *Madame Butterfly,* Mimi——"

There was an immediate hush. A moment later I found that Mimi was the heroine of *La Bohème.* Up till then I'd always believed that Mimi was Madame Butterfly herself.

I withdrew from the circle of opera-lovers, but the incident left its mark.

Suddenly, it seemed a dreadful thing not to know whether Puccini or Rigoletto wrote *The Magic Flute;* not to be able to quote, off-hand, what else Tosca said, if he did say anything else, when he said good-bye.

I resolved there and then to learn the plot of one opera in its entirety, right down to, and including, all gypsies, courtiers, and vassals concerned in the fray.

I decided upon *The Ring of the Nibelung* (Richard Wagner, 1813-1883). What attracted me to *The Ring* was the discovery that the full performance lasts for three nights, with a preliminary evening, or *Vorabend,* and that Wagner wrote the four parts back to front. Anyone, I reasoned from this, who knew what *The Ring* was about would be able to hold his own in any kind of opera talk.

I bought a book on the subject, and now I can tell you the plot of *The Ring*. In four parts. (1) The Rhinegold. (2) The Valkyre. (3) Siegfried. (4) The Twilight of the Gods.

There is nothing to this, really, if we keep steady.

The characters involved in the first part are the Gods, Wotan, Donner, Froh and Loge. Wotan is the chief of the Gods; Loge is the God of Fire; Donner and Froh are brothers to Freia, who is, of course, the Goddess of Youth and Beauty.

Wotan has promised that Freia will be given to the Giants Fasolt and Fafner, in exchange for the giants' work in building Valhalla.

But Wotan is here in disagreement with his spouse Fricka. Fricka doesn't want Freia to be handed over to Fasolt and Fafner —Fracka doesn't want Frissa to be handed over to Fanholt and Fosser—*Wotan* actually doesn't intend to hand over Fisser to Frosser. . . .

It will be easier, I think, to take it from the moment when the curtain goes up.

The scene shows the bed and the flowing waters of the Rhine. The three Rhinedaughters, Woglinde, Wellgunde and Flosshilde, are swimming about guarding the Rhinegold.

Woglinde sings, *"Weia! Waga! Woge, du Welle, Walle zur Wiege! Wagala weia! Wallala Weiala weia!"* Then three contra-bassoons add a B flat, and Alberich appears out of the bowels of the earth.

Now Waltraute, Gerhilde, Helmwige, Siegrune, and Grimgerde begin to talk about the Rhinegold. No, they are the Valkyrs, or rather five of the Valkyrs. The other three are Ortlinde, Schwerleite, and Rossweisse. *And* Brünnhilde, of course. They come later. We are dealing now with the Rhinedaughters, Woglinde, Wellgirdle, and Rosshasser. . . .

At all events, Alberich hears the Rhinedaughters say that anyone who renounces love, steals the Rhinegold and makes a ring—(n.b. *Ring*)—out of it will have supreme power over the world. Alberich steals the gold, and *now* we've arrived at the scene where Wotan doesn't want to hand over Freia to the giants Fasolt and Fafner, or, at least, apparently intends to but is in fact going to play a trick on them through Loge, in order to please Fricka, who didn't want Fasolt and Northolt to build Wallala, because Wosser . . .

It occurs to me that I have paid insufficient attention to Alberich. Alberich is the chief of the Nibelung, who live in the underworld. He is symbolic of the lust for power, and is attended by Mime, a dwarf.

As Mime has appeared, perhaps it will be as well for me to spotlight him too. The name is pronounced Mee-meh. It is obviously of the first importance not to call him Mee-mee, or you know what.

In "Siegfried"—that is, Part 3—Mee-*meh* rears Siegfried, who is the son of Siegmund and Sieglinde, who in their turn are the children of Wotan, who in order to beget a hero who will slay Fafner, who has turned himself into a dragon to defend the Ring of the Nibelung, which he received from Wotan as a ransom for Frica, has turned himself into a human being called Wälse. That is, *Wotan* has turned himself into a human being called Wälse.

Anyway, this Wotan (Wälse)—Siegmunde-Sieglinde-Mime-Siegfried sequence leads up to the first meeting between Siegfried and Brünnhilde.

Brünnhilde is the daughter of Erda, the Goddess of Wisdom. Wotan had something to do with this, too, and then gave Brünnhilde a horse, so that she could carry dead heroes to Valhalla.

Now, Brünnhilde, as a punishment laid upon her by Wotan for having tried to protect Siegmund against Hunding, who robbed Sieglinde and then married her, has been cast into a profound slumber, and surrounded by a ring of fire. Siegfried breaks through the fire, and plights his troth to Brünnhilde with the ring which he wrested from the giant Fafner.

But, Alberich, it will be remembered, laid a curse upon the ring, and upon all who held it, when he renounced love, having heard the Rhinedaughters Hoglinde, Baglunde and Gobtrante telling one another that anyone who renounced love, captured the Rhinegold and turned it into a ring would have supreme power over the world.

This is the scene revealed to us as the curtain rises upon the *Vorabend*—the preliminary evening before the three major dramas.

We see the bed and the flowing waters of the Rhine. The three Rhinedaughters, Woglinde, Wellgunde, and Flosshilde, are swimming about guarding the Rhinegold.

Woglinde sings, "*Weia! Waga! Woge, du Welle!*"

What an extraordinary thing! I seem to have got back to the beginning again. Just a moment. After *Wotan* finds out that Brünnhilde has been trying to protect Siegmund, who is her brother-in-law by her previous marriage to Erda, the Love Goddess, from Hunding, who is also married to her mother-in-law Sieglinde. . . .

How cool it is here by the Rhine! I wonder what would happen if my foot slipped . . .? Sinking . . . Sinking . . . Waving fronds. No flowers. No artificial respiration. By request.

"Weia! Waga! Woge du Welle!"

Smiling sweetly, I drift away, bottom up to the world.

BACK CHAT

Perhaps because of the veritable tattoo of blows that has been rained upon it in recent years, what with inflation, deflation, reinflation and so on, in addition to Lord Longford and J. C. Superstar, the British back is not at all what it used to be.

The British back, once the toast of such places as India for its straightness and sturdiness, is now no more than a tottering column of displaced and decaying vertebrae, liable to "go out" at the drop of a hat—trying to pick it up, that is—and never come back.

I don't, at this moment, know any British citizen whose back is not "out"—this "outness" leading to symptoms of such staggering diversity that one can stand on one leg for ever listening to the list.

Once the British back goes "out" it brings on blinding headaches, agonising gravel in the neck, piercing pains in the wrist, elbow and upper forearm, a dragging ache between the shoulder-blades, grinding discomfort in the pelvis, flaring torture, all down the leg, of the sciatic nerve, terminating in an almost total numbness of the feet save for super-sensitivity of the toenails. A full house, indeed.

We know a beautiful woman whose back used to "go out" so far that she took to standing with one foot in boiling water and the other in a bucket of ice, and that didn't do any good, so that every surgeon in London had a slash at every one of her vertebrae and that made it worse so her husband took her to New York where they threw all her old vertebrae away and made her a new lot out of the bones in her right leg and now she's back again and barely able to reach forward, once every three minutes, for the glass of red wine which some ass told her would "clear up her trouble in no time".

I know people who hang for hours at a time from bars and that doesn't make any difference, apart from pulling their collar-bones up over their eyebrows. I know a man who has been trying, for weeks, to hang from one of these bars by his feet, and hasn't made it yet because his feet are too small and he's too heavy. He's mad enough, too, not to wear a crash helmet while he's at it, so it's really doing him harm.

Some people go to other people round the corner who are marvellous with backs and they get a quick, expert twist and walk out with one leg longer than the other, which spoils the hang of their trousers.

It's a serious matter, this universal back trouble, because the whole universe seems intent upon telling me about their backs when, in point of fact, when it comes to blinding, agonising, piercing, dragging, grinding, flaring and terminating no one has got a back that's gone farther "out" than mine.

I've had it in a plaster cast, sloshed on too loosely by an orthopaedic genius so that I had to hold it up by the lower rim when I walked. In the end I made a couple of shoulder straps from a pair of braces and undressed, even when alone, in the dark.

I took it to a Harley Street specialist who led us down to a cellar, put my head into a kind of horse-collar, hauled on a rope until my head ground into the ceiling, leaving my feet, owing to my unusual height, still on the ground. "Lift your feet," he said. I said, "Not on your life," and that was the end of that treatment.

But despite all this suffering I still stand on one leg for hours, listening to other people telling me about theirs. Like the other morning, waiting for a taxi in Sloane Square. Total stranger, noting a certain stiffness, launched out at once into his own symptoms, when suddenly I was seized by a stab of agony the like of which even I had not known before. It was exactly as if someone had seized a nerve inside my left knee, and a little above it, given it a sharp wrench with a pair of pliers, put the pliers on one side and then fallen to enlarging the hole with a saw-toothed breadknife. Cries were wrung from me—"Aargh—gaw—gurgh—grimpf . . ." Sweat pouring, everything.

The stranger watched the performance with detachment. "I," he said in the end, "get that in *both* legs—and at the same time . . ."

If you were the only girl in the world, and you had back trouble, I'd leave you.

A French Connection

THE OT HOUNDS

"It's hot weather," he announced suddenly, sitting up and looking keenly around.

It was a surprising performance, in view of the fact that we had been sweltering in it for hours, and it seemed to alarm his wife.

"No, it isn't," she said quickly. "It isn't at all. You're not to think about it."

Something was going on here that required elucidation. "Why are you so astonished at the heat of the sun so suddenly?" I asked him. "And why are you telling him not to think about it and that it isn't hot?" I asked her. The mind was working slowly but fairly surely in the blissful semi-stupor of an endless Riviera lunch.

He looked at me with an appearance of pain. "Not *hot* weather," he said. "Ot weather. Ot with a capital O."

"Please don't," she said urgently. "You haven't for ages, and you know how tired you get."

His eye ranged over the harbour and the crowds of late holiday-makers strolling up and down. "They'll be running freely now," he said. "The time of year and the weather conditions," he told me "are just perfect now for Ots. Sudden heat in mid-September brings them out in droves. Round, plump Ots looking for bargain prices because the season's over—" He leant back in his chair and raised his feet a couple of inches off the ground, his knees bent and spread wide. Then he lowered them again, tenderly, as though the action gave him some sensual pleasure. "Lovely," he said.

After a moment I said, "I imagine if I knew what an Ot was that all the rest would fall quickly into—"

"By God," he cried without warning, "there's one!" He sprang to his feet and threw down the last of his brandy. His wife, equally excited, swung round. "A beautful one!" she exclaimed. "Just look at those lovely thick little legs!"

He gave her a look of passionate appeal. "Could we hunt it?" he begged her. "Just this one. I think—" He hesitated, as though not daring to go on. "I think it might be a Royal," he said in a sudden rush.

I couldn't make out what they were even looking at.

"I think so too," she breathed. "Tally-ho!"

"Tally-ho it is," he said.

A moment later he'd paid the bill and we were off, tracking what for me could have been the Invisible Man.

"Just," I said, "so that I can get the absolute maximum possible pleasure out of this Ot hunt, could you tell me what we're hunting?"

"That one there," she said. "Look at him. An absolutely perfect specimen."

Wandering along ahead of us, dazed by the heat and the glitter of the yachts tied up along the quay, was a round, fat little man who could only have been English. The shorts were khaki and knee-length. The feet were encased in red woollen socks and stiff, brown leather sandals. He wore a shiny blue shirt and a Frank Sinatra straw hat perched on top of his head. He was hot and weary, and probably lonely, with the diffident half-smile of someone looking for a compatriot in a dazzling and frightening foreign town.

"So that's an Ot," I said. "Could you tell me," I asked her, "why he's called an—"

"Do you want me to turn him, Master?" she asked her husband, very business-like and crisp. "We don't want him wandering down to the end of the jetty. There's nothing there for him to sit on."

"Good idea," said the Master. Master, presumably, of the Ot hounds. "We really want to get him on one of the benches on the Croisette."

She gave him a nod and set off quickly after the Ot. We stopped, to watch developments. She walked past him and then paused to examine one of the yachts. Hopefully, recognising her to be English, he gave her a shy little grin. When she came back again he was following her, respectfully, hoping only for the opportunity to exchange a few words in the English language. "First bench beyond the bus stop," she murmured to us as she went by.

We set off in leisurely pursuit. "Now," I said to the Master, gripping him firmly by the arm, "you will tell me what is an Ot."

He replied frankly and immediately. "An Ot is a round, fat man who sits on benches and his little legs go up into the air and then he takes off his hat and wipes his forehead and says, 'Ot, ennit?' If he performs the whole sequence correctly he's a Royal. All right?"

At once I knew that I would always recognise an Ot, instantly, and for the rest of my life. "Go get him, Master," I said.

He accelerated slightly to pass the Ot and to join his wife on the first bench after the bus stop. The Ot approached them, gave a shy little grin, and sat down. His little legs went up into the air. He lowered them, took off his straw hat, wiped his forehead and said politely, "Wonderful weather, isn't it, for the season of the year?"

The Master was inconsolable for the rest of the day.

NE TOUCHEZ PAS MAMAN DANS LE VENT

During the night the wind had been going slowly mad, and now, in the morning, it had reached a crisis of hallucination.

It shrieked out of a crystal-clear blue sky, with not a cloud in sight anywhere.

It seemed to be coming, in the main, from the north-west, yet there was no shelter from it even in the lee of a south-facing wall. It whistled over our heads and then doubled back on itself, a living thing intent upon sweeping everything off the face of the earth.

The extraordinary thing was that if it hadn't been for this demented wind it would have been a beautiful morning with the sun blazing from this cloudless sky, already hot at nine o'clock.

We decided it was an ideal day for the beach, that it was only in the mountains that there was no shelter from the shrieking mistral—except that it still seemed to be operating in the big square in Antibes.

A thirty-foot banner, announcing sombrely enough that this was the day of blood—for blood-donors—had come adrift at one end above the flower-beds in the centre of the square and was lashing itself like a huge whip. An old woman, made deaf and blind by this fearful wind, walked straight into the banner and was knocked off her feet. It was a moment or two before anyone went to help her. The mistral had turned everyone in on themselves.

The beach was infinitely worse than the mountains. Sunbathers, huddled behind umbrellas and deck-chairs, were being lashed by flying sand. It stuck to their sun-tan lotions and got into their drinks. Every time one of them stood up the others buried their heads in towels and flapping newspapers. Yet the sea was sapphire-green and unruffled. One could see twenty miles across the bay to Cap Ferrat and in the further distance the line of the snowy Alpes was as sharp as the edge of a razor. Absolute hell in blazing sunshine.

We endured the beach for a couple of hours, with the wind tearing over us and then doing this impossible trick of doubling on its tracks and howling back in again at sea-level, and then decided to have lunch on the terrace of the restaurant. Inside, French families in Sunday clothes ate decorously in the still gloom, but we had lunch outside because the sun was there, and it was changing our English pallor.

Lunch on the terrace was considerably worse than sunbathing on the beach. We weighted down the table-cloth with rocks, but it still flapped with pistol-like reports. Fish soup blew out of our spoons into one another's faces. Pieces of bread took off like snipe from the basket. One of us, recklessly venturing upon a green salad, had to hold it down on his plate with the flat of his hand.

It was notable that the two waiters—one to hold the door open and the other to sprint in and out with plates—betrayed no apparent interest in the extraordinariness of our situation. They were merely tight-lipped, turned in on themselves by the mistral. To brighten their lot one of us ordered four cheese soufflés. "There's no need to serve them," he explained. "Just stand at the door and we'll catch them in our mouths as they fly past." The waiter only said that cheese soufflé was off.

Round about three o'clock we decided that the only thing to do was to go home and stuff newspapers under the doors and pull the curtains and ride out the gale. The others went off to the showers to try to clean the fish soup and the sandy sun-tan lotion out of their hair. I was waiting for them in the car-park when a large, dominant lady drove up and sprang out of a small saloon, leaving two frail little old people in the back. She disappeared into the restaurant.

A couple of minutes later the frail little old lady, after struggling with it for some time, succeeded in opening her door, only to have it smashed shut again by the fury of the mistral. Then the frail little old gentleman had a go at opening his, with the same result.

They held a despairing consultation and then both of them tried to open the door on his side. The mistral allowed them to get it about half way, and then showed them who was master again.

I thought, in the blazing sunshine, they were probably going to die of heat-stroke. I went over to the small saloon, prized open the door on the old lady's side, put my back against it and helped her out. She very, very nearly blew away. I only just caught her arm in time and then the door slammed, almost amputating the foot of the old gentleman.

Gripping the little old lady with one hand I opened the door again and helped the little old gentleman out. He nearly blew away, too, so that I found myself, in the shrieking wind, standing there with my arms round two tiny little strangers, whose heads came up to my waist.

I was wondering where to put them when the large dominant lady suddenly materialised, and went mad. It had, it seemed, taken her nearly half an hour to get her father and mother into the car outside their residence in Vallauris and now I, a person altogether unknown to her and for reasons which she couldn't possibly guess at, had let them out.

I gave her back her father and mother, making sure she had a firm grip on both of them, and retired to my own car, regretting that the mistral hadn't turned me in on myself, as it had done everyone else.

SOMETHING NASTY IN THE BOUDOIR

The girls came downstairs in their nightdresses, holding cigarettes rather stiffly between their fingers. Both had obviously been lit at the same time.

It looked like a deputation of some kind. They had the appearance of persons with news to impart and, judging by their expressions, which were a combination of fear and hysterical amusement, the news was of a substantial nature.

My hostess and I had been sitting in the garden, still velvety warm at midnight, trying to identify, in a lazy way, the source of the many whistlings and pipings that fill the darkness of the Alpes Maritimes in high summer, but now we turned in alarm to greet the deputation.

They presented their case without preamble.

"There is," said Miss B., "a sort of lizard in our room."

"And the trouble is," said Miss P., "it moves rather quickly."

I found the eyes of all three ladies centred gravely upon me. Their gravity said, more clearly than words, that swiftly moving lizards in bedrooms at midnight were the exclusive concern of men, that ladies could merely announce their presence and then withdraw, to speak casually of other matters, until the bedroom was once again lizard-free.

"What sort of lizard is it?" I enquired, taking partial control of the situation.

"It's sort of flat, with big eyes," said Miss B.

"And it's got little feet with pink toes," said Miss P. "And it runs very quickly," she added, emphasising once again the more unwelcome feature of the little visitor, although large eyes and pink feet were already beginning to play their part.

"Well," I said, "we'd better go and have a look at it."

It was crouched in a corner of the ceiling, looking down at us with flat, black reptilian eyes, but it didn't seem to be a lizard to me. It was about half an inch wide and three inches long and it did have little pink feet, but there were tiny suckers on the end of each toe. Little suckers—if it fell off the wall—that would fasten on to your eye or your tongue—if your mouth was open. . . . A'hem.

"It's not doing any harm," I said. "Let's just leave it there. It'll probably go away."

An extraordinary sequence of yippings and squealings broke from the girls. They jumped up and down, hugging themselves in dread. If it fell off the wall while they were asleep, they shrilled, it would fasten itself on to their eyes, on to their mouths. It would be *awful.*

"Well," I said, "I'll give it a bit of a rootle," thinking that the first rootle, or nudging, would precipitate the beast into his widely publicised burst of speed. Straight down my throat?

Our hostess said, "I'll get the new ceiling brush. It's nice and soft." I think she meant it was soft enough not to provoke the animal into eating us alive.

While she was getting it I opened the cupboard and took out the box which had contained the presentation cake of soap from last Christmas. The box had been prettily decorated by the donor with gold paper and sticky tape with a motif of holly. Just the thing for catching lizards with pink feet in.

I removed the lid and found another forgotten present inside, a large red handkerchief with white spots. I gave this, for some reason or other, to our hostess, in exchange for the new ceiling brush, which was made of blue nylon, with a long black handle. Written across the head of the brush was the legend, baffling in its contradictions, "Qualité Kilt". But then, with the golden box and the lizard's pink feet, everything was beginning to get a little out of focus.

I stood on a chair and with extreme delicacy touched the extremity of the lizard's tail with Qualité Kilt. "Moving rather quickly" didn't come anywhere near describing the creature's reaction. With the speed of light it waddled down the wall, the tail and the pink feet a blur. "Waddled" is a slow-sounding word, but this creature speeded it up no end. It disappeared under one of the beds, as the four of us got jammed in the door.

When we'd sorted ourselves out our hostess and Miss B. retired to the other bedroom, where they sat on the sofa and initiated a sparkling conversation to take their minds off things. In the lizard's den Miss P. was kind enough to move the bed to give me a clear look at our quarry.

Once again, it was in the corner, and now it was panting hard, the little ribs pumping in and out like, indeed, those of the hunter.

I abandoned the golden box and Qualité Kilt and threw a towel over it and it had glued itself to the wall and I had to pull and it gave a little squeak that turned my mind, but it came away. I released it in the garden and went upstairs to report the All Clear.

Our hostess was wearing the spotted handkerchief, knotted into a remarkably chic looking little bonnet. I couldn't understand it. "Do you always wear that," I said in the end, "for lizard hunting?"

"Not always," she said, brightly casual. "It was just that I couldn't think of anything else to do."

DEUX GAULLES

It would have to be allowed that under any kind of formal cross-examination one might not be able to reveal too profound an appreciation of the virtues and vices of the political system instituted by General de Gaulle.

Under pressure, one would also have to admit to certain gaps in one's knowledge about the precise function of M. Georges Pompidou, the Prime Minister. Is he, for instance, allowed to take a cup of coffee with General de Gaulle as frequently as Mr. Harold Wilson sips tea with the Queen? Furthermore, is he—unlike Mr. Wilson—debarred from speech while so doing?

Is M. Couve de Murville—if that's how his name be spelled—the French Foreign Minister or the Chancellor of the French Exchequer, presuming that either or both of these posts exist in the administration of France?

No precise answer to these questions can spring to the minds of many thinking persons in the British Isles, and in this soft impeachment I include myself.

Yet my interest in the future of General de Gaulle could not be warmer or more personal.

"Funny," you say, in the popular music-hall vernacular. "Funny."

A warm and personal interest in the future of General de Gaulle sounds like presumption in one who, by his own testimony, is somewhat ignorant of the precepts of de Gaullism. Nor, you might say, is there anything in the public persona of this cold and remote figure to promote either warmth or a personal interest. Yet the truth of the matter is that in France or, rather, in a remote corner of that great country, General de Gaulle and I sink or swim together.

I made this discovery by chance one morning on entering the little shop that serves the village in the Alpes Maritimes where I spend so much of my time not on holiday, as so many envious persons suppose, but in concentrated pursuit of the literary Muse.

I entered this shop as soon as it opened, at 7.30 a.m.—(British food stores please note)—and took the *patronne* by surprise.

Before she could arrest herself she said, *"Bonjour, M'sieu Charles!"*—although in fact I misheard it the first time. I thought she said, *"Bonjour, M'sieu Chat,"* or, "Good morning, Mr. Chat." Or, taking it a little further into what I presumed to be the *argot* of Provence, "Good morning, Mr. Tomcat"—a possible reference to her conception of my activities in the area.

It was while quizzing her, rather slowly, about the matter that she revealed that she had called me *"M'sieu Charles",* for the reason that I so closely resembled General de Gaulle both in height and—she blushed with a measure of embarrassment—in the length of my nose.

She and her husband, she went on to say, always spoke of me in private as M'sieu Charles and she was desolated that it had now slipped out.

For my part, of course, I was delighted, because to be addressed by your own name, or anyone else's, in a French mountain village is an extreme rarity for Anglo-Saxons. The polite form is "M'sieu" or "Madame", so that one always has a feeling of remaining indefinitely anonymous. But here I'd been presented with "M'sieu Charles," just as though I'd lived in the village all my life.

For the last two years, therefore, I have been "M'sieu Charles" not only to the *patronne* and her husband but also to many of the regular customers in the shop. It's a delightfully warm greeting but it is, of course, impossible for me to tell whether the warmth extends to *le grand Charles* himself.

I only know that I love him and I hope passionately that he will come back for another seven years because with someone called Mitterand President of France I'll probably lose my identity and go back to being a mere M'sieu again.

The trouble lies in the proud nature of my namesake. If he is rejected by France he's going to go straight home to Colombey-les-deux-Eglises and shut the door and never come out again, and where will that leave me? Ex-Msieu Charles? It's unthinkable. It would turn me into a ghost.

The ideal, of course, in the fearful event of the General being rejected, would be for him to turn into a Grand and Genial Old Man, like Winston Churchill in his retirement. The armed police would be withdrawn from the forbidding fortress in Colombey-les-deux-Eglises and the house and gardens would be thrown open to the public. The General's massive gestures on television, the two hands held out to indicate that he alone holds France secure between them, would be transformed into the open arms of Father Christmas, welcoming everyone in. Even Madame de Gaulle might be able to rustle up a smile. Think, then, of the universal love and affection that would descend upon the lofty and long-nosed head of the other *grand M'sieu Charles.*

But, as I say, I don't trust my namesake's potential for geniality in the event of failure, so therefore, with 50 per cent of France, I cry with heart and voice, *"Vive de Gaulle"*! For ever.

A HEN ON MY SHOVEL

As is the custom in Southern France—one unchanged by experience or advances in technology—the builders had been having a second bash at the plumbing, apparently bypassing their earlier system and constructing a new one of infinitely greater size.

A mound of yellow rock and clay perhaps four feet high and thirty yards in length now bisected the olive grove, suggesting that a start had been made upon excavating an Underground line rather than the mere laying of a drain pipe.

I was delighted to see this splendid mess, crying out to be flattened or shifted or turned into something else, because of all the joys that life in the sun provides none is greater than navvying. The exercise of pick, shovel and wheelbarrow empties the mind of all speculation normal to it, like what about the Inland Revenue and how can I possibly face up to the labour of writing a letter?

Pick it, shovel it into the wheelbarrow, wheel it gently away, tip it out and start the whole blissfully soporific process all over again. The sun shines on the pallid, urban torso. Muscles come to life that have been employed in the city only for hair-tearing or burying the face in the hands. But above all else the mind is empty, simply directing the body to pick it, shovel it, wheel it away and tip it out somewhere else, until the end of time.

And now I realised that this enterprise could be especially rewarding, because in place of merely tipping it out somewhere else it could be tipped out to form a ramp leading down from the road, and a new and badly needed entrance for cars. This made it perfect. Instead of creating a new pile of rubble somewhere else all this mess of rock and clay could be turned into an orderly construction and of a practical nature, and one that might posibly be even pleasing to the eye.

I began picking it, shovelling it into the wheelbarrow, putting on a short burst of speed to push the barrow up on to the road and then tipping out the rubble to make the new ramp and then I was joined by the hen.

This bird's appearance was almost coincidental with its death. I'd raised the pick in the air and was about to bring it down when this hen suddenly appeared, right in the middle of the target area. A large, plump hen with bronze, dark-blue and black feathers and a bright red comb. Obviously someone's favourite hen, a good layer and mother.

By this time the pick was already half-way down. Impelled purely by instinct I tried to throw myself to the right. The urban muscles responded only sluggishly. The pick buried itself in the ground, almost parting the feathers of the hen's posterior. The bird made a contented clucking sound, looking up at me with what appeared to be approval.

This was indeed an odd bird. All the other hens I'd known had been hysterical creatures, ready to dissolve into panic flight at the distant waving of a handkerchief. But this bird stood her ground even as a pick-axe whistled down but a bare inch away from her egg-laying machinery.

I moved her a little with my foot and prised out the pick. Immediately, she began her congratulatory clucking again and started scratching for insects in the loosened earth. My obligation was clear, to keep the pick going and lunch continuously coming up.

We began to work together as a closely knit team, almost too closely knit for comfort, really, because the hen missed death from the pick three times out of five, and on the other two occasions she was standing on the shovel. Once we ran into a nest of worms and I had to wait while she pulled them out, laboriously, one by one.

It had to be allowed that quite a lot of the blissfully soporific quality had gone out of the work, that certain undesirable tensions were building up, almost urban neuroses establishing themselves, so much so, indeed, that I should really have got rid of the hen, driving her away with a volley of stones. If I had, the man wouldn't have run into the tree.

This mishap occurred in the most curious way. I'd actually loaded the hen into the wheelbarrow. She'd been standing on the shovel, as usual, and I'd just put her on the pile of earth in the wheelbarrow with the last shovelful, where she settled down at once and started scratching away. Even when I picked up the wheelbarrow and moved off with it to the site of the ramp she showed no signs of alarm. There even seemed to be evidence of pleasure in her beady eye at the unfamiliar sensation of movement.

Coming to the slope up to the road I put on my usual burst of speed and then it happened. The hen became suddenly agitated by the acceleration and tried to scramble out of the wheelbarrow. In so doing she knocked off the rake which I'd balanced on top of the load. Still running, I'd just got the wheel of the barrow on to the road when I stepped on the prongs of the fallen rake and dealt myself a lethal blow between the shoulder blades. I let go the barrow at the moment when a small English saloon car came round the corner. Seeing an unattended wheelbarrow coming at him the driver took evasive action and struck a tree, cracking his near-side headlamp.

I bowed, in French fashion, from the waist, said, "*Je m'excuse, M'sieu,*" and withdrew into the house.

Explanations, in English, about the hen would have appeared too fanciful, it seemed to me.

WITH LORD AND LADY LOBSTER

We were scarcely moving along the Croisette in Cannes, blissfully stunned by bathing, by blazing sunshine and a long, long lunch when Lord Lobster—a pseudonym won during the course of the meal—shuffled to a halt and said to Lady Lobster, "I feel the time has come, my little dove, to buy you that long promised watch."

He cautiously extended a weary arm and pointed to the window of the most expensive looking jeweller's shop I'd ever seen.

"And where better to do it," said Lord Lobster, "than in there?" He leant forward and peered into the window, shrouded in gloom by its awning. "It looks quite clean," he assured us.

"No, thank you," said Lady Lobster promptly. "I feel like an old skate in the bottom of a dirty rowing-boat. I'd prefer to be wearing my pearls and a clever little silk suit before I went in there. It's not," she went on to explain, "that I mind feeling like an old skate. It's just that lovely watches look better on one if one is looking lovely. And you too," she added without warning, addressing an elderly and expensive French couple who appeared to object to our monopolisation of the jeweller's window.

They moved on, looking alarmed.

"Perhaps," I said, "we're all in slightly too raffish mood for the serious inspection and possible purchase of costly watches. How much did you want to pay?"

"A couple of hundred quid," said Lord Lobster, not without pride. He'd made rather more than that in the casino the previous evening.

"I'd quite like to see that happening," said Madame Moules. "A touch of the bon ton," she explained, "is always welcome." She was sitting, on the edge of the pavement, on the large basket in which we had our bathing things, a lot of leeks with long fronds, a chicken and a huge loaf of bread. A somewhat gypsy-like ensemble.

"Perhaps," I said to Lord Lobster, "you'd like me to go in first, to make sure they've swept the carpet? Or, perhaps, you'd rather I didn't go in at all?" I was wearing only a pair of shorts, and carrying a string bag containing potatoes and a beach-ball. I was also burdened with a door-mat which we'd bought in the Monoprix that morning.

"We'll all go in," said Lord Lobster firmly. "These people know class when they see it."

They certainly knew something when they saw us. They froze. They became instantly wary. Three large men, very light on their feet, quick movers, by the look of them. And a fourth one, in an alcove at the back. He slid a hand under his desk, and kept it there.

Lord Lobster looked around with mild disdain. The brim of his Panama hat was slightly detached, as it had been for years. "Do you do watches?" he enquired, peering at a case full of them.

The biggest man behind the biggest desk motioned to the other two. One of them shut the door leading to the street. The other put four frail, gilt chairs very close together. Lord Lobster's party sat down, arranging our impedimenta around us as neatly as possible. One of the men took my door-mat and propped it against the wall.

"Do we have to have the door shut?" asked Lord Lobster. "I'm sweating."

The big man behind the desk said, "It is against the noise of the street, so we hear ourselves talking."

"Shovel 'em out, then," said Lord Lobster.

I lit a cigarette. One of the other men silently handed me a tiny marble ashtray, with a malevolent look.

Lord and Lady Lobster examined, and rejected, a large number of watches. Then he leant forward, under the detached brim of his Panama.

"Don't you want to know if it's for a gentleman or a lady?" he asked.

"But yes," said the big man. He was losing ground all the way.

"Lady," said Lord Lobster. "My lady wife."

Eventually, the big man found one that seemed to please. The other two were still standing tensely and silently behind us. The watch was £250.

"Traveller's cheques," asked Lord Lobster tersely, "French francs or a fiddle on an English bank?"

The big man got more flustered than ever. "First," he said, "I must ask you some questions, please."

"You may ask," said Lord Lobster graciously, "but I may not answer."

They'd hardly got anywhere before Lady Lobster said, "I don't like it after all, and I want to go home. I'm going off," she explained to the big man, who couldn't have known about the skate trouble.

"Of course you shall go home," said Lord Lobster. We all got to our feet, picking up our disordered luggage. One of the silent men almost snatched the ashtray from my hand. The other one opened the door.

We looked back, when we'd got some way down the street. All four of them were watching us from the door.

We heard afterwards that they'd recently had their third or fourth raid in a matter of weeks.

It explained a good deal.

THE DARK AT THE TOP OF THE STAIRS

"I'm afraid," said the lady, coming out into the garden in a bikini, "the lavatory in the upstairs bathroom isn't working."

I looked at her over the rims of my sunglasses and below the brim of my new cotton hat. The sun was hotter than it would ever be again—in Bognor Regis or Skegness next year.

"Please," I said, "This is the last holiday I'm going to be able to take on the Riviera. Next year it'll be water-wings at Mevagissey. Please do not ask me just to look at the lavatory in the upstairs bathroom. I must stay in the sun."

"I think it's the ballcock," she said. "It's probably just got a bit of grit in it."

"There's a new plumber in the village. We'll get him to have a look at it."

"What a good idea," she said. "Why don't you go down and see if he's there?"

I left the car in the garage and walked a mile down the hill—in the sun. A notice on the door said that the plumber was closed for the month of August. The sun was on my face as I walked the mile back up the hill. The lady was dozing on a long chair, already nut-brown.

"He's shut," I said, and was easing myself into my own chair when she said, "If you just took the top off the cistern you could have a look at it."

The upstairs bathroom faces east. It was almost gloomy in there. I took the top off the cistern and fiddled with the ballcock. The valve was undoubtedly blocked. I replaced the top and went downstairs again—into the sun. "I can't do anything," I said, "without a Stilson. It's a kind of wrench," I explained. "Plumbers have them."

"I'm sure they'd have one in that lovely ironmonger's in Grasse," she said. "It's only ten o'clock."

I drove to Grasse, with my right arm out of the window—in the sun. The ironmonger's was plunged in gloom even deeper than that of the upstairs bathroom. I had to wait twenty minutes to be served with a Stilson wrench.

She was wearing a shady hat when I got back. "Almost too hot," she murmured, stretched out in the sun on the long chair.

I went up to the gloom of the upstairs bathroom and with the help of the Stilson removed the ballcock in its entirety, after turning off the water with the tap above the cistern. I brought the ballcock down to the garden and examined it for a while, in the sun.

"We want a new one," I said, and added immediately, "but it will not be necessary for you to advise me to go back to the ironmonger's because I'm half-way there already."

Even the doorway of the ironmonger's was in shadow now. Inside you could scarcely see your hand in front of your face. It took a long time to get a new ballcock, with which they didn't supply a ball. When I got back to the upstairs bathroom I found that the ball which I'd removed from the old apparatus wouldn't fit the new one. I was half-way out of the gate, on my way back to Grasse, when she said :

"It's nearly twelve o'clock. They'll be shut. Why don't you leave it until after lunch?"

We had lunch, owing to the excessive heat, in the shade of the orange tree. I managed to get some sun on my foot by extending my right leg as far as it would go.

After lunch, when I got back from Grasse for the third time, I put the new ball on the new cock and tightened everything up hard with the Stilson.

I turned on the water and it gushed out of the two joints between the ballcock and the tap above the cistern. Also, the cistern flushed itself when it was half-full. The new ball was too big. In rising it tripped the flushing mechanism prematurely.

I turned off the water and turned on the light, the better to see what I was doing. On the hill behind the house I could see a happy and prosperous French family basking in brazen heat beside the azure waters of their new swimming-pool. They were all as brown as berries.

Dear Mr. Callaghan, I've now got to go back again to the stygian gloom of the ironmonger's to try to get a smaller ball for the ballcock and with the way things are going I know this smaller ball will be too small and that the washers, to stop the leaks, will be too big, so that I'll have to go back to the ironmonger's again and again and again, probably until Christmas. But your new and miserable travel allowance begins on November 1st.

For God's sake, therefore, flash me £500 in traveller's cheques before the blow falls. We get a little sun at Christmas down here.

By that time the lavatory in the upstairs bathroom will surely be in working order.

A ROUGH OLD GENERAL

During the French General Strike of 1968, when the students were spending so much educational time throwing paving stones at the Paris police, we were in the South also suffering hardship and inconvenience, alleviated in part by the fact that Nice Airport was almost closed to aerial traffic, thereby preventing compassionate friends from London arriving with food parcels, medicines and petrol, for our relief.

The following report, composed at the time, indicates, superficially, what we had to endure.

* * *

The weather here has been patchy in the extreme for the French General Strike.

Round about now we should be sitting in the shade, pointing out to one another the enervating quality of the heat and the exceptional dryness of the ground, and advancing from there into a comprehensive destruction of the character of the Mayor, who year after year fails to provide us with sufficient water for our vegetables, but in fact—ever since the students started things in Paris—we have been subject to weather conditions not dissimilar to Wigan in August.

That is, a more or less continuous overcast, leading to sudden and torrential rain.

It has put us out. The General Strike, we tell one another, would be just tolerable if the sun was blazing down as it should do at this time of year, and we were able to complain with fire and passion about the shortage of water, but as things stand we've got nothing concrete to level our indignation against.

Round about the time that the workers took over the Renault factory two parties developed in the village. One held that the almost continuous rain was good for the earth; the other maintained that the tender young shoots of the tomato plants were being drowned in an excess of unseasonable moisture.

Suddenly, however, the sun would come out, the ground would begin to steam, we'd start to couple up our hoses, and then the rain would come back again. It came back, in fact, on the same day that President de Gaulle returned from Rumania, leaving us with so much to talk about that we could scarcely apply our minds to anything specific.

Once, we talked for perhaps three hours about a Spanish workman who had been seen buying ten kilos of flour in Pré du Lac, while his wife, in the establishment next door, was stocking up with an equal quantity of sugar. We agreed, fairly early on, that it was only the foreigners who had panicked, but that it was only to be expected of them, because of their invincible ignorance, and then we said the same thing, comfortably, over and over again.

Of course, it wasn't all as easy as this. One or two of the older ladies got a touch of the cafard, rather in the way of hens getting their back feathers ruffled by an unexpectedly chilly puff of wind. Madame T., for instance, said she couldn't bear to think of the noise being made in Paris by students tipping over motorcars, and many of us shuddered in sympathy. We were all relieved by her decision to walk down the hill and to take a cup of coffee with her sister-in-law, as an antidote to this *crise de nerf*. She was certainly easier in herself when she came back again, incidentally letting slip the information—provided by a friend of her sister-in-law's cousin —that row upon row of shelves in the Supermarché in Cannes were standing empty, as a result of various urban elements hiring whole vans to drive away perhaps a thousand tins of sardines per head. In full, plenary session we agreed that an occasional sardine was quite interesting and tasty, but that too many of them would be bad for the liver. That night a policeman was shot dead in Lyons, and the older ladies were driven to making whole batches of fresh ravioli, to keep a return of the cafard at bay.

We have, of course, had no post for more than a week, while at the same time seeing a great deal of the postman. The heavy rain has promoted a tremendous harvest of snails in the long grass bordering the lanes around here, and the postman—a young and eager lad—hunts them all day long in his large, black DS.19. Perhaps his official position gives him a private supply of snail-hunting petrol, because petrol is getting a little short.

We held many discussions on this subject. In view of the fact that the Customs are on strike at the frontier post in Menton, some people hold that it would be worth while to drive into Italy and to bring back enormous quantities of loot, including several hipbaths full of petrol, but then the other side maintains that while we were queueing to get over the border the strike might be settled, and we would have missed lunch to no purpose. It's very difficult.

The telephone has also become uncertain. The exchange has a tendency to say that you can only ring a doctor, so that we all ring one of the three doctors and tell him to ring our friends and ask them to come to dinner on Tuesday, and *merci mille fois, M'sieu le Docteur.*

It is, in fact, now Tuesday morning. Miss Beryl Gray, that distinguished ballet dancer, hopes to leave Nice Airport for London this very afternoon. I am entrusting this message to her, in the hope that she will be able to take off.

In the meantime I think the sun is struggling through, and the sea is already beautifully warm.

It's certainly been a rough old General Strike down here.

With Pinafore and Hammer in the Home

DEM BONES, DEM BONES, DEM GREY BONES

After a while, the trot round the corner with the Red Riding Hood basket to the supermarket, shuffling about in their deep freeze and coming up with yet another pre-cleaned, pre-cooked, pre-carved, gaily packaged little television supper—merely heat and eat—promotes, particularly in the absence of a television set, a feeling of over-dependence on the enfeebling facilities of the modern world.

At a headlong pace, words tripping over themselves, I rush to state that deep-frozen, pre-cooked, gaily packaged little television suppers are beyond question the reverse of being physically enfeebling, packed as they are from colour picture on the front to simple instructions on the back with nut-brown goodness, vitamin-wise 100 per cent glutamate pure. The enfeeblement is to the spirit, the sensation of the loss of the manliness that sent the caveman, with a club, on the track of dinosaur giblet minestrone with noodles, dinner gained by work, courage and imagination, nutriment torn from nature by the sweat of the simian brow.

The memory returned of an Aran Island legend, wherein Pat Mullen, the Man of Aran himself, resolved to settle his commissariat problems by cooking, at one blow, enough stew to last him for three months and to this end he furbished up a forty-gallon oil-drum and set it upon a great turf fire and all the people of Aran came to their king with pigs and sheep, some of them skinned, and ducks and hens and threw them in tribute into the mighty pot and bushels of potatoes and onions and cabbages went in and for a week there was great drinking and singing while the cauldron bubbled, and for good measure at the end the king tossed in a boulder-size lump of rock-salt, and when the ceremonial tasting came the enormous stew was that powerful they had to take it out into the middle of Galway Bay in a hooker and drop it into the deep. . . .

A more continental type of stew, I calculated, going easy on the rock-salt, wool and feathers, might well serve to get me off the little telly suppers and back among the men who struggled for their food.

Big saucepans, suitable for big stews, turned out to be prohibitively expensive. It was as though there were a tax on size in cooking, as though it were a threat to the nation's food resources for a man to require a saucepan large enough to hold a cow's leg and a stone of mixed vegetables. I got one in the end, not very large, for 28*s*. 11*d*., after dodging pots retailing at anything up to a fiver, even if they did have non-stick, aluminiumized, even-heat-distributive bottoms.

The butcher was interesting on the subject of meat for stews. He said he wished he'd been on the "Panorama" programme when Dimbleby was doing the butchers. He'd have told him a thing or two. "Everyone's gone crackers," the butcher said, itemising one of the things he would have told Dimbleby, "buying fillet steak for stewing. Natural they think the price of meat is high." I came out with a heap of fragments at 4*s*. 6*d*. a pound and fippence wortha bones—a huge, glistening, blue-white knuckle and a chopped-up shank as long and as thick as your arm.

The preliminary stages of the manufacture of stock were alarming. The boiling of the beautiful blue-white knuckle and the pinkish, ivory shank threw up a fearful, mud-coloured scum. It was as though, in pursuance of the haute cuisine of the Aran Islands, I'd thrown a ton of murphies straight into the pot out of the sod. At the end of two hours of low simmering the glistening bones were grey and muddy themselves, seeming to threaten anthrax or foot-and-mouth disease. Straining was obviously required, and here, failing a strainer, the first, amateurish improvisation broke out. A glazed, brown coffee-pot with a filtering device. The stock stuck in the filter, but with a toothpick to clear the filter holes I managed to get quite a lot of it into the coffee-pot, somewhat grey still in colour but looking more anthrax-free. I wrapped the boiling bones in newspaper and put them in the dustbin, feeling like Hare acting under the orders of Burke, scoured the saucepan and filled it with stock from the coffee-pot in four strained helpings. Coming out of the spout, it looked like a lot of coffee I've seen in various places.

Ready to go now, a great, nourishing, self-made, simmering mélange of meat, potatoes, leeks, carrots, onions, substantial clove of garlic and herbs sounding like a society wedding—Rosemary Thyme and Basil Fennel. It bubbled and fenelled away all day, filling the residency with the scents and sounds of a factory ship in attendance upon a whaling fleet.

I dined upon it, in it, off it, in solo state at the fashionable hour of 7.45 that night and even after four helpings, decreasing admittedly in size, made gratifyingly little impression on the basic mass.

Indeed, the surrounding soup, or stock, was by now so rich that it could have endured 100 per cent dilution and retained every shred of its identity. Little telly suppers, it was plain, would not be required for a long, long time.

A new problem, however, by now has become apparent. Running a big, permanent stew is like owning a big, permanent dog. That is, you've got to keep it exercised. You can't go out and leave it or it pines, goes sick. For the last three days I've been too busy to give my stew a run. It looks bad, and probably is.

Failing Galway Bay, I may have to sink the whole suffocating saucepan in the Serpentine.

DISGRACE ABOUNDING

The tide began to ebb in a south-easterly direction early on the morning of Christmas Eve, carrying with it one or two unimportant bits of driftwood like a table lamp, a small stool and a plastic tray, transported more for their lightness and mobility than for any specific purpose.

They made little difference even to the sparse furnishings of the new flat but at least it was a start, though I had to think for a while before being able to analyse what it was a start towards. In the end I decided it was a start towards saving the eventual furniture removers trouble.

It was not the best of reasons, seeing that furniture removers, accustomed to shifting double-beds and grand pianos, would be little inconvenienced by a table lamp, a small stool and a plastic tray, so I had to work on it a little harder, coming up in no time with a much more rational justification. I was, in fact, saving myself trouble, by distributing these small objects around the new home while there was still room to do so. After all, when the official removers had finished, the place would be cluttered with table and chairs and cupboards and all that, and it would take hours to sort everything out.

So I went back for some more bric-à-brac.

In the lift and on the landing I met several of my fellow tenants and we wished one another all the compliments of the season. They said I must drop in for a drink any time and I said I'd be giving a substantial farewell party before the New Year, because I wouldn't be moving until round about January 10th.

This time I packed a lot of old clothes into three suitcases, the kind of stuff I never really wore and felt it would be handy to have out of the way. Curiously enough, I found myself listening this time, with the front door partially open, to make sure that the coast was clear, before smuggling the suitcases into the lift and out into the car. I had a subconscious feeling that people looking forward to a farewell party some time after Christmas might not understand these apparent signs of premature departure. I also felt it would take too long to explain the disused nature of the wardrobe, which was merely being got out of the way.

In the new place I put the old clothes away in the newly built-in bedroom cupboard and sat on the new sofa in the new sitting-room. It felt very much unlived in. No pictures. No magazines lying around. No bottles or glass. No sign anywhere, in fact, of Christmas cheer.

I went back to the old place, with a large shopping basket, to get some glasses and a bottle or two, and found in the letter-box an invitation, delivered by hand, to attend a Boxing Day party in the flat of some old friends on the third floor. It wanted an R.S.V.P., but I knew there'd be time for this later.

I put a couple of bottles and a lemon and the spare ice-bucket into the basket, and then on a sudden impulse took down the three pictures in the bedroom and wrapped them in a blanket. I was glad to be able to get all this out into the car and away, unseen.

I put the blanket, neatly folded, on the floor of the empty new bedroom and had my first drink in my new home. It was beginning to enclose me more warmly, to become, in fact, a home. All at once it occurred to me that if I had a mattress and one more blanket and a couple of pillows I could camp out on the floor and wake up on Christmas morning in the new place—surely a good omen for the future. It would be, of course, merely a temporary measure—I'd be back in the old one to give this farewell party—but in the meantime it was an irresistible idea.

I had a struggle to get the mattress into the lift, but once again I got away with it, unseen. From the other flats came the thunder of Christmas celebrations. Everyone was much too busy to notice that one of their number was leaving—and I suddenly saw it with absolute clarity—for ever. The furniture removers would have to deal with the bed, the chest of drawers and the rest of the heavy stuff, but everything that would go into the back of a Mini-Traveller was going now, however many trips it took.

I got back to the old place, on my fifth trip, round about six o'clock that evening, to collect some chairs, when I saw leaning against the wall outside the flat opposite me a tangle of holly and ivy leaves and a large branch of a tree, discards from their Christmas decorations. I removed the large branch, at the same time as the chairs, tidying up for them and giving myself something with which to decorate the bare white walls of my new patio.

What with Christmas Eve and everything I got back to the old place, to collect the dining-table, round about three o'clock next morning, to find a note pinned to my door. In the event, it said, that I had inadvertently removed a branch from outside their door, could I kindly put it back, as it was intended to form the centre of their decorations.

I returned it round about 4.15 a.m., with a letter of apology, leaving it outside the door. I should also like to apologise, here and now, for not replying to the Boxing Day invitation, but I've been too busy.

I should like to think that many people in the old place will remember me, as we all advance on our separate paths into a bright New Year.

FLASH IT ON THE WALL

It was possible to tell at a glance that this great and glittering emporium had gone out of its way to create an atmosphere of hope, to promote the illusion that here one could find exactly what one wanted in as short a space of time as twenty minutes.

Acres of glass, open staircases, indoor vegetation, a fountain in the courtyard and spotlights picking out the subtleties of texture and design. And, above all else, the various wallpapers pasted on to immense sheets of hard-board, hanging vertically on hinges like the pages of a giant's picture book.

"But what," I said, looking round with child-like wonder and delight, "about this! What a marvellous idea, to spread the stuff out so that you can get a look at it."

The interior decoration expert was fingering a length of curtain material hanging in majestic folds from a wire loop in the ceiling.

"Yeah," she said.

The curtain material was almost royal in its splendour, a rich blend of purple, crimson and gold.

"Were you thinking about that for the master bedroom?" I enquired, suffering a slight fall in euphoria as a result of that somewhat lack-lustre "Yeah".

"I wasn't thinking about it at all," she replied abstractedly. Then she said, with unexpected vehemence, "I've spent some of the best years of my life in here."

I realised that the fingering of the royal curtain material was just a limbering up, a flexing of the muscles and the mind for the task ahead.

"I'm sure we'll find something on these splendid boards," I said, consolingly.

The first set of boards were splendid indeed, but somehow not quite—not exactly—right. We went through them again, impeded by two predatory ladies in mink who were clattering the boards as though they were playing chemmy.

"Perhaps," I said, "we might move on to Contemporary." I'd noticed the sign on the way in.

"Why don't we do that," said the interior decoration expert. It was, at least, an improvement on "Yeah".

The Contemporary boards were very exciting. At the first run-through I picked out three, with special emphasis on a marvellous, sea-green, glowing paper with a nubbly finish, almost like silk. "Almost perfect," I said, "for the living-room, complementing the foliage in the patio, once it gets going."

The interior decoration expert responded by nodding, twice, and then pointing towards what turned out to be a price list, let into a small glass case. The sea-green paper was 102*s.* 6*d.* a roll.

I had to ask her if that was a lot. "You might be able to judge it," she said, "by the fact that the Lessors of your new apartment are prepared to decorate the living-room with two coats of emulsion paint or wallpaper at twelve and six a roll."

We moved away from Contemporary and rattled through Figured, Traditional and various other groupings without, once again, finding exactly what we wanted. I had a feeling that the feet and the back were giving out. "What do we do now?" I said.

She squared her shoulders, preparing—it seemed—for something she had always known was coming. "Now," she said, "we sit down in front of twelve books of wallpaper, each of them weighing a ton, and we go through every page, looking for the one out of every hundred which might possibly be suitable for our purpose. You take that one and I'll take this . . ."

Ten minutes later I'd got to the end of the first book, stunned to discover that wallpaper could come in what looked like a million different patterns and not one of them exactly right. And I still had another eleven books to go.

"You know," I said, looking round at the boards and the indoor vegetation and all the lightness and brightness, "these people have really burst themselves to ease the burden of this revolting task, but they still haven't gone far enough. What they ought to do is invent a kind of magic lantern and then you put wallpaper slides into it and project them on to the walls of the room you're trying to decorate."

Suddenly, I became excited. "This is a wonderful idea," I said. "It's perfectly easy to make the equipment. You've only got to—"

The interior decoration expert looked up, removing a pencil from between her teeth, another page of wallpaper half turned.

"There's no point in chattering," she said severely. "Just keep looking. Let me assure you, there is no other way out."

We're still on the treadmill, slowly turning pages, but at the back of the mind still flickers on this wonderful idea of magic wallpaper slides.

There *must* be another way out.

COME EARLY, PEARLY GATES

I'd been writing letters for some time, the gentle levers necessary to pry myself loose from my surroundings, prior to taking a short or, probably, rather longer break in the sun.

Dear Sirs,

I am in receipt of your small account of even date and have to inform you that I am about to leave the country on a brief but exceedingly important business trip which will pay more than handsome dividends to both of us. I look forward to settling your account, and doubling my usual order, on my return.

Yours, etc. . . .

A gentle slithering away from the claws, leaving behind sensations of warmth, goodwill, even expectation, so that the claws would sheath themselves for a sufficient period of time at least to allow me to sail from Dover, however savagely they might try to scratch later on.

The telephone rang, as it had been doing almost continuously since lunchtime. I picked it up and spoke firmly, getting my blow in first. "This is not Poynder and Barlow of East Cheam, and neither am I their Mr. Tarporley. There's a fault on this line, so kindly dial the exchange." After five consecutive requests for Mr. Tarporley, of Poynder and Barlow, I had turned against their whole organisation.

A faint, female voice at the other end said, "Oh." It found the courage to persist. "I—I was looking for the person who advertised a flat to rent—"

It came out in a torrent of ingratiation, a whole jugful of double cream. "My dear madam, how delightful to hear from you. You're speaking to him—me. That is, I'm he. You'll find it just what you're looking for. I can thoroughly recommend—" I used the secondhand car salesman's technique, the clinching of the deal before it had even started. "You've got yourself an absolutely charming apartment."

She used the technique that ages secondhand car salesmen before their time. "I wonder if I could just see it first?" We made an appointment to view that very evening, at five o'clock. She said her name was Mrs. Gates.

I swept all the letter litter off the table, and put the typewriter under the bed in the other room.

Flowers! Was there time to rush out and buy flowers? Great masses of daffodils or chrysanthemums, or whatever vegetation might be in season. But there was nothing to put them in. Keep them in the sink and then present them to Mrs. Gates? "Dear Mrs. Gates, this is just a small tribute in exchange for your great kindness!"

There seemed to be rather a lot of pipe tobacco, smoked and unsmoked, on the sitting-room carpet. The windows were a bit murky. Too much old bread lying around in the kitchen. I went into a flurry of activity, sweeping stuff under the settee, shovelling newspapers into the cupboard, scrubbing curry marks off the kitchen door with the corner of my handkerchief. Delay your entrance by another twenty minutes, Mrs. Gates, and everything will be beautiful for you!

At 5.10 p.m. I knocked an ashtray off the windowsill. It fell down behind the radiator. I tried to poke it out with a wooden spoon and the spoon fell down too. Mrs. Gates would never rent an apartment that had spoons and ashtrays behind the radiator. I forced my arm down behind the radiator and my elbow got stuck. But seriously, painfully stuck, so that I couldn't get it out.

Mrs. Gates, is that you? I'm frightfully sorry but I can't open the door because I've got my arm stuck behind the radiator but the porter can open it for you and then you can look around and please don't mind me—

Leaving skin behind I extricated my elbow, sitting sweating on the settee. Mrs. Gates would not wish to rent an apartment from an overheated occupier so I shot into the bathroom and the towels were fearful, so I shoved them under the bed with the typewriter and put out some fresh ones for Mrs. Gates.

By 6 p.m. I had decided not to charge Mrs. Gates for the use of the telephone, and to throw in lighting, heating and laundry as well. Not at all, Mrs. Gates—it's my pleasure, I assure you.

By 6.30 p.m. I had come to the conclusion that the sensible thing to do was not to charge Mrs. Gates any rent at all, but to pay her some nominal sum like £2 a week for watering the plants and forwarding mail, during the period of her tenancy. I could compensate her for any additional expenses incurred on my return.

Mrs. Gates, in fact, failed altogether to put in an appearance.

I can only say she missed a real snip.

DRAWERS IN GOOD RUNNING ORDER

The events of last Thursday, when I considered them the following day, seemed to me to represent the essence of what is wrong with modern Britain.

I didn't have time to come to this conclusion on Thursday. I was too busy.

Thursday began on a hopeful note. For some time past a stripped pine chest of drawers in the living-room had been getting bigger and bigger. Not, of course, in the physical sense, but more in the way of an optical illusion. It just looked as if it was getting bigger and more inconvenient every day.

Then I had the clever idea of selling it back to the lady from whom I'd bought it. She's in the used furniture business, and you don't come across a stripped pine chest of drawers in good running order every day.

She sounded, however, a little guarded on the telephone. Didn't actually remember having sold me the piece, not much demand, might be able to allow me ten, etc.

Ten in the wallet looked a lot more desirable than a chest of drawers that was getting bigger and bigger, so I said it was a deal, and when could she send round for it?

The awful woman said she wouldn't be able to do that. I'd have to deliver it myself.

It's not easy for one man, single-handed, to transport a large chest of drawers from a lower ground floor apartment to the roof of a car, particularly when three stone-idle house painters are leaning against the railings watching him, without making even a microscopic gesture of assistance. Their attitude suggested that they didn't fully understand what I was trying to do.

I made the chest of drawers fast to the roof of the car with string, rope and electrical flex, and drove very slowly to the other end of the town, to find that since I'd last called on the furniture lady some busybody, probably Barbara Castle, had caused a wire fence to be erected along the whole length of the pavement.

I saw the furniture lady through the window of her shop, telephoning someone, probably telling them she'd just come by a very desirable chest of drawers. She gave me what I took to be a wave of encouragement.

Single-handed, I took the chest of drawers off the roof of the car, manoeuvred it over the fence, and set it on the pavement.

The furniture lady came out, looked at it, and spoke. "Oh, dear," she said, "you couldn't have bought that from me. I'd never handle anything like that." Then she assembled a haymaker, and let me have it. "I'm afraid I couldn't buy it," she said. "You'll have to take it away."

I'll say this much for her. She did help while I was wrestling the chest of drawers over the fence and back on to the roof of the car. She came to the door of her shop and said, "If you take the drawers out it's easier," and then she went in again. I did, and it was.

On the way home I called at the off-licence to collect six large tonic, a bottle of vodka and a bottle of brandy. I put them in one of the drawers in the back of the car.

Home again, single-handedly I once more wrestled the chest of drawers off the roof of the car, down the area steps, along the passage and back into the sitting-room. Then I went back to get the drawers themselves, beginning with the one containing the drink. The kerb outside my house is rather high. I tripped over it and fell, with the drawerful of drink held out in front of me. Every single one of the tonic bottles broke, foaming over the pavement, but fortunately the brandy and the vodka remained intact.

I should like to point out that it was the rush-hour. A number of office workers, hurrying home, were good enough to walk round rather than over me. They seemed unconcerned.

I knelt on the pavement, in a pool of foaming tonic, and put the brandy and the vodka back in the drawer. I rose to my feet and the bottom fell out of the drawer, the glue probably having been loosened by the tonic water. The brandy and the vodka fell straight through the frame and smashed themselves to pieces on the pavement. Five office workers averted their gaze as they hurried by, stepping gingerly over the sea of broken glass, and the pool of tonic, vodka and brandy. None of them spoke.

Some time later, however, I was addressed by an old lady while I was brushing the broken glass into the gutter. She said, "A little boy lives round the corner's good at sweepin'. He'd show you how to do that."

The whole business a perfect microcosm of Britain today. Too many technocrats too free with advice, and too few stout-thewed workers to get on with the actual job.

FOLLOW THROUGH ON THE FLIES

The lady suddenly yelled, "Go away, foul flies, or I'll murder you!"

She sprang out of her chair, incensed, and ran round the patio several times, flailing her arms and making snatching motions with both hands.

I drew my chair back a little, to give her greater freedom of movement. "Did you catch anything?" I asked her.

She sat down again, out of breath, but her eyes were still darting around, looking for the enemy. The flailing and snatching seemed, however, to have dispersed them for the moment.

"It's just one of the joys," I said, "of the beginning of summer."

"Foul," she said. "I can't stand them." Without warning, she slapped her own arm. It looked painful, and she missed.

"Why don't you do something?" she cried.

I stretched my legs out again, more comfortably. "Women," I said, "always seem to me to have a disproportionately passionate attitude towards our little whirling friends. An occasional fly or two seems to convince them that they're in the presence of corruption. They feel sure that a leg of lamb has gone off or something unspeakable has died under the sink. I'm more like a contented old horse in a field. An occasional swish of my tail or, rather, hand, is as far as I feel it necessary to go anti-fly wise. You might do well to adopt the same, almost Buddhist philosophy."

She spoke with extreme seriousness, emphasising each word. "Go and get something," she said, "which will deal with them. Now." She had an afterthought. "But not flypaper. Wherever you hang flypaper, if you hang flypaper fifty feet above the ground, it gets into people's hair. Instantly," she added, with the greatest emphasis yet. "So go and get something else, now."

The man in the hardware shop round the corner had the same contented, Buddhist horse philosophy as myself. "Never get rid of 'em in the open, sir," he said, with satisfaction. "Stands to reason. It's their natural habitat. I could give you a lot of sprays and suchlike, but they'd be for indoors, more. No," he said, "flies are here to stay, out of doors anyway. Specially at this time of year."

"I'm giving a friend lunch on the patio," I said. "But she's unable to come to grips with these self-evident facts. But the trouble is the table's already laid and we don't want to have to shift it all in again."

"Women," he said, "are always very hot on flies."

Talk about the brotherhood of man!

"Tell you what," he said suddenly. "What about a couple of fly-whisks? Nice little plastic jobs. Give her something to do."

The patio was reeking when I got back with some sour smell.

"It's vinegar," she said defensively. "I splashed some around, but it hasn't done much good. What are those horrible things? What revolting colours."

"Fly-whisks," I said. "Would you like the tomato red, or the acid green?"

She took the green one, doubtfully, and without warning smashed it against the wall. The fly effortlessly looped the loop and escaped.

"Your back swing's too quick," I said, "and I think your grip's a bit tight. You want to avoid tension. A flick with the wrist should bring about the best result."

I flicked at the table and missed by several inches. "It obviously takes practice," I told her.

We sat in silence for some time, with our whisks at the ready. "That vinegar of yours has driven them away," I said. "It's like fouling up the water-hole on safari. We want the big tuskers to come down to drink, don't we?"

She didn't say anything. We resumed our vigil, the whisks poised for action.

After a while I said, "Fly-hunting puts rather a stopper on general conversation, doesn't it?" I nailed one with a lovely, back-handed flick. "What do you think about the shameful failure to make use of the National Theatre site in South Kensington?"

She replied by smashing her whisk down on my left arm, breaking her instrument in half. The fly flew away. I examined the glass of my wrist-watch with fairly tender care. "Now," she said, "I'll have yours."

In the end I gave her my tomato-red fly-whisk. We lunched in silence, punctuated by futile slaps.

Women are not only neurotic about flies. They also simply cannot grasp the technique of the slow back-swing, followed by the wrist flick with follow-through and I said so.

It was a relief when she broke the second fly-whisk over my head.

Taking What Comes

A CASE FOR A WHITE SICK CAR

"But you don't want all those toys on a picnic," I protested. "A picnic is a sort of . . . toy . . . itself . . ."

I couldn't put it into words, but I wanted to thin out their luggage.

They stood round the car in a silent circle, Brigid under an open umbrella, Mister Phanie carrying a shopping-basket filled with plasticine, Gewaan a large, stark-naked doll in a cot, Guy supporting with difficulty a full-size shovel.

"Just leave it all in the summerhouse," I said. "It'll be there when we come back."

"But what shall we do at the picnic without our toys?" Brigid said.

"What do you do at picnics anyway?" I asked. I did, in fact, want to know what they thought was going to happen.

"Eat and read," said Gewaan. She looked more like Pola Negri than ever, with her long, black fringe, straggling side pieces, and sultry brown eyes. At five Gewaan—Gwen to her parents—looked, astonishingly, as though she'd be at home on a leopard skin couch.

"If you're going to read," I said, "why don't you bring some books?"

They looked at one another with what I estimated to be embarrassment. I had been guilty of an illogical process of thought.

"Daddy," said Brigid, brightly changing the subject, "did we nearly make tea?"

"The tea is in the basket," I said carefully, "if that's what you mean."

"I want a drink of orange lemons," said Mister Phanie—a child, christened Stephanie, with all the vivid colouring of a white mouse.

"Jelly," said Guy. He was the youngest, a square, brown boy capable of infinite unsmiling pursuit of whatever fancy might enter his mind.

There was no jelly in the picnic-basket, and no orange lemons either, if it came to that. I bundled the four of them into the car, before I had to remake the meal. I put the umbrella, the basket of plasticine, the doll in the cot and, finally, the shovel, in with them.

"Guy's going to garden and garden and moan the lawn," said Brigid, apropos, apparently, of this last piece of equipment.

I'd decided to take them to a place along the river where the water was shallow enough for them to paddle. I didn't feel like organising games of tig.

The four of them stood in the back of the car, Gewaan, unconscious of our close proximity, breathing on my neck. She must, recently, have eaten a whole bag of bull's-eyes.

"Daddy," said Brigid suddenly, "do you know? Mister Phanie makes terrible bodies, like legs!"

I examined it carefully, searching in a wide orbit for a clue. I'd almost decided it was some acrobatic trick, when I remembered the plasticine.

"You mean she models things?"

"Horrible old lions and ladies and squills," said Mister Phanie enthusiastically. A hand appeared, holding a worm-like piece of multi-coloured plasticine with a white knob on one end.

"Is that the horrible old lion?" I asked, overcoming a lack of interest.

"It's a squill!" Brigid cried indignantly. "Like what we saw on the grass when it was having its breakfast!"

Mister Phanie's white-topped worm was a *squirrel*! "It's just like a squirrel," I said. "Mister Phanie's very clever."

As we turned into the field leading down to the river I said "squill" and then "squirrel" several times very quickly to myself. They sounded maddeningly alike. Then I began to think that people lit pipes with squills, and found I couldn't remember what the word really was. I was on the verge, probably, of a breakdown when Brigid said, "Daddy—Daddy"—the familiar, imperious opening—"do you know? White cars are white sick cars."

I parked our own car carefully by the river bank, and turned to look at them. They stared back politely.

"What do you mean," I said, "white cars are white sick cars?"

"They take you to hospital," said Guy. Ambulances!

"When you were coughing the other bit," Brigid added.

I considered it, encouraged by my success with the white sick cars. Could "coughing the other bit" be a specially severe cough —"the other bit" being taken in the sense of something extra or additional?

"How do you mean," I said, "coughing the other bit?"

Brigid looked put out. Then she said, "I can't think it," and turned to Gewaan. "Shall we play ring-a-rosies and see if we all fall down when we go straight?" she asked.

Gewaan said, "I think my dolly will be sick every day—really."

I intervened. "Get out of the car," I shouted, "play ring-a-rosies —anything!"

They descended with infinite care, passing the umbrella, the basket of plasticine, the doll in the cot and the shovel from hand to hand. Then they sat on the running-board of the car, in deep shadow.

Brigid said, "Daddy—Daddy—are we having a picnic—real—with bread-spreads?"

"We've a rug," I said. "You don't use bed-spreads for picnics."

"Oh, don't *say* that!" she cried. "Bread-spreads is like what Mummy puts on bread out of the bockle!" Like a watchmaker, with minute patience, I took it to pieces, to discover eventually, from Gewaan, that the reference had been to sandwich-spread.

Keeping my emotions nailed right down, I laid out the rug and put them on it, and removed Guy's shovel. I was passing round the bread-spreads when the swans appeared, round the bend of the river. At first sight there were so many of them I thought it must be some special occasion, like a swan-upping. I counted them, and found there were twelve. They came forging ahead in two irregular lines, and then suddenly they were all clambering up the bank, lurching from side to side on flat black feet. Their necks were stretched out. There was a deadly purpose about them. They obviously knew about picnics.

"Quick, children!" I cried. "Into the car!" Without bothering about what happened to the bread-spreads or the cake or anything else I bundled all the food into the rug, together with Brigid's umbrella and the plasticine basket, and started to run. The three little girls ran with me, with Guy bringing up the rear, impeded by his shovel.

In the safety of the car, with the windows up, Brigid was the first to speak. "Daddy—Daddy," she said, "do you know? Those swongs are called Clammy and Jammy and Nammy and Pammy and——"

"Stop it," I said.

"I like swongs better," said Guy, without adding than what.

"Eat your picnic," I told them, "and keep quiet."

Almost daintily they began to eat cake off the rug. Intermittently the swans tapped on the windows with their beaks.

"Brigid . . ." began Mister Phanie. I waited, suddenly tense.

"Do you know," said Mister Phanie, "I call my daddy 'Concrete'."

I half turned round.

"Do you?" said Brigid indifferently. "I call my daddy 'Office Work'."

The swans, and the children, were astonished at the speed with which I drove out of the field. A man can take so much, and then no more.

FLASHING AFTER A BRUSH

So far, I, undressed, have come rushing at women twice. One of these occasions was connected with a shaving-brush.

I was lying in the bath one morning, when I remembered that I had left my new shaving-brush in my overcoat pocket. The overcoat was hanging in the hall.

Everything else was ready and in position. Shaving-mirror and soap; new razor-blade; toothbrush and paste; hairbrush, comb and brilliantine tin; packet of ginger biscuits and a copy of *Forever Amber* on a chair beside the bath. When I wash I like to *wash.*

Everything was ready, then, except the new shaving-brush. I lay submerged for some time with just the nostrils and the whites of the eyes showing, trying to think of a substitute for a shaving-brush. Perhaps if the soap were rubbed on with the hand, and worked in? Or the tooth-brush might be adapted to serve the purpose? The only difference between a toothbrush and a shaving-brush is that one is shorter and harder than the other, and the handle is fastened on in a different direction. But the toothbrush, properly employed, might be induced to work up a lather. I might even, by accident, invent a new kind of shaving-brush, with a long handle and a scrubbing motion. . . .

All this time I knew I would have to get out of the bath, and fetch the shaving-brush out of my overcoat pocket.

I got out of the bath, in the end, at a quarter past eleven. At that time I had a hairy kind of dressing-gown that set my teeth on edge if I put it on next to my skin. I ran out of the bathroom, roughly knotting a shirt about my waist.

In this flat the bathroom, bedroom and sitting-room led off a passage. I ran lightly down the passage to the door, where my overcoat usually hangs. Then I remembered I had left the coat lying on a chair in the sitting-room. I ran more rapidly back along the passage, leaving footprints on the carpet. Already, I was becoming chilled and a little pimply. Passing the bathroom door I put on an extra burst of speed, and entered the sitting-room nearly all out.

It is difficult under such circumstances to make a precise estimate of the passage of time, but I think that a fifth of a second elapsed before I saw the charwoman standing by the window. She must have been dusting the bureau, but when she saw me she froze dead.

I, too, froze. Then I said "Waah!" and tried to leap out backwards through the door.

The charwoman very nearly got there first. The thought must have flashed through her mind that she would be better off outside in the passage, convenient to the main staircase, and so with a kind of loping run she came across the room.

We arrived upon the mat inside the door simultaneously. The mat went from under us, and we came down. I fell heavily on the feather duster which she was carrying, and the bamboo handle snapped. I thought my leg had gone.

We lay together on the mat for several moments, not shouting or anything, just trying to piece together in a blurry way exactly what had happened.

I came to my senses first. I was younger than she was, and probably more resilient.

I jumped up and made another break for the door. To my surprise I found it was shut, and not only shut but locked. I wrenched at the handle, conscious in the most alive way of my appearance from the back. The door was unyielding. I caught sight of a Spanish shawl draped across the top of the piano, and in a trice I was enveloped in it, an unexpectedly flamboyant figure.

Afterwards I remembered that the door opened *outwards*. I had gained the impression that it was locked by unthinkingly pulling it towards me.

And now the charwoman was also back on her feet. But to my horror I saw that she was taking off her housecoat—slowly and deliberately. It seemed to be her intention to disrobe. But why?

I watched her, wide-eyed. She folded the housecoat into a neat square. She placed it tidily in the centre of the table. "That," she said, "is me notice—and now me husband will have to be tole."

I fortunately never saw her again.

NOULDED INTO A SHAKE

When I was a tall, sensitive boy at school I once sent up for a booklet about how to be a ventriloquist.

I was always "sending up" for things—variable focus lamps, propelling pencils with choice of six differently-coloured leads, air-pistols discharging wooden bullets, scale model tanks with genuine caterpillar action, tricks in glass-topped boxes, and so on—anything, I suppose, to vary the monotony of straight games and education.

The booklet arrived at breakfast time one morning in a large square envelope. I told the other boys it was a new stamp album, and got on with my shredded liver poached in water. I wanted the voice-throwing to come as a real surprise.

We had twenty minutes after breakfast in which to get our things ready for first school. I had a quick run through the new book.

It was called *Ventriloquism in Three Weeks*. On the first page it explained that the word ventriloquism came from the Latin *ventriloqus*—"a speaking from the belly". There was also a drawing of a schoolboy smiling pleasantly at a railway porter carrying a trunk. From the trunk came hysterical cries of, "Help! Help! Murder! Police!"

It was just the sort of thing I was aiming at. I slipped the book in with my other ones, and hurried off to first school.

In the next fortnight I put in a good deal of practice, sitting right at the back of the class, watching my lips in a small piece of mirror, and murmuring, "Dah, dee, day, di, doy, doo."

It was necessary, however, to be rather careful. Dr. Farvox, the author of the book, suggested that it might be as well to perform the earlier exercises "in the privacy of one's bedroom or den." Dr. Farvox was afraid that "chums or relatives" might laugh, particularly while one was practising the "muffled voice in the box".

The best way to get this going, Dr. Farvox said, was to experiment "with a continuous grunting sound in a high key, straining from the chest as if in pain."

He was right in thinking that this exercise ought to be performed in the privacy of the bedroom. It was inclined to be noisy—so noisy, indeed, that I was caught twice straining in a high key from the chest during practical chemistry, and had to pretend that I'd been overcome by the fumes of nitric acid.

But, in the end, it was the easy, pleasant smile that terminated my study of what Dr. Farvox described as "this amusing art".

It happened one Saturday morning, in the hour before lunch,

ordinarily a pleasant enough period devoted to constitutional history. Bill the Bull, who took the class, was usually fairly mellow with the prospect of the weekend before him, and there was not much need to do any work.

As was by now my invariable custom I was seated right at the back of the room with a large pile of books in front of me, and the mirror lying on the desk. I was working on the Whisper Voice, which had been giving me quite a considerable amount of difficulty.

"Lie down, Neddy, lie down," I whispered, watching my lips closely in the glass.

"It's due in dock at nine o'clock."

Not bad.

"Take Ted's Kodak down to Roy."

There it was again—the old familiar twitch on "Kodak".

I sat back, relaxing a little, and smiled. Dr. Farvox was strongly in favour of the Smile. "What the young student," he said, "should aim at from the first is an easy and natural expression. He should Smile."

I smiled. Smiling, I whispered, "Take Ted's Kodak down to Roy."

To my absolute horror I found myself smiling straight into the face of Bill the Bull.

He stopped dead. He was in the middle of something about the growth of common law, but my smile stopped him dead in his tracks.

"Well, well," said Bill, after a moment. "How charming. And good morning to you, too."

I at once buried by face in my books, and tried to shove the mirror and *Ventriloquism in Three Weeks* on one side.

Bill rolled slowly down the passageway between the desks. He was an enormous Welshman with a bullet head, and very greasy, straight black hair. He took a subtle and delicate pleasure in driving the more impressionable amongst us half mad with fear at least five days a week.

"Such pretty teeth," said Bill. "How nice of you to smile at me. I have always wanted to win your admiration."

The other boys sat back. They knew they were on to something good.

I kept my head lowered. I'd actually succeeded in opening my constitutional history somewhere near the middle, but the corner of Dr. Farvox was clearly visible under a heap of exercise books.

Bill reached my desk. "But who knows," he said, "perhaps you love me too. Perchance you've been sitting there all morning just dreaming of a little home—just you and I. And later, perhaps, some little ones. . . .?"

A gasp of incredulous delight came from the other boys. This was Bill at his very best.

I looked up. It was no longer possible to pretend I thought he was talking to someone else.

"I'm sorry, sir," I said. "I was just smiling."

Suddenly, Bill pounced. He snatched up Dr. Farvox.

"Cripes," he said. "What in the world have we here? Ventriloquism in three weeks?"

He turned a couple of pages.

"Scholars," he said, "be so good as to listen to this."

He read aloud: "To imitate a Fly. Close the lips tight at one corner. Fill that cheek full of wind and force it to escape through the aperture. Make the sound suddenly loud, and then softer, which will make it appear as though the insect were flying in different parts of the room. The illusion may be helped out by the performer chasing the imaginary fly, and flapping at it with his handkerchief."

"Strewth," said Bill. He looked round the class. "We'd better get ourselves a little bit of this. Here am I taking up your time with the monotonies of constitutional history, while in this very room we have a trained performer who can imitate a fly."

Suddenly, he caught me by the back of the neck. "Come," he said, "my little love, and let us hear this astounding impression."

He dragged me down to the dais.

"Begin," said Bill. "Be so kind as to fill your cheek with wind, and at all costs do not omit the flapping of the handkerchief."

"Sir," I said, "that's animal noises. I haven't got that far yet."

"Sir," squeaked Bill, in a high falsetto, "that's animal noises. I 'aven't got that far yet."

He surveyed the convulsed class calmly.

"Come, come," he said, "this art is not as difficult as I had imagined it to be. Did anyone see my lips move?"

They cheered him. They banged the lids of their desks. "Try it again, sir!" they cried. "It's splendid!"

Bill raised his hand. "Gentlemen," he said, "I thank you for your kindness. I am, however, but an amateur. Am I not right in thinking that we would like to hear something more from Professor Smallpox?"

They cheered again. Someone shouted, "Make him sing a song, sir!"

Bill turned to me. "Can you," he said, "Professor Smallpox, sing a song?"

It was the worst thing that had ever happened to me in my life. I tried to extricate myself.

"No, sir," I said. "I haven't mastered the labials yet."

Bill started back. He pressed his hand to his heart.

"No labials?" he said. "You have reached the age of fifteen without having mastered the labials. But, dear Professor Smallpox, we must look into this. Perhaps you would be so kind as to give us some outline of your difficulties?"

I picked up *Ventriloquism in Three Weeks*. There was no way out.

"There's a sentence here, sir, that goes, 'A pat of butter moulded into the shape of a boat.' "

Bill inclined his head. "Is there, indeed? A most illuminating remark. You propose to put it to music?"

"No, sir," I said. "I'm just trying to show you how hard it is. You see, you have to call that, 'A cat of gutter noulded into the shake of a goat.' "

Bill fell right back into his chair.

"You have to call it *what*?" he said.

"A cat of gutter, sir, noulded into the shake of a goat."

Bill's eyes bulged.

"Professor," he said, "you astound me. You bewilder me. You take my breath away. A cat of gutter——" He repeated it reverently, savouring each individual syllable.

Then he sprang up. "But we must hear this," he cried. "We must have this cat of gutter delivered by someone who knows what he is at. This—this is valuable stuff."

He caught me by the ear. "Professor," he said, "why does it have to be noulded into the shake of a goat?"

"Well, sir," I said, "if you say it like that you don't have to move your lips. You sort of avoid the labials."

"To be sure you do," said Bill. "Why didn't I think of that myself. Well, now, we will have a demonstration."

He turned to face the class. "Gentlemen," he said, "Professor Smallpox will now say, 'A pat of butter moulded into the shape of a boat,' *without moving the lips*! I entreat your closest attention. You have almost certainly never in your lives heard anything like this before."

He picked up his heavy ebony ruler. His little pig-like eyes gleamed.

"And," he went on, "to make sure that Professor Smallpox will really give us of his best I shall make it my personal business to give Professor Smallpox a clonk on the conk with this tiny weapon should any of you see even the faintest movement of the facial muscles as he delivers his unforgettable message."

Bill brought down the ruler with a sharp crack on my skull.

"Professor," he said, "it's all yours."

I don't have to go into the next twenty-five minutes. The other boys yelled practically on every syllable. I got the meaningless words tangled up, and said, "A cack of rutter roulded into the gake of a shote."

At times Bill was so helpless with laughter that he missed me with the ruler altogether.

When the bell went for the end of the hour he insisted on being helped out into the passage, wiping his eyes with the blackboard cloth.

After that, I gave up ventriloquism, feeling no recurrence of interest even after reading Bill's observation on my end-of-term report: "He ought to do well on the stage."

SAVED BY THE BELL

When Miss Courtney said she would come up to my flat for a few minutes I was so excited I got my finger caught in the lift.

I put her in the armchair with her back to the window. Then I thought it would be better for both of us if she was on the sofa. I arranged the armchair so that she could put her feet up. It took us some time to settle down.

We didn't say anything at first. Indeed, it was all I could do to breathe. Then I said: "Comfy?"

Miss Courtney nodded. Then she smiled, "I could be comfier." I was about to slide my arm along the back of the sofa when I heard the men marching out into the yard. I hurried over to the window.

One of them had hooked a ladder into the third floor of the dummy house. Four or five others were grouped about an instructor down below. I couldn't catch what he was saying, although I opened the window and leant right out.

"They're going to do some practice with the hook ladder," I told Miss Courtney. "Don't quite know what it's going to be yet."

"Are they?" said Miss Courtney. "Whoever they are."

"They're firemen," I explained. "We're overlooking a fire-station."

"Oh," said Miss Courtney, "lucky us."

I turned back to the window in time to see the fireman come

down the ladder in a series of short jumps, both feet together, one rung at a time.

"He's with both feet together," I reported to Miss Courtney. "I think it's for toning up the leg muscles."

To tell the truth I was puzzled. I was pretty familiar with the routine by now, but this practice was one I had not seen before. I couldn't make it out. Why feet together? Perhaps the man was supposed to be carrying an unconscious person on his back. But these short jumps would surely put a great strain on the fireman, and on the ladder. I explained this to Miss Courtney. But in the end I told her not to worry.

"After all," I said, "it's probably just an exercise. He's probably toning up his calf muscles."

"If he gets them into any kind of condition," said Miss Courtney, "ask him to bring them up here."

I thought she was joking. "You don't really want anyone to come in, do you?" I said. "I mean, we don't want any interruptions, do we?"

"We certainly don't want the fire-brigade," said Miss Courtney. "They'd have nothing to put out."

For a while we sat quietly side by side, without saying anything. I took her hand. "Miss Courtney," I began, "Mavis . . ." At that moment someone started the engine of the fire-escape. I can always tell the difference between the pump and the fire-escape. The fire-escape has a higher, more whining note. I dropped Miss Courtney's hand and leaped for the window. "All aboard!" I cried excitedly, "it's escape practice." The long aluminium ladder was snaking into the air, the motorman on the engine watching it intently.

"Oops!" I cried. "He's just missed the chimney of the married quarters." I turned to Miss Courtney. "One of these days he's going to knock over that chimney and *then* he'll get what-for from his wife."

"I'm surprised to learn that he has time for a wife," said Miss Courtney.

"But of course," I said, "lots of the firemen have wives, and children, too. I often see them playing on the balconies overlooking the yard. Sometimes I can even see what the firemen are going to have for dinner."

"Boiled instruction manuals?" said Miss Courtney.

"No," I smiled, "of course not—just soup and meat and things like that."

The man working the escape swung it round towards the dummy house. "They're going to do a trial lowering," I reported. "There's a long rope on a pulley attached to the head of the ladder. There's a sort of leather belt on one end of the rope which they strap round the waist of the person who is being rescued. Then the men below take the weight on the rope, and lower the person safely to the ground."

"No doubt putting their helmets over their faces for fear they might see anything," said Miss Courtney.

"I think they're going to lower one of the firemen," I said. "Wait now—yes. . . . Oh, dash it, they're going to use that old sandbag again."

"Dash it for me as well," said Miss Courtney.

"Yes," I said, "yes, it's the sandbag all right. There she goes. Easy now. Lower away, men, Bristol fashion. Hurrah! The lovely lady is saved!"

"That's right," said Miss Courtney.

The firemen disengaged the sandbag, but they seemed to be dissatisfied with the working of the ladder. They shot it up and down several times.

"You know," I said, "I often think of what might happen if the real alarm went while they were holding one of these practices. While they have the ladder fully extended, I mean. Imagine what would happen if they got over-excited when the alarm bell rang and tried to drive the escape out of the yard without lowering the ladder. It might easily carry the whole fire-station away."

"Please," said Miss Courtney. "You're making my mouth water."

I took her hand again. "What an anxious life it must be for the firemen's wives," I said, "waiting all the time for the bell to ring, and their men to go dashing off to the blaze."

"The wives must spend a lot of their time," said Miss Courtney, "just waiting."

"The strain must be terrific," I agreed. "But I suppose they get used to it. After all, it's only very seldom that a fireman gets killed or injured."

"Do you have the exact figures?" asked Miss Courtney.

I had to tell her I couldn't be sure about them.

"That's funny," she said, "I thought you would certainly know the figures, over an average five-year period, for firemen killed or injured on duty. I mean, I thought you were practically a fireman yourself."

I had to laugh at that. "Oh no," I said, "I'm not really in the fire-brigade. Although, I'm so interested in it, I suppose you could call me an honorary fireman."

"I'll do that," said Miss Courtney.

We fell silent again. Then Miss Courtney said, "Listen, what were we talking about?"

I couldn't quite follow her. "When?" I said. "Do you mean about me being an honorary member of the brigade?"

Miss Courtney did not speak for a moment. Then she said : "No, before that. Before all these fires broke out."

I was puzzled. "Well," I said, "I'm not sure. I think I asked you if you were comfortable—comfy, I mean."

"That was it," said Miss Courtney, "I thought I hadn't been mistaken. Well, now, if you will be kind enough to hang your smoke-helmet and electric torch in the passage, ease off those hip-boots, loosen the tunic . . ."

At that moment the alarm went. I leaped for the window, counting, "One, two, three, four . . ."

The fire-station was in a controlled upheaval, someone shouting, the quick shadows of the crews flashing down the pole. The station doors rumbled back. The engines sprang to life with a roar. At the same moment their warning bells rang out. As I counted eight the engines swung out into the street, the men still scrambling aboard, pulling on their heavy boots and helmets.

At my end I went into my own routine. I grabbed the log-book out of my desk, and filled in the details.

Time of Alarm: 15 hrs. 27 mins. 5 secs.

Time of Departure: 15 hrs. 27 mins. 13 secs.

Type of Engine: Heavy pump and escape.

Direction of Departure: South-east.

Remarks: Wind : Force 2. Cloudy and drizzle.

There was nothing more I could do until the engines returned. I would then have to enter the time, and make a note of any casualties, or damage to enquipment.

"Pretty exciting, isn't it?" I said, turning to Miss Courtney. But Miss Courtney was not there. The door was open. She had gone.

I suppose she thought she could catch up with the engines by grabbing a taxi, or something. It just shows how much the ordinary person knows about fire-fighting. The engines, of course, would have been miles away by the time that she got out into the street.

FOUR IS A MOB

It's got to come to all of us sooner or later, and I got mine in a cupboard on the top floor of a house belonging to people called Cartwright, in the early spring of 1932.

Daphne Oakes was her name, a strapping girl from the sunlit beaches of Sydney, Australia, and she looked upon love as healthy exercise.

We were members of a house-party, gathered to celebrate a hunt ball in the Cartwrights' home. Major Cartwright was the M.F.H., and the house was packed to the roof with human horses and hounds.

As soon as I arrived I found I had to bunk in with the Master himself.

Mrs. Cartwright said, "I'm afraid you'll have to bunk in with Bob and Daph will bunk in with me." She gave a light, screaming laugh. "It would never do," she cried, "if Daph were to bunk in with you!"

Daphne Oakes came bounding up. I'm afraid I'll have to come right out into the open here, and admit that she was not exactly a girl. Rising thirty-five, I should say, but as strong as a kangaroo. She looked, indeed, quite like a kangaroo, bleached and sunburned, with her longish nose, short, compact arms, and powerful springy legs.

It was easy to picture Daphne, startled, leaping away through the bush, except that nothing, save a sudden explosion, could possibly have startled Daphne Oakes.

She was in favour of my bunking in with her. The others seemed to know that this was humorously intended, for they laughed loudly as she wound her arms around my neck. I backed away, being only seventeen, and they laughed more loudly than ever. Except one of them—a human horse who had been introduced to me as Maxwell Crump. Mr. Crump glowered. He had black, crinkly hair coming down almost to his eyebrows, and black, crinkly hair on the back of his hand. I had already marked him down as a slow starter in conversations not dealing directly with things on four legs.

Crump took Daphne away, and then gradually the party broke up, to change for dinner and the ball.

I accompanied Major Cartwright to our room. There was a small camp-bed in the corner, and on this I laid my suitcase.

Major Cartwright cleared his throat. He blew several times, and harrumphed, and then he said, "Bathroom's down the passage. Better nip in before the ladies get powder all over the shelf." Powder on the shelf seemed to be a grievance with him, for he added a moment later, "Stinkin' stuff—gets up your neb."

I was as clean as a new pin, but I went down the passage and waited in the bathroom for ten minutes. When I came back the

Major was wearing underpants, a boiled shirt, and a pair of astoundingly red, bare feet.

I dressed quickly—we were continually getting in one another's way—and left him to it. He was having difficulty with his tie, but I thought it wiser not to make an offer of help.

The others were already gathered in the drawing-room—Daphne Oakes in electric-blue, convulsed with laughter, and slapping people on the back. We went in to dinner; then the band arrived; and the other guests; and the ball was under way.

For the first couple of hours I kept clear of Daphne. I was a reserved boy, and contented myself with partners in pink taffeta, as young and modest as myself.

I couldn't have been thinking when I let myself in for the Paul Jones, because there in the inner ring was Daphne, doing an aboriginal war-dance, pawing the ground, and shouting for music.

She nailed me on the first lap. I was about to join hands with a young lady carrying a bead bag when Daphne shot between us. "Come on, Tommy," she cried, "let's go!"

I had no idea why she thought my name was Tommy. And a moment later I found I had no idea what she thought she was trying to do. We flayed our way round the ballroom, jerking and leaping, making hay of the other couples.

I tried to steady her by taking a firmer grip. Daphne, assuming this to be a sign of ripening friendship, tried to get inside my shirt. Her eyes were bright. A fine flush mantled her powerful cheek.

Near the door I rode her into a pillar, and brought her to a halt. "Shall we," I said, "sit this one out?"

Daphne looked at me. Her eyes narrowed. "Certainly," she said, and dragged me into the hall.

The staircase was jammed with dancers eating ice-cream, and fanning themselves with programmes. We threaded our way through them, and came out on the first landing.

"Up here," said Daphne. We mounted the second flight of stairs.

"Come on," said Daphne. We reached the top floor.

It happened like lightning. There was a door under the stairs that led up to the attic. Daphne threw it open. She shoved me in. Then she fell upon me like a ton of bricks.

It was like nothing I had ever known before. I had previously been conducting a delicate courtship with a young lady in Dublin called Brenda Poole, but that had been a matter of sighs, and hand touching as if by accident. This, however, was murder, pure and simple.

There was no gleam of light in the cupboard, but I tried to fight her off. I sprang back and fell over a vacuum cleaner. Daphne Oakes came after me. I'd never struck a woman before, or even thought of doing so, but now I doubled my fist and let her have it, hoping to catch her in the eye.

I must have struck a bedroom jug on the shelf above her head, because there was a crash and a shower of broken china. Then I found the door. I leaped out on to the landing, and fled for my life. I got as far as Major Cartwright's room, shot into it, and wedged a chair against the door. Then I sank back, trembling, upon my bed. I'd lost my tie. All the studs had burst out of my boiled shirt. So far as I was concerned the ball was over.

I was still sitting on the bed an hour later when Cartwright came rattling at the door. In that time all manner of thoughts had seethed through my mind. Should I become a monk? I didn't know. But one thing was clear. I should have to tell Brenda Poole about what had happened, and, at the least, emigrate to Australia, in the hope of picking up a job. I made a rapid emendation—China. The thought of being cooped up in Australia with Daphne Oakes brought me out into a cold perspiration all over again.

I jumped up and took the chair away from the door. Major Cartwright blundered in. He looked at the chair, and then he looked at me, but it clearly meant nothing to him. He was a broken man. "By God," he said, "I'm glad that's over."

He wrenched off his tie. His collar burst open and writhed round the back of his neck. "Pack of gabblin' wimmin," said Major Cartwright. Then he cocked an eye at me. "Better cut along to the bathroom, boy," he said, "before they mess it about with their fol-de-rols."

I was getting tired of being sent to the bathroom by Major Cartwright, but I did as I was told. He was hot and peevish. He was not a man to be argued with.

I opened the door of the bathroom, and there was Daphne Oakes. I gave a scream, and tried to jump out into the passage. She slammed the door with her foot. "Come here," she said, "you mad, mad boy."

I snatched up a backscrubber. I told her I was dead beat. I told her I was engaged to be married. I said I was getting a glass of water for Major Cartwright. I announced I was going to be sick. Daphne Oakes advanced upon me, showing her powerful teeth.

I kicked her on the leg. I threw open the door, and tore down the passage to the Major's room. But Daphne beat me to it. She slipped past me, turned the key in the door, and dropped it down the front of her dress. "Now," she said, "come and get it if you want to go to bed."

I walked away, making for the head of the stairs. Daphne followed. She stopped at the door of Mrs. Cartwright's room. "I'll be here if you want me," she said. "The bed next to the door. Good night, Romeo."

I made no reply. I walked straight down the stairs and into the sitting-room. I locked the door and put the writing-desk against it. Then I lay on the sofa and tried to go to sleep.

By 2.45 a.m. I'd had enough. I'd left my dinner-jacket in the Major's room, and my boiled shirt offered no protection against the draughts of the night.

I decided to go and get the key. I decided that, whatever the consequences might be, I would creep into Mrs. Cartwright's room in the hope that the awful Oakes had left my key on the table beside her bed. It was a wild plan, but it had been a wild night.

I waited for another hour, trying to keep warm under a pile of satin cushions, and then I climbed the stairs. I removed my shoes outside Mrs. Cartwright's door, opened it stealthily, and crept into the darkness on hands and knees. All reason had left me. It didn't matter any more what happened. I only wanted to be safe in my own camp-bed, with the Major watching over me, and our door locked on the inside.

I crept straight into something large and hot and solid. I shot out my hand and touched a face—a leathery, whiskered face, and a mass of crinkly hair. Maxwell Crump!

I felt my hand imprisoned in a vice. "Who the hell," hissed a hoarse voice, "are you?"

Then I heard Daphne Oakes. "By damn," said Daphne, "it's Tommy!" I heard a gasp of laughter suddenly smothered by a pillow.

The grip on my wrist tightened. "What's he doing here?" hissed Maxwell Crump.

Daphne subdued another paroxysm. "Perhaps," she whispered, "he wants me to come for a walk!"

At that moment Mrs. Cartwright turned on the light. Mr. Crump and I pressed ourselves into the floor. The side of Daphne's bed came down to within an inch of the carpet. There was nowhere to hide.

"Sorry to wake you, Daph," said Mrs. Cartwright—"I've got frightful wind over the heart."

A series of despairing noises proved this to be true.

"It must have been the claret cup," said Mrs. Cartwright.

Daphne sat up. "I've got some bicarbonate on the dressing-table," she said quickly. "Let me get it for——"

Mrs. Cartwright jumped nimbly out of bed. "You stay right there, dear," she said, "I'll get it myself."

Crump put his head under Daphne's counterpane. I saw he was wearing tennis-shoes and a dressing-gown. I tried to get under the bedside table. Then Mrs. Cartwright sailed across the room. On her head was a slumber-cap, tied with pink ribbon under her chin. Her face was thickly coated with cold cream. She wore only the top part of a pair of striped pyjamas that must have belonged at one time to her husband, the M.F.H.

She padded swiftly to the dressing-table, picked up the bottle of tablets, turned round, and then obtained a grip on the situation.

Mrs. Cartwright was a heavy woman, but she tried to leap into the air. She screamed. She was still screaming when she came down. With a galvanic bound she reached the curtains, threw them round her, and brought the whole lot crashing down on her head.

Crump and I tried to get out of the door. We got tangled up in one another and came down again.

There was a loud, splintering crash at the other end of the passage. A bull's roar, the thunder of feet, and suddenly in the entrance to Mrs. Cartwright's bedroom stood her husband, holding a broken chair.

He stopped, seeing his wife's room filled with people. He examined us minutely, one by one. Then he said, in a low voice, "Some damn fellah locked me in. Couldn't open me door." He looked at his wife in her slumber-cap and cold cream, draped in the curtain.

"Heard you screamin', Effie," he said. "Thought I could lend a hand."

Mrs. Cartwright made a splendid effort. She took a deep breath.

"It's all right, dear," she said, "go back to bed. We're only —only playing a game."

Major Cartwright looked at her heavily. The world, as he knew it, had come to an end. No rhyme, no reason anywhere. No recognisable sequence of cause and effect.

"I see, m'dear," he said. Then he added, "Don't get cold." He looked at the broken chair in his hand, and set it carefully against the wall. "G'night, all," he said. We heard him go down the passage. He stopped for a moment outside his own door, and then went in, closing it gently behind him. Then there was silence.

"Well," said Mrs. Cartwright brightly, looking at the ceiling,

"I suppose we'd all better get off to bed. I'm sure Daphne will be able to explain everything quite satisfactorily in the morning."

Crump and I rose to our feet. We kept our eyes on the floor. We stepped aside to let the other out first.

I kept on walking. I walked down the stairs, I took someone's overcoat off the peg in the hall, I put it on over my boiled shirt, and walked a mile and a half to the station. I caught a milk train to Dublin soon after dawn.

A week later my suitcase arrived. It was neatly packed with the clothes I'd left behind. But there was no covering note. No communication from the Cartwrights. Nothing.

I sent back the overcoat by parcel post. I didn't bother to write a note either.

There didn't seem to be anything to say.

AN ATTRACTIVE IMPEDIMENT

From my earliest days I have enjoyed an attractive impediment in my speech. I have never permitted the use of the word "stammer." I can't say it myself.

This surprising phenomenon has assumed, in its time, a wide variety of different forms, and the ability to change its nature without warning.

For instance, I used to have for several weeks at a time what I came to call the "muted gibbon" cry. It used to go, "May I—awah awah—awash my—ahah ahah ahah ahah ahands please?"

Then, suddenly, I would awake one morning to find that I was back again in the happy inhalation days. All at once I would begin to speak while breathing *in,* having found it impossible to produce a word even as structurally simple as "Oh" while breathing out. This sounded like wind blowing under a door, and it was a sharp man who made anything of it.

Soon the inhalation method gave way to the impassive. Upon finding myself held up I would abandon all further effort to produce anything at all, fold the hands neatly in the lap, allow the face to become expressionless, and wait for the next word to arrive, possibly out of the air.

The snag to this device was that the audience never really knew if the show was over. Once, I got into one of these quiet times in a railway carriage, while talking to an elderly stranger about bicycles. I had been remarking upon the difficulty of riding bicyles into the wind, and was preparing to reach even more deeply into the subject when everything shut down. It was my intention to say, "One feels so like turning round and going the other way," but I got locked on "one."

Under the new system I blew the boilers down at once, and sat back looking absolutely impassively at the floor. The elderly stranger, having had one or two previous examples of the same thing in the earlier part of our discussion, sat back to wait. But after, I suppose, nearly a minute, he became uneasy. He leant forward. "Excuse me," he said earnestly, "I don't want to embarrass you, but could you—er—possibly tell me if you've finished?"

I made no attempt to speak. I shook my head very slowly from side to side, without altering by an iota the blankness of my expression. Unfortunately, he had to get out at the next station, before I could come through to him again. He did so with the most abject, stumbling apologies, knowing that I was still working away. The incident may have given him some incurable complex. For me, it was just another chore in the daily grind.

Several cures were tried. Once, I spent two months lying on a psycho-analyst's sofa in Harley Street, pouring out the story of my life in a loud, clear, and absolutely uninterrupted voice. At the end of the hour I would rise to my feet and try to bid the doctor good afternoon. Nothing happened. No word emerged.

We abandoned the course by mutual consent. We parted, as a matter of fact, by gesture. I wanted to say, "Well, good-bye, doctor —don't let this upset you," but the shut-down was complete. By some curious kind of transference he too became afflicted, and turned rigid in the middle of the sentence, "You will probably find things easier soon." The word "find" very nearly choked him. In the end we waved at one another reassuringly, with the veins standing out on our foreheads, and then parted for good.

In its time this trick has involved me in a number of unusual situations—the most unusual of them undoubtedly being Mrs. Gilbert's lunch party. (It is necessary to create fictitious names. Some people are more sensitive about this matter than others.)

Mrs. Gilbert rang up one morning and said, "I hate doing this. I'm one short. You've got to come to lunch, but you're to make absolutely no attempt to speak. Even if someone asks you a direct question you are to remain silent, and pass it off with a shrug, or something—*you* know."

"It's all right," I said, "there's no need to panic."

There was a pause, and then she said, rather seriously, "I *can* trust you, can't I? It's most important. The First Secretary of the Legation is coming, with his wife, and I don't want them to think we're mad. What makes it rather worse is that Theo is coming, too. He practically asked himself, although why *he* wants to go out at all I can't imagine."

"Oh," I said, "I see it now. Theo's coming along—Theo the Whistle."

"Don't *laugh* about it," said Mrs. Gilbert. "I'd die of shame if by some impossible chance you both began together." (Theo was rather worse than I was. He filled in the gaps, or built himself up for further effort, with a short melodious whistle.)

"You can trust me," I told Mrs. Gilbert. "Not one single word will emerge."

"I know *that,*" said Mrs. Gilbert, "but are you going to *try* to say anything?"

"Not a word," I reassured her. "Trust me—no chat."

"Very well, then," she said. "A quarter-past one for half-past. And—*be careful.*"

The other guests, including Theo and the First Secretary, were there when I arrived. I kept a mile clear of Theo, and bowed, without speaking, upon being introduced to the diplomat. Mrs. Gilbert looked quite cheerful as we went in to lunch.

I found myself seated beside the diplomat's wife on my left, and a rather brisk matron in a large flowered hat on my right. Theo was immediately opposite. It was clear that he had had his orders too. His eyes were on his plate. From time to time he put his hands across his mouth, as if to remind himself of his duties.

I discovered almost at once that the diplomat's wife could only say, "Yiss, pleece," in English, and that all the rest of her remarks had to be presented in her native dialect. That seemed to look after her. There was no chance of *her* starting anything. But the matron in the large hat was another matter altogether. First crack out of the box, even before the soup had appeared, she turned to me, centred me squarely with her eyes for a moment, and then said, "What do *you* do for a living?" I found out afterwards she prided herself upon her lack of self-consciousness.

I shrugged my shoulders, and made a vague gesture with both hands. What I wanted to say was, "In all probability, a damn sight more than you do," but I was under sealed orders.

"H'mm," she said—"nothing? Well, well, that must be very agreeable for you. And quite delightful for your poor father."

With that, to my relief, she abandoned me, and applied herself to a retired soldier on her right.

The lunch continued upon its placid, meaningless way, Mrs. Gilbert establishing herself powerfully with the First Secretary, and the rest of them aggravating themselves with some stuff about bridge and pedigree dogs.

And then, suddenly, it happened—out of a clear blue sky. At one moment they were all chattering away—Mrs. Gilbert, the First Secretary, the brisk matron, the retired major—and at the next there was complete silence. The whole lot of them dried up, practically together. They sat there, looking at their plates, and it was obvious that none of them would ever speak again.

I got going at once. I had no moment of hesitation. I had been sitting there for nearly an hour, contributing nothing, and now that the emergency was upon us it was clearly up to me to save the day. I had no memory whatever of Mrs. Gilbert's orders.

At this time I was having the muted gibbon call, with rotation. That is, my head turned ponderously from right to left, and then back again, with the effort of speech. It humped the muscles on the back of my neck like a bison, and in fact rendered any attempt at articulation completely out of the question.

But I threw myself into it. I set myself to say, "I went bathing yesterday, and the water was as warm as toast." I became locked at once. My head turned slowly to the left, the rich blood already pounding into my face. I met the terrified gaze of the diplomat's wife, tried to smile at her, emitted three "ahah ahah ahah's" instead, and then found myself centred upon Theodore, immediately opposite me. To my absolute consternation I saw that he was busy too. The fool had thrown himself into speech as well, and was now whistling away in short, piercing trills, with his eyes clamped firmly shut. My head ground round to the right. "I awah awah awent . . ." I said to the brisk matron, and then my head started its journey back again. I caught a glimpse of Mrs. Gilbert out of the corner of my eye. Her lips were moving in prayer. I had time to think that she was lucky to have them moving *at all,* when I became based upon Theodore once more. He must have played the whole of "The Bluebells of Scotland" by this time, but he was as far away as ever from saying anything.

It went on through all eternity—Some of the guests leaning forward with bright smiles, and the perspiration running down their faces, others suddenly exhibiting nervous mannerisms of their own, twitching or plucking at their clothing, or coughing loudly, but all waiting to hear what either Theo or I might have to add to the fund of human knowledge.

Mrs. Gilbert broke it down into the end. Her voice, when she found it, came out in a scream, but she managed to speak. The guests leaped in their seats as if shot, but she'd done it. In another moment the whole lot of them were chattering away again—high-pitched, nervous stuff—but at least it was coming out. Theodore and I let ourselves unwind slowly, and the rest of the lunch played itself out without incident.

To this day I have no knowledge of what Theodore was trying to say. For all I know he may have been bathing too, and, like myself, found the water warm as toast. But that is Theodore's secret, and as far as I am concerned he can keep it.

A SCUFFLE IN THE SAC DE BOUSCULADE

The gentleman of style, before departing for the Riviera, spends many thoughtful hours of trial and error amid the Italian-American haberdashery of Shaftesbury Avenue, fingering the linen-nylon tapered trouserings, the beach-shirts with the pineapple or other tropical motif, light-weight jackets with reversible shawl collars for the cocktail hour, casual moccasins for promenading, intricate sandals for the *plage,* straw jockey caps and boaters and then, two days later, he's strolling about Cap Ferrat, Beaulieu or St. Tropez wearing, if he has any sense, a pair of shorts and five shillings' worth of rope-soled *espadrilles*.

The Italian-American haberdashery lies in his suitcase at the hotel or villa, undisturbed save for the nesting activities of ants. What appeared to be garments of gossamer texture in the heat of the London summer turn out to be the equivalents of chain-mail in the furnace of the Côte d'Azur.

So here is this previously well-dressed gentleman, free of all restraint or inhibition in his scruffy shorts and canvas slippers, and the only cloud on his azure-blue horizon is the fact that every time he sits down, or stands up, everything, including his passport, travellers' cheques, cigarette lighter and loose change, falls out of his pockets, for the reason that shorts are not constructed for the secretion and transport of urban paraphernalia. So this man, previously free of all restraint and inhibition, walks about clutching both his side pockets while urging friends bringing up the rear to keep an eye on his passport in the pocket on his hip. Sitting down, or standing up, involves making a complete inventory of all possessions. The taking out of a handkerchief can divide one's capital in half. Small French children are as quick as the next at getting their little feet on top of rolling, loose change.

Happily, there is a solution to this torment. What every sensible man will be wearing on the Riviera this season, shortly after he reads this, will be *un sac de bousculade,* or scuffle-bag. I could even come right out into the open and say that it's a handbag for men. Rather a lot of bags are creeping into this exposition, but I find that a large, zippered sponge-bag makes the best scuffle-bag because even the *avant garde* boutiques of the Riviera are not as yet making male handbags, though of course they will be on sale everywhere from Menton to Marseille before the end of the week.

My own *sac de bousculade* now contains my passport, travellers' cheques, scissors, a purse, a bottle of vitamin pills, two pipes, a tobacco pouch, a cigarette lighter, a packet of pipe-lighters, a handkerchief, a noggin of cognac, a comb, a small notebook, a penknife and a pair of bathing-trunks and even at that, as a *sac de bousculade,* it's only in its infancy. *Le bon Dieu seul* knows what else will be in it by the time I leave here at the end of the month.

The original invention of this daring reticule must be credited to an Englishman who some years ago, lost to all sense of conscience and duty, sold up everything he didn't want in England to buy everything he did want in Villefranche, like a motor-cruiser, a villa, wine at 2*s.* 6*d.* per bottle, total idleness and absolute peace of mind. He took to a sponge-bag for his accessories after finding that the pockets of shorts distributed an almost continuous stream of currency over the side of the cruiser, a matter of special irritation to him as it was absolutely the only flaw in his indolent, disgraceful and glorious way of life. He referred to it, however, only as "my little bag". It was I—and I want it to be remembered in the form of a percentage when full production gets under way—who gave it the name of scuffle-bag, or *sac de bousculade,* and simultaneously invented a new Riviera divertissement, not an easy thing to do on this pleasure-crazed coast. It is, simply, to *bousculer,* or to get right head-down into your sponge-bag and have a really good scuffle around. The thrill of discovery, the contrapuntal chinking of pills and keys and fountain pens and money add up to hours of deeply satisfying pleasure in the cafés or on the beach. If one is fortunate enough to meet a fellow *bousculadier* it is also possible to enjoy a *jeu de bousculade,* challenging him to match your bric-à-brac piece by piece, and scoring a point if he cannot do so. To this end I've just added an ashtray to my *sac.*

One word of warning to novice *bousculadiers* coming fresh to their work. Do learn the French for, "My faith, gendarme, someone's knocked off my scuffle-bag and it's left me completely up the spout!"

It will, almost certainly, come in useful.

THE OUTSIZER, OUTSIDE

Whatever Colin Wilson had to say about it—and it's all so long ago I cannot clearly remember his message—I'd rather be an Outsider than an Outsize.

What was the matter with the Outsider? Something about a man agonisingly aware of the chaos underlying the order in which most of his fellow men believe?

That's only a fleeting attack of the jigs in comparison with the screaming, bulging meemies that descend upon the Outsizer, when he's having a day on which he finds himself to be twice the size of *all* his fellow men and particularly women. Fellow women? Get on.

One of these days started for me with trying to buy a pair of shoes.

At no time in the history of the world have men's feet had a wider choice of pouch. There are winkle-pickers and spade toes, moccasins and loafers, two-tie-wing-tips, bronze Cordovans, Mexican huarachas, Italian casuals, even elastic-sided, ecclesiastical chukka boots, presumably for clerics who wish to play polo, but they're only made for men—and clerics—with feet the size of ants. So, at least, it seems to the Outsizer, putting in a request for a moccasin-type, reversed-calf casual with concealed elastic gussets in Size Twelve E, or, failing that, anything equally casual that will fit.

Nine shoe shops in a row—*nine*—and small, ant-footed assistants coming from every corner to gaze, shuddering, at the great, sad plates, curled and gnarled, overflowing the edges of the fitting-stools. "No, no—nothing at all, nothing in sports or casual wear, not in that size, no demand, you see. . . ."

"Have you any other kind of boot, shoe, pouch, holster or other leather artifact that would contain these feet?"

They produce a pair of black, square-toed things with brass eyelets which D. H. Lawrence's father might conceivably have worn while attending Sunday service in a colliery town in 1852, or whenever it was. No bronze Cordovans, no huarachas. The Outsizer is out, cut off by his monstrous dogs from any part of the fashionable, moccasin-casual life of the ant-feet, dancing along the Promenade des Anglais in their Northampton *espadrilles*.

Feeling like Frankenstein, I clumped away, the great plates slapping on the echoing pavements, to make a purchase—half of lard and a tin of pepper—in a small, general store. It was Outsizer day, all right. The store seemed smaller than ever, and it was filled with tiny women. The proprietress's chin appeared to rest on the counter. A minute, female shopper backed away from beneath my elbow. Three more huddled in a corner beside the potted meats, gazing up in dread. I'm six feet five and nearly always have been, but now on Outsizer day I'd clearly got bigger. It was as though King Kong had lurched in, casting a monstrous shadow on the tiny scene. Total, breathless silence—the women looking for somewhere to run. It was then I found I'd lost the 10*s.* note set aside for the half of lard and the tin of pepper, tiny things in themselves.

Something prompted me to look out into the street, to see a woman four feet high pounce upon my note and stuff it into her shopping bag. I had to bend nearly double to shout into her ear, to establish ownership of the currency. The other midgets huddled more tightly together. King Kong was going berserk.

The size of a creature so vast in such close proximity scattered the note-whipper's natural acumen, and she gave it back. We re-entered the shop together, all the other midgets backing away. A moment later I pocketed the note-whipper's change, in mistake for my own. I felt fifty feet high, uncontrollable as a rogue gorilla. Bereft of all sense, I picked up the shopping basket belonging to the midget beside me and started out of the shop. Squeaks of outrage, as if from mice. I went back in again, gave the basket back to the wrong midget. In leaving, I stepped on the note-whipper's foot. I fled, round the corner, colossal, Brobdingnagian, bulging, sweating, and nearly trampled a little child to death, playing in the road. It was time to separate myself from miniscule humanity until this terrible Outsizer feeling passed away.

I went for a walk in the park, stepping delicately so as not to shake the trees. It's a curious park, silent and empty, fenced off into wide paths wandering through tangled undergrowth. A good place for giants, where they can do no harm.

The bird suddenly appeared in front of me, a baby bird too young to have a tail. It flopped about on the path, helpless on its stubby wings. Seeing the giant, it turned in tiny, heroic defiance, opening its beak in an inaudible yell. Holding my enormous breath, I shooed it back through the fence. The undergrowth looked vast, inviting, all-concealing, safe. The fence was low enough for me, a giant, to step over. "Make room, bird," I said, "I'm coming in." One leg raised, then a roar like the last Trump.

A park-keeper. "Come back out of that! What you think you're doing? Git back on the path, like everybody else!"

Like everybody else? He didn't know he was talking to a man Outsize.

PACKING-PAPER SHIRTS

Death, of course, would be going too far, but I cannot help hoping that the typhoon which raged through Hong Kong the other day gave two Chinese haberdashers in Nathan Road at least a *frisson* of fear, a brief stab of anxiety to remind them that there are forces in the universe bigger than themselves, that punishment on a cosmic scale can be handed out for sin.

I hope that they are contemplating what happened to Sodom and Gomorrah as they try to restore order among the miles of shirting material on their shattered shelves.

I also hope that the fearful, soup-like waters of the sampan harbour were blown up as far as their emporium, mucking up their miles of shirt material so that they had to wash them foot by foot, and then iron them, so that they could see the visible evidence of their guilt—probably a shorter route towards this desirable goal than the chance of a message from their non-existent conscience.

The six shirts which they hypnotised me into buying have all returned from the laundry now, with the collars on all six of them looking like corrugated packing paper.

Haughty Jermyn Street shirt-makers would, no doubt, maintain that the material was the merest shoddy in the first place and that people who buy shirts in Nathan Road, rather than in Jermyn Street, well deserve whatever they may get. Such people know nothing of the rigours of selecting shirt material in Nathan Road.

When I made my choice I was standing with knees partly bent and head buried on the chest, being fitted for a suit in a fitting-room the size of an upended cabin trunk, obviously constructed for very small Chinese. The ceiling, at any rate, was a foot too low to accommodate a fully grown barbarian as, indeed, was the Chinese tailor. He had called for a box to stand on and even then he was on tiptoe, examining the hang of the jacket from the shoulders. The temperature was 93 degrees in the street, and twice that inside the trunk.

Into this tiny inferno, then, another Chinese inserted himself, carrying numerous bolts of shirting material. He closed the door, struggling with one hand behind his back, out of deference to two Indian ladies buying saris a few feet away. "Velly nice shirr matelial velly goo velly chip," he said, and began to lay out his wares. The tailor by now was sawing away at the sleeve of the jacket, standing on tiptoe on his box, so the shirt man hung a lot of the stuff off him, and off my unoccupied shoulder and then off and around himself. Very soon the three of us were swathed in stifling miles of cotton, poplin and silk. It felt like standing in a cauldron of giant spaghetti. With the addition of meat-balls and tomato sauce we'd have made a dish for a starving cannibal king. Indeed, I was practically boiled into a meat-ball already, though the two Chinese remained cool and underdone. It was under these conditions of *haute* human *cuisine,* unknown in Jermyn Street, that I made my choice of material, and I do have to allow that when the shirts were delivered to the hotel as early as the following morning in a handsome cardboard suitcase they looked very smart indeed. But now they've all come back from the laundry with collars like corrugated packing paper, and I hope the typhoon struck those haberdashers hard.

At first I suspected that the honest British laundry might be at fault, but a short session of personal ironing proved this not to be so. It also proved that honest British laundries know a lot more about the ironing of shirt collars than do people who are led to suspect their efficiency by double-crossing Chinese haberdashers—another reason to hope for a good, hard strike by the typhoon.

A somewhat makeshift ironing plant set up on top of the refrigerator, with a tablecloth folded several times over the bread-board, and an iron borrowed from the lady next door. The first touch with the iron caused the first collar to take on an indelible, pinkish blush, incomprehensible in origin until I saw on the tablecloth a faint but obviously still active stain of grocer's Beaujolais. That was one shirt down and five to go.

Having refolded the tablecloth to obtain a clean working surface, I ran the iron lightly over the second collar, pulling it out tight to smooth the corrugations, and in no time at all the collar had turned dark beige. Iron too hot. Two down and four to play.

I put the iron into half an inch of cold water in the sink, being in a hurry to get on with the job, and when it had stopped sizzling I passed it lightly over a new set of corrugations and on the crest of every one there appeared a black streak of grease, transferred from the frying-pan to the sink and then to the iron and finally to the collar of the shirt.

I stopped, then, while I still had three shirts to wear, even if the collars did look like corrugated packing paper.

In the course of time the ruined ones will, no doubt, be used for polishing the car—one can only hope without deleterious effect. It would be unfair to the innocent inhabitants of Hong Kong to wish upon them another typhoon.

EARLY MORNING TEA TIME

Of all the times for refreshment in the home early morning tea, to the conservatively minded, is the one that must be run to inflexible rule.

To those to whom tea is served the slightest deviation from the norm works like sandpaper upon a nervous system already strained by the ascent from the soft valleys of sleep to the dizzy and jagged heights of consciousness.

Such persons have their "own" cup, which is used for morning tea and for nothing else. The handle fits their flaccid morning finger, the circumference of the rim exactly matches the half-open, semi-waking mouth. Give them a larger or a smaller one and they actually get up, coming down as far as the kitchen, to ask what the hell is going on.

For those who make their own tea the pattern must be just as rigid. While they are making it the kitchen has to be devoid of human kind. If they are accustomed to having the tray set for them by somebody else, a missing teaspoon can lead to a clashing in the cutlery box that will—and is intended to—wake the whole household.

But however diverse may be the idiosyncrasies of the two groups, they are passionately united upon one point of order. If morning tea is served, or made, at 8 o'clock that is the precise time at which it will occur, and until that precise moment no unusual disturbance of any kind must take place.

People waiting for tea in bed are prepared to tolerate, even to enjoy, the popping of gas and the chinking of tea-cups, knowing it is all for their own good. A sudden, inexplicable and almost inaudible conversation, however, with someone who may or may not be the milkman, infuriates them to the point of getting up and shouting for silence down the stairs.

In the same way, for those who make their own tea, a premature cry of greeting from above, or the running of a tap when the whole household should be asleep, is as shocking an intrusion upon their semi-consciousness as the firing of a gun.

This tenderness towards abnormal noises before the rigidly fixed hour of reveille makes things difficult for the man who suddenly finds himself awake and alert two hours too soon, round, say, about 6 a.m., or the middle of the night for persons still sleeping in the vicinity.

Many men with a tendency towards rough husbandry often find

themselves awake at this comparatively early hour. They could, of course, think or read a book or even try to go to sleep again, but the silence, the emptiness of the early morning world is too exciting. The very thought that everyone else is asleep spurs them out of bed, to polish the stainless steel sink so that for the first time in weeks it will be really stainless, to shine to a mirror-finish three pairs of shoes, to have a slash at the recipe for marmalade presented in the evening paper of the night before. The world is young and fresh and uncluttered by human beings, and what is more, at 6 a.m., it will be hours and hours before any of them are awake, to ask questions, to object, even to place a complete embargo on the task in hand.

For the man who is interested in housework—and this is the time of his maximum interest, because there is nothing more interesting to do—6 a.m. is the hour of challenge.

It's a challenge, because the job must be chosen with care. Whatever it turns out to be it must provide the stimulus of a dramatic change in the appearance of the object, whether it's a dusty fire grate handsomely black-leaded, or all the kitchen cupboards painted blue. At the same time it's a job that must be conducted in almost total silence, if sleeping people are not to be aroused. The man intent upon finding some interesting job doesn't really mind if they stop sleeping. What he does object to is their astonishment and indignation when they track him down to the kitchen and discover him inventing a new and almost silent method of chopping parsley at 6 a.m.

The dilemma that faces him is that absolutely every job around the home creates some kind of noise and that at 6 o'clock in the morning it sounds ten times louder than it does at midday. Ten times louder and fifty times more inexplicable.

The cleaning of the sediment from around bathroom taps with a strip of emery paper sounds to someone in the room above, suddently awake and staring at the ceiling, like the rhythmic gnawing of a horde of rats, already half-way through the wainscoting on their way to get him, if it happens at 6 o'clock on a black winter's morning.

I remember waking one morning in January—it was no more than 5.45—with the click that occasionally precipitates some of us out of bed and into the kitchen or sitting-room before we're really awake, turning on both taps in the sink full blast to clear away some coffee dregs from the night before and suddenly being struck, in the graveyard hush of a January morning, by the tremendous Niagara of sound that can be created by water, gushing at the wrong time, from two taps of comparatively small bore. I shut them off quickly, and waited for reprisals.

After the Niagara, on this particular occasion, I decided to leave the sink alone until general morning gushing broke out and looked around for something else to do.

On an impulse, I opened the door of the medicine cabinet and a bottle of iodine fell into the bath with a crash like a double-decker bus going through a plate-glass window.

I turned on the cold tap very gently, to keep the geyser quiet, with the intention of washing the worst of the iodine away, and at once the bathroom was filled with a hoarse groaning like the last bubbling gasp of a giant syphon of soda-water with a cast-iron and rusted spout. I shut off the tap very quickly.

This would have been the time, particularly after the iodine reversal, to go back to bed and at least lie there quietly until hot water could safely be used and a proper job done on the bath, but some of us seem actually to thrive on disaster. It drives us on to get one job done, finished, perfect and complete.

I lined the bath with newspaper to suck up some of the iodine, and to deaden any further concussions, and then I removed everything from the medicine chest and scubbed it out with a nail-brush and sponge. I threw away a number of nearly empty pill boxes and bottles, nothing on their labels giving a clue to the long-forgotten ailments they'd been intended to alleviate. I threw away a styptic pencil, which had grown lumpy, like a stalagmite, several exhausted tubes of shaving-cream and a tin of ointment which had turned grey, if that was not its original colour.

In the end the medicine chest was gleaming white, its contents spare and efficient with nothing surplus to foreseeable requirements, and I couldn't wait to get my hands on something else.

I returned to contemplate the debris, including the iodine-stained newspapers in the bath, thrown up by the hour of early morning tea. It was notable that one of the few things that hadn't happened since 5.45 was a cup of tea—a perfect example, indeed, of the flexibility of rough husbandry.

A PAIR OF WRITING TROUSERS

As mild, gentle and kindly old Winter gave way to savage and bitter Spring the writer's thoughts turned, with some urgency, to —trousers.

Trousers, however inverted it may seem, became uppermost in my mind.

The plain fact of the matter was that the ceaseless grind at the desk throughout the winter had rendered us unmistakably thread-bare behind. And, therefore, under the present weather conditions, chilly. A serious matter, because by contra-calefaction, or whatever it's called, heat was being withdrawn to the colder pole from the mind, leaving that power house working at about half its normal capacity.

A new pair of writing trousers was required with maximum speed. To the layman, "writing" trousers might not seem to be all that different from what he would call "ordinary" trousers—and that demonstrates pretty clearly the commonplace nature of your average layman's intelligence. The two types of trousers are, of course, as different as chalk from cheese.

A great deal of a writer's time (92%?) is spent about eighteen inches away from the desk, with the elbows propped on the knees to support the face, which is buried in the hands. Writing trousers must, therefore, be of substantial texture, to cushion the tender meat of the thighs from the elbows' penetrating points. Furthermore, they must be unfashionably baggy round the knees. While, you see, we are sitting with our faces buried in our hands we are, in fact, couchant. The feet are well back under the chair, to provide leverage for the spring to the typewriter when, if ever, the errant word comes into view. The modern, so-called "slim line" in trousering simply does not permit of this position. Slim line trousering creates a ligature round the knee that speedily puts the feet to sleep, exposing us to the possibility—in mid composition—of actually falling off our chair.

Okay, layman?

So I was faced with this big decision. The capacious and woolly pair of writing trousers, in which I had been working for years, had to go. They had begun by being part of a rather unfortunate tweed suit, one that hadn't quite worked, as it were. They had then served for a couple of years on the golf course, not unattended by comment, before finding their true niche, eighteen inches back from the escritoire.

Clearly, it would be impossible to buy their like ready-made. They would, in fact, have to be run up by my chap—in Notting Hill Gate, rather than Savile Row. IN CORDUROY!

The thought of corduroy came to me like a thunderclap. Corduroy—absolutely made for the job. The ribbing would give me a firm grip on the chair and would, furthermore, prevent my elbows slipping off my knees—a serious hazard for the writer because when the elbows go the forehead strikes the edge of the desk with agonising force, disorientating everything.

So I went to see my chap and said, "Good morning, I want a pair of trousers to write in."

Obviously, he thought I wanted to write something *on* the inside of a pair of trousers, because he said, hesitantly, "Perhaps—white flannel, sir?"

"No," I said. "Corduroy."

He sucked his teeth very quickly, perhaps thinking of the effect of corduroy on the nib of an expensive fountain pen.

I'd had enough of this nonsense. "I want a pair of corduroy trousers to wear while I'm writing," I said firmly. "Fairly tight behind to grip the chair, but generous in the knee so I can get couchant."

"Corduroy?" he said, with distaste. "We might find it somewhat—inflexible."

"You make 'em, mate," I said. "I'll flex 'em."

(This is why I go to Notting Hill Gate, rather than Savile Row. They understand man's talk at the old Gate.)

"On your own head be it, sir," my chap said sombrely.

I thought of a humorous remark, but let it go.

He really got cracking on the corduroys. They arrived yesterday. I slid into them and took a turn up and down the passage, breaking them in. It was extraordinary. Somewhere in the immediate vicinity someone was cracking a whip. Or running a flexible stick along some close-set railings. Or a porcupine was fighting some wire netting. Then I realised that it was my baggy corduroy knees, whisking themselves together, piercingly, with every step I took.

There's a nice thing. Now I've got *noisy* writing trousers.

As if things weren't bad enough already.

DAMN!

One is not, of course, a libertine or anything excessive like that, but the sight of this delicately matured piece of crackling, sitting all by itself in the corner, was so arresting that I gave my hostess but the most perfunctory of greetings before weaving swiftly through the crowded room to slot myself right in beside it.

"Good evening." I said. "And who are you?"

Not a second wasted. Getting the spade into the work without a second's delay.

The lady turned to look at me through lowered lashes—admittedly false but lushly cemented into place. Perfect heart-shaped face, framed by smooth blonde hair, shoulder length, something after the style of Rita Hayworth. But, brother, ever so more so.

When she spoke it was in a voice so husky that I came within an ace of bursting into applause. The content, however, was a little lowering, even a little abrupt in tone.

"*Parle pas Anglais,*" she said.

Something of a setback. After all this time in France a fair measure of badinage is available to me in the French language but the more delicate subtleties, the telling and elegantly turned subjunctive, the suggestive but gracious compliment rather tend to elude me. The level rather closer to, "What about it, duck?" than, "I drown myself in the twin pools of your mysterious, moon-stone eyes."

However, the lady had said, rather curtly, that she didn't speak English, so that it was up to me to flash a subjunctive or two in her own language.

I asked her if she was alone. "*Mais non,*" and she indicated with a soft white hand a distinguished looking elderly gentleman on the other side of the room. She was wearing a wedding ring.

"Your husband?"

"Not exactly," she said, in an absolutely level voice.

In fact, the few remarks she had delivered had all been in this curiously unemotional form. Nor, after the first moment, had she looked me in the eye. A less sanguine disposition might almost have come to the unthinkable conclusion that the lady was bored, and so bored, indeed, that if I didn't leave in the next couple of seconds, she would.

I decided to pump some steam into the atmosphere. "I do hope I don't disarrange you by talking to you like this without an introduction," I said, "but the fact is that there are very few beautiful women on the Côte d'Azur, particularly during the winter months."

The lady produced a cigarette. I lit it for her. Once again she didn't look at me, accepting the service without noticing it, as though I'd been a manicurist, working on her nails.

"The French girls mostly have very long noses and very short legs," I went on. "In fact, their legs are so short that their knees seem to be joined on to their bottoms. I can't imagine what happens when they try to run."

This mildly risqué anatomical chat continued, to my regret, to leave the lady as unmoved as ever. You could even say that things were getting worse. Through the smooth blonde hair I could see the lovely line of her jaw tighten for quite a moment or two, as she held back what could only be a yawn.

The only thing to do was to put my foot right down, drive the accelerator through the floorboards. So pointed a brush-off was not to be borne, after so little provocation.

I leant in a little closer. "As, at the moment," I said, "you're sitting down it isn't possible to check the facts with a hundred per cent accuracy, but from what I can see of it from here your knees rather definitely aren't fastened to—your knees are not attached in this unfortunate fashion."

At last the lady turned to me, but there was no warmth in it. Only disdain, like a duchess unforgiveably importuned by the boot-boy.

"*Non*," she snapped, disposing in one word of a filthy suggestion, and all further conjecture about it.

At that moment I found my wife was standing above us. I struggled to my feet and, at a loss, said, "Darling, this is Madame—", and had to leave it at that.

Madame C. looked at the other one for a brief moment. *"Bon soir, Monsieur,"* she said, and moved on.

Like a lot of coal falling downstairs everything dropped slowly into place.

The other one was a chap.

CLARENCE HOUSE — AT LAST!

My eye flashed down the third column on Page 3 of the *Sunday Times* last Sunday, rapidly misreading as usual the smaller headlines.

Thus "AIR SHOW CRASH FILMS FOR INQUIRY" became "AGE SHOW CRUSH FILMS FOR ENQUIRERS" and "ROAD CLOSED BY FLOOD THREAT" turned into "ROAD CLOSED BY FOOD THREAT"—perhaps a mass distribution of sausage rolls by the Granada service station on the M.4. which had put the great motorway out of action.

Then, immediately below this, I saw that I had succeeded the Lady Jean Rankin as Lady-in-Waiting to Queen Elizabeth the Queen Mother.

The hurried eye took in the brief paragraph which comprised the Court Circular, and there it was, clear for all to see: "Mr. Patrick

Campbell has succeeded the Lady Jean Rankin as Lady-in-Waiting to Queen Elizabeth the Queen Mother."

A moment later, of course—and an anxious one it was, too—I saw that it was really someone called Mrs. Patrick Campbell-Preston who had succeeded the Lady Jean Rankin, but the shock lingered on for quite some time. It lingered so long, indeed, that in this state of alarm I began to make plans for taking up my new appointment, hampered in no small measure by my present exile in the South of France.

When this kind of major posting comes the first necessity is to try to find out why one has got it, in preference to anyone else. Only in this way can one enter upon one's new duties with the confidence required for their proper execution.

On the other hand, other important factors are also involved, like the strong possibility of becoming subject all over again to British tax, the repurchasing of a domicile within handy distance of Clarence House and, speaking of Clarence House, what the Lady-in-Waiting would have to do there when she (he) was in it.

The agenda seemed to be so full that I decided to take first things first: i.e., to find out why I had been chosen as the first male Lady-in-Waiting to the Queen Mother. Evidently, so far as the Royal Family were concerned, my qualifications must have been of the highest, seeing that there must have been any number of female ladies queueing up for the job.

The obvious thing to do was to give Philip a tinkle at Buck House, presuming upon having lunched with him on several occasions some years ago at an organisation called the Thursday Club. Presuming? Presuming nothing. If the new Lady-in-Waiting to a chap's mother-in-law can't ring him up and ask him what's the score, the whole social élite has gone to pot.

But how to go about it, without having the telephone number to hand?

"Je voudrais parler personnellement au Duc d'Edinboourg, chez le Palais de Boockingom, à Londres, mais malheureusement je connais pas le numéro."

And then the imperious one at the local exchange barking out, as usual, "Comprends pas! Faut parler Français!" As if I wasn't.

All much too difficult. Better just to accept the honour graciously, almost indeed as though I had been expecting it for some time and had even been wondering what had been keeping them at Clarence House.

Perhaps, the financial side? A discreet telephone call to my predecessor, the Lady Jean Rankin, to ask her what the screw, if any, was like, and the perks—also if any, including possibly free accommodation, with meals of course, in the attic.

Little point in that either. The post of Lady-in-Waiting to the Queen Mother has an honorary flavour about it, suggesting that you've got to bring your own loot. And very right and proper, too. But would my accountant concur in this opinion? After all his trouble in getting me out would he regard it as a fiscally viable proposition to find me once again on the back of his neck, admittedly in a highly exalted position but one producing the absolute minimum in the way of scratch?

"Hello? Mr. Ive? Look, something rather odd has just turned up. Perhaps you've read about it in the papers? No, no. Not in the nick here. As you say, not at the moment. But, look, I've just been appointed Lady-in-Waiting to the Queen Mother and I've been wondering if it would be a fiscally viable proposition for me to —Under no circumstances? Certainly not? Thanks a million. I was just wondering . . ."

What a relief not to have to wonder any more, to come out of the state of shock, and to wish Mrs. Patrick Campbell-Preston the best of British luck in her new job.

THE GREASY WOLVES ARE COMING!

The eye is poached and yellowish.

The demeanour is gritty and abrasive.

The frame is slouched and profoundly reluctant to move.

"Is this the way," you enquire crisply, "to return from a morally illegal holiday in the sun? You should be fighting fit, ready to roll up your sleeves and work, work, work, so that this great nation of ours may once again hold her head high in the—"

Ah, shaddap.

I've got a liver, mate. A real French liver, in prime condition, imported free of duty, and don't think for a moment I've been living it up on fiddled francs.

Three-and-a-tanner's worth of black pudden did it—or started it. Malign and mocking Fate did the rest.

I laid out the 3s. 6d. on about a foot of pudden through a sheer whim. In French it's called *Boudin,* and the agreeable assonance with "pudden" caught my fancy. Black boodin—black pudden. *Plus ça change, plus ça la même chose.*

I had six inches of pud, fried in olive oil, with a substantial acreage of fresh, fried bread for breakfast the following morning, personally cooked to placate the appetite of a shark. I'd been gardening with a pick-axe in baked clay since 5.30 a.m., in blazing sunshine, and by 7.30 was ready for something tasty. Even if the pud—or bood—had been suspended in salt water I'd have beaten a shark to it.

Next morning, I had the second half of the delicacy, after a rather shorter period of pick-axing owing to certain social events of the night before. Suspecting that the *boudin* might be a little heavy under these conditions, I added some green bacon to the dish, crisply fried, to lighten it. A mug of strong black coffee, without sugar, assisted the commodities down.

By midday, if any word or deed of mine could have precipitated global atomic warfare, I should not have hesitated to speak or act.

It seemed to me, judging by the taste in my mouth, that I must have been drinking diesel oil the night before and enjoying it sufficiently extravagantly to have taken in at least an imperial gallon.

I sat sweating in the sun, looking for a dog to kick or a child to strike. One of the adult members of the household incautiously approached me with a request for a light. My response was so comprehensive and so firmly negative that he backed away in dread and fell over a chair.

During the afternoon my mood declined in *bonhomie,* even from this comparatively low point, and by popular request I retired to bed at 7 p.m. with two bottles of Vichy water which, after consumption, floated for the rest of the night at the base of the oesophagus, unable to combine with the diesel oil. I got up at 4.45 the following morning, mainly to get away from the wolves, dripping with goose grease, which had pursued me every time I closed my eyes, but also to engage in a frenzy of pick-axing which I hoped might have the same effect on the liver as riding a horse.

It was then I became aware of the smell of cooking, coming from the house next door. *Nom d'un chien! Boudin!* Madame B., the charming little old lady who does for us, was preparing a substantial breakfast for her son. I moved away to another part of the olive grove, to continue the pick-axe therapy in fresher air.

At 7.30 a.m. I placed my breakfast—a peach and a glass of lemon juice—on the garden table and was just sitting down to it when Madame B. came shyly through the gate. She carried a small earthernware pot. *"Pour vous, M'sieu,"* she said. *"Vous avez bien travaillé."* She lifted the lid. *Boudin!* Kilometres of it, lying on a bed of sauté potatoes. Lukewarm. "I will put it in the oven for you," she said. "It is better when it is hot."

She did so. Then she got her brushes and things out of the cupboard and slowly and methodically began to polish the tiles. In the room with the french windows opening out on to the garden, and on to my breakfast of a peach and a glass of lemon juice.

I tracked our hostess down to the bathroom, and pounded on the door. "Madame B.," I shouted through it, "has just arrived with a load of boudin for my breakfast and now she's polishing the dining-room floor and I don't want to offend her so what'll I do?"

There was a brief silence. The voice said, "Nosh it." Then water burst from both taps to drown laughter of the most ignorant and vulgar kind.

I noshed it, Madame B. watching the consumption of every mouthful with love and pride.

I wouldn't mind a pint of diesel now. It might alleviate the heavy-duty back-axle grease with which my system is lined at the present moment and—to judge by the impermeable consistency of it—for the next six months.

PUTTING A SOCK IN IT — WHERE?

Yet another dark, oven-hot morning in yet another hotel bedroom, packing, dressing, breakfasting all at the same time, as we seem to have been doing ever since Christmas, in Geneva, Paris, London and Manchester, and now I couldn't find my sock.

I opened the door of the wardrobe and said, "Have you seen my sock."

"Shut it," she said. "I was doing my hair in it."

I examined both sentences in their entirety. Nothing came through.

"The door of the wardrobe," she said. "It's got a mirror on it. I was doing my hair in it."

"Where," I said, "is my sock? You must have seen it. It's got a huge suspender on it. White. Looks like a bandage. Where is it?"

With a hairbrush and comb in one hand she drank tea with the other. "Put on another pair," she said.

I became enraged. "This room," I said, "is not large. There is one built-in cupboard behind or under which my sock cannot be. There are various drawers which I have already searched, even to the extent of lifting the lining paper, without finding my sock. I have stripped both beds, looked under the mattresses, looked under the beds themselves, pulled them away from the wall, and I still can't find my sock. I must have entered this room last night wearing two socks, and now I have only one. Therefore, you must have packed it and therefore I'm going to unpack everything you've packed and tear it all to pieces until I've found my sock . . ."

I was shouting towards the end of it. Traffic beginning to thunder outside, roasting central heating, general corrosion of nervous system from the night before, and now the idiocy of standing in bare feet, shirt and trousers with only one sock and the car coming at any moment to take us to the airport. "WHERE IS IT?" I bawled.

She unpacked everything with meticulous care, searched each item and repacked them all over again. Absolutely no trace of a navy-blue sock with a huge white suspender attached to it. She became mildly interested. "Perhaps," she suggested, "you threw it out of the window." And opened the window and peered out. "It's not there," she said.

"A sock," I roared steadily, "with a huge white suspender attached to it simply cannot just disappear. Before I go out of my mind provide me with a theory which might, just conceivably, cover its loss. It doesn't matter how fanciful it is. JUST SPEAK!"

At that moment the telephone rang with the news that the car was at the door. I put on another pair of socks and all the rest of it and rode to Manchester Airport in steaming silence. We checked in, bought the papers and walked down the long greenhouse to Gate 26. We sat down on the window-seat thing and suddenly I shot six inches into the air. Something very, very sharp indeed had pierced my lower back.

She began to laugh, sliding rapidly down into hysteria. "You've found it," she gasped. "You've found your sock. Oh no—no . . ." She gripped her middle, fighting for air.

With hauteur I put my hand under my jacket, under my overcoat, and felt around the back. There seemed to be a piece of material looped around my belt. Undoubtedly the toe of the missing sock. With the huge white suspender hanging from it. With the catch broken and jagged teeth reaching out to penetrate the tender flesh the very next time I sat down.

"Oh no," she moaned. "No no—I don't believe it—it's too—too good . . ."

Underneath the jacket and the overcoat I tried to unwind the sock from my belt. Before I could get a grip on it the flight was called and we were swept down the stairs and out into the rain. Stampede across the tarmac, into the plane and up in the air again as I sat down. I really thought she was going to die.

As soon as we took off, of course, turbulence broke out and the stewardess ordered us to retain our belts and to remain seated until further notice.

I only mention all this so that the other passengers on that flight will know why an attractive woman in a fur coat spent the whole journey in an apparently mindless paroxysm of idiot laughter.

All Abroad!

GULLIBLE TRAVELS

"Hello. Fred here. D'you want to go to Hong Kong?"

I was surprised by the speed of my double reaction. I knew, of course, I would accept instantaneously, but in the same flash of time I know I hadn't got a thing to wear.

I realised something else as well—that when women said they hadn't got a thing to wear they really meant it. I saw, with absolute clarity, that it wasn't vanity or the desire to show off or even social panic. It was simply that the nature of the invitation whipped them out of the world they lived in, or could rise to at a pinch, cancelling their entire wardrobe at one stroke, leaving them with literally nothing to wear, in the sense that everything they already had would prove to be insufferably hot, cold, light, heavy, bright, dark, thick or thin, promoting physical discomfort so intense that it would be almost a joy to stay at home.

I must have hesitated for a moment because Fred said, "You trying to say yes?"

"Yes."

"Fine. Thursday. We'll be in touch."

He rang off.

Hong Kong. The steaming Orient. Punkahs? Small, smooth, almost weightless Chinese flickering like swift fish around the legs—through the legs—of huge, sweating, meaty, red-faced people from the West, bulging with mashed potato and stew. . . .

I rang him back at the Airline Office.

"I'm afraid he's just gone out to lunch, sir. Could I help you?"

"Well, I was just wondering. Perhaps you know I'm going on this Hong Kong trip? I was just wondering if it was going to be very hot there?"

"I'm afraid I couldn't say, sir. Will I have him call you back?"

"No no. It doesn't matter. Thank you very much."

"Thank you, sir. Goodbye."

I almost rang back again to ask her not to tell him I'd phoned to ask how hot it was in Hong Kong. In his job he travels the world—Tokyo, Mexico, Rio, Peru. He wears lightweight American suits. He's ready for anything, always. I didn't want him to think that I wasn't in the same cool condition. He probably had a lot of other things to do, anyway, arranging this trip.

Hong Kong. The mysterious East. The inscrutable Orient. Susie Wong? Little Lotus Flower of the First Water. Or was that Japan?

I had one fairly good dark suit, not too heavy, that would do for the evenings—and at that moment I realised I didn't know how long we were going to be there for. Three of my six white shirts were in the laundry, and wouldn't be back until Saturday morning, by which time I'd be on the other side of the world. If that was where Hong Kong was. Where was it—really?

I found a tiny world atlas at the back of a *Pears' Encyclopaedia.* On the flat it didn't look all that far to Hong Kong. Across Germany, Turkey, Iran, India, Thailand and we were there. Then I remembered driving from London to the Riviera and feeling that even London to Dover was nearly enough, and that afternoon the interminable straight roads of Northern France and by the evening I'd got as far as a place called Troyes. Over dinner I looked at the map. I'd done about a third of the journey, having been on the move since early morning.

Sitting there at the table I suddenly felt the size of an ant, but a microscopic ant, an almost invisible speck, occupying an incalculably tiny area of the world. For the first time in my life I truly realised that the world was round, that you could go on and on and on for days and weeks and months, passing limitless millions of people on the way, and finish up where you'd started from. Driving from Dublin to Galway or even London to Inverness gave you no feeling of the roundness of the world. You had to be on a Continent to begin to appreciate it.

Calais to Troyes looked to be about 250 miles. But Turkey alone was four times as wide and India twice as much again. It was impossible to think about it. All I could do would be to present myself at the airport like a parcel, and let the airline handle me from there. But wrapped in what? Three white shirts, a fairly lightweight suit, two pairs of flannel trousers and a hacking jacket. I was going to arrive in Hong Kong looking as if I'd walked there, with some tattered, sweat-soaked rags in a broken suitcase by way of a change.

I knew what sitting in an aeroplane, even from Dublin to London, could do to your clothes. Cigarette ash everywhere, coffee and drink spilt, probably fruit salad in the lap, everything crumpled into premature old age. How much worse, then, after passing over Germany, Turkey, India, Thailand—and another thought—getting out at oven-baked, tropical airports, swept by sandstorms, alive with mosquitos. Sweating, bitten, lumpy, shirt collar too tight, trousers with two huge and sodden bags on either knee.

Whatever else happened I had to keep one shirt unused, and the dark suit, in case there was some great formal dinner party when we arrived in Hong Kong. Perhaps I could wash one shirt in the lavatory on the plane. But they were poplin. They'd never dry and even so they'd have to be ironed. The Chinese were great laundrymen. I could hand the shirts to room service when I arrived, saying I'd like them back in half an hour. How to say it, to avoid all possibility of misunderstanding? "Velly clean. Chop chop." Ludicrous. And utterly ludicrous to reduce this great adventure to a lot of female fussing about clothes.

Madame thought so, too, when I told her about it that evening. "Just go out," she said, "and buy some."

Agitated as I was I succeeded in being patient. "You know perfectly well I can't buy anything off the peg. I'm the wrong size."

"Not all that extraordinary."

"But I am!"

All my life I've had this problem, people thinking I can just go into a shop and buy a suit or a shirt or a pair of shoes. I know they're wrong, but they never believe me.

My trouble is that I'm a quarter of an inch under 6 feet 5. This might be all right if it was evenly distributed, but in fact it's nearly all leg. My legs are two inches longer than any ready-made trousers I've ever been in, so that the only way I can cover my socks is by lowering the seat between my knees. Furthermore, one arm seems to be longer than the other, because I've got a 2-inch drop on my right shoulder, and even the shorter arm is an inch longer than all ready-made shirt sleeves, and if I can't show a little shirt-cuff I simply cannot bear to be out in the thing.

At the other end I've got difficult feet. They're almost round, like an elephant's. Lengthways they're size ten and sideways size twelve. No manufacturer, in my experience, has ever brought off the feat of combining these two sizes of shoe into one. It is, therefore, agonising pinching or slopping along in huge boats that soon begin to turn up at the ends like Turkish slippers.

"You got a very smart pair of shoes about a year ago," she said. "That place in Brompton Road. Try them again."

"They took about six months to break in. I'm certainly not going to go hobbling around Hong Kong in boiling heat with my feet being squeezed up my legs into my knees."

"If the worst comes to the worst you can always wear a loin-cloth."

My anxieties redoubled themselves. "We're probably going to have to attend all kinds of cocktail parties and things on the Peak. That's where all the English people live, in shantung suits and silk shirts. It's like Sunningdale, only worse—"

"Oh, for God's sake," she said. "You're getting a lovely free trip to Hong Kong."

"It'd be all right for you if it was you. You've got all kinds of cool dresses and things, but for an unfortunate man of my size it's extremely difficult—"

But we'd had this discussion too often before. "What agony to be you," she said, bringing this one to an end.

Later that night I came to the conclusion that in the circumstances this was very nearly true. To be thrown into a tizzy—the word struck just the right note of feminine hysteria—by having nothing to wear for flying to Hong Kong. It came, of course, from having lived too long on the thin northern edge of the world. Too many years in Ireland, a small dot in what often felt like the middle of the vast, grey Atlantic. An island as remote in every way from the bazaars of Calcutta, from the plains of Persia, even from the Riviera, as somewhere like Tristan da Cunha, equally drenched by drifting rain.

I was an islander, in thick trousers and a jersey and a mackintosh, looking upon driving to Dingle as an adventure, still waiting to be sure that the world was round.

By now I'd learnt that we were going to spend the weekend in Hong Kong. We would leave London on Thursday morning, arrive in Hong Kong the following afternoon and start back again on Monday—just a weekend on the other side of the world.

By the time I'd finished my shopping quite a number of gentlemen's haberdashers in Regent Street had been told about this bold adventure, but only one of them got the benefit of my actual custom. From him I bought a white, alpaca jacket, the sleeves of which surprisingly enough almost covered my hands. I also bought two very thin, floral sports shirts with short sleeves and a pair of black shoes made of woven, openwork leather thongs. None of them were anything like what I'd been hoping to find and, indeed, were so tasteless and generally unpleasant that I knew if I were ever driven to wearing them in London it could only be with the accompanying explanation that I'd bought them almost for nothing in Hong Kong.

We took off from London and landed almost immediately afterwards in Frankfurt, where some more journalists came aboard. They scarcely had time to complain about having to pay for their own drinks before we landed in Vienna, to be joined by half-a-dozen Austrian newspapermen. This was an inaugural flight and the airline was intent upon getting the maximum publicity for it.

We left Vienna and landed in Istanbul, where for the first time I got out of the plane, wearing a white shirt and grey flannel trousers. It was like stepping into an oven. The airfield was a sandy waste, with a wind from a furnace blowing across it. Turkish soldiers wandered about, carrying machine-guns. The adventure was really beginning.

In the airport building—a large, battered shed, shimmering in the heat—I cashed a travellers' cheque for £10, receiving in exchange Turkish lira. The notes were thick and pulpy, almost like soft cardboard. I cashed the cheque because I'd already used up my English money, and wanted to buy my first drink in Turkey. I had a cognac—seeing that the word was universal. It tasted of pepper and brown sugar. The barman gave me some smaller but even thicker notes in change.

Shortly after leaving Istanbul I asked the stewardess for a bottle of beer, and "What's that in Turkish lira?"

"I'm sorry, sir," she said, "but we don't take Turkish money."

I couldn't believe it. An international airline would surely accept any currency in the world.

"I'm sorry," she said, terminating the discussion at one stroke, "but not Turkish."

In the bar in Istanbul I'd felt myself easing pretty comfortably into the role of world traveller, but suddenly now I was right back where I'd started—a panic-stricken islander, penniless and a thousand miles from home.

I examined my Turkish money again. The printing was blurred and messy, even the colours had run. It looked as if the barman could have printed it himself. I wondered if I could change it into Lebanese money in Beirut, the next stop. But then I'd have about £9 worth of Lebanese whatever-they-were which wouldn't be acceptable in Karachi.

All at once, and quite clearly, I saw myself going mad, cashing travellers' cheques at every stop and finishing up in Hong Kong with a dozen different kinds of currency that not even the hotel would accept.

Social anxieties about having nothing to wear had given way to the straight terror of not being able to get anything to eat.

I sat huddled in my window seat, looking down at the brown whorls of the deserts of Arabia, knowing that I was really only up to travelling to Dingle, and even at that I'd want to be careful to keep my head when I got there.

I was saved by the man sitting beside me. "If you're really lumbered with all that Turkish stuff," he said, "I can lend you a tenner till we get there." In excessive gratitude I tried to give him a travellers' cheque, but he waved it away.

"Too complicated," he said. "Just give me the cash in Hong Kong." He knew his way around the world. I'd seen that his wallet was full of pounds and dollars.

We landed in Karachi, and into poverty the like of which I'd only seen before in the West of Ireland. Paint was flaking off the bus that took us to the airport building. It had lost a wing and one of the tyres was nearly flat. Litter was blowing around everywhere. One of the windows in the bar was broken. The barman's white coat looked as if he'd been delivering coal.

I ordered a cognac for myself and for the man who'd lent me the money. The barman poured it from a Hennessy bottle. It tasted of pepper, Tabasco sauce and brown sugar. "That," he said, "is one and one half English poun."

"Well," I said to the other newspaperman. "I certainly shan't be coming here again in a hurry."

He scarcely bothered to smile. He probably knew that a teaspoonful of alleged brandy cost 15/- in the airport bar at Karachi, and would have had a bottle of beer if left to his own devices.

Through the night we flew across India to Calcutta. I slept for a few minutes at a time and then woke again to listen to the roar of the plane. After Hong Kong it would go on without us to Tokyo, Honolulu, San Francisco, New York and back to London, where it would begin again. Frankfurt, Vienna, Istanbul, Beirut . . .

It was no longer possible to doubt that the world was round. Also, there was evidently a very great deal of it.

I stayed in the plane at Calcutta. It was too early in the morning for cognac and to drink tea in India seemed to be altogether too much of a good thing.

Later that morning we landed at Bangkok. The fence outside the airport building was lined with hundreds of tiny Thailanders, none of them seemingly more than five feet tall. They giggled delightedly as they saw the scruffy Western giants tottering down the steps of the plane. In the airport building the minute Thailand air hostesses with their little golden faces and lilac coloured uniforms were almost edible, two or three to a mouthful, beautiful beyond belief.

I sat down carefully in an armchair in the lounge, not daring to move about, feeling myself to be—in comparison with these small, quick, golden little people—hopelessly uncoordinated and of a truly monstrous size. The heat was stupendous. Sweat dripped even from the ends of my trouser legs, while the hurrying Thailanders remained as crisp and as fresh as ginger biscuits.

It was even hotter in Saigon, when we landed there a couple of hours later. This was before the Americans had entered the war and the whole country had been enveloped by it, but nevertheless there was a feeling of jumpiness around. A number of people ducked when a car backfired, and none quicker than myself. Once again I was distressed by my huge Western size. Standing so high above the Vietnamese I felt like a target that no one could miss. Many Americans were later to feel exactly the same way.

We flew on over the China Sea, and began to lose height. After thirty hours of flying we were nearly there. All at once the sea was covered with mountainous but heavily wooded islands. As we came down still lower the trees were all round us and even above us. The plane rocked about, then steadied itself. Just ahead was the long runway, a single strip of concrete running out into the sea. Everyone held on to something fairly tightly as the plane put down. I gathered afterwards that it's always a pleasure to land without incident in Hong Kong.

Outside the airport building there was a bus with our destination written along the side of it—The Peninsula Hotel. The Chinese driver took us at a fearful speed through streets alive with millions of people straight to the Miramar. After a splendid altercation with nearly everyone in the bus he drove us very slowly to the Peninsula.

It was plain that he still didn't believe it.

The Chinese commissionaire said, "How are you?" So did the receptionist. The liftboy said, "How are you?" too. And so did the pageboy who carried my bag. The very old Chinaman whom I found in my bathroom said nothing. He seemed to have some official purpose there, because he had a bucket and a mop, though he wasn't using either of them.

We looked at one another in fear for quite a long time. He said something in Chinese, pointing to the bath with his mop. I thought he might be some kind of bath attendant, waiting to get to work on me. I shook my head and pointed to the door. He pointed to the bath again, with his mop. I shook my head and on a sudden inspiration gave him one of the smaller notes from my Turkish store. He looked at it, gave it back and left the bathroom, muttering.

I turned on the hot tap. Not a drop of water emerged. The cold one was also dry. There was no doubt that I was face to face with the mysterious East, and with no means of finding out what it wanted, or was prepared to give me.

Next morning I put on the white alpaca jacket and the open-work shoes. I looked like the driver of a coach on an outing to Folkstone on August Bank Holiday. I put the jacket away, never to wear it again, and put on one of the new floral sports shirts and sauntered out on to the Nathan Road to do some bargaining.

Alternating with the shops selling jade and jumpers decorated with diamanté were others dealing exclusively in money. Their frontages consisted of a small brass grille, with a face behind it, surrounded by large advertisements for rates of exchange. I pushed my Turkish lira through the first grille I came to. It was pushed straight back again. A Chinese face said, "Cullency too soft," and beamed as though it were the best news it had been able to hand out all week. I tried it again, next door, with the same result, and decided to abandon further horse-dealing on money market.

At midday I had an appointment to meet a distinguished Englishman at the Hong Kong Club. I crossed on the ferry with a million Chinese and on the other side pushed my way through two million more. Already, in Kowloon I'd seen half-finished blocks of flats occupied by swarming Chinese families, with thousands more waiting in the street for the next floor to be put on so that they, too, could move into the empty shells.

I was refused entry at the door of the Hong Kong Club. The hall-porter said, looking at my floral sports shirt, "No tie. Go please to bar at back. How are you?"

When the distinguished Englishman arrived he was wearing a beautiful white shirt, a regimental tie, a beige silk suit, boned brown shoes and a Panama hat. The temperature was 102 degrees.

After a jolly weekend I left the mysterious East on Monday morning and after the now familiar kangaroo leaps around the world arrived at London Airport the following afternoon, wearing the cleaner of my two florals.

There was a bitter wind blowing, accompanied by gusts of freezing rain.

The taxi-driver looked at me. "Where you bin, then, mate?" he wanted to know. "The good old Costa Brav?"

"No," I said. "Just a weekend in Hong Kong."

He closed an eye. "And I'm Susie Wong."

He might well have been, for all I'd seen of her.

Next day I took my Turkish lira into the bank, £10 worth of them, less the price of the cognac in Istanbul.

After interminable deliberations, much of them conducted out of sight somewhere round the back, the cashier gave me £3 15s. in English money.

INTREPID AIRMAN

A split-second after he'd said it I could not remember the exact sequence of words or, indeed, what the words themselves had been. I was too busy trying to massage my heart back into some sort of working shape, an instinctive gesture performed with the speed of light.

He'd said something like, "Good morning. This is your Captain speaking. I'm afraid we've run into a little trouble."

Or else he'd said, "Good morning, this is Captain Scott speaking. I'm afraid we're in serious trouble."

At 16,000 feet over Liverpool, half way to Dublin on what had been up till now just a routine flight.

Probably the interval after his opening statement wasn't all that long. He'd paused only for the briefest of moments to choose how best to put the rest of his message. But in that second I had time to massage my heart back into action, take a look at both the starboard side engines and to check the position of the nearest emergency escape exit. A fast and efficient worker in a crisis.

I was trying to see if the port side engines were on fire, when our Captain resumed. "I've only just been informed of this," he went on, "but it seems that they are digging up the runway in Dublin, so that we won't be able to land there."

A notable advance over the previous situation. At least the aircraft was still in running order. But for how much longer, if we were unable to land?

"We have several alternatives," the Captain continued. "We can land at Belfast or Shannon, or on the short runway at Dublin."

"Make it Belfast or Shannon, birdman," I said to myself. "Or Manchester, or good old London. Do not go near the short runway in Dublin."

"If we use the short runway at Dublin," the Captain went on, "we'll have to fly round for about an hour and a half to use up fuel and lighten our weight. There is no danger whatever because we'll still have enough fuel left to get back to Manchester, if we decide against landing in Dublin. I shall keep you informed. Thank you."

There was a click, and the intercom shut down, and I could see the whole bunch of them up at the front end sweating into their uniforms, coming to grips with approaching death.

We were not exactly dry-palmed in the passenger compartment. The large American woman sitting beside me had not, however, grasped the full extent of the emergency. "What did he say?" she asked me. "I don't hear so good." I explained the situation to her, sounding—I fancied—as calm and efficient as the Captain. But I was trying to remember the perimeter of Dublin Airport. Thank God, there were no mountains. Mostly fields with low hedges. Few trees. But there were roads. Perhaps people were getting into a bus in O'Connell Street at this very moment, and the bus—a big, solid, double-decker bus—was going to be right there, at the wrong time, just as we became short of runway . . .

The Captain was speaking again. We were going to land at Dublin, though an hour and a half late, as this would save us time in the end. He apologised for the inconvenience. He should have been informed before take-off that the main runway had been damaged by "jet-blast", but this had not been done. He assured us again that there was no danger of any kind.

I wondered if he'd thought of the double-decker bus. I then wondered if I could sue the Manager of Dublin Airport—if I got out alive. Then I began to think seriously, in approximately the following form:

"Change places with this big American woman so that she can see out, see if we're getting short of runway, and then I'll be in the aisle, closer to the door . . . move into the first-class section where there are fewer people and tell them I'll pay later, if the need arises . . . if I hadn't been kind and loving and generous and hadn't started for Dublin to see my mother I wouldn't have been burnt alive so watch these generous gestures in the future, if there is one . . . what blithering ass forgot to tell London about the hole in the Dublin runway, definitely sueable on waste of time alone . . . who'll get the insurance money, have I made a will . . . I don't think the Captain ought to be strolling up and down the aisle reassuring the passengers with that charming smile, he's got more than enough to do up front . . . steward, may I have a brandy and dry ginger, please . . . with the compliments of the Company? . . . thank you so much, may I have another one . . . the least they can do . . . but better keep stone-cold sober, for that last hysterical, scrambling rush, before the explosion . . . what did I ever do to deserve this . . . how sorry, how very, very deeply grieved everyone will be . . ."

We landed in perfect safety, with yards of runway to spare. The memory of fear was wiped out instantly. But it was several days before I could shake off the recollection of the somewhat unworthy thoughts that had occupied my mind in what could have been my last hour and a half on earth.

BROTHER PATROS IN THE BASKET

There is a small town round about the middle of Greece called Meteora.

Like almost all small Greek towns the main street of Meteora is made of mud and deep, water-filled potholes, whilst on either side of it a superb metalled road leads to Salonika in the north and Athens in the south. The potholes begin where the town council takes over responsibility for the highway.

The potholes, however, don't really matter to the town council because when they are not sitting on very hard chairs outside very small cafés they are trotting about on horses, donkeys or mules, so that Meteora looks very like a Wild West frontier town. It is even surrounded by Red Indians in the form of thousands of gypsies, living in ramshackle tents on the outskirts, with at least two horses and seven children per man.

Meteora is also filled with what sounds like seven cocks per hen. They do not wait for the dawn. They go off intermittently all night long, led by a senior citizen whose crow, probably owing to shortage of breath and lack of teeth, goes, "Ark-a-google-erg!"

All these things would make Meteora remarkable enough, and yet it's got one more feature so extraordinary that it obliterates all the others.

Meteora lives in the shadow of about a dozen immense rocks, some of which must be at least a thousand feet in height. They shoot straight up into the air at the back of the town. And to make things still more dizzy and vertiginous there are several monasteries perched on the very top of these monstrous columns, with monks still in residence, probably clinging to the inside walls. And—though even to write it down makes the toes curl inside my shoes—at least one of these monasteries has no visible means of access, save for a rope bag, monk-size, on the end of a long, long line.

I wouldn't have known about this if I hadn't found a picture postcard in a souvenir stall up at the top, where a new road looks after the tourist traffic. The postcard, in full colour, shows a black bearded monk in his brimless tophat and long black robe looking out through the mesh of the bag, supported by what looks like a thin piece of clothes line in the middle of a brilliantly blue and howlingly empty sky. The monk seems to have an umbrella and some assorted vegetables in the basket with him, but the really striking thing about the picture is the expression on his face. It is one of a sadness so profound as to be unreproduceable by any other face in any other circumstances whatsoever.

You can see what has promoted this melancholia, so tragic that no words could possibly describe it. I can feel every fraction of it now myself just by looking at the postcard, even with Meteora a thousand miles away . . .

I was awoken that morning by Brother Thermos stirring me with his boot, as I lay on my simple palliasse. "Brother Patros," he said, "I have good news. Father Spiros has chosen you to go down to the village. We've run out of matches."

Instinctively, I snatched at the stout rope that bound me to the wall, a safety precaution I've taken ever since Brother Skouros slipped out of the window whilst turning over in his sleep. "Not me, Brother," I told Brother Thermos. "The honour is too great. You go."

What with one thing and another it took them nearly an hour to get me into the basket, and it was only when I couldn't get out that Father Spiros gave me the full shopping list. Not just a box of matches but a gross. Plus a stone of spuds, one doz. cauliflower, two packets of custard powder and a bottle of milk. I protested that the line couldn't possibly take all this, and me as well, but Father Spiros pointed out that this kind of bulk purchasing would save me having to go down again for at least a week. At the last moment, just as Brother Thermos started to lower away, Father Spiros shoved in my umbrella. "You might need it," he said mysteriously, though it hasn't rained in Meteora since last year.

Well, I did my shopping and then I had thirty-seven ouzo on the house against the return journey, but now they've all drained away. Because I'm half way up, 893 feet above the ground, and the first strand of the line has just gone. I feel ineffably sad. I told them this bulk purchasing wouldn't work but they wouldn't believe me. It's all so silly. If only Father Spiros had said I could use my umbrella as a parachute it wouldn't be under the spuds, and I wouldn't be sitting on *them*. So sad.

"Ark-a-google-erg!"

I hope that old rooster's underneath me when I touch down. He might serve, fractionally, to break my fall . . .

THE RIGOURS OF SNICKIFF

The freezing smoky air, the yellow arc-lights, the Wagnerian clangour of metal are reminders of Manchester, Bletchley and Crewe despite the fact that we are still far to the south of those gritty, Arctic cities, here in the railway sidings in Avignon.

The car, that safe little travelling home, has just been driven aboard the train at 35 m.p.h. in bottom gear, the engine screaming beneath the leaden foot of an Algerian in blue overalls. The tail-lights, leaping and bounding, disappear down the long iron tunnel of the flat trucks. One waits for the crash as the Algerian drives straight into the car at the head of the line, or clean off the other end, but there is no answering concussion so that all is presumably well. Or as well as things can be for the foreigner, facing the rigours of Snickiff in the middle of the night, and in particular the rigours of Snickiff's second-class *couchettes*.

The Société Nationale des Chemins de Fer Français, or S.N.C.F., or Snickiff offers the service of their *trains-couchette* between Avignon and Paris to save motorists the labour of a two-day journey through France. "Awake refreshed," they say, "at your destination in the morning."

This consummation might well be possible if snickiffing didn't go on throughout the night.

Snickiffing is a process of nerve-erosion practised by all French railway officials and all French railway travellers upon all foreigners travelling on French railways, and it continues without cessation until the destination is reached.

Step aboard, *mes amis,* into Coach No. 11, holding in our hand a flimsy and illegible pink folder that entitles us to awake refreshed in *Couchette* 85 in the morning.

The corridor is impassable, filled with French fellow travellers looking out of the windows at the fascination of a railway siding by night. All of them have safely secured their own *couchettes* and now, by standing in the corridor, are snickiffing the foreigners still in search of theirs. Many of them are already in night attire and could easily be in bed, but they prefer to snickiff in the corridor.

It takes a long time to push past them, in search of *Couchette* 85, because each of them has to be apologised to separately and then they have to reply. When I arrive at *Couchette* 85 I find it's a top bunk and an elderly Frenchman is asleep in it propped up against three pillows and wearing a black, Homburg hat. The other five bunks are occupied by persons who complain, in sharp, querulous French, about the opening of the door and the intrusion of light. A perfect snickiff in view of the fact that they, and the man in the hat who is occupying my bunk, are the only passengers who have retired. All the others are standing in the corridor and I have to push past them again, apologising to each one separately and awaiting their reply, in search of the attendant, so that I can get the old gentleman in the black Homburg turfed out.

The attendant is besieged by French travellers who have already found their *couchettes* but don't like them, and want to move somewhere else. I get to the attendant eventually and show him my ticket. He glances briefly at the illegible writing and tells me it's the wrong date. I explain that the date has been changed and that it says so here and in the middle of it he suddenly snickiffs off into the next coach.

I've been sitting for an hour on a prop-up seat outside the lavatory when the attendant materialises without warning, beckons impatiently, wrenches open a door, thrusts me in and drags it to again behind me, leaving me in darkness amid the sound of at least three people breathing heavily in deep sleep. A snickiff right up to snuff.

The lowest, left-hand bunk appears to be unoccupied. I slide into it sideways on to what I first presume to be a dog but which quickly turns out to be a small female child. By the time its screaming has been silenced, *mille pardons* offered and I've hoisted myself into the top right-hand bunk I've been snickiffed into a state of such abject servility that I lie without breathing for twenty minutes on a bunk from which both pillows and blankets have been removed. I feel around in the rack for some covering, find a blanket, pull it and find the other end is wrapped around the feet of what turns out to be a woman in the opposite bunk who apparently feels, and tells her husband down below, that I am attempting to interfere with her virtue. His grunt is non-committal, but hostile to us both.

In view of this it's some time before I have the courage to struggle out of my trousers, under the blanket, but the heat is fearful and they're going to be unwearable by morning. In a tinkling cascade my lighter, my keys and all my loose change fall out of the pockets down the side of the bunk, presumably on to the man below, but he makes no sound.

I spend the rest of the night rehearsing the morning's *pardons,* snickiffed wide and staring and permanently awake.

THE ADVERTISED TIME OF DEPARTURE

Here we sit in a giant Pan-American silver bird, whistling across the Atlantic to New York, at 600 m.p.h. getting ever closer to the riots, murders, demonstrations, muggings, sluggings and police charges that seem to animate that great city, and of course at any moment the man beside us may produce a gun and apply it to the pilot's sense of discretion so we'll all finish up in Brazzaville or Paraguay, but at least until that happens we are enjoying the sense of peace that comes from being helpless to direct one's own affairs.

A pleasant change.

It seems only yesterday that Madame wrenched me away from some gentle autumnal pruning under the brilliant blue skies of the South of France. "Last winter," she said, "you nearly fell to pieces reading paperbacks in the same chair. You rose only to eat and to haul yourself up to bed at seven o'clock. This winter will be more active."

So the dreadful preparations went ahead. That astonishing piece of equipment the dinner-jacket disinterred from the cellar, mildewed after two years' hibernation. The house swept and polished and the shutters closed. I was standing in the garden, trussed in socks and shirts and collars and ties, holding an overcoat as heavy as mediaeval armour, waiting for Madame to emerge, when I heard her saying, "Dah—dah—dah." Her voice was much deeper and hollower than usual, signalling—I judged—some emergency. A moment later she walked out into the garden, stiff-legged, and with a jaw that didn't seem to work. "Ra," she said, the teeth clenched, "in tha."

Evidently, there was a rat in the kitchen. Shortly afterwards I was in there too, with André, our neighbour, Madame Marie, the *bonne,* Jaca the boxer dog, Charlie the cat and a selection of offensive instruments. The animal element, having been thrown out repeatedly in the past, now thought they had been dragged in to be murdered, and tried to get out. In no time at all we had the huge fridge in the middle of the tiny kitchen, the stove dragged away from the wall, plates crashing, Madame Marie screaming,

André banging around with an iron spike and myself shouting instructions while standing on a bucket in the corner.

We only just got to Nice Airport in time, much too hot.

We arrived in London and unpacked very quickly, as we always do, but this time it was too quick because the lock fell off Madame's large suitcase, her smaller Revelation shut itself almost flat and the zip became jammed on my green-canvas folding-over gentleman's suiting bag. In less than a minute we had no usable luggage at all.

Next morning I put the useless bags in the hall and rang down to the porter for a taxi. He laughed, the indulgent laugh of a man with loads of lovely bad news. "No taxis today, sir," he said. "It's the State Opening of Parliament and the Underground brothers are out on strike. I'd forget it, if I were you."

Madame and I scuttled along the streets towards Victoria, carrying these huge, flapping, empty bags. We found a taxi instantly, and told him to go to a reliable luggage repairer in Pimlico Road, only to find that the premises had turned into an antique shop. We sat in the taxi, not wanting to let it go, with the three empty bags, wondering what to do next when Madame, ever resourceful, said, "Peter Jones."

At the entrance to that emporium she said, "Good luck. I'm off to do something useful." And left me on the pavement with the luggage.

It wasn't easy to struggle through Ladies' Cosmetics, burdened as I was, to the Luggage Department, but there a nice man did something tricky to the Revelation, which caused it to expand to its full size. He also gave me the address of someone in the wilds of Gloucester Road who would repair the others. I left the Revelation in his care and fought my way out through Ladies' Cosmetics again, meeting with many a pained enamel stare.

I arrived at the new repair shop on foot, only to find that it was closed for repairs to itself. A notice on the door gave, however, the address of a branch office still open for business.

I tried to board a bus, only to find it was unlike any bus I'd ever seen. Single decker, and a piece of mechanism that said, "Enter." I couldn't oblige, with the two bags, so I trotted all the way to the new shop, who received the luggage. Then I ran back to Peter Jones, through the Ladies' Cosmetics, picked up the Revelation, out through Cosmetics again and back to the flat, where I discovered later on that I'd left all my lingerie in the side pocket of the green canvas sack.

All is now safely gathered, however, as we howl across the

Atlantic in this Pan-Am projectile, bound for New York or possibly Cuba or Tel Aviv.

And to think that if all this hadn't happened I might have got through half-a-dozen Denis Wheatleys by now.

THE DOORS OF THE COCKPIT

"Do I not know him!" exclaimed the dark girl. "He tore the biggest strip off me—but the biggest—for taking six bottles of orange squash aboard in Brazzaville."

"The Brazzaville stuff," said the fair girl, "is even worse than the glue they load you with in Karachi."

I leant closer to them. Brazzaville? Karachi? What could they be at?

"I wasn't genned up," said the dark girl. "I'd only been round the houses before—London, Paris, Rome, etcetera. I didn't know the stuff was so concentrated that the bods were going to use all my fresh water. When Georgie finds I've none left for my washing up he practically throws me off the aircraft."

So that was it! They were air hostesses. But what a fascinating thing to know—to go easy on the Brazzaville orange juice because it makes the passengers drink all the water intended for the washing up. I extended my ear even further. Here it was, straight from the horse's mouth—the revelation of what really went on behind the closed doors of the cockpit.

"You never know where you are with Georgie," said the young man sitting between them. "I was navigating for him once when we were coming into Hong Kong. Gerry was co-pilot—his first trip. He hadn't landed a Seven with a full load of bods before, but Georgie told him to go ahead and bring her in. Needless to say, the monsoon was firing on all cylinders. Sheets of rain. You couldn't see a thing——"

I found myself groping for my seat-belt and pressing my feet on the floor.

"Anyway," went on the young man, "Gerry slipped her in over the mountains. His ADF was bang on."

I relaxed a little. This was good news.

"The only trouble was he was about 200 yards to the left of the runway. Tom's the engineer, so what does he do? He gives her the gun, thinking Gerry doesn't know what he's doing."

"Engineers!" said the dark girl. "Talk about chips on the shoulder. They always want to fly it themselves."

"I thought," said the young man, "we were going round again. We were really doing a rate of knots. Georgie starts bawling out Tom, and in the middle of it Gerry suddenly gives her full flaps, slips her sideways, and lands at about a million miles an hour.

"But he brings her up beautifully, just short of the end of the runway. That's when Georgie blows his top. 'That,' he roars, 'is the worst landing I've ever seen!' It was quite unfair, of course. After all, Gerry *had* got her down——"

I crept out of the pub, feeling my way along the wall, making sure the ground was solid before advancing the next foot. It's better to keep the doors of the cockpit closed.

THE GENERAL IN A GREEN SILENCE

There were three different kinds of policeman outside the gates.

One was a fresh-faced lad of pinkish complexion, sitting astride a motor-bike. He wore a white crash helmet, and the stubborn look of policemen everywhere who don't quite know what they're doing, but are determined to do it.

The second one was half-way towards being a plain clothes man, in that he had a sports jacket above the navy-blue uniform trouser.

The third one had everything. Full uniform, a peaked cap, pale face and a walkie-talkie apparatus that was working, because he murmured into it continuously. Round about twenty-four years of age, and intent upon becoming the youngest superintendent in history.

The gates themselves were rusty white, and didn't quite close over the cow-trap bars. The avenue mounted straight ahead for perhaps five hundred yards, until it disappeared over the brow of the hill. At the other end of it was General de Gaulle and Tante Yvonne, beyond all reason immured in the soft, green silence of County Kerry.

"Hello, there, then," I said to the three representatives of the Garda Siochana.

The one on the motor-bike polished his handlebars carefully. The walkie-talkie operator, still intent upon promotion, registered my appearance in one glance, and for all time. The semi-plain clothes man nodded, without saying anything.

"Is he in there still?" I asked, just to keep the situation alive.

The dismounted ones slowly turned their backs, and kicked

small stones in an absorbed way. The motor-cyclist removed a speck of rust from his petrol tank with a fingernail.

"Well," I said, "I'll just nip up and have a little chat with him. I speak French, you see," I said, reassuringly.

I opened the gate. It was stiff and rusty. The three policemen watched me struggling with it. I closed it behind me and started walking briskly up the wet avenue. I wondered how long it would be before they realised what had happened.

I'd covered about a hundred yards, when the voice said, "That's enough, now." I stopped, with one foot in the air, turned round and walked back to the gates. The semi-plain clothes man opened them for me, politely.

"Thank you," I said. Then I added, defensively, "I only wanted to say good morning to him."

The three policemen nodded. They understood, without condoning the near-offence. All of us kicked some stones for a while.

Round the bend in the road, pedalling his bicycle with extreme care, mastering a highly complex piece of machinery, came an ancient Kerryman. Old, brown monkey face, one tooth in the top jaw. Large, thick, purplish overcoat, despite the fact that it was warm and sunny. He stopped, and dismounted. It took quite a long time. He leant the bicycle against the wall. He went up to the young policeman with the walkie-talkie.

Looking at the ground, he said, "Is de Frenchie in dere yet?"

The young policeman said, "Yeah."

The old man digested the information, then nodded to himself a couple of times, confirming what he knew already. He remounted his bicycle—an elaborate, creaky operation—and rode carefully away.

The policeman and I found our eyes briefly entangled. We looked away from one another. Then, with care, we kicked some small stones for a while. All four of us were wondering what in the name of God was going on.

This feeling of incredulity saturates the air of the little village of Sneem, just down the road from the General's guarded gates. Casey's pub is packed all night long. A surprising number of young people. Pretty girls in near-mini-skirts talking about Dublin fashion. In the corner five old farmers playing halfpenny nap. But everyone has an air of preoccupation. It's as though the General were a live and visible man from Mars. Something incredible dropped into our midst. We don't talk about him, because there's nothing really to say, but he's there all the time, looming, in the way that he's loomed over Europe for so many years.

A small car comes down the avenue in the middle of the morning. A middle-aged priest is sitting in the back of it. The chauffeur wears a dark blue uniform, with a peaked cap. A dozen newspapermen jump into their cars and follow Father Flavin into Sneem.

When he gets out I see that he's tall and white-haired. Pale blue eyes, gentle, bothered but trying hard to please. He answers questions. Yes, the General and his lady took Communion. They were both looking well. No, they didn't say when they were coming out. Or at least the interpreter didn't say anything about it. He himself couldn't venture an opinion about the General's next move.

We all stand around in the middle of the village street. It's as though we were trying to catch non-existent flies in our bare hands.

Father Flavin, having courteously made sure that we have no other unanswerable questions to put to him, opens his gate and walks up the neat path to the temporary haven of his house. He feels that he should have done more, but of what? The General hasn't really helped. He's only loomed.

I find the French journalist talking to the uniformed chauffeur, in French. The chauffeur must be the General's own! I ease in on him.

"Bonjour, M'sieu."

The chauffeur is short and grey-haired and suntanned. He doesn't exactly fall flat on his back with shock at finding himself addressed in his own language in the middle of the village of Sneem. He says, *"M'sieu?"*

"Le Général," I say, *"il s'amuse bien, quoi?"*

The chauffeur helpfully, says, *"Mais oui,"* and waits with polite patience to see if I have any further enquiries. I can't think of one. He gets into the car and drives away.

Some of the newspapermen go across the road into Casey's. We go back towards Heron's Cove Hotel, but by way of a change we leave out the gates this time and take a small road down to the right. It leads to the shore of Kenmare Bay. From here we can see the hotel. Two grey gables. A rather prim and proper looking house. Not very big and not very old. A couple of open launches are tied up to a buoy, a couple of hundred yards out to sea. In one of them half a dozen men are sitting. My companion says, "They're the poor sufferin' eejits from *Paris Match*. They've telefoto lens as long as your arm. All they've got is a few mackerel. They've been there for a week."

Round the corner comes the fresh faced copper with the motorbike. He stops beside our car, but doesn't look at us. Once again he polishes the handlebars with his glove. We get into the car, feeling that we've infringed the regulations by looking at the hotel with our naked eyes, and drive back again to the gates. The copper rides along slowly behind us, looking at the road. Once again everyone is moving about like automatons, driven pointlessly from place to place by the invisible, untouchable, *grand Charles.*

During the course of the afternoon a car arrived with a square-jawed man in the passenger seat. He was smoking a small, patent pipe, looking very continental. The coppers had the gate open from the moment they saw him coming. The car swept in and up the drive so quickly that he didn't have either the time or the inclination to give the police even a nod.

They had the gates open again for his return, half an hour later. I said to the young man who was driving our car, "Follow him."

"What for—?" he was genuinely puzzled.

"Never mind. Just do it."

We followed the other car down the road. It turned into the Great Southern Hotel, in which I was staying. The square-jawed man got out and began to stroll in an unhurried way down to the little jetty. I let him get well away from the hotel and then I pounced upon him.

"Bonjour, M'sieu. Vous êtes an ami du Général de Gaulle?"

He turned round, looking put out. Something had just happened that was beyond his comprehension.

"What's that?" he said.

I said, "I'm sorry. I thought you were French. I saw you calling on the General a minute or two ago. What were you doing there, anyway?"

He laughed out loud, in relief. "Don't mind me," he said. "I'm only the Chief Superintendant of the County." We shook hands, for some reason, and he walked away.

That night, in Casey's, I was discussing, with Mick Casey, that distinguished, retired, all-in wrestler, the virtues of Mick MacManus's showmanship technique in the ring, when a wild looking man with a strangely contorted face shoved a copy of the evening paper into my hand. He made short, sharp grunting noises. I realised that he was dumb, and that he was trying to convey something to me that was to him of the first importance. I gave him back the paper, to get rid of him, but he pressed it upon me again. Then he seized my hand and began to pull me towards the public bar, making gestures as though he were throwing darts. I saw then that the paper wasn't important. It was just an introduction.

His violence and his contorted inability to speak frightened me. I shook him off and ran out into the darkness of the village street, where I concealed myself behind a car. He came after me, looking for me with angry, impatient gruntings. He gave up the hunt after a while and went back into the pub.

Next morning the hall porter was convulsed with laughter. "I'm told," he said, "that Dummy gave you a right run around last night."

"He's a hard case," I said. "He wanted me to give him a game of darts."

"That's only the half of it," Tom said. "He thought you was General de Gaulle."

After a moment, I said, "How did he tell you? Did he write it down?"

"No, no," Tom said. "We talk with the hands. The old sign language. You know?"

In a kind of way it was the closest I had yet come to our quarry, but it was the following afternoon before the General and I came face to face.

I was late on duty at the gates, having fallen into conversation over lunch in the hotel with an Englishman and his wife. They had arrived in Parknasilla three weeks ago, intending to stay for one night, but had become entangled in the intense social life that the presence of the General has created and now she saw no prospect of ever getting him out. He said, through the third bottle of rather good claret, "I'm readjusting, you see, the whole former process of my thinking. Let me tell you how I was from, say, fifteen onwards."

She said, "Darling, could you not start at twenty-one?" He wasn't in favour of it, so that it must have been round about four o'clock when I reported for duty at the gates of Heron's Cove. And just in the nick of time. The three resident coppers were tense and alert, apparently on the verge of having something to do.

The semi-plain clothes man even spoke to me, unprompted. "He's out," he said, "and he's comin' back anny minyut."

The whole myth had suddenly become reality.

Five minutes later the General and his lady arrived, in a small black English car. They were led by a police car, and followed by the cars of the newspapermen. The whole procession had been tearing around the countryside for about an hour.

The General was sitting on the left-hand side of Tante Yvonne. As the car slowed for a moment, to get through the gate, I bent down and caught his eye.

"Vive la France!" I shouted, carried away.

The great monolithic face eased a fraction. There was almost the suggestion of a smile. He raised the two hands in their famous, all-encompassing gesture, and then he and Tante Yvonne were swept away.

Under the circumstances, it seemed to me to be an outstanding interview.

IN THE HOME OF THE GNOME

A small, discreetly opulent restaurant, with the lighting striking exactly the right note between intimacy and being able to see what you were at.

It had been planned for its precise purpose. The tables had been placed, scientifically, so that you could speak above a whisper and still not be overheard by your neighbours, while at the same time, without straining your voice, you could let them have an earful of what you were talking about, if such a strategem happened to be part of the master plan.

Even the maître d'hôtel was perfectly cast for his job. Old, rolypoly, red-faced, slightly tetchy in manner—a man who'd heard it all before, who'd seen them come and seen them go and whose only remaining interest in his customers was that they should enjoy his excellent food and drink. It was plain that one could speak freely, while he was bending over the table, without—as it were—rocking the boat.

The serving itself was done by a young girl as carefully chosen as the rest of the ingredients. Fresh-faced, innocent, supremely competent, her sole desire could only be to do her job as well as possible, with a view to laying aside a nest-egg for her marriage to a reliable young man. No eavesdropper, she.

"Thooper thet-up," I said to Madame, as we sat down.

She silenced me with a financial look—for where should we be but right in the heart of Gnomeland itself, right in the middle of Zurich, up to the neck in Kreditanstalts and Bundesbanks and les Banques de Quelquechose.

Exciting, more particularly, as we were about to dicker with a Gnome in person, actually a good-looking, dark haired young man, somewhat above average height. Four languages, of course, and charming in all of them.

Not to go into the contest entirely unarmed we had incorporated into our team an expert handler, manager or agent—an elegant lady stockbroker, who lives near us in the South of France.

Instantly, the two ladies rejected the Gnome's offer of a bottle of champagne by way of an aperitif, so firmly, indeed, that I couldn't squeeze even a dry Martini out of the situation for myself. It was clear—as if it hadn't been clear before—that we were on business bent, a large part of the business being to introduce our handler, manager or agent to the Gnome, and from what we hoped would be their mutual understanding to do ourselves a bit of good.

A short silence fell after we'd ordered lunch. To fill it, I said, "So this is Zurich, the Home of the Money Wrench," and got Madame's heel along my anklebone by way of commendation.

A moment later I found there was no need to keep the party going with the lighter kind of conversation because our lady aide and the Gnome had serious work to do: i.e. to find out and to lay bare the metal of the other.

She: "A friend of mine in New York, J. Strangler Stockbaum, was talking quite interestingly about United Electronic Plumbing, Inc. Spot forward reversible debentures, of course."

He: (having nodded, once, at the mention of J. Strangler Stockbaum) 'Vielleicht, aber on ne sait jamais about the chances of consolidatory refunding."

Me: (an aside to Madame) "Perhaps, but one never knows about the chances of—"

Madame: No words, but a look that would have corroded concrete.

After that I let the experts continue without further assistance, because all at once I felt entirely at home, in Zurich, in this discreetly opulent restaurant, because it was exactly the same as the pub beside Harold's Cross dog-track in Dublin.

The same exploratory feelers: "Your man said that John-Joe Kelly might be up with a good one from Clonmel for the hurdle." And the same counters, aimed at further elucidation: "Maybe so, but th'other fella tole me that the Tralee boys, if the price was right, was thinkin' of havin' a go with the brindle."

All the Kreditanstalts and the Bundesbanks and the Banques de Quelquechose—there was no mystery about them. They were engaged, one and all, in the holy process of trying to find a nice, long-priced winner.

When lunch was over I asked Madame, "How did we do?"

"I did fine," she said. "He's going to send me a huge box of lovely Swiss chocolates."

"Is that all? Big deal."

"Ah," she said, "but he wanted to know if I'd rather have white or dark truffles in the centres."

I suppose I'll find out, sometime, what really happened.

THE STEAM CHICKEN LINE

This enormous young man said, as though the idea had come to him quite suddenly, "Let's go and have lunch tomorrow with Joanna in Minorca."

I said, "We did that a couple of weeks ago, and we bear the marks to this day. If you leave here at dawn, fight your way through the queues at the Spanish frontier, drive like a maniac down the Costa Brava through half the population of the British Isles and struggle through the city of Barcelona it's just possible to catch the evening boat to Mahon, where you arrive at breakfast time the following morning after a sleepless . . ."

"I am not speaking," he said severely, "of old-fashioned conveyances like motor-cars and steam packets. We shall travel in an aeroplane and be there in a couple of hours."

"There is no such thing," I said with equal severity, "as getting anywhere by aeroplane in a couple of hours. Strikes, civil unrest and faulty radio beacons get in the way. Obviously, you didn't read my column last week. Fourteen hours from Dublin to Nice . . ."

"Ah," he said, "but that would have been by vulgar commercial airlines. I've got my own aeroplane. Take-off tomorrow morning 11 a.m. All right?"

This, provided someone else is playing for it, is the way to do it. At Nice Airport there was the usual small hold-up for passport flashing, and then a rather longer but more unusual one while our host cadged a jar of ice from the barman in the Departure Lounge.

Then, while hundreds of people queued up in front of us for planes that would never leave, we slipped out through a side-door into a huge and entirely empty bus, which drove us straight out to the waiting, twin-engined Beagle. Along the side of it was painted in large black letters a mysterious legend. It said, "The Steam Chicken Line".

It was not reassuring, particularly as I thought that our enormous host might be intending to drive the thing himself. At the controls, however, God be praised, was a smaller, neater, young professional pilot, called Graham.

The five of us climbed aboard, into accommodation infinitely more spacious than that to be found in jumbo jet. I was even able to stretch my legs without getting them tangled up in the tree-trunks of our host.

Graham turned round in the pilot seat. "There's just one word of warning," he said. Instant terror, to be relieved a moment later when he said, "If you're opening the champagne it's liable to be fizzier than usual owing to the altitude."

We took off like a little yellow bird, or a Steam Chicken. It was extraordinary to watch, through the windscreen, the runway speeding back behind us like a road and then gradually falling away as we climbed into the air. The airport tipped sideways as we turned south. Then the blue sea came level below us and we were buzzing along in our own drawing-room at 210 miles an hour.

Rupert poured whisky, on the grounds that we didn't want to be bothered with the fizzier champagne, while Tolly dealt with the ice. "Certain West Africans," he said, "refer to everything that moves by power as 'steam'. They also call everything that flies, 'chicken'. That's why we're The Steam Chicken Line." It was, in a way, an explanation.

Two hours later the flat, brown island came into view. Rupert said to Graham, "Did you ring for a taxi?"

Graham nodded. He had, too, by radio. Our sense of luxury became Byzantine.

At first I'd intended to say to Joanna, who had had no warning of the visitation, "I've just come back for my toothbrush." Then we thought to increase her sense of unreality by pretending she wasn't there. In the end the excitement became too much for us and we simply called out, "Is anyone at home?"

The effect was entirely satisfactory. For several long minutes she was unable to speak, looking at the five of us in turn and blinking, trying to bring us into focus. There were already two other guests for lunch and a leg of lamb on the spit, so that there was just enough for eight.

We left for Nice again at 4 p.m., and were home in time to give a small dinner party of our own. During the course of it one of the guests said, "If you tell us any more about having had lunch in Minorca today I'm going straight home."

It was impossible to blame him.

GULLIBLE DE TROP AT ST. TROP

It is round about 7 o'clock in the evening, the time in St. Tropez when everyone saunters up and down the quay, looking at the yachts.

To save space the yachts are moored stern-in on the quay, so that the passers-by can get a good look at the general décor of the various deck-saloons, as well as the quality of the owners and their guests.

Quite a number of these strollers are yacht owners themselves, intent in a gentlemanly way on seeing what kind of mess the others have made of their furnishings this year, or what ghastly kind of friends they've got themselves stuck with.

Once up and down is usually enough, and then everyone retires to their own boat, to sit on the after-deck and to discuss the catastrophes that have overtaken the others. For this ceremony one wears one's smartest summer clothes, and smartest summer manner, in case some of the people taking it in from the quayside are yacht owners themselves.

On many of the after-decks standing-up cocktail parties are going on, with white coated crew members moving among the guests with trays. The English Language, in its more strident aspects, lies like a tangible layer of sound upon gatherings of this kind.

Next door, identifiable by a couple of Ferraris and a Maserati on the quay, are a group of languid Italians accompanied by beautiful women dressed not so much for boating as for the theatre in New York. They lounge about in extremely expensive cane chairs, conveying by their exquisite indolence the fact that they are well accustomed to millionaire yachting and to the heat of the Mediterranean night—unlike the English who have to stand up and yelp about it.

The English often feel like bunging a tomato at them.

Next down the line is an American yacht. Three elderly men sit on the after-deck, smoking cigars. Their wives must be ashore, picking over scarves and costume jewellery in one of the countless boutiques.

If you're English, or Italian, you always feel that cigars before dinner are not quite on and that in any case a cigar aboard a yacht is perhaps just a little too much.

Further down is a French boat, filled with very brown young men and very brown young women. They are drinking very chic whiskys on the rocks. One feels that somewhere or the other they have been bathing all day in the nude. In an absentminded way they fondle sections of one another as though they were still wearing no clothes. They are probably waiting to go up to Bardot's pad or she is coming down to them.

The other nationalities, apart from the Italian men, try not to watch them too closely. There is a general feeling that what they are doing is not really yachting at all.

Seven o'clock in the evening in St. Tropez, and there we are sitting on the after-deck drinking Pimms, with plenty of fruit and vegetables in our glasses so that the chic-ness of our refreshment will be readily identifiable to the watchers on the quay.

"Did you see what that dreadful old Turk has done this year?"

Maggy, our hostess, has been ashore all afternoon having her hair done by her favourite Jean-Claude, to whom she always goes when she's in St. Trop. He's done her proud, a great mound of pinkish spun sugar, immovable with lacquer in the evening breeze.

"He's actually gone," she continues, "and built himself an Elizabethan library in his deck-saloon. Panelling and leather-bound books and all that sort of thing. And, my dears, do you know—he's actually got an open fire as well! With huge logs all blazing away—on an evening like this."

Richard, her husband, joins in. He spent a lot of time this afternoon on the telephone to his broker in London. The telephone is on the bar in our favourite restaurant. You can see it from the street. I passed by several times and he was still there, speaking urgently into the phone, wearing rather a small yachting cap.

"The really funny thing was that he was wearing a smoking cap—an extraordinary looking plum-coloured arrangement with a tassel hanging down over one ear—"

"And he was smoking, too!" cries Maggy. "A huge curved pipe like—like Sherlock Holmes."

"Learning the English way of life," said Richard, smiling comfortably.

Everyone laughs.

Wolf, the German deck steward, appears. He sidles forward and breathes urgently into Maggy's ear.

Various attempts have been made in the past to call Wolf "Volf", which is the way he pronounces it himself, but they've been abandoned. There was a lack of consistency about it which led to too many misunderstandings, so that he is now simply called Wolf. He doesn't, however, look like a wolf. He looks a very nervous, pale blond young German with slight homosexual tendencies, if he ever had the courage to give way to them. Much more of a Volf, in fact, but that cannot be helped.

"Oh, Wolf," Maggy says petulantly, "don't be tiresome. The chef will simply have to turn it down. We're not nearly ready yet. And we want some more ice."

Wolf shivers away. Some of us have got sympathy for him. The chef is a large, dark-complexioned, passionate man who may be either Rumanian or Greek. At all events, no one understands whatever language it is that he speaks, so that he is driven to communicating with his fellows in rudimentary French.

We can hear him at meal-times, because the galley is right below the dining saloon. From time to time he roars, "Christoos!" or "Merde!" or "Putain!" He must be very frightening in that enclosed space.

To prevent Maggy getting on to the servant problem I say to Richard, "Do you remember the time we went into Tangier and it was pissing rain and you sent Wolf ashore with ten quid to buy some drugs?"

I became aware, a second too late, of the presence of the Colonel and his lady. They are visitors from another yacht and while they're not yachting they live in Wiltshire, where the Colonel is Chairman of the local Bench.

I am already regretting my description of the weather conditions in Tangier, and now feel I should take the sting out of the rest of it.

"We only wanted something light, like adulterated keef. None of us had ever taken drugs before and we just thought it might be fun—with the rain, and all that."

"I see," the Colonel says, without, however, pardoning the contemplated offence.

"Well," I rattle on, "nothing came of it in the end because Wolf came back without any. He said the price had doubled since he'd been in the drug-smuggling business and he didn't want to waste Richard's money."

Several seconds go by before Richard says, "Who's for another Pimm?"

After this we settle ourselves again and Richard and the Colonel begin to discuss the possibilities in the Malaga area. They are wary, however, of the unreliable Franco, the Gibraltar situation and the prohibitive charge on property dollars.

Commercialism of this kind seems to me to be out of place on this lovely yacht, in glamorous St. Trop and on this hot Mediterranean night. Anyway, I'm quite gay on the Pimms.

"What about the time we were in Malaga," I say to Richard, "and you and I and Maggy and that curious financial friend of yours set off in a horse-drawn cab to look for a night-club called the Pam-Pam. We jiggled through Malaga, bowing and waving like Royalty to our many fans and admirers, and when we came to the Pam-Pam it was shut. Bolted and barred with the shutters up. We asked the driver what had happened and he said, 'Il Padrone e muerto,' or however it goes in Spanish. And your curious financial friend said, 'The boss has kicked the bucket? Well, ask him why his sobbing wife can't carry on?' And you in your rough Spanish put the question to the driver who replied by pointing up to Heaven with his whip. We got it. It was Good Friday and by 'Il Padrone' he was having reference to Our Redeemer—"

In that instant I remembered Maggy's warning about the Colonel's lady, about her close relationship to the Duke of Norfolk and her devout, if high, Catholicism, but it's too late.

The Colonel's lady appears to be about to rise to her feet, with the intention of departing, but the yacht lurches so suddenly that she is thrown back into her chair.

The lurch has been accompanied by a loud crash and this is now followed by a passionate cry, "Jaysus—me foot!"

Everyone runs up towards the bow. I bring up the rear. I don't like the sound of that accent, and with reason, as it turns out.

With the propeller still churning away in reverse a dingy little ketch is grating away at the immaculate white side of Richard's yacht. The ketch might also have been white, but many many years ago. A line of indescribable laundry hangs from a piece of string between the mast and the forestay. Amidships is a young man with flaming ginger hair, wearing a pair of filthy flannel trousers and nothing else. His bare foot does indeed appear to be wedged between the yacht and the smaller boat.

"John-Joe," he bawls again, "me foot. It's cot. Will yez knock off the —in' ingin for Jaysus sake— !"

The engine stops. The smaller boat swings clear. The young man, cursing foully, tenderly nurses his foot with one hand. He looks up and sees me retreating into the wheelhouse.

"Holy Mother!" he cries. "It's Paddy. Paddy Campbell from Dublin."

Wild with excitement, his injured foot forgotten, he shouts down into the ketch's cabin, "John-Joe—Norah—Bridie—come up owa that! It's Paddy Campbell. The hard man himself. Doin' the lord on this —in' big t'ing here!"

His companions appear. To judge by their appearance they've been at sea for a long, long time, and it's been an unusually tough trip. Jean-Claude, faced with the matted locks of Norah and Bridie, would have had the vapours.

But all of them are delighted to see me. "Holy Mother" and "Suffering duck" ring out in the warm night.

John-Joe remembers that first things come first. He has a dark grey hand on the gleaming teak rail of Richard's yacht.

"Hey, Paddy," he says urgently, "is there air of a chanst of a botla shtout? Jaysus, we're —in' pairched."

The Colonel and his lady have withdrawn to the safety of the stern. Maggy's in the wheelhouse, pretending it isn't happening. Richard says to me sternly, "I shall be glad if you will tell your friends to pull away. The harbour regulations do not permit double-berthing."

As it turns out a moment later there is no reason for him to be so toffee-nosed because there is a sudden roar of rage from down below, followed by a scream and Wolf erupts on to the deck as if propelled from a gun. His pale blue eyes are rolling in terror. He grabs Richard by the arm of his immaculate blue blazer and sobs out, "Cook—epileptic attack—hess knife—Herr Gott—Herr Gott—!"

The evening peace of St. Trop—tenuous at the best of times—has been shattered, at any rate in our section, for at least another twenty-four hours.

Old Brave-New World

GULLIBLE FROM PEN TO PHILLY

Someone knocked politely on the cell door. After a moment, there was the jangling of heavy keys. The door opened and the Superintendent came in. Behind him, with the keys, was the Sergeant.

"Good morning," the Superintendent said. He looked at the breakfast tray on the bed. "If you've finished," he said, "it will be all right for you to go home. I'm just off myself, as a matter of fact. We've had a busy night."

He'd shaved, but he looked very tired.

There was a movement in the narrow passage outside the cell. "Oh, by the way," the Superintendent said, "I'd like you to meet my colleague. He'll be—looking after you from now on."

A younger and leaner Superintendent came in.

I said, "How d'you do." We shook hands.

The other Superintendent said, "You will be in court this morning, won't you? Ten o'clock. The West London Magistrate."

I said, "I've already explained about that. It's going to be very difficult."

"I strongly advise you to attend—sir," the Superintendent said. He didn't want to go into it again. He put out his hand. "Good-bye, sir." He went away, followed by the Sergeant.

The new Superintendent and I stood irresolutely in the passage.

To say something, I nodded towards a hand-written notice stuck on the door of the cell opposite. I'd looked at it several times during the night through the spyhole in the door of my own cell. The notice read: "The Ice Box."

"That's not your torture chamber, is it?" I said, trying to smile. The new Super managed a laugh. "No, no," he said. "We've got a lot of stolen refrigerators in there. One of the lads just stuck up the notice for a joke."

In the middle of my other troubles it was a kind of relief.

He wanted to get on with his day's work. "Well, then," he said,

"I'll see you later. Your car's in the garage. If you'd like to follow me—"

A couple of minutes later I was driving home. Five hours before I'd also been driving home, when the young policeman stepped out of the shadows and put up his hand. Later he described it as "just a routine check". It was a routine check that landed me in a cell—"over-tired in charge of a motor vehicle".

Even now, ten years later, I still call it "over-tired in charge". The reality is too shameful.

I drove home. The car was exactly the same, but my own circumstances had changed out of all recognition.

Five hours before I'd been looking forward to flying to America for the first time. A week in Philadelphia at the expense of Pan-American Airways, which had already flown me so many thousands of miles. But the plane was due to leave London Airport at 10.30 that morning, and if the Law had its way I'd still be in the West London Magistrates' Court at that time.

In many ways I'd had as busy a night as the gentlemanly Superintendent. I was incapable of applying my mind to the problem.

There'd been an old and greasy copy of *Woman's Mirror* in the cell. I'd read every word of it and then slept for about twenty minutes, to wake and to begin pacing up and down not thinking about the locked door. Now, I couldn't think about Philadelphia either. There was about an hour and three-quarters before the plane took off, either with or without me. I didn't know which it was going to be.

The moment I got home I rang Madame, the most sturdy person in an emergency. I woke her up, but she grasped the situation immediately. She even had time to say, "What bad luck. But don't worry. I'll shop around for a legal eagle and call you back."

I thanked her hysterically. At that moment my own solicitor was probably waking up and yawning in some outer suburb, but both his suburb and his telephone number were unknown. I thought I'd once heard him talking about Sevenoaks. Or was it Haywards Heath? It was nearly 9 o'clock. There was no time to track him down.

Still torn between Philadelphia and the Court I was packing when Madame rang me back. "You're off to Philadelphia," she said cheerfully. "I've just caught a barrister in his bath. He says you've only got to write a letter to the Magistrate explaining the position, and tell him you'll be back in four days' time, or whenever it is, and it'll be all right."

"He's sure?"

"He says he's sure."

"Thank you more than I can say."

"I won't keep you. You must be busy. Have a good trip."

I wrote the letter very quickly but the typing was awful so I wrote it again, more carefully, and signed it as legibly as I could. I took a taxi to the court—it seemed easier than the car. There was a policeman outside. I pressed the letter into his hand, without speaking, and jumped back into the taxi again, in terror of being seen by the Superintendent, thinking he was certain to arrest me. The taxi left me back at the flat. I was waiting on the pavement with my suitcase when the car arrived from the airline at 9.30 a.m.

Someone else was in it. Another journalist, a fat jolly man whom I'd seen around several times before. We exchanged greetings, and drove off in silence. I know he was looking at me with a certain curiosity, but I didn't meet his eye.

Suddenly, I realised we were driving up North End Road and at any moment would be passing within a couple of yards of the court I'd just left. And, almost certainly, just at the moment when the Superintendent arrived.

I crouched right back into the corner, ducked my head and covered my face with my hand.

After a moment the other man said, "Not feeling too good? Rough night."

"The worst," I said, without looking up. I wondered, in the days and nights to come in Philadelphia, if I'd be able not to tell him what had happened. I didn't want to tell anyone and then, in the next second, I wished to God I'd gone to the court and got it over. It was senseless to go tearing off to Philadelphia. Then I had another, altogether terrible thought.

The Superintendent only had to ring the airport police. I'd be arrested at the immigration desk and probably be given a prison sentence. Three months. I thought of the five hours I'd spent in the cell, the tiled walls, the bright light, the thin blanket on the hard bunk . . .

I must have groaned or made some sound of despair because the other man said, "Not much further now." Then he added sympathetically, "They'll probably give us a nip before we take off."

I thought of the nips that had got me into this situation, and didn't know if I wanted one or not.

We were given one in the airline's V.I.P. lounge. Several of their representatives were there to see us off. I could scarcely talk to any of them, still shaking from the business of going through immigration. A number of hard-eyed men had been standing around, looking very like detectives. The immigration officer had given me a glance so penetrating that when he handed back my passport I thought he was signalling to the plain-clothes men. I stood in front of the desk, holding my passport, waiting for the hand to fall on my collar, until the immigration officer said, "That's all, sir—move along, please."

Evidently, I was going to be allowed to go to Philadelphia, whatever they proposed to do to me when I got back. For a split second I wondered what the rest of my life would be like if I didn't go back at all, if I borrowed some money and went to rich friends in New York. I could get a black-market labour permit—

For that split second the laden weight of sick misery lifted. I was planning to do something of my own volition, something that hadn't happened since the young policeman stepped out of the shadows and put up his hand. It was gone as quickly as it had come. I knew what was going to happen. I was going to trail round Philadelphia for four days, with the weight getting heavier and heavier, and then I'd return to London where I'd be fined something like £50, and I'd lose my driving licence for a year. If nothing worse happened because I hadn't attended the court . . .

I read a number of English newspapers, as we flew across the Atlantic. In all of them was the story of a well-known actor who'd been arrested in exactly the same circumstances as myself. I'd forgotten about the newspapers. Perhaps because I worked for one the others wouldn't use it. I couldn't even think about it. It was just another thing to be faced when I got back.

When we landed in Philadelphia the temperature must have been in the nineties. Standing in line for the Customs I knew I was going to faint. My knees were going to give way and I was going to fall on my face on the concrete. I'd finish up in some unimaginable hospital and be shipped straight back to London from there, leaving me with nothing to write about Philadelphia and in the airline's debt for the rest of my life.

A policeman in shirt sleeves with black glasses stood in front of me. The butt of an immense gun stood out from the holster strapped to his side. "March, buddy," he said. "We ain't got all day."

Before I had time to think that he was arresting me I saw what he meant. I was holding up the queue. I shuffled forward, filling up the gap. In comparison with the courteous Superintendent this policeman—this cop—was very frightening indeed. America was obviously not a place to be arrested in.

After Customs the fat, jolly journalist and I stood for quite a time in a huge cavernous hall full of milling people—the men in shirt sleeves and even the old women in light summer dresses. Again I thought of sliding away, of losing myself among them, of never going back to London, but I knew it wouldn't work. America, seen for the first time, was more foreign than any country in Europe, and I looked utterly foreign in it. There was no chance of hiding here.

We were claimed in the end by three genial young men from the airline office. In a car as big as a boat we drove into the middle of Philadelphia. A surprisingly large number of the shop windows were boarded up, and looked as if they'd been like that for a long time. One of the young men said, "The city centre's dying. Everybody's moving out to the suburbs."

Under different circumstances I could have been interested, and asked him questions. Now, like the big cop with the dark glasses, it just seemed further evidence of the ruthlessness of America. I couldn't think of anything to say.

"Still," the young man said, "we've got some good eating houses left." He seemed to share a joke with his friends. "I guess you'll like this one," he said.

For a moment, in blazing sunshine, I thought we were going to have dinner. Then I realised it must be lunch. We'd left London at 10.30 a.m. But it was probably only about midday in Philadelphia.

In terror, I began to work backwards. I hadn't been in bed, apart from the twenty minutes on the hard bunk in the cell, since the night before last. And now we were going to have lunch and then be shown all over the city. Later on there would probably be a cocktail party, and a dinner party and then a nightclub. If I began drinking again I was certainly going to fall down as much from exhaustion as anything else—and finish up for the second time in a cell.

For lunch I resolved to eat as much as I could, and drink as little as possible.

The restaurant was decorated, successfully, to look like an English chop-house. The waiters wore red coats and kneebreeches—and the manager came from Dublin.

This was the treat that the young men from the airline office had prepared for me, because the manager remembered me well from the old days, and there was a bottle of Jameson on the table to welcome me.

I remembered him, faintly, too. "Slainte," we said to one another, and had the first one. We reminisced for a while. After two more Jameson, he said, "Would you ever come into the back office a minute? The wife's in there and me mother and she'd love to meet you again?"

The proceedings in the back office took nearly an hour. When we left the restaurant at about four o'clock I didn't immediately recognise the fixed grin and the glittering, glassy eye that met me in a mirror.

We called on the City Hall, where I met Police Chief Petersen. "This guy," someone said proudly, "can spot a crime a half hour before it's committed." I shook him confidently by the hand. He punched my bicep in a playful way and I steadied myself against a table.

We examined the Food Produce Centre and the Schuyikill River and the Liberty Bell. We had dinner somewhere or another and I don't know what time it was when I said to the young man, "I'm sorry, I've absolutely got to go to bed. You see, I spent last night in a cell in London and I didn't get a lot of sleep."

He took it very well, or, perhaps he was thinking more of his own commitments. Outstanding among them was the necessity to get the fat, jolly journalist and myself to a café from where someone called Frank Ford ran an all-night radio show. When we got there, to be interviewed by Mr. Ford, the young man hoped we would be able to mention the name of the airline as favourably and as often as possible.

"Just do this one thing for me," he said. "Then you can hit the sack."

The programme must have been on for some time because the café was jammed with people, many of them in a state of high excitement. At a table on a dais at the end of the room sat a man with silvery-grey hair and a humorous, intelligent face. He had a telephone receiver to his ear, but the voice of the woman he was talking to was broadcast by a loudspeaker on the wall behind him. It seemed to be a general discussion, because the café audience joined in. The subject was public transport in Philly, and no one thought very much of it. Once again America seemed to be raw and violent and ruthless. I wondered, half-consciously, what they would think of us.

The fat and jolly journalist was very good. He'd read a lot about Philadelphia and got several rounds of applause for his enlightened opinions. I was almost asleep when Frank Ford nudged my elbow. I opened my eyes. He was holding a piece of paper. Written on it was, "Campbell fresh from pen. in London."

The young man must have passed it up to Ford in the hope of rousing me into taking some part in the show.

Ford said, "Mr. Campbell—I'm informed you've arrived here straight from the penitentiary in England. We've got a penal reform problem here in Philly. Tell me, how do you find things over there—from the inside?"

He was laughing. He was a very nice man. Quickly, he smoothed it all over and we went on to talk about first impressions of the city and so on, but I couldn't help wondering how many people listened to the programme, and how many newspaper reporters.

Next morning, I didn't have the chance to find out. I was still asleep when the phone rang. It was my agent, Irene, calling from London.

"It's just purely a formality," she said, "and there's no reason at all for you to worry, but I think I ought to let you know that there's a warrant out for your arrest."

The receiver actually fell out of my hand and rolled under the bed. I was crouched on the floor when I picked it up again. Irene was saying, "Hello—what's happened? Are you all right—?"

"There's a warrant," I said, "for my arrest?"

She said again that it was purely a fomality, because I hadn't answered to my bail, but she assured me that the Superintendent was being very nice about it, and I wasn't to worry.

I thanked her for letting me know and got back into bed again, where I lay rigidly on my back for some time with my eyes shut.

The phone rang again. It was quite a long time before I picked it up. "Yes—?"

"Mr. Campbell?"

"Yes."

"You don't know me but my name is Frank Somethingorother and I'm your host for the day. You want to meet me in the lobby in a half hour?"

"Yes. Thank you—"

"How shall I identify you?"

I thought of several ways in which he could identify me. Debauched, terrified, demented. I said, suddenly, "I look like a mad ferret about nine feet high."

There was a longish silence. Then he said, "Would you oblige me by repeating your identification, sir?"

"Tall," I said. "Wearing a dark-brown suit."

"Fine," he said, reassured. He gave me his identification, which included his weight—one hundred fifty-two pounds.

That day was interminable, and the next and the next. With a warrant out for my arrest I partnered Mrs. Frank Somethingorother at a dinner dance in a hotel. The dance began at six, and we had half a bottle of Californian white wine among five people. With a warrant out for my arrest I sat in the Theatre-in-the-Round, the only person not laughing at the hilarious clowning of Miss Carol Channing. Knowing I was going to be arrested at London Airport I sat up all night in the plane that took us home, staring at the back of the seat ahead of me.

We passed over Ireland in the dawn. It looked very green and fresh and innocent. If only I'd never left . . .

There were no policemen to meet me at Heathrow. Only my own solicitor. He looked sad. He said, "The Superintendent tells me he won't execute the warrant for your arrest provided that you report at the police station at five forty-five tomorrow morning. I think you should do that," he added, for fear that I might contemplate returning to America. "Your case comes up at ten."

I was early for my appointment. It was just after 5.30 a.m. when the door of the cell slammed behind me.

The copy of *Woman's Mirror* was still there.

It felt as if I hadn't really been away.

The subsequent proceedings were shorter than I'd expected, but at least I had correctly estimated their result.

I wouldn't mind going back to Philadelphia some time, just to see what it's like.

NEW IN NEW YORK

We had stood and shuffled along and stood and shuffled along again for exactly an hour in the immigration hall at Kennedy Airfield while a small, uniformed official with grey cropped hair and a relaxed, smiling manner minutely examined every page of the passports of the people ahead of us. He also read every word of the immigration forms, of the Customs declarations and of the vaccination certificates that were presented to him by the Persians, Greeks, Israelis, Irish, French, German, English and Bessarabian travellers who were united, in a polyglot way, in believing that it ought to be easier to enter the Land of the Free.

After he'd read every word of the documents he then referred to a grey-backed volume, the size of a huge telephone book, which presumably contained the names and descriptions of the thousands of people all over the world whom the F.B.I. considers to be a threat to the American way of life. All we Bessarabians and Greeks and Persians and Irish turned out, however, to be pure. After he'd passed us and we had thanked him he said, "It's my pleasure. Welcome to America." The process had taken seventy-two minutes, during which we had moved ten yards. In the Pan-American plane that had flown us here we would have covered something like 600 miles in the same time.

The Pan-Am hostess who had whipped our baggage through Customs without us even seeing it apologised as though she, personally, had been responsible for the delay. The whole airport, she explained, was being extended to receive the new giants that would be flying by February. In the meantime, the reconstruction work was making things difficult for the present passengers.

Outside our hotel, two hours later, the porter said that rain made things impossible for everyone in New York. "When it rains," he said, "you wanna stay home."

It certainly seemed impossible to get a taxi. An endless succession of enormous yellow cabs lurched past in the downpour, either engaged or with their "Off Duty" signs glowing on the roof. Every doorway on West 44th Street held three or more people, trying to wave them down.

After half an hour of it we phoned our friends in Sutton Place, several miles downtown, to say we couldn't make it. A moment later the infinitely obliging black porter rang us to say that he had a cab. We phoned Sutton Place to say that we were on our way, got into his immense yellow hippopotamus and found that the driver spoke no word of English of any kind. Nor, it seemed, did he know where Sutton Place was, not having heard of it before.

He said something that sounded like, "Thinca pla?" Then he added doubtfully, "Okkay", and drove off.

We turned into Fifth Avenue and started down it, encased in yards of yellow metal, the disproportionately small windows opaque in the streaming rain. On either side of us and for miles ahead and behind were more monstrous limousines and elephantine yellow cabs, covering the surface of the city with never more than two people in each.

At every light there was a traffic jam and every jam was discordant with the hooting mooing of these huge beasts. Then the jam would break and the pachyderms would heave themselves out of the potholes and sunken sewer covers and roll on, still hooting and mooing, to the next one. Shortly afterwards we found we were mooing *up* Madison Avenue, instead of down. I said to the cab driver, speaking very slowly and distinctly, "You—must—ask—the—way—to—Sut—ton Place."

He nodded, without turning round. "Thinca pla," he said, and drove on slowly in the wrong direction.

We became a little desperate. I wound down my window, about to ask the cab driver next to us in the jam, when he shouted fiercely, "Taalk, willya," and drove on before I could. All the beasts behind us mooed, and we too moved on.

We got there in the end, to the cost of about £4 10s., to find our host and hostess in the most beautiful apartment on the 18th floor, with picture windows overlooking the East River and the Elevated Highway. They had their feet up, watching the lights of the hippopotami crawling along. Every minute or two the lights would converge, as two monsters crashed together. Then all the other lights would flow round them, like a river round a rock. Our friends said they watched every evening. It was a pleasant relaxation after work.

This is a city unlike any other I have ever been in.

It's monstrous—and it's absolutely magical at the same time. Or it would be absolutely magical if we could alleviate our hunger with something that tasted of food.

HERBIE AND HIS WHISTLE

A Saturday night dinner party in an elegant clapboard house in Connecticut—the equivalent, perhaps, of Sunningdale, England.

The level of the conversation, however, was louder. So much so that when I wanted the salt I had to lay my head back and bawl for it and even that passed unnoticed, and during the first course, too.

Our American friends were having their weekend unwinding. getting unwound by the usual giant pre-dinner drinks.

Opposite me was a large, genial, sun-tanned man of about fifty, wearing very expensive and tastefully chosen casual clothes. We had already had some chat about golf. I think he'd even asked me to join him any weekend at his cottage in Palm Beach. I could call him Herbie.

It seemed, so far as it was possible to identify the subject in the uproar, that people were talking about Spiro Agnew, and his veiled threats about censoring the Press and the TV newscasters. The voice of our host, an enlightened TV producer, was as audible as any.

Without warning the room was split by a whistle so deafening that it could only have been some mechanical source. Except that it had come from the lips of Herbie, and straight at that. No hands, no fingers. Just a piercing whistle, from between his unusually powerful teeth.

It created a moment of silence, a benefit that hadn't seemed possible a moment before. Herbie filled it instantly, however. "Censorship!" he roared. "It's the silent majority of decent Americans who've been censored. They oughta be called the silenced majority. They've been silenced by the goddam liberals!"

The conversation became general pandemonium again, but I found myself roaring at Herbie, "You've got everything back to front. No liberally minded person ever silenced anyone!"

Herbie killed that stone dead, with his whistle—this mind-blasting sound as alarming as a siren. He glared at me for a moment, making sure that the whistle had had its effect, then he bawled, "I know you. You're one of these goddam, long-haired, effete intellectuals!"

"Thank you," I roared. "A most gracious compliment. I've never been called an intellectual in my life."

Wheeep! It was the most paralysing one yet. Almost before the shattering sound had died Herbie was back in business. At the top of his voice he informed me that there were sixty-two million decent white, Protestant Americans struggling to raise decent families on only fifteen thousand dollars a year, but they were silenced by not being intellectuals and consequently unable to make their plight known. "They can't taaalk," Herbie bawled, "not like you clever guys!"

Then something very strange happened. Herbie, having made his point, whatever it was, suddenly—but really suddenly, instantly—became his old genial self again. He smiled, almost shyly, at me, and took a huge tug at his drink.

I knew what it was like, though I hadn't seen it for years. It was just like Hitler, in the Sport Palast in Munich, taking a breath after a successful paroxysm of screaming.

I was surprised to find myself screaming in turn. "You know what you are?" I shouted at Herbie. "You're a Nazi. A book burner!"

WHEEEP! And then he roared back, "You bet your life I am. And if you start writing any intellectual books and stuff about America I'll make goddam sure that it's all burnt. And there's another thing I'll do for you, buddy boy. A British journalist's a good friend of mine, and he's also a good friend of your boss Roy Thomson and if I give him the word Roy'll see that your ass is shifted out of Fleet Street so quick you won't know which way it went and that, buddy boy, will be the end of you because you'll never work again. . . ."

At this point I felt myself clutched from behind by a hand trying to get inside my shirt. It turned out to be Herbie's wife, a tall, elegant lady swaying a little with a plate of food in her other hand. Oblivious to Herbie, she breathed into my ear, "I just love your English accent." It served to break up the political discussion. Herbie and I did not meet one another's eye for the rest of dinner.

After they had gone our host, the enlightened TV producer, said, a little tightly, "There's a lot of those guys around, but now they're being led from the top, not like Joe MacCarthy, who was out on his own. Herbie makes two hundred thousand dollars a year. He's got weight."

It was quite frightening. So much so that I won't mention the producer's name, nor give Herbie's real one. Just in case. . . .

HAPPY PIE SHOW

The telephone rang in the shoe-box office of this large, shambly literary agent—an elderly woman hung round with beads and gold-rimmed glasses on a chain, a bulging handbag open on the floor beside her, into which she dipped continuously for yet another cork-tipped cigarette.

For the past fifteen minutes or so, without any kind of contract between us, she had been dissuading me from attempting to write for any American magazine, on the grounds that "your English sense of humour just doesn't jell over here, but you all come over thinking you're gonna make a pile of dough."

In fact, Madame and I had been shopping round New York looking for a half-human agent in case there might be some chance of disposing, on the larger market, of some of the reams of stuff I'd already written. This shambly lady was the third that morning.

Now, she relented a little. "Of course," she said, "some of your stuff is just dandy. Real delicate—like Winnie-the-Pooh—"

It was wrung from me. "Winnie the sodding Pooh—!" I cried—and it was at that moment the telephone rang, cutting short further protest.

The lady listened. Her eyes widened. She even removed her cigarette. "That's Mr. Frost?" she breathed. "Mr. *David* Frost? And you wanna speak to *him* . . ."

Madame said briskly, "I'll take that."

The lady actually stood up, awe-stricken. "You sit right down here, my dear," she said to Madame. "Right here—" She handed Madame the telephone, as though it were a silver chalice. Continuing to watch it she placed herself beside me on the excruciatingly uncomfortable guest chair. "Gee," she said, "David Frost, in person, right there on *my* telephone—"

Madame, at the desk, conducted some crisp negotiations. She turned to me. "All right for Frostie Friday night?" she said. I said, "Well, we're not doing anything else, are we?" When we left, the shambly lady came out into the corridor with us and pressed the bell for the lift, observing repeatedly what a great privilege it was to meet, personally, personal friends of Mr. David Frost.

This was in the days when the lad was at the peak of his American output, conducting a chat show that ran five nights a week, on a nation-wide hook-up, at the prime time of 8.30 p.m.—an enterprise of such intensity that it might have confused a computer.

We watched the programme one night before I was due to do my bit and within a couple of minutes had made two discoveries. The first was the difference between Frost in London and Frost in New York.

Here, in New York, there was no trace of the London Grand Inquisitor—the pursuer of Sutro and Savundra, the searcher after truth who had reduced the Archbishop of Canterbury to comparative silence in repeated attempts to get His Grace to define the nature of the Protestant Faith. Here, Frost had turned into a kind of Mid-Atlantic Wilfrid Pickles—a genial, chuckling, happy host putting everyone at their ease, everything very relaxed, almost aimless—until, that is, the purpose of the discursive and innocent chat became clear.

The fact is that everyone who appeared on the Frost show had something to sell. A writer with a new book, an actress with a new play, a comic hoping to break into the big time in Las Vegas—and everyone guaranteed nation-wide publicity.

It was just the thing that Madame, running the business, had been hoping for. I had no American publication to advertise. No word of mine had appeared in an American magazine. "But you get in there with Frostie boy," she said, "and flash that stammer. You never know your luck."

John Berendt, from the show, came to call, to ask what I wanted to talk about. Young, thoughtful, rather serious, and after a couple of minutes obviously doubtful about the potential weight of my contribution. I assured him that David and I had done a lot of chatting together for the B.B.C., and that all might be well.

He rang the following day to say that by chance he'd had to ring Ned Sherrin in London, and that Ned had given him a list of things I might like to talk about. Ned, who had launched me in "Not So Much a Programme . . ." hadn't forgotten where we'd been.

His list read: "First TV performance, with stammer: Telephoning: Irish Navy: *Irish Times*: Cinema and TV writing: Ireland."

Only the first and third items inspired me, as I was already relying on them myself. The rest threw up fragments of half-remembered anecdotes, most of them lacking either the beginning or the end.

On the evening of the recording Madame and I walked rather silently west along 44th Street towards the Little Theatre, just round the corner from Broadway. The Little Theatre was small indeed. Above the entrance the Frost smile beamed from a poster, showing a lot of teeth.

We were shown down a very narrow flight of concrete stairs, into a passageway. Stencilled on the wall were the words, in big letters: BOMB SHELTER. On our left was a low opening. Someone, for safety's sake, had padded the lintel with foam rubber, attached with sticky tape. We entered a big cellar, its size reduced by being divided into a number of hardboard compartments, like loose-boxes. The dark green walls were little more than head high, some way below the level of the roof.

My loose-box contained a large mirror, surrounded by make-up lights, a shelf beneath it, two upright chairs and a small couch. There was also an ashtray, but nothing else. The central heating must have been in the middle eighties.

Madame and I sat there alone for some time. She chatted brightly, as one does to a loved one waiting, in the lobby of the hospital, to be shown to his room, in preparation for a serious operation.

I thought tenderly of Television Centre, Wood Lane, Shepherd's Bush. The smiling commissionaire, saluting. The jolly ladies in Reception, with a warm welcome. Then the Hospitality Centre, the big room with drinks and sandwiches and the other performers. Light badinage, an encouraging word with the producer and the waitress producing another drink, unasked. . . .

We sat there in our roasting loose-box, in this bomb shelter under Broadway, listening to the hip talk and knowing laughter of the band in the box across the aisle.

John Berendt appeared, sat in the remaining chair, and talked

—I think—about the New York theatre. A lively, dark-haired, pretty little girl called Audrey Eisman came in, and sat on the floor. She and Madame had already talked together on the phone. "This job," Miss Eisman said. "When I started it I was tall, blonde and beautiful. Look at me now." Everyone laughed.

I wished I had even one joke to make of that sharp, short, funny, New Yorkerish kind.

Someone else put their head in and said I was wanted in make-up. Coming out of the cubicle was the tallest member of the British group, the Scaffold. "Next for shaving," he said, as much in need of a sharp New Yorkerish joke as myself.

A preoccupied girl wearing her street coat drew two pale lines from my nostrils to the corners of my mouth. With a sponge she painted my face beige, in a couple of seconds, then whipped off the cloth around my neck. "That's it," she said, and disappeared.

At Television Centre, Wood Lane, there's about an hour of colour testing before a show. Make-up girls write notes about your complexion. Sometimes you are asked to change your shirt, tie or jacket because it clashes with someone else. Before you go on the girls are there in the wings to retouch the make-up it has already taken them twenty minutes to put on. And in the stomach there's always a drop of something relaxing and nourishing.

I went back to the loose-box, wondering if the beige paint was dripping on to the collar of my blue shirt.

Peter Baker, Frost's producer, appeared. He used to work for a London daily paper. He was in shirtsleeves, composed but looking grey and exhausted. "You're on in a couple of minutes," he said.

Miss Eisman showed us back up the concrete stairs and into something called the Green Room. There was a small colour TV set and hard cinema seats for about ten or twelve people. It was very cold in here, after the loose-box. The Scaffold were performing on the screen in harsh, primary colours. They got a round of applause when it was announced that one of them, Mike McGear, was Paul McCartney's brother. The band struck up, deafeningly, on the other side of the Green Room wall. Suddenly, I was standing behind the curtain, with the Scaffold coming off. They were followed by David Frost. He grabbed both my hands in both of his. "Lovely to have you," he cried softly. "Great. Splendid. Happy pie show!" It was the first time I had seen him in two years.

I said, hurriedly, "You won't forget the stammer bit—tell them I may not be able to speak. . . ."

"No, no. Lovely. Great. Smashing." He bounded back on stage.

Buttoning my coat, fixing my tie, I was scarcely aware of his introduction : ". . . want you to welcome . . . most welcome visitor . . . writer in his own right . . . therefore a big welcome for . . . Mr. Patrick . . . Campbell. . . . !"

I walked on, briefly aware of a two-tiered audience, a scatter of applause. Then David seized me by the hand again. "Welcome!" he cried, with immense enthusiasm. "Lovely to have you. Great. Smashing. Marvellous. Come and sit down."

We shook hands again several times as he led me to a semi-circular dais. Four swivel chairs in some kind of yellowish, furry moquette. Tomato-red carpet badly worn in front of each chair. We sat down. David said something about the stammer. I began to talk about my arrival in New York, found I'd lost the stammer, and droned on and on. David, hunched in his chair, long legs wound round one another, listening intently, thinking hard how to help me along, to get a laugh from the silent audience. Suddenly, he said, "Right. We'll take a short break right here."

The commercial came on. During it David said again, "Lovely to have you. Smashing. Marvellous. Great." He looked even more exhausted than Peter Baker. On the board on his knee I saw the suggestions made by Ned Sherrin. They had been typed out verbatim.

After some more chat Pat O'Brien came on, the Hollywood star who has played so many Irish priests. A lot of very funny Irish stories, completely professionally done. And a young comedian called Morty Gunty, with stories of his own. Then it was all over.

David came round the back with me and saw Madame waiting there. A kiss on both cheeks. "Lovely to see you again. Great. Marvellous. Happy pie show!" He was gone.

Madame and I walked back together, along West 44th Street. A drunk with cropped hair and a face beaten into a pulp came lurching up to her. I stepped between them. He cowered away. He'd been hit enough already. He went lurching off up Broadway. His tattered mackintosh was split from the collar at the back, all the way down.

There and then, amid the blazing signs of the Great White Way, remembering the evening and watching the back of the poor, battered drunk, I saw what a struggle it must be to fight your way to the top in the raucous, tender, ruthless and yet incredibly buoyant City of New York.

FAT TUESDAY TAILS

"Dat man tink he gonna see de p'rade sittin' in dat caw. Lawdy, lawdy. Dat man sittin' in dat caw ain't gonna see no p'rade, no, *suh!*"

His tone had been censorious, but suddenly he laughed, for no apparent reason. "He-he-he-he-he." It was a parody of Ole Black Joe. Or, perhaps, just his natural laugh.

We sat in the back of his huge, battered old taxi in our London clothes, hemmed in by thousands of bedraggled young people in the French Quarter of New Orleans. Nearly all of them were drinking from bottles or beer cans. Whenever we moved ahead a foot or two a bunch of them jumped on to the boot of the car, weighing it down.

The grey-haired old taxi driver seemed hardly to mind. "Dose hippies," he said placidly. "Dey come in all ovah de town. Stoodents. Lawdy, lawdy." Suddenly, he did his giggle again. "He he-he-he."

By our time it was five o'clock in the morning. We'd been travelling since shortly after midday, whistling through the air in the unimaginable comfort of Pan American's flying hotel, the 747, drinking champagne cocktails, looking at films, conquering the world at 600 m.p.h. in two capacious armchairs, speeding off to Mardi Gras in New Orleans. And now we were stuck right in the middle of it, and had been for two hours, crawling round and round the Vieux Carré, trying to get to the Royal Orleans Hotel, wherever that might be.

Madame said, fairly tartly, "Have you any idea how much longer this is going to be?"

The old man giggled again. "Don' yoh worry, ma'am. Ah git yoh dere. Yes, ma'am. Ah git yoh dere good. Yes, suh."

The South, seeming to be a parody of itself, had been creeping up on us all day. We'd landed at Washington, gone through Customs and got back into the Pan Am drawing-room that had swept us so effortlessly from London. But now it had been taken over by Delta Airlines, for the trip to Atlanta, Georgia, and the Delta girls were dressed in trouser suits, each one different to the other. A very pretty dark girl, with ribbons in her hair, said, "Yawl want somethin' to drink?"

Everyone was yawling in the airport at Atlanta. All in shirt sleeves and summer dresses, unburdened by luggage, because Americans use aeroplanes like buses. When we landed at New

Orleans an elegantly dressed woman handed the man she had come to meet a large dry Martini across the barrier. Mardi Gras had begun. And now it looked as if we were going to spend it in the back of this ancient taxi, or at least until such time as "dose hippies" fell down or went to bed.

The sign said we were on Bourbon Street. Through the long hair and the jeans and the old army jackets we saw that the doors of the strip joints were wide open, with the girls bumping and grinding away inside. I knew I was the only man in New Orleans wearing a collar and tie. We were halted outside The Absinthe House—people pouring drink over one another inside and on the pavement. We'd never felt so far from home.

Two hours and forty-five minutes after leaving the airport—a matter of fifteen miles—we crawled into the garage at the back of the Royal Orleans. It was filled with huge American cars trying to get out, past an encampment of hippies monitored by police. Handfuls of dollars to the taxi driver, garage attendants and two hotel porters, and then up to the reception desk with our luggage miraculously intact. At eleven o'clock at night the foyer was swarming with people, hippies mixed up with elderly matrons and huge men from some golfing society wearing green peaked caps, all of them with a glass in their hand.

The wonder-working Pan Am people had booked us a room from London, No. 626. I opened the door and found the room strewn with other people's clothes—after eighteen hours of continuous travel. Madame poured a stream of machine-gun fire down the telephone. A porter appeared with the right key, No. 624. Huge, beautiful room in soft green and white. I opened the curtains. On the other side of Royal Street was a balcony, decorated with streamers and tinsel round the exquisite iron trellises. The balcony was occuplied by a demented female figure in fancy dress, pouring drink into the throats of the hippies below and with the other hand waving a flag made of gold lamé.

I drew the curtains again. Circumspectly, we went to bed, after brushing our teeth and very nearly saying our prayers.

Two days later, against every conceivable law of probability, I found myself standing on the corner of Camp and Common, in the city of New Orleans, preparing to enter the premises of Joe "Fit 'em All" Gemelli for the purpose of hiring not only white tie and tails, but also white gloves, for the celebration of Mardi Gras the following night.

Right there on the corner of Camp Street and Common Street, where I belonged.

Moiphy, an almost square man with a red face, white hair and an electric-blue suit, had everything ready for me, concealed in a long brown paper bag, having taken my measurements earlier in the day. I said to Moiphy, "May I try on the coat?" He seemed surprised. "Surely," he said, "but that's your suit." He provided a further explanation. "Come from the warehouse," he said. "That's it. Nineteen dollars fifty."

There was no time for further discussion, or to change the thing if it didn't fit, because it was already 4.15 and at 6.30 we were expected to attend a cocktail party at the Boston Club in *full evening dress*. As a preliminary to the fabled delirium tremens of Mardi Gras, when a whole city goes mad in the hysteria of licensed debauchery.

Holding up my long paper bag of goodies to keep them out of the mud, I pushed my way through the swarming crowds that had already blocked the old French Quarter for the past three days and nights. Thousands of furry young men and women, nearly all of them with emerald-green glass bottles, wrapped in newspaper, of Boone's Farm Wild Grape Wine, from which they drank as they walked and threw away when they were empty, spreading everywere a carpet of broken glass. They seemed mostly to be students, rather than genuine hippies, and appeared to be harmless, except that their numbers made it impossible to find a taxi in the Vieux Carré. We'd already found out that if we wanted to get anywhere we walked—even, as was shortly to happen, if you were wearing white tie and tails, and white gloves. Through the licensed debauchery of Mardi Gras.

In our room in the Royal Orleans Hotel, right in the middle of the old town, and almost next door to Antoine's famous restaurant, Madame was about halfway advanced towards getting into her ballgown—at 4.45 on a sunny afternoon, with the screams and yells of Mardi Gras, the crashing of breaking glass, the shrilling of police whistles, going on immediately outside our window.

"I will not," she said as I came in, "repeat not, wear long white gloves for a cocktail party, even for the Boston Club."

I opened my parcel, to examine the potential deathtrap of a hired boiled-shirt, and found that Moiphy had given me a soft-fronted, piqué article, with collar attached, but of a kind I had not imagined could exist. The collar was simply a soft circle of material, about an inch high, with the wings forming part of the same bandage. The white tie was a made-up one, with a large tin buckle.

We fingered it, in turn. With this lot on I was going to look, if anything, like a Pakistani night-cleaner at London airport—in the hallowed premises of the Boston Club, Canal Street, New Orleans.

"That," I said, "is me, for Mardi Gras. You could try not to look."

There was, indeed, no other way out. We had become totally enmeshed in deep southern hospitality, but of the most exclusive and aristocratic kind, through the extreme thoughtfulness and generosity of a man we didn't know.

Before leaving France we'd met an American at a lunch party, mentioned we were going to Mardi Gras, and that did it. On his return to Philadelphia he'd rung a neighbour of his, who knew a lot of people in New Orleans. The neighbour got in touch with them immediately, with the result that on our arrival I found I was a temporary member of the Boston Club and the New Orleans Country Club, that we had invitations to cocktail parties and grand balls that resident millionaires would have given their right arms for, and that furthermore Mayor Moon Landrieu had conferred upon me Honorary Citizenship of the Crescent City, made official by a gold paper stamp.

We had a look at the Honorary Citizen, in his costume. The points of the tailcoat stuck straight out from the body. The top of the trousers appeared above the V of the white waistcoat, while its points extended far below the points of the coat. Even with the braces braced up to kill there were folds of trouser above the shoes.

The back of the neck was indescribable, the bandage-like collar being invisible beneath the straps and buckles of the white waistcoat, and the straps and buckles of the white tie.

I tried on the white gloves. They reached halfway up the backs of my hands, and looked not unlike mittens. I took them off.

"All right," I said. "Let's go."

Mardi Gras was beginning to swing on Royal Street, as Boone's Farm Wild Grape Wine took hold. Drunks lurched into puddles left by the recent rain and fell down on the broken glass. People threw bottles from the beautiful iron trellis-work balconies. Blue-helmeted police prowled about, swinging heavy nightsticks. A youth with a red blanket over his head lifted it repeatedly to cry, "Howl! Howl!"

Through this lot Madame, in a fur coat, long silk dress and silvery shoes, picked her way tensely, trying to avoid the mud, the beer cans and the broken glass, followed by her escort, whom most of the revellers seemed to take for some kind of clown figure, for he was accosted by none.

After perhaps half an hour of this march we reached the heavily guarded doors of the Boston Club, showed our passes and were allowed in.

(It is worth noting, as evidence of the exclusive nature of the club, that a wealthy and cultured Frenchman has been refused membership, for ever, on the grounds that he is a distant relative of the late "Tiger" Clemenceau, whom the old French families in New Orleans hold to have been disloyal to *La Belle France*.)

The Honorary Citizen and his Doxie, however, were welcomed with open arms, thanks to the good offices of the man we'd never met in Philadelphia, and all the infinitely kind people he'd contacted on our behalf in New Orleans.

We'd already met three or four hundred of them the previous day at the Country Club, where the Sunday Sinners had given an immense cocktail party in surroundings straight out of a film set. Colonial mansion, huge trees, unexpendable wealth and another Bloody Mary every five minutes. A Dixieland band of ancient coloured musicians made conversation almost impossible. Some of the Sinners began to dance in the enormous entrance hall. A white-haired matron, plunging about without reference to the music, cried out "Ah just adore that niggah jazz!"

A black barman, with an impassive face, poured Bloody Marys from a jug until the tomato juice overflowed and soaked the white tablecloth, dripping on to the floor.

Lunch was served, for 500 people, but it was really more like breakfast. Scrambled egg, hominy grits, sausage and bacon, buns and waffles accompanied, after all those Bloody Marys, by iced water and coffee.

Now, in the Boston Club, we met many of the Sinners all over again, and the friends of their friends and the Queen and the Maids at the court of Rex. The Queen, a shy girl with dark eyes and a longish nose, and the Maids were indistinguishable from English debs. I asked one of the saucier looking Maids how the Queen had been selected. Fairly tartly, she replied :

"Our Father which art in commerce."

By now we'd almost begun to understand the real heart and core of Mardi Gras, as the Boston Club sees it.

It has nothing whatever to do with broken glass, pot puffing, drag queens and free love in the streets. Rather it is an entertainment only fractionally more *louche* than a Buckingham Palace garden party.

It began in earnest in 1857, with the birth of "the Mistick Krewe of Comus", and, in quick succession, of Rex, Momus, Proteus,

Hermes, Pandora, Mokana and so on. They are all exclusive men's clubs, some much more exclusive than others. The word "Krewe" is pure invention, and "Mistick" covers the secrecy which surrounds all of them.

Every year a leading citizen is secretly selected to be Rex, King of Carnival by the Captain and his secret committee. The privilege is said to cost Rex only about $2000, contrary to popular belief. His identity is announced only at the last moment. On Fat Tuesday he emerges from his den at about ten o'clock in the morning and on his Royal Float leads a four-hour, six-mile procession through the city, pausing at the Boston Club, where his Queen awaits him on the gallery.

Just below Rex, in the colour cards, is Comus, who also gives a ball on the night of Fat Tuesday. The whole thing culminates in the cavernous Auditorium, where the courts of Comus and Rex are joined, on the last night of Mardi Gras.

For some people it cannot come too soon, because the carnival balls begin on 17th December, and carry on right through until 15th February. The parades, disrupting the city almost in its entirety, begin on 23rd January, and continue until Mardi Gras. And long before all this even begins the next year's carnival is being organised.

It is a season which is undoubtedly more fun for the chaps than for the girls. Indeed, some of the girls we met in the Boston Club, which is rigorously barred to them for the rest of the year, were almost impolite about the goings-on.

It seemed that after this white-tie cocktail party we had been invited to the Ball of Proteus, as exclusive as the grand balls of Comus and Rex, to which we had also been bidden. One woman, hearing of this, said to Madame, "My, honey, you've sure got it made." Not all of them, however, were as envious.

One lady, of sophisticated French extraction, said to us:

"You're gonna go to Proteus? You'll get your ass bored off. And you're gonna get your ass bored off again tomorrow night at Rex. If I were you I'd take a bottle of Scotch in bed."

We were about to take her advice when I was approached by a gentleman who said he'd just heard I came from Dublin, and might be interested to know that though he was a Catholic, he was a member of the once rigidly Protestant Kildare Street Club, in that very city.

That took up some reminiscent exchanges, so that it was almost midnight by the time we'd battled our way back to the Royal Orleans, through the increasingly delirious crowds. The police had put up steel barricades along the pavements, jamming the people against the shop windows. They stalked up and down the streets, piercingly blowing their whistles at the more abandoned revellers, who blew plastic horns back.

It looked as though another parade was on the way. We'd just got into bed when it started. Shouts, yells, whistles, sirens, brass bands, jazz bands, motorbikes with blaring exhausts, and all the time the juddery sound of breaking glass.

I watched it from the window for a long time. Floats twenty-five feet long and two storeys high representing Cyclops, Frankenstein, Medusa and other laughter-makers, and the people on floats throwing beads and other trophies to the clutching hands of the crowds, fighting one another for them. When I went back to bed, as the uproar died away about 3.00 a.m., I was glad of the protocol of the Boston Club, which had kept us off the streets, for one night, at least. It looked like being a long haul tomorrow.

We clocked in again at the Club, in immaculate business suits and fur coats, the following morning at about 11.30. The litter on Royal Street was perceptibly higher, the furry young people momentarily defeated by exhaustion. But a drag queen was having a splendid time on the corner of Bourbon, in bright sunshine, a spangled bikini and a towering headdress, daring anyone to pluck a feather from it. Sobriety was not present.

Things were steadier in the Club, with what looked like the same Dixieland band from the Country Club once again playing for dancing. Madame and I armed ourselves with a Boston Club Punch, which felt like neat 100-proof Bourbon, and went out on to the balcony to get a good place from which to watch the parade.

A fireman checked us at the door. It appeared that no liquor was allowed on the gallery, that Madame had to take a seat, that I had to stand at the back with the other gennelmen *after* I'd put out my cigarette, and that the premises had to be vacated by 3.00 p.m.

On Canal Street, down below, what was afterwards calculated to be more than a million people raved and grooved and drank and hugged one another, smoking cigars and cigarettes and pot, while we sexless, drinkless and smoking aristos surveyed the scene with interested smiles. The rabble enjoyed another bonus. Today being the day of Mardi Gras they were allowed to wear masks and costumes in the street, such folly being illegal up till now.

The parade began with a selection of police squad cars, six Rex lieutenants on horseback, masked and in full costume, followed by the Ross Volunteer Company, Texas University, a military drill team that did things with rifles that would have earned them life in the glasshouse at Pirbright.

Then we had the Pennsylvania Military College band, followed by the Captain on horseback in gold and amber. He is responsible for the whole parade and his name is never mentioned, possibly not even by his wife.

Six more Rex lieutenants and then the King of Carnival himself, a distinguished lawyer called Leon Sarpy on a golden float, heavily made up and wearing a golden crown, wig, beard and whiskers. He made regal gestures to the crowd, waving the sceptre in slow motion, moving the other arm horizontally, bent at the elbow.

He stopped in front of the Boston Club stand, to give flowers to the Queen and to his real wife, and a short address over the microphone, inaudible to the gennelmen standing at the back. Then he moved on his floating throne on up Canal Street, making the same regal gestures as before.

(The next day the local paper, the *Times-Picayune*, was to record the fact that "He was stared at by gleaming eyes and hoarse voices yelled greetings his way", and that, furthermore, after a good night's sleep, he had "a light breakfast consisting of a soft-boiled egg, one piece of toast and two fingers of milk". It isn't all Bloody Marys and Mint Juleps, being a King.)

After the royal float came his Majesty's own band wagon playing Rex's National Anthem, "If ever I cease to love". Then a huge, papier-mâché cow, the Boeuf Gras, pronounced burr-grah, surrounded by masked cooks who flung glass beads and silver dollar-sized doubloons into the crowd, who fought for them like wolves.

These doubloons, in gold-finish for Rex, silver for Proteus, and so on, are specially minted every year, at the estimated cost of more than a million dollars.

The maskers on the Rex floats distributed 500,000 of them this year, many of them straight into the faces of the ladies on the Boston Club gallery, with heavier shot in the form of glass beads to follow. A number of picture hats were unbalanced as the ladies struggled for them among themselves.

The beads and the doubloons are as much part of Mardi Gras as the white ties and the tails. The throwing of them symbolises the break-down of all class distinction, and adds greatly to the merriment.

After the Burr-grah came another military marching group from the University of Florida, followed by the first float to demonstrate the theme of the parade, "A Tribute to Jules Verne". After that came the Rice Owl Band from Houston, Texas and then an enormous papier-mâché submarine, none other than Captain Nemo's *Nautilus*.

From this erupted a doubloon that, threading its way through the ladies in front, completed its journey by striking me on the forehead. Unobtrusively, I retired into the club premises again, to the punch counter, to emerge at intervals to watch the Tulane University Pershing Rifle Drill Team, the Biloxi High Indian Band and various giant figures in further celebration of the clairvoyancy of Jules Verne.

Some considerable time later the parade was wound up by His Majesty's Royal Calliope, featuring on top of it a jazz band known as Sharkey's Combo. Madame, smoking like a furnace and dehydrated to the very soul, arrived at speed at the Club punch counter, where I had two lined up for her, the very least I could do.

We had lunch in an almost empty restaurant on Royal, with a lot of not bad Californian Burgundy, while the crowds had hot dogs and wild grape wine in the street outside.

After a prostrate afternoon in bed we began to get dressed again, for the Grand Ball of Comus in the Auditorium, due to begin promptly at eight of the clock. The Auditorium is an immense grey building resembling a railway station, and is not widely admired.

My dress shirt, white tie and waistcoat now looked more like discarded bandages than ever. Madame, slipping into a Norman Hartnell number—*for Mardi Gras!*—said, "A lady friend in the galley told me that the Dook and Duchess of Windsor attended the Carnival some years ago and, just like you, the Dook didn't bring his tails. The sleeves of the coat they found him only just covered his elbows, so you ought to be laughing."

I pulled on my mittens and looked sombrely at the Pakistani night-cleaner in the mirror. "Come on, honey chile," I said. "Yawl is fixed to go to de bawl?"

The previously elegant lobby of the Royal Orleans was blocked off with wooden barricades and armed police twirling their night-sticks. There were a lot of young furries and people dressed as chimpanzees and so on, including a nun in a see-through habit with a glass of bourbon in either hand, doing a rudimentary can-can. But, of course, no taxis, and we had about a mile to walk.

I shouted at the reception desk, the cash desk, the three doormen and all the porters. "No, suh," they said. "There's no way . . ." For a moment I thought of tearing off my bandages and melting away into the Carnival, but we had too many obligations. A taxi appeared. I ran round the back of it and grabbed the driver by the arm. "The Auditorium!"

"De Auditorium! No *suh.* Dere's no way."

"Ten dollars."

"Foh ten dollahs, suh, I take you to de moon."

All the way there the crowds leant against the radiator and sat on the boot. They were perfectly good-humoured and not very drunk, but they made an impassable barrier. We arrived at the Auditorium twenty minutes late, clutching our sheaves of tickets and invitations, and were prevented from rushing into the Comus ball, in place of the Rex, only by a last-minute inspiration upon the part of Madame, in her long white gloves, who found the right door, thereby probably saving us from being black-balled by the Boston Club.

We entered together, and were instantly separated for the next four hours. Three charming ladies fell upon Madame and bore her away to the ballroom, while a lithe young gentleman took charge of me, herding me firmly downstairs.

I had no idea whatever of what was going on. We entered an enormous locker-room filled with men removing their white ties and tails and robing themselves in spangled plus-fours, glittering jackets, caps and masks, attended by old coloured valets with bourbon in paper cups, in preparation for whatever arcane ceremonial was about to take place above.

It turned out that these gentlemen were called the Maskers. I was introduced, by my keeper, to dozens of them, many of them already wearing their bland, blank, pink, slightly smiling masks, all identical. Another glass of bourbon came with each introduction.

The writing began to appear, in large, day-glo letters, on the wall. I begged my keeper to allow me to rejoin my wife, on the grounds that a certain unsteadiness was developing that might be relieved by dancing, or even sitting down without a glass in my hand. The young man said he would escort me there at the appropriate time.

I have a frank confession to make. The Honorary Citizen of the Crescent City of New Orleans became, in that immense locker-room, ineradicably stewed, wandering between the blank, masked faces with a paper cup in his hand, like a moth-eaten tiger caged in a zoo. He also got hold of a joke. "It's the Wrecks' Ball," he told the blank faces. "Not the Rex. Let m'spill it . . . spell it . . . out foh yawl!"

Even the masked faces seemed to take on a look of disapproval. There was a perceptible drawing away from the infected area, which briefly included my keeper. I found refuge behind a locker for a while, sitting on a shoe-box with a nice old valet called Jackson, who had a bottle of Scotch of his own, or his master's. Neither of us were able to venture upon the labour of speech.

Four hours after my imprisonment in the locker-room my keeper assisted me back to the Ball. In the meantime someone had nailed a large, live magnolia to one lapel, and a bunch of coloured ribbons to the other.

We entered the ballroom. I was aware of an immense stage brilliantly lit and covered with slowly moving figures in fancy dress. I thought I heard a piercing English voice remark, "My dear, Gala Night at Fred Pontin's," but was unable to track down the source. Then, for the first time in four hours, I came up against Madame.

She took one look at the thing before her, wrapped in dingy piqué, bedizened with flowers and ribbons, and said, "Oh dear. Well, I suppose it was bound to happen."

She had not been so fortunate. What had happened to her was this. At the very heart of the crazy wine-sodden festival of Mardi Gras, in company with hundreds of other ladies, all caparisoned like medieval chargers, she had sat in the same seat for four hours. She had had one drink, in that time, in a Ladies Only bar. She had not been permitted to smoke. She was compelled to wear her long white gloves. She had danced five times, having been "called out".

I said, "Whassa?"

"The ladies," she replied precisely, "are referred to as Call-outs. The Maskers, on the ballroom floor, apply to the ushers, who are known as Blackcoats, to call-out the lady of their choice. The Blackcoats pass the message to the lady and she takes one turn round the floor, before being returned to her seat. The Masker then gives her a present from his reticule. I got a shiny, chalice thing, some doubloons, a bookmarker, a memo holder and a mirror. That poor girl on the other side of the aisle sat there the whole night without being called-out *once*."

"I'll call her up—out . . ."

"Even if you could you're not allowed to. Not yet. Not until the courts of Rex and Comus are joined, which ought to happen any minute now, I hope." She measured her words with care. "The last time I ate, that food passed my lips, was at 2.15 this afternoon. It is now 12.35 a.m. You didn't happen to fall over a sandwich down below, did you?"

"Not a crumb . . ."

"And," she said, "there is one other thing. No lady can go to the lavatory without being escorted by a Blackcoat, and I don't know a Blackcoat sufficiently well."

"Gaw . . ."

At that moment there was a clarion note on some instrument or other and hundreds of the figures in fancy dress began manoeuvring in slow motion across the ballroom floor.

It was the peak moment of Mardi Gras, the joining of the court of Rex and his Queen, and all his Dukes, maids, pages, and officers, with the court of Comus and his Queen and all his similar supernumeraries. It was a lengthy business, with Rex bowing to Comus, the Queens bowing to one another, and the dukes and everybody else doing ditto.

"I curtsied to the Queen," Madame said, "about twelve hours ago. When I got back to my seat a lady said, 'That must put yawl just exactly in mind of your Palace of Buckingham.' "

"Cor."

It must have been round about 1.30 a.m. when the welding of the two courts came to an end, and for the first time the ballroom floor became available to non-Maskers and non-Blackcoats. I was making for it somewhat uncertainly in the wake of Madame when a courteous Blackcoat stepped in front of me. "D'yawl mind putting on your gloves?" he said.

I pulled out two crushed paper-cups from my trouser pocket, and my mittens, put them on, got a grip on Mr. Hartnell's creation, and sketched in some of the rudimentary outlines of a rhumba, out of deference to Mardi Gras.

Madame said, "I think everyone else is waltzing. I know I am. Cinderella, I believe you've had this Ball."

We found someone who drove us part of the way back to the hotel. We walked the rest, through the weaving drunks and the mountainous litter of the remnants of Mardi Gras. Already, mechanical shovels were sweeping up the beer cans, the broken beads, fragments of clothing and ton after ton of shattered green glass.

Next morning, we saw in the *Times-Picayune* that out of the million-odd people who had gone mad the previous night only thirty of them had been arrested, two for obscene behavour.

"They were lucky," said Madame pleasantly, "to have found the opportunity."

In the city itself, that day, it was pleasantly warm, the sky was an innocent baby-blue, with fluffy cloud accessories, and here and there people were walking to work in an abstracted manner, bearing on their foreheads the penitential mark of Ash Wednesday.

Apart from the green sheen of powdered glass in the gutters—the remnants of the tons that the Sanitation Department had shifted during the night—there was no sign that the whole city had been given over to debauch the night before.

Not that the debauch is all that debauched, in comparison, say, with Piccadilly Circus on the night of the Cup Final, or the pubs of Dublin after Ireland has beaten England at Landsdowne Road. The hundreds of thousands of young people, who come wandering into New Orleans for the occasion from all over the United States, are certainly responsible for damping down the potential excesses of their elders, simply by the sheer weight of their passive numbers.

A reveller who's been thrown out of The Absinthe House, by his friends rather than by the management, and who wishes to get going again in Wanda's Bar, will have an hour-long struggle to get there, through hordes of teenagers rather damply chanting, "Peace—and Love".

The Deep Southern traditionalists think the police should keep them out of town, an impossible task. The hotel proprietors think so, too, complaining that their bookings were badly affected this year by the paying customer's fear of hippie rioting. The Mardi Gras conservationists, emotional and financial, have another worry—the increasing popularity of the Mistick Krewe of Bacchus.

This club, one of the sixty-five that provide parades, elects as its King not a local dignitary but someone rather more glamorous from Show Biz. This year it was Phil Harris, the comedian, with the result that the Bacchus Parade was the gayest and furthest-out of the lot. Too much of this, the traditionalists feel, might possibly lead in years to come to the slow disappearance of the Grand Balls, the white ties, tails and tiaras.

It's as though the older and richer people feel that if Mardi Gras were to die, or even become changed in any way, the city of New Orleans would die with it. The young businessmen, on the other hand, maintain that Mardi Gras itself is killing New Orleans: "You can't find a top executive in his office more than an hour a day three months before the damn thing begins, and you see two million dollars thrown away in the streets."

It's a curious thing to find so much dissension behind the fabled abandon of Mardi Gras, and specially in a city so beautiful, so softly self-indulgent as New Orleans, at least as far as the old French Quarter is concerned.

The day begins for a lot of the inhabitants with breakfast in Brennan's, a two-storey pink house with a trellised balcony and a big, leafy patio at the back. For breakfast, the first course is called

"An Eyeopener", either a Bloody Mary, or a Sazerac, which is made with bourbon and "a little mystery", after the glass has been coated with absinthe. For breakfast.

If you wish to lunch or dine in Antoine's, one of the world's most famous restaurants, do nothing as vulgar as ringing up to book a table. Proceed up the side-alley, ask for your own waiter, and he will lead you to the table of your choice.

In the Garden District there are exquisite, pre-Civil War houses, colonnaded and imposing, separated from neighbours by a narrow path, because dry land is scarce in soggy New Orleans, where the water is so close to the surface that the citizens are buried in vaults above the ground. When it rains, as it does, torrentially, the water must be pumped out into Lake Pontchartrain. And the Mississippi, 140 fet deep and the colour of pale tomato soup, wanders in great sweeps throughout the city, held in by embankments twenty-five high.

The inhabitants have a method of dealing with the damp. When making a tour of the city you leave each house with a "walker" in your hand, a disposable plastic glass of whisky. In many of the cars there are fittings to hold the passengers' "walkers" and, naturally, the driver's as well.

When I told one young man about the breathalyser test in Britain he said, "I guess yawl is real backward ovah theyah."

In a Common Market Garden

SOFTLEE SOFTLEE

There are nine people—four more than last week—living in two houses, but all eating in one, at least twice a day.

There are three cars, but everyone wants to avoid the third one in which hens or something equally feathery have been in residence.

The drive down to the village takes about five minutes—or a quarter of an hour of rather tight-lipped backing and advancing if the other two cars are coming up because the road takes only one car at a time, and is full of hairpin bends.

Under these circumstances the prudent guest abides by the old adage, "Softlee softlee watchee position".

It is dangerously easy to earn a black mark.

One might, for instance, come down the hill from the non-eating house, having overslept, at the foully self-indulgent hour of 10 a.m., and slide into the kitchen in search of coffee only to find five virtuous persons in there who have already breakfasted and are now nobly preparing lunch. The wise thing to do is settle for a glass of water in the cloakroom, meticulously drying the basin after use in case someone else has just spent twenty minutes cleaning it. After that one should retire to the furthest corner of the olive orchard and quietly gather kindling wood for the evening fire until the crime of looking for coffee at 10 a.m. has been pardoned or forgotten.

Volunteering to perform services for others can run one head-on into sin.

A., for example, might have to go to Grasse to collect some laundry and asks if there is anything he can do for anyone while he's there. There turns out to be five separate commissions he can perform. There is a spare wheel to be collected. A new dustpan is required. There may be, at long last, some fish in the fish-shop in Pré du Lac. Someone else wants three postcards carefully chosen, not the usual local views. The fifth task is to change some hand lotion which the owner thinks was purchased in the chemist's beside the car-park, though it might also have been in the Monoprix.

A., who thought he was going to get a good mark for making the offer and then merely collect his own laundry, jibs. He doesn't, for a start, know the French for dustpan, while the hand lotion business is clearly beyond anyone's powers to negotiate, particularly as the lotion owner apparently doesn't even know what kind of lotion she would prefer to the existing one, always provided she could find the shop in which she'd made the original purchase. Why doesn't she come with him and buy her own cursed lotion?

The lady says she is perfectly prepared to do this, if he is genuinely incapable, but she refuses to travel in the hen feathered car, particularly as someone—and she has a pretty good idea who it was—has removed the clothes-brush from her room without—she mentions it only in passing—having asked her permission. She is prepared to go in the big car, or not at all.

Someone suggests that if the big car is going it might just as well go on down to Cannes, having collected the spare wheel in Grasse, because there is always fish in the Cannes Monoprix, and he's damned if he can face another beef stew tonight.

A voice suggests that he might, perhaps, like to take over the catering just for one day, in that buying two meals for nine people, preparing and cooking them, might provide an interesting break in his normal routine of sitting with his feet up on the table drinking pastis while other people are chopping their fingers to the bone on his behalf.

The victim, thus attacked, says that he tried on five separate occasions yesterday evening to get into the kichen, to get the cutlery box and lay the table, but was unable to do so because there were seven people in there already, five of whom were perceptibly doing nothing whatever.

In the middle of the ensuing discussion the ninth member of the party staggers in from the olive grove, ostentatiously bent double under the weight of a basket of wood which he has been gallantly chopping with the axe personally purchased by himself while everyone else—he has just noticed—has been finishing off the crate of white wine which he personally collected from the *Alimentation* only that very morning.

A piercing cry from the hostess interrupts this complaint. Would he kindly look at the tiles which she has only just finished polishing, working like a slave on her hands and knees! They are now covered with mud. The wood chopper puts down the basket. Chips and shavings burst out of it. Someone, seeing a good mark coming up, rushes for the brush but it's disappeared. Some thoughtless person has left it in the other house . . .

But the sun shines on and on and the blessed silence of the mountains is broken only by the tinkling of the sheep bells among the olive trees.

Softlee softlee watchee position, because this is the place to be.

A BASH AT THE BULLETIN

The blackboard in the kitchen was originally started as a method of warning helpful people that certain jobs had already been done, and was of special benefit to the nervous system in the early mornings when superfluous questions tend to rile.

Messages used to appear like, "Yes, I have already refilled both oil stoves and brought up more wood from the cellar, and I know that more paraffin is required." Or, "Kindly do not inquire if I'm having orange juice because I've already had it, and yours is in the fridge."

It developed from there into setting out plans for the day which might not be immediately acceptable to everyone and should therefore be studied in silence and without argument. An example of this genre was, "I am going to Cannes at 8 o'clock this morning to collect the trunk. This means that four people may accompany me there, but owing to the size of the trunk only one can come back. Kindly make your arrangements in accordance with these indestructible facts."

As the blackboard was comparatively small it had to be allowed that the early risers got a disproportionate amount of space so that, with a large number of people in the house, the system soon began to fall into disrepute. One morning, for instance, I wrote, "There is absolutely no point in leaving this house at 11 o'clock with the intention of visiting the Matisse chapel, cashing some travellers' cheques, buying a present for your mother and getting something for lunch because everything in France shuts from midday until 2.30 p.m. The last hour for departure, to execute such commissions, is 9.30 a.m." The next time I looked at the board someone had written under this helpful injunction, "HITLER GO HOME", disguising his or her handwriting with capital letters. Subsequent oblique questioning of the other members of the household failed to establish the identity of the malcontent.

After that I left out advice, confining myself merely to writing down things required for the commissariat, until last Monday morning, two days before our return to London. Suddenly, with only two days to go, there were so many things to do that only a master-plan could deal with them. Having woken at 5.30 a.m. I got to work on it alone, before argument and counter-suggestion could break out, and by 7 o'clock I'd completed it to my entire satisfaction.

I wrote it down on the bulletin board, using handwriting as small as possible, to get it all in. The master-plan went as follows:

"Leave here 7.30 a.m. with trunk for Cannes station and three empty paraffin tins to be returned to shop en route in Grasse. This means only one passenger possible. After tins and trunk dealt with buy padlock and chain in Cannes for garage door. On way back book taxi in village and arrange with garage to take car battery . . ."

There was a great deal more of it, involving a brilliantly designed swoop on the pottery shop in Vallauris, for last-minute present buying, on the way to leaving one of the party at Nice Airport, on their way to Rome. It carried me down to the bottom of the blackboard, where I wrote "P.T.O.", preparatory to setting out the arrangements for calling on the builder in Valbonne to see what he was going to do about the septic tank, whilst incorporating in the circuit the delivery of a rubber-plant in a neighbouring village—a Christmas present which had been overlooked in the general rush.

By now it was approaching 7.45, so I decided to nip down to the *Alimentation* in the village to get bread and cheese for lunch, putting that matter safely out of the way.

When I got back one of the ladies was drinking tea in the kitchen in a trance-like, semi-conscious state which belied the report given to me by her husband that, "She's not only up and dressed—she is also awake."

She looked at me with hooded eyes as I greeted her, and went back into her cup of tea. I took down the bulletin board, to get on with my P.T.O. on the other side and saw that someone had written "Hair 10.30" right across it.

The beginnings of fear began to establish themselves. "Did you do that?" I asked her. "Is that your hair?"

She nearly turned herself inside out with a yawn. "It was all written on," she murmured, more than half asleep, "on the other side."

"What do you mean—'Hair ten-thirty'?"

"Having it done," she said, "ten-thirty in Nice."

"But you can't possibly. I've got to get the trunk to Cannes and the paraffin tins to Grasse—"

The lady came awake with a snap. "Oh, yes I can," she said crisply. "You don't think I'm going to go back to London like this."

The heat of the discussion roused the other two ladies, who

reported equally crisply that they, too, were going to have their hair done in precisely the same salon, and at the same time, and that I would kindly wait for them and drive them back for lunch.

I wiped out the master-plan with a sponge and in place of it wrote a single word the shadow of which will undoubtedly remain upon the bulletin board for some years to come.

ROUND AND ROUND THE POMPA

When friends have had the energy, the imagination and the currency to transform a ruined farmhouse in the South of France into a charming and almost inhabitable little villa, this is the time for other friends to gather round them, thereby avoiding hotel bills, and to put the final polish on their dream.

There is, in fact, nothing that one friend will not do for another, provided that the party of the second part is the owner of a villa in these marvellous mountains, removed by twenty minutes from the now totally demented bedlam of the coast road and by a million decibels of noise.

All that we hear in our village is the urgent chirruping of crickets and the equally urgent scratching of paintbrushes against cement. There is also from time to time passionate discussion between the contractor, the plumber and the electrician who come boiling up the mountain in their vans and spring out of them denouncing one another even before they come to rest.

The marked Midi accent of the three contestants makes it difficult to follow the thread of their debates, but their alignment is abundantly clear. As of now it's the plumber, solo, against the contractor and the electrician, with the electrician waging a private feud of his own against the plumber. For a moment, a couple of days ago, the plumber called the contractor "*un petit bourgeois*". The electrician said he agreed with this, as a matter of broad general principles. This led the contractor, as far as one could gather, to discharge both of them on the spot. All three of them returned, however, the following day in the old set-up of plumber versus the contractor-electrician bloc, and took forty-eight minutes, timed carefully by myself, to reach an impasse about the plumber's alleged failure to ring somebody up about "*la pompa*".

Everything agitates itself around the *pompa*. While there is enough electric current to light the house there is insufficient power to drive the *pompa*. The power will, in fact, not be here until some time next month. This was known to all three parties when the *pompa* was installed five weeks ago, but all three of them thought that the other two were going to do something—it remains unspecified—about it.

The contractor, the electrician and the plumber stand, therefore, for about an hour every day pointing accusingly at the *pompa*, and at one another, while the inhabitants of the villa try to squeeze past them to fill buckets from the outside water-tap which is, mercifully, working. Sometimes they pause in their discussions to watch me staggering over broken ground carrying a large dustbin filled with water. They comment—I think with admiration—about the *puissance* of the *M'sieu* who is able, all alone, to carry so great a burden, and then they turn to rending one another all over again.

Last Tuesday morning was full of promise. The electrician arrived at 7 o'clock, by which time the rich English had already been painting one of the bedrooms for nearly an hour. He connected some wires to the power line which runs along the road, ostentatiously examined his watch and then spoke for 4½ minutes—I make a point of timing these discourses—about the plumber's congenital inability to arrive anywhere within thirty-six hours of the arranged time of the rendezvous. He then left in a passion of rage, with the ultimatum that he would return only when the plumber had installed the pump.

Seventy-eight minutes later—again the time is exact—the plumber arrived with the pump and spoke for nine minutes flat about the electrician's incurable impatience which rendered any attempt at cooperation with him absolutely impossible.

He then installed the pump, after putting the electrician's wires well out of the way, and left in an excess of rage even greater than the electrician's. It is too early yet to say whether they have given one another a *coup de téléphone*, and the contractor seems to have disappeared altogether.

These confusions, however, which would be intolerable in the grey climate of England, are under these blue skies and a temperature of 80 glorious degrees but an amusing diversion in the day's work—or an amusing diversion, at least, for the guest who has not had to lay out serious currency for the pleasure of hot and cold running water.

The absence of this facility, on the other hand, does make it difficult to remove the white paint with which I have covered myself, and the other painters, while painting the ceiling in the master bedroom. We are all, in fact, pretty well permanently speckled in a way which suggests that we may be suffering from some contagious disease.

This, in a way, is an advantage. When we go down to the sea the other hundred thousand bathers move well over, to allow us to get into it.

BULLOCK AWAY, MON BRAVE

It was really no more than a matter of politeness, the introduction of a new subject to lubricate this meeting with a casual acquaintance, when our bearings had begun to run a little dry on the subject of forest fires.

We had agreed, some time ago, that forest fires on the Riviera look very frightening, particularly by night, but that, taken all in all, they do surprisingly little damage, except to the trees, and then our own combustion died and we stood silent, two English-speaking persons in an *alimentation* filled with talking French.

"By the way," I said, "have you any idea where I could get one of those?"—and showed her the broken knob off the cooker.

Her reaction was instantaneous. "Oh, dear," she said, "you haven't got one of those, have you?"

My reaction was equally quick—a sudden falling into the state of alarm familiar to all transient visitors to the Riviera when faced with the superior wisdom of a permanent resident.

"The cooker is fine," I said. "It cooks beautifully. It's just that the knobs are a bit fragile. But surely it can't be all that hard to get another one?"

"I'd say impossible." Her smile was warm and, indeed, helpful. "But, look," she said, "don't let me depress you. I'm sure we can find a way around it. Come and talk to my husband. He's outside in the car."

Instead, he was just getting into it, looking disgruntled. "Rabbit," he said, as soon as he saw her, "for no apparent reason is eight francs a kilo today when it was only seven fifty yesterday. I told the butcher he could keep it." He gave me a preoccupied nod of greeting.

For several minutes—I found it a long time—they discussed the question of whether or not it would be worth driving down to the Monoprix in Cannes, where rabbit appeared to be permanently established at 7.45 francs, and then resolved it by deciding to have two slices of veal instead.

"By the way," she said, including me once again in the conversation, "he's looking for a new knob for their cooker."

His manner brightened immediately. "Knob broken on the

cooker, eh?" he said, "I don't suppose you've got it with you?" he asked hopefully.

He was fractionally disappointed when I gave it to him, but brightened again at once. "Oh," he said, "you haven't got one of these, have you?"

"The cooker is fine. It's just that the knobs are a bit fragile."

He threw the knob into the air and caught it several times, thoughtfully. "This, *mon ami,*" he said, "is a really tricky one, believe me." Without warning, and with a flow of words promoting a chain reaction that threatened to go on for ever, he told me a story about a refrigerator they'd bought in 1952, from the handle of which they'd received electric shocks during wet weather. The end of the story seemed to be that they'd bought a new refrigerator in 1961, the handle of which was free of electric shocks whether the weather was wet or dry.

After that, it seemed impolite to bring up the irrelevant matter of cookers, so I said I had to be getting along.

"*Doucement, doucement,*" he said—he still had the knob of the cooker—"just hold your horses, old man. I'm thinking." After a moment he said, hesitatingly, "Ye-es. Ye-es, I think so." His manner became confident in the extreme. "I think we can just about manage to swing this one for you. You know the Rue du Courgette in Nice? Well, just on the corner there's a little *bonneterie* with a charming little girl behind the counter. What's her name, dear—Marie, something like that?"

His wife thought that Marie was the dark and unhelpful one, and appended an anecdote underlining Marie's unhelpfulness. He became a little impatient about half way through it. "Anyway," he said to me, "it's the fair one. Well, her brother works next door in the *agence*—"

"The agency for this cooker?" I said quickly.

"Good Lord, no. He's the one we got our fridge from. A most obliging chap, speaks a little English. He knows everyone in the household appliances game in Nice, and if you slip him five francs or so he'll do all the telephoning for you."

"All what telephoning?"

His manner became patient, resigned, remaining friendly only with an effort. "My dear chap," he said, "you've got to do these things the French way. There's no point in bullocking your way in. They're a tricky lot, you know. You've got to match 'em, point for point. I remember the time when our front door fell off and—"

A long time later, in Grasse, in the window of a household appliance shop, I saw the same cooker that we have. I bullocked my way in and they let me have a new knob, from a drawer filled with them, for 2 francs 50. They said they kept plenty in stock because the design was poor but would be greatly improved in the new model.

It certainly takes a little time to get to know one's Coast.

MR. RAKE AND FREDA FLORADORA

Let us be frank about it.

One has known a small measure of fame. One has, in all fairness, to admit, with a gentle deprecating smile, that journalism, television, a book or two has thrust one, however unwillingly, into the outer edges of the limelight. One's name has become a little—known?

Well and good. So be it. It's the way of the world. Fine while it lasts. But dross, my masters; dross, when one contemplates what could lie ahead.

And what is this shining radiance that beckons one on, to change in its entirety one's way of life? What peak of achievement, of ambition, still lies ahead? What summit of fulfilment?

A change of sex? The Church? Taking up the oboe?

None of these things.

I simply want to become known as the man who keeps an acre of Provence neatly raked, and utterly weed-free. A whole acre and believe me, *mes copains,* that's a lot.

This acre, containing twenty-three olive trees, has been a knee-high jungle of brambles and monstrous, flowering weeds for the past fifty years. The home of field-mice, lizards, hens and half-savage cats, to say nothing of enormous armoured beetles, flamboyant caterpillars, tree-frogs and worms as thick as your thumb. A brazen offence against the virtues of neatness and discipline.

Last winter it was ploughed up by a large man whose seat overflowed the tiny wheels of his miniature tractor. This summer the weeds are marching back again, revivified, made more luxuriant than ever by the aeration of their roots.

I was contemplating their dead battalions the other morning in the furnace heat of the sun, watching Fishmonger's Reject almost burgeoning before my very eyes. None of the inhabitants around here seem to know the scientific name of the weeds that cover the landscape, perhaps because they are so used to them, so that I've had to classify them, in English, myself.

Fishmonger's Reject is a particularly revolting specimen. Steely-blue in colour, it has a smell of old haddock, with some strongly human undertones, and it grows six inches overnight.

The other morning, however, overcoming my repugnance, I took a specimen of Fishmonger's Reject between finger and thumb, applied an upward pressure and was literally transported to find that the whole noisome thing came out sweetly and gently, including its foot-long and dead-white root. In a moment I'd cleared a whole patch of Reject, roots and all, guaranteeing that with normal vigilance it would never return.

My new profession had been born!

Swiftly, I cleared more and more, making the discovery that Freda Floradora came out just as sweetly as Fishmonger's Reject. Freda is odourless, but she has a sickly yellow flower and a root like a stomach-turning, long, pink worm. False Verbena, however, proved tougher work. The jade has a smell of verbena, but coarsened beyond measure, putting one in mind of Dorian Gray on a bad night. She has roots like a tree, that must be dug out.

My time-table now is set. Five a.m. to six every morning plucking Fishmonger's Reject and Freda Floradora, and digging out False Verbena. Six to nine, raking the area smooth and level. Nine to nine-ten, breakfast. Nine-ten until it gets too hot, removing the endless tons of stones, thrown up by the raking, in a wheelbarrow, and tipping them out somewhere else, and then back again, eagerly, on the job at four, when the sun has lost some of its fury. Already, I have cleared a space the size of a tennis-court and there is so much—so gloriously much—still to be done. And when it's finished, I can begin all over again at the beginning.

It is profoundly satisfying work, repetitive, mindless, making only light demands on the body, but it brings sweet order out of howling chaos, a most worthy cause.

And already I have gained a name. The other day, I heard an old woman passing by on the road say to her friend, "*Voilà—M'sieu Râteau!*"

Mr. Rake! Quite charming. A Rake, doing only good.

Now, I only need someone to pay me for it, in francs.

WHAT WE REALLY NEED

"What we really need," she said, "is that heavenly looking carpenter from the village."

"Since we first began to need that heavenly looking carpenter," I replied, "so many years of hopeless unfulfillment have gone by that even his lustrous eye has begun to fade. There are silver threads in the hair that once was black as night. His saw is blunted and he's probably lost his chisel. I will do the job myself."

"It's a brand-new door."

"What difference does it make if it's brand-new or falling to pieces, when all you want is a hole in it? You might even say that the action of cutting a hole in a brand-new door tends to age it, that in fact a brand-new door with a hole in it is a contradiction in terms, and that therefore—"

"Oh, all right," she said. "But try, just for once, to get it straight."

With the usual difficulty I disentangled the tin box with the tools in it from the mass of miscellaneous cleaning rubbish in the cupboard under the sink. I realised, not for the first time, that what I really needed was a bench with all the tools hanging neatly from hooks in the wall above it. I also really needed some more tools. The ones I had, however, had done a lot of good work in their time, and they'd do it again.

I got a stool and sat looking at the garage door for some time, planning the operation. The vertical cuts would be comparatively easy, running down the edge of the planks. They would also, of necessity, be straight. The lower cut would also be straight, along the edge of the bottom batten. The straightness of the top one would be the only problem.

I saw that I really needed a T-square, to mark it along the door parallel with the batten. I also really needed a good, thick carpenter's pencil, to draw the line. Instead, I removed the hacksaw blade from its holder and, using it as a ruler, scratched a line across the door with the screwdriver. It looked straight.

I fitted the drill into the brace and thought, not for the first time, that I really needed one for wood. This particular drill had been designed for boring holes in stone or concrete but curiously enough the softer wood had always defeated it.

Thirty minutes later I'd bored three holes fairly close together in a vertical line down the edge of the first plank. What I really needed now was a thin, sharp chisel and a light hammer to join the holes together. Instead, I used the materials available: to wit, the screwdriver and the shifting spanner which has served as a hammer ever since the hammer disappeared.

Eventually, I was able to insert the hacksaw blade into the hole and began to saw, downwards. At this point it occurred to me to have a look at how things were going on on the other side of the door, so I opened it and out of the garage stalked, indignantly, the two cats for whose convenience this cat-trap was being made. They went away, put out by their temporary imprisonment, and by the banging.

I then saw that the banging, with the screwdriver, had rather severely splintered the wood on the other side of the door. The outside, of course, where it would show. I saw that I really needed a small plane, some sandpaper and a pot of the original varnish to repair the damage, but all that could come later.

After sawing away with the hacksaw blade for some time it became clear that I really needed a proper, narrow-bladed saw because it was impossible to control the hacksaw blade by holding it in the bare hand, which was becoming slippery with blood, but it was too late for all that now.

I finished the cat-trap as darkness was falling. The square hole had a slightly rhomboid appearance, with one corner higher than the other. There was also a good deal of splintering round the orifice, rather as if the hole had been made by a single blow with a large axe, which would certainly have been quicker, but at least cats could pass through it.

I caught them and put them down in front of it. With remarkable agility they sprang on to the roof of the kitchen and entered the house by the bedroom window, a route they had not employed before.

What I really need now, in addition to everything else, is two rather more intelligent cats.

DESPERATELY, ALL MORNING

The voice cried piercingly over the garden wall, "Darlings—been trying *desperately* to phone you all morning!"

It was tossed over the wall in the way that a hat, in the immemorial bar-room tradition, is thrown into a saloon, to see if it's going to be thrown out again. A kind of sighting shot, a testing of the temperature of the water.

Madame and I said nothing, shelling beans quietly in the sunshine. But we exchanged the kind of look that passes, perhaps, between two hard-bitten Commandos, snug in their foxhole, whose trained ears detect the advance of trouble.

And trouble, of course, it must be, because the voice was the voice of none other than the toast of the Coast—the (unfortunately) irrepressible Dinky Scrimgeour-Scrivener, so far off her normal Antibes-Cannes beat, up here in the mountains, that she must have had some very special request to make of us, one that would cost (us) quite a lot of time and probably money to fulfil.

A moment later it was plain that the matter was urgent, because suddenly Dinky was right in amongst us, without even the small formality of touching the goat bell at the gate. "Darling!" she cried again. "Fearfully sorry banging in like this, but I was so near I just had to."

At this the miniature poodle in Dinky's arms went off like a miniature siren—a thin scream that pressed our eardrums together in the middle. Dinky paid no attention to it whatever. Through the scream she gave us her wistful, little-girl smile, the one that asks to be forgiven for naughty presumption—a considerable technical achievement for a lady in the middle, restless fifties.

"That's all right," Madame said in her level kind of voice. "It's nice to see you."

Both of us were trying to estimate, with a speed of computers, what it was that Dinky wanted; or what it was that we had of which she required the use. And, of course, to head her off before she got us jammed in a cleft of non-existent moral obligation.

In a split, silent second we came to the following conclusions, though not necessarily in the same order.

Dinky probably didn't want to remove Madame T., the lady who does for us, nor Marcel, our handyman. To get them to her villa on the coast, and home again, would have occupied the services of one of her three cars at a time when it might be needed for something more important.

Dinky probably didn't want to remove our builder, and his three remaining workmen. Her villa is constantly being repaired and enlarged by a resident team of masons, plumbers and electricians and it seemed improbable, even if she wanted a few quick shelves put up in the servants' hall, that she would go to the trouble of stealing our lot.

She couldn't want to borrow our car, our cat, my pick-axe or Madame's silk suit, and yet here she was—all the way from the coast and a little on edge. In fact, she was so on edge that she suddenly silenced the poodle with a rap on its lug and came to the point, albeit with a number of detours.

"You see, darlings," Dinky said, "ever since we got back from Capri, Alexis has been terribly difficult. You know?"

We didn't. We'd never heard of Alexis and could only guess that he must be new.

"So the darling boy," said Dinky, "saw this advertisement in some English newspaper for some marvellous new kind of lawnmower. It floats in the air or something. And so he wanted one immediately."

Alexis— a new and rather special gardener?

"But the trouble is," said Dinky, "they cost twice as much here as they do in London." Then she played her ace, pretty quickly. "So I thought," said Dinky rapidly, "that as your dear little daughter is driving down here fairly soon with her little friend she could possibly just slip one of these lawnmowers into the back of the car and of course it's going to be difficult for you with so many girls but Alexis has masses of the most divine boy friends and of course I'd settle up with you later."

Madame settled up instantly. Back of daughter's car already bursting with contraband, etc., etc., leading to extreme shortage of cash, etc., and in any case divine boy friends perhaps not quite ideal for man-hungry English girls . . .

Dinky left before Madame had finished. We went back to shelling beans.

"It's always so sad," Madame said presently, "when they think you can't see them coming."

TWO AND A HALF OF HIS

A man whom we know vaguely brought another man to see us the other day whom we didn't know from Adam.

The stranger wore an excellently convoluted Panama hat. It was mature and as individual to him as the bullet-holed, sweat-stained, dusty old stetson of the television trail boss. A small work of art, on its own.

The rest of him was very good, too. Sun-bleached alpaca jacket, with a pair of secateurs in the breast pocket and a few skeins of raffia trailing from one of the side ones. Baggy old corduroys, even in the heat of the southern summer, and a stout pair of brown walking shoes. And the whole thing set off by a red and yellow silk square round the throat. I. Zingari? At any rate he looked like a clean, spare, lithe, gentlemanly old cricketer who had turned, with dashing Corinthian brilliance, to rather expert gardening in his later years.

It turned out that he was justified in the amount of time he must have spent upon perfecting his appearance, because this was exactly what he was—Fairlie Hardy, from Monte Carlo, an absolute genius with flowers.

As they came in through the gate the friend introduced him

in a voice so hushed with reverence that he might have been handling Fairlie Hardy on a professional P.R.O. basis. "You know," he whispered to me, after the introduction, "the Rothschild place on Cap Ferrat."

I said, "What's he doing here, then?"

"Nothing at all," the friend said cheerfully. "We were just passing by and he said he'd love to have a look at your garden." The friend went so far as to give me a little touch of his elbow. The right eyelid almost closed. "He always reads your jottings in the *Observer*," he said.

I was about to deal with this misconception, demolishing the revolting "jottings" on the way, when I saw that Fairlie Hardy, the genius with flowers, was at it. He stood in the middle of our small, walled garden, in which geraniums grow like weeds, and his left hand, with the fingers sensitively and delicately curved, was raised to about shoulder level, the fingertips almost visibly tasting the air.

After a moment, Fairlie Hardy was able to analyse his emotions with sufficient accuracy to give them expression.

"Persuasive," he said, giving it the weight due to the only possible word.

Madame has a special look that she gives people on such occasions as this. It's quite narrow, perhaps nearly steely. She doesn't speak, but the head is placed a little on one side. Her attitude says, very clearly indeed. "Kindly wash out your mouth and then, omitting the rubbish, begin again."

Fairlie Hardy got it straight between *his* eyes. He cleared his throat. "I mean," he said, "it speaks to me. It tells me—I like it well."

"That's good," Madame said, closing the subject like the door of a safe. But Fairlie was courageous. "Perhaps, though," he said, "just a hint too great a profusion of the Pelargonium Peltatum. Might I suggest Trachylospernium Jasminoides?"

"We had some of that," Madame said, "but it died."

They fought it out steadily from then on, toe to toe. Fairlie said the new lawn was full of Mullumbimby Couch Grass. Madame said she liked the colour. Fairlie said that one of our mimosa trees—he called it "Acacia podalyriaefolia"—was going to get much too big for the place it was in and Madame told him that before that could happen she would "lop it until it squeaked".

During Round Nine the friend said to me, "I told the old goat it wasn't going to work." He was resigned, rather than bitter.

"You mean," I said, "Fairlie Hardy thought he was going to

remake the entire garden, seeing that we're new here and he hoped we wouldn't know any better."

"He wouldn't do anything himself," the friend said, defending Fairlie's reputation, "but the nursery in Cannes would give him ten per cent of their nett for the introduction."

"And what's yours?"

"Two and a half of his," said Fairlie's friend.

They left, after drinking a whole litre of wine each.

We gave our Pelargonium Peltatum a good watering that evening. It made the whole garden look fresher.

ONE OUT—ALL OUT

The electric razor ceased to work so abruptly that I knew at once what the trouble was. Probably, it had been coming on for some time. The armature electrode had simply detached itself from the wattage conductor, or some damn thing like that, and now I had half a face shaved and the last safety razor blade had been used yesterday for cleaning paint off a window.

I was putting the electric razor back in its case, with the intention of doing something about it some other time, when Madame called down in a fair fury from the upstairs bathroom, "What's wrong with the pump?"

I'd been put out myself, so I called back with some asperity, "What do you think is wrong with the pump? Give me a basis for diagnosis."

"I can't hear you."

"What's wrong with it?"

Women.

"There's no water in the tap and I can't rinse the laundry. Please go and look at it—no wait, you needn't bother. There's no electricity. It's the strike."

I should have known there was nothing wrong with my armature electrode. Of course it was the strike. We'd been waiting for it ever since the near-revolution of last May. The Syndicalists—the sinister French word for trades unionists—had done it again. It was March 11th, and there would be no electricity in the whole of France from 9 a.m. till 5 p.m.— leaving me with half a face shaved and her with the laundry unrinsed, and both lavatories out of action. *Quel malheur*!

At about ten we went down to the village to get some food and found that both the greengrocer and the butcher were in darkness, and because they were in darkness they'd closed their doors. It was something we hadn't allowed for, so we went home again.

I went down to the study to write some letters. It's always rather dark down there, as it faces east, so I switched on the table lamp and nothing happened. Then I noticed that nothing had happened either to the electric fire, which I'd just plugged in, so I went upstairs again and found that she'd erected the ironing-board in the kitchen and was shaking the iron, trying to make it work.

I was just about to unplug it, to do some running repairs to the armature electrode, when simultaneously we remembered the facts.

We went and sat in the living-room for a while. There was no point in going down the hill again to get the newspapers because even if there had been any they wouldn't have arrived, and in any case the bar that sells them, being in darkness, would also be out of business.

I said, "For jollity, let's put on the—never mind it doesn't matter."

"The record-player?"

"Do not speak about it."

At midday the clouds came piling up again from the east, the way they've been doing for weeks. She said, "I'm terribly cold."

I said, "We've got no wood left and I'm sure the wood-merchant is in darkness, and shut, so we're done."

"We could have the elec—" she said, and stopped.

There was a pleasant diversion during the afternoon. Geoff arrived with his pump. Thanks to the torrential rain that has been falling on the Côte d'Azur there is as much water in the plastic cover over the pool as there is in the pool itself, and I've been meaning for weeks to get rid of it.

We lifted the pump out of the boot of Geoff's car—it weighed a ton—and carried it into the garden. While Geoff primed the suction end of the hose I unrolled the other to the furthest corner of the garden and put the spout into the gutter that runs down the road. There were hundreds of gallons to be got rid of and I didn't want to get our bit of land soaked.

Then Geoff plugged in the pump, and nothing happened.

The three of us looked at one another without speaking and then went inside and in the cold, semi-darkness, had a drink. The ice in the fridge, of course, was nearly melted, but it served.

At five o'clock that evening the main pump sprang to life, so did Geoff's, the iron burnt a hole in the ironing-board and the following morning I found that the electric fire and the table-lamp had been on in the study all night.

General de Gaulle apparently made a great speech about the whole thing, but I haven't been able to get down to buy a paper.

Incredibly, the car battery is flat.

CRISES WITH LEMON TREES

Without wishing to intrude—clear evidence that it's going to happen—a personal note into this socio-political column, I have to make the statement that I'm a five-hour man.

Get me into the basket at 10 p.m. and I'm awake, tiger-eyed, alert, rippling all over, at 3 a.m. the following morning. If anyone else was awake at that time he could set his watch by the clang of my eyelids, as they snap open.

I learnt the trick in the Navy (Irish), where we had four-hour watches, in Dublin Bay. I was in command of the Port Control vessel, so that a rough but kindly word to the shy young sailor who came before me gave me an extra hour in m'hammock, and him half a dollar per night. I've been a five-hour man ever since.

It's like those round, segmented boxes of Swiss cheese. Two and a half segments for sleep, twenty-one and a half for consciousness, in the daily round—fixed and unvarying. It's something of a burden, really, one that requires careful handling. Slot me in too soon, say at 7 p.m., and I'm alert and rippling at midnight, all sleeping done. Only to fade at 3 p.m. that afternoon, to awake at eight, having missed dinner, and all hope of human companionship until 10 a.m. the following morning.

Picture if you will, then, my consternation the other night on getting the opening clang at 8.42. As the searchlight, tiger eyes looked at my watch by the flicker of a match, I knew that something fearful had happened. Basketed at 7.45 p.m., exhausted by the unseasonable weather, I was due to surface like a Polaris missile at a quarter to one the following morning. But now it was 8.42, on the Wednesday, with Thursday as yet untouched.

The antennae that stand all over me, like fur, on awakening, quickly told me the cause. It had been raining all day but now a car, coming up the hill past the bedroom window, was doing so in dead silence, wheel-wise. It should have been splashing in and out of the potholes, the tyres squishing through the mud. Instead, it was proceeding in thick, cocooned silence, apart from the murmur of the engine. It could mean only one thing. SNOW!

Snow on the Côte d'Azur, on the eleventh of March. *Pas croyable.*

I lay there in bed, and I could almost hear the soft flakes silently fall upon, among other flora, the two lemon trees that I should have covered in November, but hadn't, on the grounds—fiercely denied by Madame—that it couldn't possibly snow this winter on the Riviera, and even if it did that the two lemon trees were now big enough to stand on their own individual feet.

Lemon trees are strange, shy, faun-like creatures. When young they stand very bare, with two or three leaves and a lot of branchy little antlers and, like as not, one socking great yellow lemon blooming proudly from the smallest twig. But they're delicate. Suddenly, they fade and die and then you've got to buy another one at round about £10, and practically breast-feed it through its adolescence. A dodgey fruit.

I lay there in bed, waiting for the snow to stop, and then—as though it were an echo of my own voice—I heard Madame beside me saying, "If you'd covered them in November the snow wouldn't be killing them now."

The cleverest doctor in the world couldn't have diagnosed her as being awake, but nonetheless she was aware of the snow, and of the remedy. "Why don't you go out and cover them," she murmured, and slipped away into deep-breathing peace.

We don't have mackintoshes, rubber boots and pixie hoods on the Côte d'Azur. Like British Rail we don't believe it's ever going to happen. I mushed out into the blizzard wearing pyjamas, two dressing-gowns, carrying over my bare head a rainbow parasol purchased on the isle of Capri for a different purpose. On the feet were sheepskin bedroom slippers.

It was very dark. Immense, fluffy flakes of snow fell from the invisible sky, making for the lemon trees as though they were magnetised. It looked like premeditated murder, in the light of the torch.

And what did our hero do? Did he strip off his two dressing-gowns, with which to drape the trees? Did he toss a coin, to decide which one of them should have the benefit of the Capri parasol? Did he even add his pyjamas, for additional protection, with the largest lemons nestling inside his sheepskin bedroom slippers?

He did not. He nipped back into the house and came out with two rolls of mauve lavatory paper, which he lashed around the lemon trees as deftly as Sir Francis Chichester repairing his self-steering gear in a gale in the Roaring Forties.

Then I went back to bed, with the glow that comes from having done well a thing that no one had ever done before.

SOOTHING SANGRIA

I came in from slashing brambles very hot, and with the feet bristling with thorns, to find that Madame had anticipated much of this condition and had constructed a cooling jug of something or other, with a lot of fruit lurking around the top.

"Now that," I said, "is one of the kindest things you have ever done, and you do a number of kind things both for me and for others."

"Thank you," she said. "I do hope you'll like it. It's sangria, a drink I learned to make in Spain."

"What a charming name," I replied. "Sangria. What's in it?"

"It is a pretty name," she answered. "It's just red wine, with a drop of brandy in it and a sip of Benedictine and other stuff like that and slices of lemon and orange and so on. It's very easy to make."

"But nonetheless," I said, "I must thank you again for having gone to so much trouble. It was considerate in the extreme."

"Do not mention it," she said. "Would you care to try a glassful?"

"Thank you."

We sat in the sun for quite a time, sipping sangria and looking at the flowers. The jug was about two-thirds empty when she said, "Oh, by the way, isn't it time you filled the salt cellar?"

I was shocked at the form of the words. "Isn't it *time*," I repeated, "that *I* filled the salt cellar? And what will you be doing while *I* am filling this receptacle?"

"Nothing," she said.

I had a curious kind of whining sound in the ears, as though something were pressing on the brain.

"So that," I said, "while I have to go all the way to the toolshed to get the pliers to remove the revolting plastic button from the bottom of the salt cellar *you* will be doing nothing."

"That is absolutely correct."

The injustice of it staggered me. Imposed upon from every direction, treated like a slave. "Do you see that cat?" I said.

"Very clearly."

"It wants something to eat. Give it something to eat."

"Go and fill the salt cellar."

"Right."

"Right."

We were both pale with fury, nostrils flaring, teeth clenched, injustice going on everywhere.

When I came back from the toolshed, having removed the plastic button, I found her performing the inconceivably lunatic act of putting the cat's food in the garden, just in exactly the right place for the dog from next door to get at it.

I literally screamed at the idiocy of it. "If you put it there the dog will have it and the cat will get nothing!"

"Not if you watch it," she yelled back, "while I get the laundry." And stamped off down the path. I went into the house to get the salt and *when I came out again there was the dog from next door halfway through the cat's dinner!* A great ugly big brute of a boxer slavering away. She came in with the laundry. "Now look what you've done," she bawled.

I could scarcely speak. "I told you what would happen . . ." Suddenly, I became homicidal. I grabbed a handful of gravel off the path and flung it at the dog and found I'd bunged the plastic button too. I aimed a kick at the dog and got tangled up in the sheets she was carrying.

"You've thrown the bottom of the salt cellar away," she cried. "And you've filthied the laundry—and I'm going to bed!"

I spent the next hour looking unsuccessfully for the button. My fury seemed to be cooling down. Then I saw her looking out of the bathroom window, preoccupied with some curious thought. She spoke. "What happened?" she said. "What was going on there, a while back?"

I'd been wondering too. "I think we got sangriaded," I said, "most dreadfully."

And so we had been. If you're trying this refreshing drink for yourselves this summer I'd leave out the brandy and the Benedictine—or wear a strait-jacket whilst partaking.

THE GREATEST LINE YOU'VE EVER HEARD

They were standing almost back to back, guarding both approaches, although it was a one-way street, and they were a great deal older than we had been led to expect.

Although it was a hot and sunny evening he carried a mackintosh over one arm, and she wore a bag-like thing on her head like a tam-o-shanter. They peered up and down the street, both ways, as nervously as though they were about to be shot at.

Madame said, "It can't last more than three hours. Try not to beat them to death."

"Let's just drive straight home," I said, "and send them a post-card to say we've fallen over a cliff."

I stopped the car beside them. "Hello, there," I cried. "It's us!"

The two heads came round, slowly and warily. For some time they examined our bright, expectant smiles. Then he spoke. "Rose Ellen," he said, "I do believe it's our two very good friends."

Under her tam-o-shanter Rose Ellen had a coarse, grey fringe, like a horse. She looked away immediately, without speaking.

He said, "This is Rose Ellen, and I'm Al. And I want you to know what a very, very great privilege it is for us to meet up with you."

His sincerity was so profound that Madame and I bowed our heads for a moment, as though we had received a benediction.

Al, still standing on the pavement, then spoke for some considerable time about the mutual friend who had brought us together. He went on to talk about the weather in Cannes, the quality of the food, and the restaurant he proposed to take us to that evening. It was, naturally enough, six miles back in the direction from which we'd just come.

It took him, as I have said, quite a long time to range over these various subjects, but during the course of it Rose Ellen made no contribution of any kind. She listened to Al with a puzzled look, as though he were speaking in a foreign language.

It didn't seem possible that we were going to spend three hours with them, just because someone had written to us about them.

"Well, then," said Al, "what say we hit the road?"

They got into the back of the car, and we drove to the restaurant. From time to time Al whistled extracts from Yankee Doodle. He appeared to be relaxed and happy. The restaurant wasn't really open when we got there, because it was still only six o'clock, but we sat down at a table in the garden. Al tapped his fingers on the table and gave us some more Yankee Doodling. Time ground on in the slowest of slow motion.

Madame said, "Why don't we drive around for a bit? I don't think this place is really open yet."

Al leapt to his feet, transported by enthusiasm. "Rose Ellen," he cried, "isn't that just the greatest idea you've ever heard! Say," he boomed, "where was that cute little bar with the wonderful view? Do you know," he said to me, "a cute little bar around here with a wonderful view?"

We drove them to a number of cute little bars but none of them was the right one so we went back to the restaurant again without having had a drink. We sat at the same table again. Al snapped his fingers. "Garsin!" he called loudly. "Get me a bottla Vittel."

The waiter brought it. Al poured himself half a glass and drank it appreciatively. "Great stuff," he said. Even if we'd wished to share it with him we couldn't have, because we had no glasses.

It was a long time after that before we ordered dinner and even longer before Al suddenly said, "Hey, people, what about a wine? Don't you think that's a great idea, Rose Ellen? To have a wine?"

Half a bottle appeared between the four of us. Al sipped his, left the rest of it and ordered another bottla Vittel. "I don't do so good on wine," he said. All at once the mineral water must have rushed to his head because he said, with the greatest sincerity he had yet mustered, "I want to tell you, sir, that this is just the greatest moment of our lives. Isn't this just the greatest moment, Rose Ellen?"

Embarrassed, I said, "Shovel over the salt, would you, Al?"

It convulsed him. "Shovel over the salt," he chuckled. "Isn't that just the greatest line you ever heard!"

We drove them home after dinner and then we went home, passing the restaurant for the fourth time that night.

They wrote to us later on from Los Angeles, to say that our dinner together had been just the most wonderful experience they'd ever had.

Incredibly enough, they probably meant it.

MANAGEMENT OF THE VOD AND TON

What I always say is that one never fully comprehends the work of management until one becomes, after a lifetime with the pick and shovel, a desk-bound manager oneself.

During the first two days I tried planning the business on paper.

(1) What jobs to find for the workers which are sufficiently interesting and easy to provoke them into completing them, before sitting down and calling it a day at 10.25 a.m.

(2) How to prevent one idiot doing the job which the other lout has already completed.

(3) The best method of stopping these two cretins from cutting the grass *before* Management has given orders for it to be done, because that's simply industrial anarchy that can lead to Management being locked out of his own shop, and a lot of silly laughter.

(4) On and on with the same obviously insoluble problems.

It was Doctor who confined me to the desk. "When you get back to France," he said, "I'd like you to take it easy for the rest of the summer. Stretch out in a long chair under the shade of an olive tree, jug of fresh lemonade beside you, not too much sun and, above all else, no unnecessary exertion."

To both of us, in that austere London hospital room, it looked like something out of Renoir.

When Matron and I got home it was drizzling, from a grey Grimsby sky. Yesterday, neighbours said, it had rained with such ferocity all day that a small bridge had been carried away near Puget-Théniers. Not since 1843 had such weather been seen in the month of June. We lit the fire but went to bed early.

It was still overcast next morning when Desmond and Ian arrived, having driven from London in tropical sunshine that began at the Elephant and Castle. They found me stretched out in a long chair under an olive tree, wrapped in two cardigans and brandy, against the damp. The tree was shedding ton after ton of white blossom, giving the Management, they said, something of the appearance of an old snowman, in June.

They looked round the garden, untended for a month. Long, leggy roses with dropping dead heads. Shaggy cypress hedges, weedy paths and grass like a field of hay. "We'll have this lot trimmed up in no time," said Desmond crisply, "but first we'll get you inside and then the workers will have a vod-and-ton."

Shortly afterwards I was stretched out not on a long chair sheltered from the sun but on the sofa in the sitting-room, with the electric fire plugged in, while Matron and the two house physicians poured down the vods-and-tons in the small, paved garden outside the french windows, laughing like anything.

It seemed to go on for a long time; and that was when Management's problems began. The workers were to be with us only for a week. Unless the vod-and-tonning came to a halt and the trimming up began we were going to lose a whole morning first crack out of the box.

After a long spell of paperwork I decided that Leadership was the answer. They were opening a second bottle of vod when I passed between them like a ghost, faint voice, "Just going to cut grass . . ." A moment later I was back on the sofa, the workers, with vods-and-tons, had gone bounding off in search of the lawn mower and Matron was at work in the kitchen. I followed her, already half-mad with overwork. "There's a can in the potting-shed called *Petrole* and they're sure to think it's petrol and they'll put paraffin in the mower and I'm sure there's no oil in the sump and the grass-catcher is in the garage and they *must* clean the filter . . ."

So it went for the rest of that sultry and overcast week. Management imprisoned in the sitting-room, too damp to be out, planning, writing lists of instructions, warnings in re. use of tools, filing, re-filing, a permanent board meeting with the Chairman the only member present. And from time to time, well wrapped up, infirm tours of the site, only to find the workers completing jobs scheduled for commencement on the previous Wednesday, 8.30 a.m. or still in bed, Friday, 11.10 a.m. Site, curiously enough, immensely improved, rather better, in fact, than normal.

They left, in heavy rain, for Italy on Saturday. Management turned its attention to Charles, Overseas Representative, and the next arrival. Postcards, cables, detailing exact nature of duty-free goods to be purchased *en route*, and *sans faute*.

Lad arrives, empty-handed. Reports fell asleep during sea passage Dover-Boulogne, woke to find duty-free shop shut.

The Chairman resigned.

THE LUXURIOUS PEASANTS

The sun, burning its way imperiously through the diamond-shaped hole in the shutter, bores through the curtain and plants a round blob like a blood-orange upon the pile of letters awaiting urgent reply in the escritoire on the other side of the room.

The time must be about 5.20 a.m. It's probably Thursday, or Friday, but the month is certainly July.

Before getting up, to take on the myriad tasks of the day, I enjoy a moment or two of commercial reflection, mainly on the subject of the escritoire. It isn't really a writing-desk but more of a table, salvaged from some old farmhouse in the hills by the rapacious antique dealer down the road. But it's an unusual shape, square-topped with rather good front legs protruding at an angle, so we drove it away and put it in the bedroom, where Madame began writing letters at it.

Within a week the wide single drawer was choked with loose sheets of notepapers, new and used envelopes, bills and all that sort of thing, and she started talking about having a proper desk, with cubby holes. That's when I began to speak of the table as "your escritoire", making it a permanent possession. In the South of France any piece of semi-elegant furniture more than two years old begins at 1,000 francs, so that if you've got a nice old farmhouse table it's wiser to regard it as your desk and grow to love it.

My interest in the matter fades. The table was bought early in 1967, so that its replacement cannot be regarded as urgent. Whether it's Thursday or Friday is, however, urgent, because if it's Thursday some people are coming to lunch.

Leaving Madame, a slow starter, still sleeping I slide my legs out of bed into the pair of shorts that has been waiting faithfully by my side all night and, indeed, all week. Fully dressed for the day I creep down the narrow, tiled stairs in bare feet, ducking my head at the bottom to effect an untroubled entry into the dining-room.

It must be 5.30 by now but already the sky is a brilliant and cloudless blue. Through the french windows I note that the old orange tree in the little courtyard is still covered with white blossom and ripe, yellow fruit left over from last Christmas. I make a mental note to thin it out next February, if I have the time.

I open the front door and there as usual is Pissoff Sharlee on the mat. He's the cat from next door. Tabby on top, an expansive white waistcoat, small black moustache under a pink nose, he looks not unlike Charlie Chaplin, but because he's constantly under our feet we added on the additional christian name. Now he believes his name is Pissoff Sharlee, so we can never get rid of him. Nonetheless, I chase him into the outer garden and round the olive tree, to supple up our morning muscles. After this short burst both of us re-enter the house at the same time.

I open the french windows into the courtyard and then walk through the dining-room into the sitting-room, to open the windows on to the balcony and the view of the mountains twenty miles away behind Nice. By leaning slightly sideways I can make sure that the Mediterranean is still there, off Cannes.

With the sun hot on my back I turn to look right through the house, at the old orange tree with the mass of Busy Lizzie at its foot, mauve and shocking pink. Sky-blue plumbago covers the sandy wall. Scarlet geraniums clamber up the nearest olive. In the courtyard something is buzzing in Pissoff Sharlee's mouth. He opens it and a large black beetle flies out. He looks thunderstruck. With a sense of utter luxury I begin to wash up last night's dinner, in the tiny kitchen beside the dining-room.

From the sink I can see our own mountain, La Mère Courmette, just down the road, her lower slopes emerald green with young oak trees. I can also see something else. It looks like the end of a large wooden telegraph pole, slowly emerging into the road from André's vineyard. It is followed by André's face, quite close to the ground. A moment later he's running up the road towards me with the immense pole balanced on his bare brown shoulder.

I call from the window, *"Bonne chance!"* *"Merçi,"* he replies, and disappears from sight.

André is the young bachelor who owns the other half of our 300-year-old farmhouse. He's been looking for the uprights for a new toolshed for some time and now he's found them, thanks to *L'Eléctricité de France.* They've been putting up some rather unfortunate concrete pylons lately but compensating for it by leaving the old wooden ones lying around. As a result a lot of outhouses and garages have sprung up in the neighbourhood, as if by magic. It puts me in mind of a task of my own.

For some time I've been doing a paving job in the garden, searching for flat stones in the terraced walls that were built by the Romans in the now abandoned olive groves above us. Unhappily, other keen gardeners have had the same idea, so that it would require a Roman legion to shift the huge ones that are left. Just across the road, however, are a couple of beauties, leaning against the fence of a retired Civil Servant from Paris.

I've had my eye on them for weeks. Being new here he probably doesn't realise the value of lovely flat stones about six inches thick. Also, seeing that they are outside his fence, they may not be his. Further, at 5.45 in the morning, he will almost certainly not be up.

I take a little stroll up the road. I lay my hand on the larger of the two beauties and instantly, blending with the early morning chatter of the cicadas, I hear an almost inaudible cough—a barely articulated, "Ah-hem."

I know where he is. He's up on his roof, adjusting his television aerial, the very first one we've ever had in these parts.

Ownership of the stones has been established, now and for all time, but of course I gave no sign of having heard the delicate announcement. I strolled on up the road and come back into our olive grove by the other gate, to find Paul, the miniature gardener, breakfasting in the sunshine with his back to a tree, sitting on a mattress which he has removed from beside the pool.

Spread out on *Nice Matin,* the local newspaper, are a small bottle of wine, a large tomato and a piece of cheese. As a starter Paul is lowering into his mouth a raw egg, straight from the shell. He completes this process and then, with the utterly charming politeness of the French, he rises to his feet and puts out his hand.

Paul is five feet high, seventy-two years of age, three jagged teeth per jaw, wearing a tattered singlet and a mad little cotton hat, but he's as dignified as an ambassador. He works for us one day a week, from dawn until dusk, for which service we pay him 40 francs.

"Bon jour, m'sieu," says Paul. *"Et comment ça va Madame?"*

He's always asking after the health of Madame. In fact, he's been propositioning her—from his height of five feet—in all manner of subtle ways ever since he came on the payroll, including managing to treat me, with deference, as her large and awkward brother.

"Va bien," I tell him. *"Elle dors toujours."*

"Voilà!" Paul cries. *"C'est la vie."*

I suspect he means that while it might be my kind of life to let Madame go on sleeping at six o'clock in the morning it certainly wouldn't be his if things were different.

Having dealt with that one he begins a new theme, raising a threatening forefinger which comes as high as my chest. *"Faut arroser!"* he shouts at me. *"C'est sec, sec, sec!"*

I tell him the garden couldn't be dry. I watered every inch of it last night.

"But not enough," Paul tells me. "You're as high as a tree and I'm as short as a carrot, but we both need water. You ask Madame," he adds, in a way that leaves him the winner all round. He returns, well pleased, to his breakfast.

I'm about to go back to the house when I notice that there's a leaf or two on the *boules* court. I get the *boules* brush from the toolshed and make the court as smooth as a billiards table. It's irresistible. No one seems to be about. Paul is still behind his tree. I let fly with three *boules,* practising the stop shot, and instantly a voice rings out, *"Bonjour, m'sieu. Vous êtes de bonne heure. Come va?"*

It's Madame Tarragoni, dimly visible in her own garden 150 yards away through the trees, but clearly audible. She's short, stocky, mostly Italian, works for us three days a week and on Sundays feeds sixteen of her own relatives, out-shouting all of them put together when she's in form.

She's *en forme* this morning and in an address of some 5,000 words, still at long range, informs me that her daughter and two grandchildren are staying, that she's making *farçis* for them and that there will be plenty left over for us and our own guests. Also, seeing that her daughter is there to look after the children, she will come personally—if still *en forme*—to do the washing-up.

I've advanced enormously since 5.20 a.m. I now know it's Thursday, since Paul is here. I've settled the ownership of the flat stones, and there's no need to worry about dinner because Madame T. is not only making it but will do the dishes afterwards. I feel like the President of a highly successful company, whose assets are growing all the time. Then I find I've got still another one. Madame is up and in the pool, doing her gentle and dreamy sidestroke!

I slip in beside her. Everyone's *en forme*. We are launched upon another marvellous day.

The Chairman and his lady, when they arrived at 7.45 a.m., were encumbered as usual with all manner of string bags, bathing things, hold-alls, notebooks and jotters, so that it took them some time to get out of the car.

They arrived for lunch at 7.45 a.m. because they live in Villefranche, on the other side of Nice, and Nice is impassable in the summer from nine o'clock onwards. Having arrived for lunch, bringing fresh croissants for breakfast, they would stay on to dinner, to avoid the evening rush, after retiring to the spare room for their afternoon's sleep. Furthermore, they treat Wednesday and Thursday as the week-end, once again in the interest of finding peace and quiet on the roads. All this needs initial planning, but you get used to it.

The Chairman struggled through the gate with his notebooks and other impedimenta. "Dreadful news from the railways," he cried, eager to impart it. "This very morning, all the first-class carriages at the *back*!" He waved several jotting pads. "It's all here on the Agenda."

He's a busy man, too. Every morning, in fine weather, he is stationed about a hundred yards out to sea from the beach and the railway station in Villefranche, intent on seeing the Paris-Rome express safely through the Beaulieu tunnel, just down the line. The engine drivers recognise his Panama hat and give him a toot as they thunder by. Thrashing the water with one hand he then raises his hat with the other and holds it aloft until the train disappears. Once, when I was helping him with the job, the engine driver gave us a toot each. "One of our very best men," said the Chairman, looking proudly after the train.

"They've put the first-class at the back?" I said to him now, as he settled himself under the orange tree. "You suspect incompetence at headquarters?"

"For the moment," he said, "I'd like to leave this matter over." He nodded towards the kitchen, where the ladies were preparing breakfast. "I'd like my wife's evidence on it, in full plenary session. But don't worry. It's all down on the Agenda."

Advancing years have caused the Chairman's memory to become

unrealiable, so that while talking—continuously—he is also making notes about what he'd like to say in an hour's time, if he can remember it. This creates agendas of immense length and complexity which are, however, always presented under the same title: "Vital Matters to be Talked About". Three random entries should give the flavour of the rest.

No. 7. A thing I think Tallulah Bankhead said to me in 1929. Discuss, if it can be recalled.
No. 33. What about the Dog Woman's Awful Friend?
No. 47. How silly would I look in a super striped blazer from Esquire, in Cannes?

As the Chairman started on his breakfast he said he wanted to begin at the bottom of the Agenda today and work his way back to the beginning, but he didn't seem to be able to find the last page so that if anyone had any important business pending perhaps they could get on with it.

The ladies began to talk about the menu for the day. An enormous Salade Niçoise for lunch, with most of the ingredients coming from our own vegetable garden, so that we really only needed bread and a few slices of smoked ham. Madame Tarragoni was providing stuffed tomatoes, aubergines, courgettes and so on for dinner . . .

"And," said the Chairman, producing a box from one of his bags, "on a point of order, a strawberry tart from us."

It was very hot as I drove down to the little food shop in the village for the bread and the ham, so I got two bottles of champagne, at 13 francs each, to mix with orange juice from our tree. Down here it's called Mimosa, very refreshing shortly after breakfast.

In view of the heat the proprietor of the food shop—a retired taxi driver and wine connoisseur—invited me into the coolness of their kitchen, where we sampled a new brand of light, white vermouth with a charmingly perfumed taste. He gave me the rest of the bottle to take home, with his compliments, so that Madame could also put it to the test. We shook hands warmly on parting, as we had done ten minutes before on my arrival.

At home, Madame and the Chairman, surrounded by bills and receipts, were assisting the work with the first Kir of the day—a cooling blend of blackcurrant liqueur and white wine. Our wine is delivered from Nice a hundred litres at a time. It costs 1 franc 80 centimes a litre, so that there is always plenty around.

"Meeting of the Finance Committee," the Chairman announced.

"Called to discover why your house taxes for the year come to 450 francs, while ours are 703. If it's because we live on the coast and you're up here in the jungle we shall move immediately. Oh, good," he said, looking at the bottles in my hand, "champagne."

I squeezed oranges in the kitchen, delighting in the feel of the cool tiles on my bare feet, and idly did some adding up of my own. By the time I'd poured the orange juice into the champagne I'd decided we were entitled to it, seeing that the provision of breakfast, lunch and dinner for four people, with just a little too much to drink, would come out at about 40 francs for the day.

I was carrying the Mimosa out to the pool, in which the Finance Committee was now meeting, when the dashing young postman with the beret and the black beard brought his yellow van to an instant halt, from fifty miles an hour, outside the gate. Greetings and hand-shakings. For him, half a glass of Mimosa; for me, one letter, from the editor of a magazine in London, requesting a piece "by November 1st, at the very outside". Despite the head-long rush and the modest reward I was glad to be able to calculate that the work, if completed, would put us about another hundred bottles of champagne ahead of the game.

Paul, the demon lover, was showing the Chairman's lady how to make a rose graft, having taken her behind an olive tree for the purpose. I joined the Finance Committee in the pool, with a Mimosa for every member. The shallow end is an ideal bar height. You can lean there with one elbow on the counter for hours at a time, with the lower part of the body gently cooled by the clear water. As Bob once said to me, "This is the best wet bar I've ever been in."

It was still only 10.30 in the morning. Obviously, this day—like all other days of this endless blue and gold summer—simply wasn't going to be long enough to contain all the vital things that had to be done. Like a couple of hours, or more, on the *boules* court.

Before we built it I used to play golf intermittently at the Club de Cannes, facing up to the labour of getting fully dressed for the event, even to a pair of socks, putting the clubs and golf shoes in the car, driving to Mougins, signing the visitors' book, trying to get the prettiest of the girl caddies and then hacking my way round in the company of a number of English stockbroking gentlemen, who seemed always to be in the deepest possible trouble.

The roof garden in their Cannes apartment was leaking into the drawing-room; every one of their four Portuguese servants was entirely unreliable; a simple service for the Rolls was prohibitively expensive and, worse, lacking in British craftsmanship; and tickets for the charity ball in the Palm Beach Casino had set them back £25 each. They were always contemplating moving on to South Africa or somewhere like that where at least the natives spoke English. It used to take me a couple of hours to shake off the memory of their problems.

Then we built the *boules* court, and now I just step out of the pool on to it, barefooted in wet trunks, with a pastis in the left hand and I play it as fiercely as I ever played golf, off a handicap of two.

These *boules* are delicious steel balls, just the right weight for a nice, smooth swing. The four players have three each, and the point is to get as near the jack as you can with all of them. Before and after each throw there are long conferences about tactics and the glasses have to be refilled and precise measurements taken, so that often darkness falls before we've got properly going. Then we switch on the spotlights in the olive trees and play on through the warm and velvety night, with little sips of cognac to keep us going.

I poured a little more Mimosa and placed upon the Agenda the possibility of going down to Cannes tomorrow, to the incredibly cheap and excellent restaurant in the Old Port to get the latest gossip from the yacht skippers about the goings-on of their demented owners.

In the end, we decided we might possibly just stay where we were, here.

Staying here, with every simple and necessary luxury to hand, costs us about £25 a week—every week for the whole six months of the summer, in the hills behind the very expensive and very beautiful Côte d'Azur.

Capital Pains

IRONMONGER'S LASSITUDE

During my years of residence in a basement apartment off Notting Hill Gate, which we called Campden Hill, I got a big hole in the wall above the mantlepiece, as a result of trying to put a nail or a hook into it sufficiently robust to support rather a pretty looking-glass, with a stripped pine frame.

Thanks to gimcrack construction this particular piece of wall seemed to be about an inch thick and made of papier-mâché. Three Rawlplugs, each of increasing size, had been inserted into the hole which was also getting bigger, and then at the first pressure of the screw the Rawlplugs had simply disappeared into the wall, falling into some bottomless cavity behind it.

I put this problem to a professional handyman and he solved it instantly. "Y'll want one of y'toggle screws on that," he said. Handymen often personalise equipment in this way. "Take a bit of y'four be two scantlin'," and "countersink y'coach-bolt, see?"

I asked him what my toggle screw was. It turned out to be a kind of butterfly nut that could be collapsed to pass through the hole in the wall and miraculously opened up the other side. "She'll hold a grand pianner," the handyman promised, and said that she could be obtained at Carters.

I was glad he'd mentioned Carters. It was ideally placed, at the far end of Tottenham Court Road, for a writer trying to get away from writing in Campden Hill. At least an hour to get there and if Carters was the same as other ironmongers at least another hour to make the purchase. It was possible, of course, that a toggle screw could have been found at the ironmonger's round the corner, but I didn't want to take a chance on it, with so much work to do.

Carters turned out not only to be ideally placed, but absolutely ideal in itself, a very cathedral among ironmongers with five or six different entrances and dozens of long counters and elderly men in caps leaning against them in a way that suggested they'd been there for ever. Of assistants, as is usual in ironmongers' shops, there was no sign.

I joined a small group at what looked like the nuts, bolts and toggle screws counter, and prepared to slip off into ironmonger's lassitude. A telephone at the end of the counter shrilled endlessly. No one even looked at it. It was possible to imagine another telephone in another ironmonger's shop on the other side of London with its receiver lying on the counter, calling Carters hour after hour after hour. It was also possible to imagine handymen all over London, drooping in telephone boxes, getting the engaged signal hour after hour from Carters and from whomsoever the other ironmonger might be. A splendid buttress against the rigours of work.

Ten minutes later nothing had changed, except that we'd been joined by a youth in an apron, carrying one of those hydraulic mechanisms that automatically close doors. He put it on the counter, but watched it warily, as though it might be about to spring into the air.

The oldest customer of all joined him in his vigil for five or six minutes. At the end of it he said, "Y'washer gorn?" The youth nodded in lack-lustre fashion. "Ah fought so," said the old man, with no appearance of triumph. We all listened to the telephone again.

The following year an assistant appeared, a bent, grey-haired man of about seventy in a brown overall coat. He carried a piece of metal of unimaginable purpose with a short length of pipe sticking out of it. He put it on the counter in front of the washer expert and they both looked at it for a long time without speaking. Then the assistant said, "That's y'five sixteenths."

The washer expert inclined himself very slightly, to look at the things from another angle. "Ah wus lookin'," he said, after a long interval, "fer inch an' a quaw'er."

The assistant said, "Ar," so tonelessly that it was a mere expulsion of breath. They resumed their study of the object without further interchange.

Time, even for a writer getting away from work, was getting on. "Excuse me," I said to the assistant, "am I at the right counter for toggle screws?"

He spoke with astonishing heat. "Jus' a minit, guv," he said. "Ah'm servin' this gent 'ere." He glared at me for an instant, and then returned to his previous condition of semi-consciousness. His moment of passion, however, had one beneficial effect. Without looking at it, he picked up the telephone receiver and laid it on the counter, where it continued to buzz rather than to shrill.

After another week a man who had the head of a hammer in

one hand and the shaft in the other said to me, "Toggle screws ain't 'ere, mate. Rahnd the corner." He pointed with the shaft of the hammer, not quite achieving the horizontal.

I thanked him, but it was plain that the stripped pine mirror would not be mounted with a toggle screw today. At least however, the morning's work was safely over.

The time was twelve-fifteen. I was steaming into the haven of lunch.

DINNER TIME

The glamour surrounding the verb To Dine has the power to corrupt absolutely. On one occasion it corrupted me almost beyond recall.

On April 24th the nice wife of a nice man called Edgar rang up to invite me to dine with them and a couple of other equally nice and amusing people on the following Thursday evening. I use "nice" here in its true sense—charming, amusing, imaginative, and fun.

By the second post that day another invitation arrived, on notepaper so solidly opulent that the writer probably had to fold it with a pair of pliers to get it into the envelope.

She began by apologising for the short notice, but said she had some difficulty in remembering my address. She went on, "Some rather amusing friends of ours have just arrived from Barbados, and we'd love you to meet them. Black tie, please . . ."

It took me a little time to decipher the signature. In the end I judged it to be "Helen Denham". A faint memory came back to me of a small, attractive woman with a crisp, forthright mind, and a large, talkative, jolly husband. They'd left me home in his Facel Vega after a party, and come in for a last drink. A lot of mutual admiration had broken out, as often happens with near-strangers at two o'clock in the morning, and we'd all agreed we simply must meet again.

The invitation was to dine with them on the following Thursday. The address was attractive, too, Grosvenor Square, no less.

If both invitations had been to lunch it is quite possible that Edgar's, having been received and accepted first, would have prevailed. When, however, the rival one—on solidly opulent notepaper—was To Dine in Grosvenor Square, with a man who had a Facel Vega, to meet some rather amusing friends in evening dress from Barbados, Edgar's never had a chance. The lights of the Denham dinner party were much too bright.

I left it until Tuesday before I rang Edgar, not because I was wondering what to say but because I judged that this late cancellation would underline the unexpected nature of the crisis in which I found myself.

"Edgar," I said, at the early hour of 8.30 on Tuesday morning —further evidence of truth—"this is a fearful thing to do to you but the Features Editor rang me up late last night and I've got to go to Paris immediately to interview a strip-tease artiste who's contemplating a summer season in the nudist colony on the Isle de Levant. Must be worth investigation, I should say——"

The explanation was getting too long and leading me away from the matter in hand. "And so," I said, "I'm fearfully sorry but I can't have dinner with you on Thursday. I don't think I'll be back in time."

Edgar, a nice man, was very nice about it. "Don't give it another thought," he said. "If you've got to go you've got to go." He laughed happily at the other end, turning the knife several times in the wound. "Stripping in a nudist colony, indeed," he said. "We can only hope the audience doesn't get out of hand. Be sure to tell us all about it," he said, laughing happily again, "when you get back."

I thanked him, too often, for his kindness and understanding. Some fiction would have to be prepared for the next time I saw him about the stripper having been arrested, but all that would keep for the moment. My conscience lightly lacquered over, but with the protective coating gaining rapidly in depth, I turned myself to preparing for the Denham dinner party. When dining in Grosvenor Square and meeting amusing friends from Barbados one likes to look one's best, and in any case by keeping busy one has no time for unrewarding introspection.

My dinner jacket looked as it always does when disinterred after three months off-duty. A full ashtray appeared to have been emptied down the right trouserleg. There was a patch suggesting Sauce Béarnaise on the right elbow of the jacket and threads of silver fox fur round the back of the neck.

It seemed a pity not to be able to remember anything of what must have been a notably jolly night, some part of which must have been spent in heavy rain. At all events, my patent leather shoes were finely sprayed with a substance that turned out to have a glue-like consistency when I rubbed it with my handkerchief. By the time I'd taken my dinner-jacket round to the cleaners, bought a new dress shirt and spent an hour on the regeneration of my shoes I couldn't really remember that Edgar had asked me to dinner at all.

On Thursday evening I began to dress at seven, having been bidden for eight-fifteen, to allow for minor accidents *en route* like button bursting or shoelaces breaking, and for once, unfortunately, got a trouble-free run. I was fully dressed, with one large vodka and tonic inside, by 7.10, and in serious danger of having another one, which I had.

On the way to Grosvenor Square I paused to have two more, merely to fill in the time, in a select public-house where I wouldn't be assaulted for wearing a dinner-jacket. When I pressed the bell of the Denham apartment at 8.20 I felt a certain heaviness in the face which suggested that I might have begun the evening a little too soon.

I calmed myself with the thought that the Denhams had certainly been flying at our last encounter, so that in their spirited company my load wouldn't show.

Ten minutes later, in Mrs. Denham's lovely drawing-room, I was trying to reverse into absolute sobriety by leaving a small Martini on the mantelpiece, untouched, while I engaged Mrs. Denham's sister Joan in conversation.

Joan was down for the night from Worcestershire and for several minutes believed me to be someone called Captain McClintock. This error—one which I straightened out without comment—explained why the Denham invitation had been issued at such short notice. The difficulty Mrs. Denham had had was not in remembering my address but in snaring a last-minute substitute for McClintock—a shrewd operator who knew when to turn down an invitation, even if it was to dine in Grosvenor Square.

Joan—a Miss Peebles—was in the late forties with so little chin that for a moment I thought she was putting it on, for laughs. Joan was keen on laughter. "There's nothing like a good laugh," she told me almost immediately, "for chasing the blues away." She had the moist, protuberant and hopeful eye of a rabbit. She was a teetotaller. "Life," she said, "is fun enough without it, don't you think?"

I said, "An occasional gargle, like laughter, does help in chasing the blues though," and when, in response to Joan's puzzled silence, I explained that "gargle" was slang for a drink, she thought it was the funniest thing she'd ever heard. She lost no time, in fact, in conveying the joke to the amusing couple from Barbados. They received it without moving a muscle, being accustomed, I guessed, to Joan's volatile enthusiasms.

The amusing couple were called Hubert and Sybil Wynander. They were in their seventies, and they were stiff and yellow. They were yellow because they'd had enough money to live in the sunshine of Barbardos for fifty years, and they were stiff because they'd been guarding their money against any conceivable erosion for the same period of time.

Sybil would have fetched, live on the hoof, about £9,000, all accessories like cigarette cases and mink capes included, and Hubert perhaps half that, though I might have been doing an injustice to his platinum wristwatch. They were very rich, and appeared to be very, very sad.

Charles Denham filled the gap, though. He was talkative and jolly, all right, though talkative did not adequately describe the torrent of words and booming laughter that poured from beneath his large moustache.

He dealt exclusively in family reminiscences of the years between 1919 and about 1923. He had been a childhood friend of the two Peebles girls—Joan and Helen—and a couple of madcaps they had been.

The only thing I gained from this debauch of memory was the information that Joan had been called Gaga in the nursery and still was—absolutely rightly, I thought—to this day.

When, ten minutes later, we went in to dinner, Mrs. Denham found fault with every item of the superbly cooked food, obviously a well-tried tactic in her war with her Spanish manservant, whose wife had prepared it. It was lightly, but bitterly done, and effectively poisoned every dish. We had one glass of hock, and one glass of claret.

About half-way through Hubert Wynander was suddenly moved to speak.

Without warning or incitement he told us about the difficulties he had had in finding an even half-way honest contractor to execute certain repairs to the heating system of their indoor swimming pool in Barbados. He took his time over it, often pausing for as much as half a minute to arrange the facts in his mind before presenting them to us.

I tried to go to sleep, with a hand partially shielding my eyes, but my elbow kept slipping off the table.

By ten o'clock the dinner party was over. Hubert didn't take brandy, because of a heart condition, and Sybil had to get back to their hotel because something was wrong with her foot.

At 10.10 p.m. I rang Edgar from the nearest call-box to tell him I'd be along in about an hour.

There was no answer from Edgar's phone. I let it ring for a long time, in case they were making so much noise they couldn't hear it. Having rung twice more from the same call-box—the second time with the assistance of the exchange to make sure the phone was in order—I had to face the fact that they'd gone out. The blackest treachery. They had asked me to dine with them at home and now had simply and wilfully gone out, leaving no message nor any means by which I could communicate with them, the swine.

What they were doing, having given me no warning of the change in plan, was dining in some new and exciting little Italian restaurant with singing waitresses in national costume, so that by now the whole place would be in a state of fiesta, with the padrone spilling out free drinks.

If, I thought, in a sudden attack of fury, Edgar had told me that was what they were going to do, I never would have become involved with the deadly Denhams, and would not now, fully accoutred for a night's pleasure, have to go home to bed. In addition, I remembered instantly, to having to invent some rigmarole about arriving in Paris to find that a non-existent stripper had been imprisoned without trial by fictitious police or, rather, that the Features Editor had lost his nerve and recalled me...

I was struck by a much more serious matter. Suppose that Edgar or his wife met either of the Denhams, or even good old Gaga, at some cocktail party and my name cropped up and they found out what I'd really been doing *after* I'd given them a version of the Paris trip?

I went home quickly and quietly, making resolutions of the highest virtue about dealing straightforwardly with all future invitations, with special reference to rejecting those from wealthy and apparently glamorous strangers when tried and trusted friends have already made a bid.

Such, however, is the frailty of the sociable human being that only a couple of weeks later I accepted another glamorous sounding invitation, as it were, blind. This, however, had a practical purpose to it—namely, to gain a couple of hours' relief from the frozen basement in which I was living at the time.

The Big Freeze of 1962–3 had set in, putting out of action even the emergency stand-pipe set up by the Metropolitan Water Board at the end of the road. From Boxing Day, in fact, until March 30th no drop of water emerged from any tap in my flat. On March 31st it began to flow again, owing to the bursting of a cistern, through the kitchen ceiling.

During this trying period I was deficient not only in water but also an overcoat, for reasons which I had to make plain to a stranger who accosted me in St. James's.

I was strolling down this fashionable street, wearing only a flannel suit, when a clubman with an astrakhan collar stopped squarely in my path, waving his umbrella, apparently enraged.

"You, sir!" he cried. "You, sir—why the devil aren't you wearing an overcoat?" The offence appeared to be all the more flagrant for having been committed in St. James's.

"I am not," I said, answering his charge in full, "wearing an overcoat because the one I had was stolen while I was conversing about the validity of faith with a clarinettist in the pub in Covent Garden at seven o'clock one morning, and I have not found the necessary drive to buy another one since."

"You——" he began. "You—you——" I think he was searching for some such word as cad, or swine, but it evaded him. He contented himself with "Pschaw!" and strode away.

He deprived me of the opportunity to explain to him that despite my lack of an overcoat I was, in fact, rather warmer than toast, due to the presence under my shirt of an Aran island jersey still heavy with its natural oils—a garment which would have been absolutely impossible outside my shirt, and particularly in St. James's. Not, of course, that I would in reality have made such an admission. There is always something a little fusty, a little close, about the thought of jerseys worn next to the skin. It's something that one prefers to keep to oneself, and above all when it's worn in conjunction with a dinner-jacket.

When this second glamorous-sounding invitation came—to the residence of an art dealer in Park Lane—I'd been sleeping and eating in the sitting-room of my frozen flat for a couple of weeks, having abandoned the bedroom as uninhabitable. The invitation sounded pretty good, although my host didn't specify the central heating and running hot water which were going to be much greater luxuries than the food and drink.

It was while I was washing in a basin on the dining-table, surrounded by the two electric stoves and the paraffin oil heater which kept me, in part, alive, that I remembered I hadn't been out for several days so that the car would certainly be frozen solid. A taxi or, much more probably, a bus would have to be taken to Park Lane where, on arrival in a lightweight dinner-jacket, I would probably be unable to speak until I'd been wrapped in blankets, or my limbs chafed with handfuls of snow. It was then I thought of the jersey under the shirt.

The Aran Island number, where one could hope for central

heating, would clearly be going too far but on the other hand a light pullover with long sleeves would surely provide a comforting insulation.

The pullover was a weathered garment, having provided for some years the outer layer of two others, since deceased, for winter golf, but it didn't show at all behind the pleated front of my dress shirt.

I arrived at the residence of the art dealer in no more than a comfortable glow, having walked most of the way, shouting at taxis.

Ten minutes later, in a room packed to the walls with people and central heating in the middle eighties, I might have been in the steam room of a turkish bath except, of course, that there I would not have been wearing a pullover.

The pullover, having begun by being feather-light and almost threadbare, had now become as hairy and prickly and mangy as the fur of an old and depraved badger, except that it seemed to smell more of goat.

In the company of smooth art dealers and their cool ladies I felt and certainly looked like some red-faced and sweating hobbledehoy who, incredibly, had intruded himself, coarse and odiferous from mucking out the cowshed, into this elegant drawing-room, and was now lousing up the whole place.

I withdrew to the bathroom to consider some remedy, having both locked and bolted the door. The obvious thing to do was to get undressed altogether and take a bath, to return purified and without the pullover in a matter of minutes. But, even if it were possible to have a bath without being detected—I could hear the voice of the art dealer's wife, "You, in there, whoever you are, how dare you take a bath in my apartment"—how could the pullover be disposed of, short of burning it on the bathroom windowsill? It should, I saw as I opened my shirt and looked at it in the mirror, have been burnt years ago. It had begun by being eggshell blue, but the front of it was now disfigured by yellowish stains probably of stout. Not the garment to be draped over the arm of a dinner-jacket, carried down the stairs to the hall and checked in with the butler.

Throw it out of the window! But the window was frosted glass with only a small panel opening at the top. There was no knowing what lay below the window or, indeed, who might be watching it.

At this point someone rattled the handle of the door, cursed and went away again. I found a bottle of after-shave lotion in the medicine cabinet and poured a lot of it down my chest, inside the pullover, and tried to get some more to run down my back. The astringency produced a chill so intense that it promised to inhibit the goat-badger confluence at least long enough for me to say goodbye to my hostess without causing her to faint.

She was standing just inside the door of the drawing-room when I returned, looking distrait. Something had gone wrong, I guessed, with the party, but I had too many troubles of my own. I was about to say goodbye when she seized my arm and said, "There you are! I do want you to meet Contessa Abracadabroff——" Or, at least, that's what it sounded like.

She towed me across the room. I put up no resistance, trying to keep cool.

The Contessa sat in a large armchair in a corner of the room, and no one was near her. For a moment I thought this might be out of deference to her rank, that one had to be presented, as it were, and then I saw why she was alone.

She was stoned. If, indeed, it hadn't been for the depth of the chair in which she was sitting she'd have been lying on the floor some time ago. Our hostess gabbled an introduction and fled. Another thing became apparent. The Contessa and I had been selected for a *tête-à-tête* because no one else would have us.

I lowered myself on to a stool beside her, trying to think of enormous cold things like Niagara or Alaska or an avalanche, and suddenly saw who she was. The Contessa was a world-famous beauty who'd been getting married to world-famous playboys, with an occasional industralist in the middle, for the last thirty years. I hadn't recognised her at first because her chin was sunk into her chest and a cloud of immensely expensive ash-pink hair obscured the rest of her face, and in any case, since her last news pictures, she'd put on a good deal of weight.

It was necessary for one of us to say something, and it didn't look as though my lovely companion was capable of making a start. "My dear Contessa," I began, "may I say how much I've always admired——"

She looked up. The eyes were immense and china-blue and unfocussed. The beautiful bones were still there, but they wouldn't be visible very much longer. She centred me after a moment. She looked puzzled. "You talkin' to me?" she enquired. Her accent had a combination I hadn't come across before—Cockney and the Deep South.

"Yes, indeed," I said. "I was just saying how much I'd always admired your pictures in the——"

"Crapola," said the Contessa, and waited for my next contribution. I decided upon a change of subject.

"You don't come to London as much now as you used to, do you?" I said.

She leant forward, peering into my face.

"Who you, darlin'?" she said. "Do I know you—who?" she added, apparently in the interests of clarity.

I said it without thinking. It came straight out of the subconscious. "Me?" I said. "I'm just an old badger who dropped in."

She looked at me for a long time, with no trace of expression on her face.

"Badger off, then," she suddenly said, with extraordinary viciousness.

Our little chat seemed to have reached an impasse from which there was no escape. "Perhaps," I said, after a moment, "you'd like to talk to someone else?"

She made no reply. She had retired again into a mood of reverie, her head down, rocking herself gently from side to side. It seemed unkind to abandon her altogether.

On the other side of the room a very good-looking young painter had been twinkling away at a number of older ladies for some time, with a lot of confident, silvery laughter. He gave us one of these bell-like performances now. I happened to know him. "Perhaps," I said to the Contessa, "you'd like to talk to him."

She raised the cloud of pink hair. Waveringly, the enormous blue eyes ranged over some of the guests. "Who's him, darlin'?" she said.

"That lad over there. He's a painter."

It took her nearly a minute to single him out, and about half a second to take him in.

"You have him, darlin'," said the Contessa, with absolute conviction. "Those little pretties are too goddam expensive."

Without warning—and it had no connection with her invitation—I was overcome by a fearful flush of heat. The cramped position on the stool had something to do with it. The after-shave lotion had gone suddenly sticky, too, adding yet another unpleasant ingredient to the goatish hairiness of the pullover. I sat sweating at her feet, blood pumping into my face. I was unable to speak, on the verge of fainting.

The Contessa examined me with what looked like concern. Then she let out a crow of laughter that silenced every other sound in the room.

"Well, whadya know!" crowed the Contessa. "I made the old badger blush!"

I was still mantled up—up to vermilion—when without further ado I took leave of my host and hostess. I noticed that he wiped his hand on his trouser leg immediately after shaking mine and then I was out in the street, dinnerless, trailing behind me through the bitter night clouds of various perfumed steam.

The telephone was ringing as I opened the door of my ice-bound flat. I picked it up and found it was not, as I feared, the art dealer asking me to return, but a nice actor who said, "Have you had dinner?"

"Nearly," I said. "I just missed it."

"Come and get it here."

"I'm wearing a dinner-jacket."

"Well, for God's sake take it off and put on a boiler suit or something human. I'm sick to death of fustian and in particular of the bloody Bard."

"What's he been doing to you?"

"I've been staggering about at Stratford conveying news from Gloucester to Worcester about Essex, wearing a variety of saucepans on my head. Come at once and we'll purge ourselves of all this."

We had about an hour and a half of excellently malicious, authoritative gossip and then he withdrew to carve the duck which his wife had laid out for him in an alcove off the dining-room.

She and I chatted away at the dinner table for some time, waiting for our portions to be served and gradually becoming aware of the sounds of disturbance in the alcove, where our host was working on the duck out of sight. Hoarse expletives, increasing in scope and intensity, mingled themselves with the clashing of a carving knife on a dish that seemed to be sliding about.

I gave his wife an enquiring look. "I think," she whispered cautiously, trying to restrain bursting laughter, "we'd better just wait and see."

Three minutes later there was a great, clattering crash, followed by the foulest obscenity we'd yet heard.

"Now," said his wife, her eyes streaming, "I think he's got it between the end of the sideboard and the wall."

He had. An amply proportioned figure with its back to us was down on all fours, poking in the gap between the sideboard and the wall with the carving knife. There was no sign of the dish or the duck.

The actor got to his feet. He pointed accusingly with the carving knife. "It's in there," he said.

"Never mind, Gloucester darling," said his wife, "I'll get it out."

Using, in the end, a large pair of scissors we managed jointly to hack the bird into three fairly equal portions and sat down to a dinner, that, having begun brilliantly, soon reached a new height of enjoyment.

"At least," the actor said, looking at the pile of bones on his plate, "it isn't flat. I hate," he said seriously—a good deal of whisky and water had been taken by way of aperitifs—"I hate flat food. You always get flat food at dinner parties. Flat slices of meat," he explained, "arranged on a sodding silver salver."

"And you begin," his wife added, "with flat smoked salmon——"

"And finish up," I said, "with flat *crêpes Suzette.*"

"It's all flat," the actor summed up. "I like mound food myself. Baked potatoes, pineapples, artichokes—anything moundy like that——"

The subject of moundy food, with deviations and variations, kept us going until three o'clock the following morning. Poor Gaga would have been quite breathless with her demands for explanation and, once the duck had got between the end of the sideboard and the wall, Hubert and Sybil would certainly have left for the safety of their hotel.

It is worth noting that, since the tea-gown went out with the Charleston, Dinner is the only meal to have an article of clothing named after it. The dinner-jacket—all part of the meretricious glitter that surrounds the verb To Dine. All persons susceptible to boredom should note that To Dine in fact merely means To Eat, and should get on with it quietly and without fuss.

I'll take a plate of piping hot moundy, myself, any time.

SHORT ON NIHILISM

"Do come in," I said. "But you may find the appointments a little austere."

He didn't come in. He looked at me as though I'd injured him. "You mean you've got nothing to drink?"

"There is that in adequate supply, but the thing is I've denuded my walls."

"I don't know about you," she said to her husband, "but I've simply got to have a look at this. Whatever it is—"

She entered the sitting-room ahead of us, looking round expectantly. "You have denuded, haven't you—" she said. "What an extraordinary effect. It's like small, blank windows."

"What happened?" he said. "Did you lend them to the Tate?"

"I got an uprush of aesthetic disgust," I said. "I sent them all off to be reframed."

He considered this for a while. "I always thought the frames were fine," he said. "You'd have done better to have them repictured."

"Why are you wearing beige socks," I asked him, "with that revolting chocolate-brown suit?"

"Why don't you go, just once, to a decent barber?"

"I don't think," she said abstractedly, "that much will come of the present discussion, but it is extraordinary to be in a room where there used to be pictures and now there are just these white blank spaces. For a start," she said, "it shows you how much dirt we must be absorbing into our lungs."

"A great deal more," he said, "than we're absorbing into our stomachs."

I gave them both a drink and he spoke in querulous vein for some time about the Budget. She interrupted him suddenly. "I'm sorry," she said, "but I simply can't stand it. It's like being stared at by six empty television screens." She got up and hung her handbag on one of the picture nails, and then stood back to study the effect. "It's called—'Effigy of a Female Person'," she said.

We examined it thoughtfully.

"It's kinetic," he said eventually. "I'll grant you that. But is it fluid?"

"It's certainly viable," I said. "But does it make a committed statement?"

He narrowed his eyes, putting his head on one side. "Painting," he said, "with solids. Fascinating. Pop art. Pop pop pop." He removed his shoe and tied it by the lace to her handbag. "It's called," he announced, " 'Divorce is a Many Splendoured Thing'."

"Don't you think," she said, "that the sole of the shoe should be pointing outwards? I mean, if it's called 'Divorce is a Many Splendoured Thing' I think there should be more feeling of rejection, a deeper melancholy. I think you're short of nihilism."

"When I called it 'Divorce is a Many Splendoured Thing'," he explained, "I wasn't thinking of divorce *per se* but more of a—more of another drink."

I gave him one and hung the bottle-opener on the picture nail beside the door. "An advanced example of the post-Fred Fazackerly school," I told them. "It's called 'I Know Where I'm Going And I'll Give You Three Guesses Who's Going With Me'."

He got up and stared at the bottle-opener so closely that his nose almost touched it. Then he backed away, framing it between his hands.

"I like it," he said soberly. "You've got your Kafka isolation bit there. It sings, with a thin whine. How much?"

"Three thousand."

"I'll take it," he said, and did so, opening another bottle of tonic.

His wife came out of the kitchen carrying, among other things, a sieve, a number of lettuce leaves and a leg of lamb, uncooked. Hung on the nail beside the door they made an arresting collage. "It's called," she said. " 'Woman's Place is in a Home for Incurables'. Four thousand pounds, delivered wrapped, C.O.D."

That did it. Within about half an hour almost every loose movable in the flat was collaged on the six nails, including a *chef d'oeuvre,* staggering in its economy, of an orange with a fork, two pens, a nail file and twelve toothpicks stuck into the skin. After a protracted discussion we were agreed that it represented modern man's futile groping for his own identity.

Shortly after that, to my surprise, they said they had to go. "But here," I said, "wait a minute, what about all this muck, all this stuff hanging on the walls?"

"Don't you worry about that, old chap," he said, at the door. "Just give Sotheby's a buzz. They'll clean up—and so will you."

ALL ILLUSION AND DECEIT

"What about Majorca, then, for Easter?" he said, pouring her some more champagne. An advertising executive, by the cut of his cool jib, the cool jib including a mohair suit in midnight-blue, with four buttons up the front of the jacket.

"I told you," she said, "I simply can't say yes or no until Thursday."

At the next table I tried to weigh up, from his point of view, the implications of this remark. She was smiling, which indicated that the Majorca proposal was acceptable, at least in theory, but on the other hand it didn't alter the plain fact that if the events of Thursday went wrong Majorca would be off.

"But you know you can tell me now," he said, with increased urgency. It was possible to guess that all of this ground had been covered before, as recently as yesterday, and that his sales technique was getting frayed.

She gave a silvery laugh. It was the equivalent of him getting on to a snake and slithering back all the way to the beginning again. "We got the most fearful rocket from the jam people this morning," she said pleasantly. "They're not going to wear that lay-out."

So she was an advertising executive, too! And in the same agency, by the sound of it.

"Never mind them," he said crossly. "That old nit Baker thinks he knows the lot. Listen, you don't have to wait until Thursday. You can tell me now."

A false move, in anyone's currency—and the lady reacted to it with asperity. "I'm going straight back to the office," she said, "if you go on about that any longer." She must have considered this warning to be final, because she followed it immediately with a charming request for some fresh strawberries.

As he turned to look for the waiter the lady accidentally caught my eye, a collision which was scarcely surprising in view of the fact that I practically had my elbow on her side plate, intent upon missing no line of the drama. On occasions like this the experienced eavesdropper creates an instant blankness in his face, a hooded remote look in the eye suggesting that his attention is miles away, concentrating on some abstruse aspect of Bergsonian philosophy.

The lady studied the structure I had prepared for her, apparently decided that it was genuine and turned back to her suitor, with the same charm as before.

"Oh," she exclaimed prettily, "clever you! They do have strawberries. How delish."

"I can always get you a pound or two," he said tenderly. "Straight from California. I know the chap—"

"I don't know," she said casually. "I'm not absolutely mad about them. Just an odd one from time to time." She allowed the waiter to decorate her plate with about 7s. 6d. worth of Devonshire cream.

The man watched this process with some melancholy. He was going to get a bill, by the look of it, for about ten pounds, and while it would certainly be charged up to the jam people's account he was equally clearly distressed by the waste, in that the Marjorcan project still refused to get off the ground. He returned to it with fresh resolution.

"If you'll come to Majorca," he said, "I'll get you one of those all-stretch American bathing-suits—you know, one of the ones with holes cut out of them all over. They haven't arrived in this country yet—not the good ones—but I know a chap—"

"You know," she said agreeably, "I always wear a bikini. I

couldn't bear the thought of elastic all over me. I'd love a brandy with my coffee."

He looked at her in the way that gentlemen in his situation often look at ladies—a way in which desire is blended in precisely equal proportions with the thought that it would be lovely to give her a stinging clump over the lug.

"Why can't you make up your mind?" he said hoarsely.

I had every sympathy for him. A trip to Majorca for Easter, nothing but the best, all paid for eventually by the jam people, a new all-stretch American bathing-suit and here she was playing hard to get.

"What about Caroline?" said the lady crisply.

The wife! The nigger in the woodpile! I was certainly getting my money's worth.

"Caroline's all right," said the man. "Don't worry about her—"

"She's not all right," snapped the lady. "I'm certain she's getting chicken-pox and if she does I'm definitely not leaving her with your mother. For Heaven's sake, she's only three."

"Mother is perfectly competent to look after her," said the man furiously, "and I'm damned if I'm going to spend Easter hanging around Surbiton when we could perfectly easily go to Majorca—"

They were man and wife. Soberly, I called for my bill, more convinced than ever that the world of advertising is shot through with illusion and deceit.

BLUNGED ON VIDKA

We met a charming Russian couple the other evening, and a quadrilateral fusion of interests broke out. None of this "love him, hate her" stuff. They were really delightful. Intelligent, imaginative, amusing—all the desirable qualities.

He was dark and she was fair, and their English was only slightly accented. They asked us to dine with them. "We will eat blinis," he said. "We will have a true Russian dinner," she said. "It will be very nice."

We presumed that they must have something to do with the Russian Embassy, and began to look forward to blinis carpeted with the best caviar.

When we arrived at their flat nothing happened, however, for quite some time. As often happens in these cases, the blazing new friendship was not quite as incandescent as it had been before. The conversation was somewhat constrained. Nor was there any trace of refreshment. I had begun, in fact, to think we'd stepped into a nest of teetotallers, when he suddenly seemed to remember his duties as host.

"Now," he said, "we drink vodka." From a cabinet containing only a limitless number of bottles of vodka he selected one and placed it with four very small glasses on a tray. He filled our glasses and said, "Straight down, in the Russian way." We did so and he immediately refilled them. I allowed a couple of minutes to pass before having another Russian go. He refilled my glass. I emptied it as we rose to go into dinner and he refilled it. I emptied it and he refilled it. I emptied it again and he refilled it and then, following my wife's thoughtful example, took the full glass with me into dinner.

On the table was a large silver chafing dish of large pancakes, or blinis. There was a big silver jug of melted butter and another of sour cream. There was also a long tray of things like smoked mackerel, anchovies, pickled herring and so on. No caviar.

Inadvertently, while waiting to begin, I emptied my glass. It was refilled immediately. Our host then explained the procedure.

"Put a blin on your plate," he began, and then she said, "One blin, two blinis."

"Put a blin on your plate, pour some butter and cream over it and then fold in piece of mackerel. Then you have more vodka. It helps with the greasy butter."

The thought of greasy butter caused me to take advance precautions. My glass was refilled. I noticed that my face was getting a little stiff and that my head seemed to be swelling.

We started on the blinis. Very nourishing. Almost, perhaps, a thought too rich. I had to pause half way through my third blin to emulsify with vodka and my glass was refilled.

By now I was really getting into the Russian way of life. I had another vodka *before* my fourth blin and said, "Surely we ought to say something Russian when we drink. Something like, Krasnayia slovolovitch !, or whatever it is. What is it?"

"I don't know," our host said. "I don't speak Russian. I left when I was three. Krasnayia slovolovitch !" He refilled our glasses.

"I don't speak Russian either," his wife said. "I was born in Lille. Krasnayia slovolovitch !" Our glasses were refilled.

This time, when helping myself to another blin, my glass was momentarily empty, so that I had the misfortune to fill it with melted butter.

The error threw me into a state of despondency. Almost crying, I said, "I'm cut off from solovolovitching. I've blindered."

"You've blunged," our host said with some severity. "The verb is irregular. I blinder, thou blinderest, he blinders, we blanger but you blunge. Krasnayia slovolovitch!"

Not to be left out of the slovolovitching I poured the butter back into the sour cream jug, washed out my glass with vodka and poured it over my blin. Then I put another blin on top of it, instead of a slice of pickled herring and I almost broke down. "I can't slovolovitch any more," I cried. "My synchronisation's all gone to blunge."

The next thing I knew I had a cup of tea in front of me with a slice of lemon in it, and beside it a plate of jam. My hostess put a spoonful of jam into her tea, but I got mixed up and poured the tea into the jam.

Next morning my wife told me I'd invited our new friends to a real Irish dinner. "Kedgeree Kathleen Mavourneen you called it," she said. "Do you know the recipe?"

By way of answer I turned my face, the size, shape and colour of a pickled gherkin, to the wall.

THE JAGGED HARE

Father, daughter and wife, with smiles like tattered spaghetti still adhering to our faces, seemingly there for the rest of our lives. Gone in the back and in the legs, able to communicate with one another only by signs.

We had been standing up too long at too many parties, shouting into too many strange faces, with too many strange faces bawling back.

"Quiet—din-din," I said, barely articulate. "Early bread. *Bed.*"

The ladies nodded or, rather, allowed their splitting heads to droop a little further towards the floor.

I gathered every inch of myself together, slotting the various ingredients into place, balanced them for a moment and then propelled the whole lot towards the telephone. I had had an idea, probably the last coherent one that would ever come to me.

I rang up this charming little Edwardian restaurant in its delightful little alley-way right in the middle of London's glittering theatre-land, and booked a table. I hadn't been there for years, but I knew it was exactly right for an evening like this. Cosy, old-fashioned, quiet and intimate—even to think of it was balm to the jiggling nerves.

They provided us with the best table in the house, a round

one with a deeply upholstered, semi-circular banquet. We sank into it. An almost invisible waiter provided us with a beautifully clean menu each—the sign of first-class service. Too spent to deal with the intricacies of an aperitif, I ordered two bottles of the delicious new Beaujolais.

We looked at our menus, drooping heads and half-closed eyes. Madame said, "I can't see it. What's the *plat du jour*?"

"Jugged hare."

"I hate it, but I'll have it."

Brigid said, "I hate it more than any sort of food I've ever had. I'll have it, too."

I said, "I hate it too much to have it. I'll have grilled kidneys and bacon."

The aspersions on the jugged hare had stiffened the waiter's back a little, but he took the order and went away. We drank some of the new Beaujolais. "It might be lovely," I said. "The jagged—the jugged her—hare." They were unable to make any comment at all.

The stuff arrived and we started on it, in silence. Suddenly, Madame's voice rang out. "Goddam it," she cried. "No! Not! I won't!"

Brigid pushed her plate away. She said, "Aaaugh!"

"My kidneys," I said, "are like used squash balls. And the bacon has been boiled in gear oil. Waiter!"

He appeared. "These kidneys," I said, "are like used squash balls, and the bacon has been boiled in gear oil . . ."

At the same time Madame said, "This hare hasn't been jugged, it's been tortured, and it isn't hare, it's elephant."

Brigid said, "Mine tastes of string, old, bad string."

The waiter, "I know it isn't very good but no one's ever complained."

Madame said, "That's all different now. Get the manager. *And* the chef."

The manager arrived. The other diners were silent, waiting upon events. The manager said the chef was too busy cooking, but could he do anything? We shouted about old, bad strings, used squash balls and tortured elephant for a long time, bursting with adrenalin, exhaustion forgotten in our outrage. The manager waited until it was over, then gave me the bill for the two bottles of Beaujolais. I paid it and we swept out. Brigid's hire-car was waiting in the street. "How long have you been here?" I asked the driver. "Half an hour, sir." I shouted at the doorman, "We told you to let us know when the car arrived."

"I know, sir," he said, "but I didn't want to disturb your dinner."

"Disturb our . . ." We left that little restaurant, in its charming alley-way, for ever.

It was strange to think of all the people inside, laughing and dining on old, bad string, just as if nothing had happened.

A COUPLE OF YORKSHIRE PUDS

"I won't tell you what it's going to be," said our host, "but it's something you don't get in France. Or, at least, it isn't nearly as good."

That identified lunch immediately. A beautiful round of pink and melting British beef, accompanied by golden Yorkshire pudding, with broccoli spears and baked potatoes, with a treacle tart to follow, with cream, and a piece of Stilton and digestive biscuits to wind the whole thing up.

And so it turned out to be. Delicious, and certainly unobtainable in France. We left at 3.30 p.m., round about the time we were able to walk, and spent the rest of the afternoon trying to speed our digestive processes by tramping round the square in the icy winds of the London Spring. Some other very kind friends had asked us to dine with them, and we wanted to be ready for it.

Our new hostess said, "I won't tell you what it's going to be, but you can probably guess, because it's something you can't really get in France."

And there it was again. A beautiful, even larger round of pink and melting British beef, accompanied by golden Yorkshire pudding in unstinted quantity, with a forest of broccoli spears and a mountain of baked potatoes, followed by a treacle tart and after that as much Stilton as we could eat on as many digestive biscuits as we could handle.

That was Saturday. Through nobody's fault we were looking forward to lunch on Sunday, in as much as it was possible ever to look forward to eating again. But this Sunday lunch was promising. Something had gone wrong with our hostess's oven, snookering the prospect of another round of pink and melting British beef, so they were going to take us out to a charming little inn they had found in leafy Bucks.

When we got there our host said, "I was sure you two must be sick of looking at restaurant menus so I've ordered lunch in advance. It's the speciality of this place and it's the kind of thing you don't get in France . . ." And so it was—again. The lot.

By Monday evening Madame and I thought we might be able to take a spoonful of something light, having left out breakfast and lunch. "I could," she said, "do an omelette. But the thought of watching it solidify—and then slopping it out of the pan . . ." We shuddered in unison.

"Let us," I said, suddenly thinking of it, "go Chinese. Three airy bamboo shoots, the merest pinch of fluffy rice, a wafer-like breast of chicken, a cool bottle of sparkling Vouvray . . ." We felt almost hungry again.

The restaurant of our choice was modest outside, and unfortunately psychedelic within. Purple and emerald décor, flickering lights, invisible menu. I said to the powerful-looking young Chinese waiter, "Something small—and a bottle of Vouvray."

A long time after that he came back with two bowls containing chopped, raw onion, and several miniature slices of what tasted like pemmican. He gave us chopsticks to eat it with, and a bottle of Turkish hock. Not much of a spread, and not too easy to get in without European eating tools, but we managed it, and the bottle of Istanbul.

When the waiter came back again, I asked him for the bill. He got a real touch of the Red Guards and snarled, "No bill—eat." He put in front of us two more little bowls, in which rested six round, greyish things which we had to spike with our sticks because they were too slippery to be gripped. We had four slipperies each, and left the rest.

When the waiter came back again, with two bowls of soup and a plate of things that looked like sausages in batter, I asked him for another bottle of Dardanelles paraffin. It looked like being a long night. And so it was. We chopsticked our way through mashed, roast duck wrapped in pancakes, the waiter having whipped the life-saving soup spoons. After a bucket of diced vegetables and small lumps of pork I begged him to give us a short break of perhaps an hour. "Not possible," he said curtly. "Chef lose timing." And placed in front of us a field of fried rice leaping with grilled prawns.

By now he had us going like brain-washed automata, ready to shovel in anything he put before us, for the rest of the night. But two courses later the road to Mandalay came to an end.

We are now going on the grapefruit diet. That is, half a grapefruit every second day.

Minding the Machine

"GENERAL COLLAPSE: PRESENT — ARMS!"

Sometimes, now, when I am overtired, or feeling ill, or someone has been sharp with me and my defences are down, the memory comes flooding back of the afternoon when I forgot what I was doing in a guard-of-honour, watched with close attention by nearly fifteen hundred people of both sexes. There were some small children there as well, but they probably didn't clearly understand what was going on.

The occasion was the opening of the new dining-hall at my old school, a handsome building with a salmon, a pig, and a turkey embossed on the entrance doors, representing fish, flesh, and fowl.

I was glad to see the new hall reach completion. Once, in the old one, I had incautiously reached behind the hot pipes at the back of my seat in search of a fork, and run my hand into something appalling. It was something old and soft and tenacious, and it might have been a former helping of tapioca, or a small animal, like a ferret, passed to its final rest.

When I say I was glad to see the new dining-hall reach completion, it would be more accurate to say that I should have been glad to see the new dining-hall reach completition if I hadn't found out at the same time that the commanding-officer of the O.T.C. had selected me to be right-hand man in the guard-of-honour, which even then was being mobilised to greet the field-marshal whose task it was to declare the new edifice open. When I found that out I wanted the new dining-hall to catch fire, and be burnt to the ground.

As soon as this project was mooted I knew it was going to be the last battle in the war between me and the O.T.C. Up till now we had fought a lively contest, with no quarter asked or given, but as yet no conclusive engagement had been reached. No sooner did I succeeed in concealing an uncleaned rifle in someone else's rack than the O.T.C. would catch me with my puttees upside-down, and both sides would retire to their lines with honours even. So it went all the time.

But this guard-of-honour business, I knew, would see the final victory go to either one side or the other. It was something too big for compromise.

When the commanding-officer picked upon me to be right-hand man he picked not upon the best, but merely the tallest soldier in the school. At this time, at the age of sixteen, I stood six feet four in my army boots—a distinction reduced in importance by my weight, which remained constant at eight stone. It is not true to say that you couldn't see me sideways, but it certainly was necessary to narrow the eyes a little.

Preparations were set in train at once. They found twenty-nine other boys around the six-foot mark—some already shaving, and with more or less permanent assignations with the maids in the sandhills—and the preliminary drilling began.

Without delay I made an implacable enemy—the Regular Army sergeant known to us off-duty as Gus.

Between Gus and me there was already but a small measure of mutual respect. During P.T. I'd corrected him once or twice in his grammar, and he'd caught me on two successive field-days shooting mud through my rifle with blank cartridges.

Now, matters came to a head. Gus, seeing me on the first parade standing in the post of honour at the end of the line, made an instant objection. He marched smartly up to Lieutenant Winter—who was, and should have remained, the games master, but was now in charge of the guard—saluted, and said: "'E carn't do it, sir. Ain't got the stuffin' in 'im." Winter, of course, had no idea what he was talking about, and it took them several minutes to straighten it out. Eventually, however, Winter grasped what was the matter. He came up to me and: "You think you can handle this job all right, Private Campbell?" I said, "Yessir," meaning, "A kind of miracle might see me through." Winter nodded to Gus as if to say, "I told you so." I think he had some idea about upholding the prestige of the middle-class.

After that Gus went out of his way to confuse me—batting on a pretty easy wicket, since I sometimes attempted to form fours on receipt of the order to dismiss. He also referred to me with unvarying persistence as "Beanpole," a masterstroke, seeing that I couldn't very well answer back, at least while I was in the ranks, and he was out in front.

"General Salute," Gus would roar—"and that goes fer Beanpole if 'e don't fold up in the middle—Preesent—*Hipe!*" "Squad," Gus would shout, "by the right, in column of fours, quick—'old up, Beanpole, yer can run if yer warnt ter—March!" By the end of the first fortnight I was getting two hours' sleep a night.

But the worst thing of all was the fixing of the bayonets. By the nature of my position, right-hand-man, it was my duty to march out in front of the squad, turn left, and then with a variety of complex gestures, fasten the knife on to the end of my rifle. The others took what time there was from me.

Gradually, bayonet-fixing began to occupy my whole life. I practised fixing bayonets on hockey-sticks, cricket-bats, yardbrooms, fire-irons—anything comparatively long and straight and narrow that came to hand. I could fix bayonets in my sleep, and frequently did.

The great day dawned, a bright blue summer's day. I had hoped passionately for a waterspout, but it was not to be.

The guard-of-honour fell in outside the armoury. There was a good deal of surreptitious polishing of buttons and setting of caps. Then Gus struck his final blow. He inspected me carefully, front and back, and then, in a terrible travesty of a refined accent, he said, "Pawdon meh, Lord Clawence, but why ain't you wearin' unifawm?" I fell for it. I shot one panic-stricken downward glance at my threadbare khaki, and realised I'd been had.

"I *am* wearing uniform," I said coldly, "to the best of my knowledge."

Gus shook his head, a long and mournful process. "Oh no, yer not, Lord Clarence," he said. "Wot you're wearin' is a crime—a ruddy, 'orrible, long-drawrn-aht crime."

"Oh, shut up," I said, "and get on with your work."

Gus was so delighted with himself that he betrayed no sign of irritation. After a short speech full of indescribable menace, he marched us on to the square via the playing-fields, the patch of grass behind the chapel, and a complete circuit of the sanatorium. My puttees began to slip, and once I walked into a tree. But we made the square at last.

It was lined with parents in top-hats and flowered dresses. The staff and the field-marshal were disposed in a row of leather armchairs.

Lieutenant Winter took over from Gus—Winter looking as if he was on his way to execution. He brought us to attention.

This was the moment. Now came the fixing of the bayonets, preliminary to the General Salute. I repeated to myself very quickly everything I knew about fixing bayonets. I was word perfect. There was nothing to go wrong.

"Fix . . ." roared Lieutenant Winter. I stepped out smartly from the ranks, achieved the regulation number of paces, halted, and turned crisply to the left. "Bayonets!" roared Lieutenant Winter.

Without a moment's hesitation I presented arms. With the precision of a guardsman I swung the rifle up to my side, across the body, a smack on the magazine, a stamp of the back leg, and there I was carved out of stone, frozen solid in the General Salute.

Perhaps half a minute later I saw Lieutenant Winter standing in front of me. His eyes were bulging out of his head. "What," he said in a shocked whisper, "what do you think you're doing?"

He took me by surprise. I thought everything was going well. "General Salute," I said out of the side of my mouth, "I'm presenting arms."

I think he danced a little. "You're not!" he hissed—"you're supposed to be fixing your bayonet!"

And then it all came back. I stared at Lieutenant Winter in horror.

"Oh gosh, sir," I said, "what'll I do?"

Lieutenant Winter, in spite of being an incurable singer of "Take a pair of sparkling eyes," and "Two little girls in blue" at school concerts, must have been an instinctive leader of men. "Come back to attention," he said, "keep your head, and I'll give you the order again." I nodded violently. I would have died for him at that moment.

He withdrew to his previous position in advance of the guard. As he walked away I went back to the beginning again, or, indeed, rather farther back than the beginning, because after orderings arms I stood at ease. With the rest of the guard still standing to attention it must have seemed to competent observers that there was nothing in the drill book that could ever bring us together again.

But Winter found it. "Private Campbell," he shouted, improvising a command unique in military history, "Attention! Guard of honour—Bayonets!"

I went through it like the mechanical man. We stuck our knives on to the ends of our rifles with a magnificent flourish and click. Then I turned left, paused, and marched stiff as a ramrod back to the comparative safety of the ranks. As I marched back I saw Gus. He was standing like a statue in the rear of the platoon. Only the whites of his eyes were showing.

The rest of the programme passed off without incident. Two days later, however, I had an interview with the headmaster. As a result of it I took no further part in military training, but on future corps days went for a walk to the village with a boy called Humphries, who had weak ankles.

On balance, I suppose it was nearly worth it.

THE HOT BOX

Once upon a time I was given an assignment to write an article about a load of archæological remains, dug up by some fool on the outskirts of Waterford.

This was in the days when the newsprint situation allowed us to devote whole columns to fossils, brass rubbings, or even the Franciscan method of illuminating manuscripts.

Caught by the Waterford job, I made a demur. No knowledge of archæological remains—very busy at the moment with an article about badminton. . . .

"Round about 1,200 words," said the news editor. "Riordan, in the public library, knows all about it."

He measured me for a moment. "You two ought to get on," he said, "like a house on fire. Or an ammunition dump exploding," he added.

I asked him what he meant.

"You mind your own business," he said.

I went along to the library, already rehearsing "Riordan," and "archæological remains." It had, of course, to be Riordan and archæological remains just at a time when my intermittent stammer was passing through a cycle which left me incapable of dealing with these initial letters.

There were two elderly gentlemen in subdued suits at the desk, both reading.

I chose the one on the right.

"Excuse me," I said, "are you Mr. M'Reer—M'Reer—M'Reer. . . ."

I was full of air, and putting in the intrusive "m"—a stratagem which often worked—but this time nothing happened.

The librarian looked up. He wore half-moon, gold-rimmed glasses, and a black woollen cardigan. He nodded towards his colleague. He also put down his book and prepared to listen—with what seemed to be a disproportionate measure of interest.

I saw why a moment later.

"I'm A'Rah—A'Rah—A'Rah . . ." began the second librarian, with his eyes tightly shut.

I'd walked into another one.

I should, of course, have given it up at once—gone back to the office, and said Riordan was on holiday.

But then the fighting instinct arose in me. My intrusive "m" against his intrusive "a." I'd tried the intrusive "a" myself, and knew that in careless hands it could bring on strangulation.

I scanned the sentence that lay before me. It contained only a number of minor obstacles.

I shot it out very quickly.

"I believe you know something abow-abow-abowbow—could you tell me what you know of the Waterford arkie-arkie-arkie—the Waterford find?"

It turned out to be rather rougher than I'd expected.

Riordan sat back. "What was that?" he said.

I looked at him coldly. He knew perfectly well what we'd got ourselves into. It was up to him to pull his weight.

Even Waterford seemed to have collapsed. I took another breath. "Man found some flints or something down south and I was told you knew something abah-abah. . . . You knew something," I said.

The other librarian had now abandoned all interest in his book, and was leaning forward intently.

"Ah, yes," said Riordan easily. "The archæological remains discovered in Waterford." You could hear every syllable, clear as a bell.

He stood up. "I think I can find you the reference. I have aboo-aboo-aboo-aboo . . ."

I let him have it. It was sheer joy.

He'd nearly torn his memo pad in half by the time that I released him.

"You have a book," I said, "which will help us."

"Downstairs," said Riordan. He loosened his collar. "Come this way," he said.

The other librarian half rose in his seat, watching us right to the door. He'd taken his glasses off, and his mouth was open.

We went down into the basement, and along a passage lined with pipes.

"By the way," I said, "what's your first name? I think I know a friend of yours."

I'd seen the card on his desk, in a brass slot: BRIAN RIORDAN. The chances were if he couldn't say book he couldn't say Brian either.

He stopped, as if shot. Convulsively, he gripped the handle of a low, barred door which had appeared in front of us. His neck began to swell. He drew a couple of long, shuddering breaths.

I watched him with interest. One foot came off the ground, and writhed about.

Suddenly, he got it. It came out like a tyre bursting.

"Jack!" said Brian Riordan.

"Can't be the same person," I said easily. "The Riordan I was thinking of is——" Everything shut down. I fought it blindly for a second. "Someone else," I said.

We went into the cellar with honours approximately even. It was a tiny room, brilliantly whitewashed, about six feet by six. A bare electric light bulb hung from the ceiling at eye level. It was very hot. Pipes ran all round the walls.

Riordan turned round. The light hung between us, very bright and dazzling.

"Where was this find made?" he said.

The stuff had been dug up in a place called Rathally. But as far as I was concerned, what with the heat, and the glare, and the congestion, it might well just have been Czrcbrno, a hamlet in the Balkans.

I tried everything—the finger tapping, the coughing, the intrusive "m," even a short whistle. Nothing happened. The light, agitated by some truant blast, swayed gently backwards and forwards. Riordan waited, leaning forward politely—exultant.

I thought I was going to faint. I had ceased to breathe. I half-turned my head—intending, perhaps, to jump upon Rathally from the rear—and then I saw Theodore Blake. He was peering through the bars, and from the look of deep peace upon his face, I knew that he, too, was engaged with the priceless gift of speech.

Theodore—of all people!

Riordan opened the gate. "Well," he said, "Mr. Bla—Mr. Bla—Bla . . ." He gave it up. Theodore came in. We moved back a little to give him room.

Theodore had lately been using an old method of my own. No sound emerged. No hint of expression ever crossed his face. He seemed to be lost in meditation. But it was then you knew that he was really on the griddle.

The three of us, tightly pressed together, the bulb hanging between us, stood there, waiting.

A full minute later Theo said, "Hello."

I'd better luck than Riordan. I said, "What are *you* doing here?"

Riordan tried to say, "What can I do for you, Mr. Blake?" and nearly made it, until the "b," as usual, beat him all ends up. He actually struck his head against the books behind him.

All this time Theodore was quietly at work. Suddenly, he got it out. "Can I have that book on Roman coins?" he said, so careful and expressionlessly that it sounded like Roger, the talking Robot.

"Certainly," said Riordan, and turned to the bookshelves.

It was certainly unfair. He must have known quite well where the book was, but he began fiddling about, pretending he couldn't find it.

Theo and I looked at one another. It was up to someone to say something. We got down to it together.

Theo won. "What are *you* doing here?" he said.

I lowered my voice an octave. "I'm gathering material on the arkie-arkie——" I couldn't go on. I simply couldn't face "archæological" again.

"On coins," I said. "M'Roh—M'Roh—the same kind of coins as yourself."

Riordan swung round from the book-case. I'd forgotten about him.

"You said you wanted the Waterford archæological remains!" he exclaimed.

"You've got it wrong," I said. "I'm doing a story abah—a story on coins." I was going to add—"through the ages"—and then abandoned it. "Just coins," I said.

The awful look of unearthly peace came over Theo's face. I knew what he was going to say. He was going to say that he'd been commissioned to write an article about coins and couldn't understand why I was doing one, too.

We waited for Theodore. It was difficult not to look at him, because we were jammed cheek to cheek, but we did our best.

Theodore looked straight ahead, motionless, carved out of stone.

"But," he said, three minutes later, "I'm doing an article about coins. Why are you doing one, too?"

Riordan opened his mouth.

"Ubu-ubu-ubu——" he began, harping on my commitment to archæological remains.

"It doesn't matter," I said. "There has been some confusion. I can easily switch over to the arkie-arkie-arkie——"

"Ubu-ubu——" gasped Riordan, "you asked me for that boo—boo-boo—that in the first pip-pip——"

It was absolutely indescribable. And suddenly Theodore joined in. On the very first word he slipped right back into his old habit—the wurr-wurr-wurr. God alone knows what he was trying to say. He simply wurred.

I don't know how long it went on for—me busy with arkie-arkie, Riordan pip-pipping, and Theo lost in the throes of wurr.

Steam seemed to be running down the walls. Once the electric light bulb bounced off my forehead with a sharp "Ponk!"

Something snapped. "Here," I said, "let me——" I couldn't say "out." I let it go. I pushed past them, fled along the passage, and a moment later was in the open air.

In my hand was Theo's book about coins.

I sent it back next day, by registered post.

MR. SMYLLIE, SIR

When, in these trying times, it's possible to work on the lower slopes of a national newspaper for several weeks without discovering which of the scurrying executives is the editor, I count myself fortunate to have served under one who wore a green sombrero, weighed eighteen stone, sang parts of his leading articles in operatic recitative, and grew the nail on his little finger into the shape of a pen nib, like Keats.

Even the disordered band of unemployed cooks, squabbling like crows over the Situations Vacant columns in the front office files, knew that he was Robert Maire Smyllie, Editor of the *Irish Times,* and fell silent as he made his swift rush up the stairs.

He was a classical scholar, at home among the Greek philosophers. He was the incorruptible champion of the fading Protestant cause in holy Ireland. His political and humanitarian views won international respect, and he spent most of his time on the run from the importunities of such characters as Chloral O'Kelly and Twitchy Doyle.

They lay in wait for him every evening in their chosen lairs in the front office and threw themselves in his path, as though to halt a rushing locomotive, as soon as he appeared at the door.

Chloral O'Kelly was a deeply melancholic youth who drank disinfectant, and was in constant need of 3*s.* 9*d.* for another bottle. Twitchy Doyle was a little old man with a straggly, jumping moustache who lived by reviewing reprints of Zane Grey. The moment the Editor burst through the front door they closed on him with urgent appeals, battling for position with Deirdre of the Sorrows, an elderly woman who believed for twelve years that she was being underpaid for her contributions to the Woman's Page. The Editor shot through them, weaving and jinking, crying: "No—not tonight—tomorrow—goodbye"—and put on an extra burst of speed which carried him up the stairs to the safety of his own room, there to deliver his unforgettable cry: "Pismires! Warlocks! Stand aside!"

I looked up "pismire" once in the dictionary and found it meant an ant. It pictured, vividly, the unrelenting tenacity of his hangers-on.

For four years, six nights a week, I worked beside this enormous, shy, aggressive, musical, childlike, cultured and entirely unpredictable human being, separated from him by only a wooden partition, in a monastic life cut off almost completely from the world.

We worked in a high, dusty room topped by an opaque glass dome. There were no outside windows, so that the lights burned day and night. Alec Newman, the Assistant Editor, and Bill Fleming, the theatre critic, shared the outside part. Then came the Editor's office, partitioned off by battered wooden panelling. I had a tiny box jammed between him and the wall, with a sliding hatch between us for the purposes of communication. When it was open I got a portrait view of the great head, hair brushed smoothly back, brick-red face, snub nose supporting glasses and a ginger moustache enclosing the stem of a curved pipe the size of a flower-pot. "Mr. Campbell, we do not wish to be observed," was the signal for the hatch to be closed.

Alec, Bill and I got in about nine-thirty every night and started to scratch around for leader subjects in the English papers. At ten o'clock the Editor burst in like a charging rhino, denounced pismires and warlocks, and went to ground in his own room.

At ten-thirty came the inevitable inquiry: "Well, gentlemen——?"

Alec assumed the responsibility of answering for all of us. "Nothing, Mr. Smyllie, sir. All is sterility and inertia."

The reply was automatic. "Ten-thirty, and not a strumpet in the house painted! Art is long, gentlemen, but life is shuddering shorter than you think." "Shuddering" and "shudder" were favourite words of complaint.

Alec made his set protest. "You're hard, Mr. Smyllie, sir. Hard!"

"Mr. Newman?"

"Sir?"

"Take your King Charles's head outside and suck it."

I never discovered the origin of this extraordinary injunction, but it meant that some disagreement had taken place between them during the afternoon and that Alec had better be careful from now on. My own orders came floating over the partition.

"Mr. Campbell?"

"Sir?"

"Prehensilise some Bosnian peasants."

"Immediately, sir."

The cryptic order had a simple origin. The Editor, seeking once to commend a piece of writing that clung closely, without irrelevant deviation, to its theme, had hit upon the word prehensile, which passed immediately into the language of our private, nocturnal life. Somerset Maugham, for instance, was a prehensile writer, Henry James unprehensile in the extreme. From here it was a short step to prehensilising an untidily written contribution. Reprehensilisation covered a second re-write. We didn't even notice we were saying it after a week or two.

The Bosnian peasant came from a discovery of mine on the back of the *Manchester Guardian*—an exceedingly improbable story about a Balkan shepherd who'd tripped over a railway line and derailed a train with his wooden leg. The shepherd, in addition, had only one eye, and was carrying a live salmon in his arms. I cannot imagine, now, how even a short fourth leader could have been written on such a theme, but for months I was dependent on the *Guardian's* Balkan correspondent for my ideas. Acceptance of this *argot* led me once to frighten the life out of the Bishop—I think—of Meath.

I'd come in very late and burst straight into the Editor's room. "I'm sorry I got held up, Mr. Smyllie, sir!" I cried. "I can always reprehensilise some one-eyed Bosnian bastards!" It was only then that I saw the Bishop sitting in the visitors' chair with his top-hat on his knee. I've never seen a man so profoundly affected by a sentence containing only eight words.

If pursuing his personal, King Charles's head war with Alec, the Editor would suddenly give him the first, interminable leader to write on some political theme, while doing the second and shorter one himself.

Silence settled in for about an hour, with the four typewriters rattling away.

Sometimes, then, we got: "Cold—cold—cold——"

Almost anything could start it off, from the mere weather conditions to some philosophic reflection that had entered the Editor's mind.

His typewriter stopped. The rest of us paused, too, expectant in our boxes. The voice rose, high and ghostly, from the Editor's compartment:

"Cold—cold—cold——"

We echoed it, still higher and thinner:

"Cold—cold—cold——"

The Editor's voice took on a deeper, tragically declamatory note:

"Cold as a frog in an ice-bound pool,
Cold as the tip of an Eskimo's tool
Colder than charity——"

There was a long pause, while we stuffed our handkerchiefs into our mouths, struggling to remain silent. The next line came out with rasping cynicism:

"And that's pretty chilly——"

He allowed this to sink in, then returned to the dramatic narrative form:

"But it isn't as cold as poor Brother Billy——"

We all joined in, vying with one another to achieve the maximum in greasy self-satisfaction, on the last line:

"Cause *he's DAID!*"

There'd be a sudden break in the mood. The voice came out with a snap. "Thank you, gentlemen, and give my regards to your poor father."

When he was writing the words poured out of him in a flood, without correction, and at times, indeed, without much thought. He'd been doing it too long. But there were occasions when he bent the whole of his courageous and intelligent mind to denouncing the rising tide of parochial Irish republicanism—notably on the death of George V.

This long-drawn-out decline was being charted much more thoroughly by the *Irish Times,* with its Unionist sympathies, than by the other newspapers. Night after night Smyllie put a new touch to his obituary leader, after the routine inquiry, "Has the poor old shudderer passed on?" Finally, the King died and the leader was sent out for setting. We were all in the Editor's room when the first edition came off the machines. He tore open the leader page to see how it looked, and gave a scream like a wounded bull when he saw that the second half of it, possibly inadvertently, had been printed upside down. Pismires and warlocks that morning were relegated to the ends of hell.

This concern for the English King got us into scattered forays with the IRA, leading once to the windows of the office in Cork being broken by a shower of stones. When the news reached the Editor he made, taking as his framework, "They cannot intimidate me by shooting my lieutenants," one of the most carefully formulated battle-cries I've ever heard in my life.

We were in the office at the time. He instructed me to give him the naggin of brandy, filed under B in his correspondence cabinet, and took a steady pull. "These shudderers," said Robert

Maire Smyllie, "cannot intimidate me by throwing half-bricks through the windows of the branch office while my lieutenants are taking a posset of stout in the shebeen next door."

When we left, round about two o'clock the following morning, however, he was in a noticeable hurry to mount his bicycle. As he swung his massive weight into the saddle one of the pedals snapped off clean. He fell off, sprang up again, shouted, "Mr. Campbell, as your superior officer I order you to give me your velocipede!"—snatched it out of my hand, leaped aboard and sped off into the darkness. I limped after him on the broken one. When we got back to his house we drank Slivovitz until breakfast, in further defiance of "the porter-slopping shudderers from Ballydehob."

In the office there was indeed at this time the feeling of a beleaguered garrison, one which prompted all of us to remain in the place until daylight, rather than face the dark streets on our bicycles. Those were the great nights of the domino games that kept us locked in combat over the Editor's desk until the charwomen came in in the morning.

"A little pimping, Mr. Smyllie, sir?" Alec would suggest, after the paper had gone to bed.

"A little pimping, Mr. Newman, would be acceptable."

No one could ever remember how it came to be called pimping, with the additional refinement of "hooring", to describe the act of blocking the game with a blank at both ends, but because of Smyllie's complete purity of mind these technicalities added a notable spice to the game.

I can see him now, his green, wide-brimmed hat set square on his head, the great pipe fuming and a glass of brandy by his side, delicately picking up his tiles with the pen-nib fingernail raised in the air.

The unspoken purpose of the three of us was to do him down by a concerted onslaught, all playing into one another's hands to present him with a blank, when his turn came to play, on both ends.

"Pimp, Mr. Newman, pimp," I would urge Alec, sitting on my right. We always used these formal titles when in play.

Alec would close one end. "Hoor, Mr. Campbell, hoor!"

If, happily, I had a suitable blank I would lose no time in playing it, then we all burst into a trimphant cry:

"Hoored, Mr. Smyllie, sir—hoored! Take a little snatch from the bucket!"

With an expressionless face, and the dainty finger-nail raised in the air, the great man would draw some more tiles from the middle, on occasion being lucky enough to find a seven, and then play it with an elegant flick of the wrist, like an eighteenth-century gallant. "That, gentlemen," he would say, "should wipe the shuddering grins off your kissers. *Nemo me impune lacessit*—and best wishes to all at home."

I left the *Irish Times* under rather dubious circumstances, intending, in fact, only to take a week's holiday in London, but I was also writing a column for the Irish edition of the *Sunday Dispatch* at this time, and thought it might be interesting to call at headquarters. As a result of this I wrote a piece about the English scene which they used in all the editions, and paid me a little more than five times what I was getting for a whole week's work at home. I sent Smyllie a telegram, saying I'd been held up, and hoped to be back soon. He countered with a letter saying he would be delighted to see the last of me if I'd send him a year's salary, in lieu of notice. I replied that I'd see my bank manager about it. I remained on in London, and the correspondence came to an end.

In the next three years I returned fairly frequently to Dublin without daring to go and call on him, until one day, I opened the *Irish Times* and saw a paragraph in his Saturday diary column, which he wrote under the name of Nichevo.

It was very short. "My spies tell me," it read, "that Paddy Campbell is back again in Dublin, after a long safari looking for tsetse fly in the bush. He is now preparing a definitive biography of Schopenhauer, and is doing a lot of field research on the subject in the back bar of Jammet's, and the Dolphin Hotel."

It was an intimation that peace had been declared. But he was dead before I could say, "Good evening, Mr. Smyllie, sir," again.

THE CONTRAST THAT KILLS

We had, during the week, a very pleasant overnight stay in the beautiful and cultured city of Cardiff.

It would be untrue to say that the primary purpose of this trip was pleasure, although of course it turned out to be exceedingly enjoyable. No, to speak frankly, but with no intention of giving offence to anyone, we went to Cardiff to publicise a book which Madame and I wrote together—an autobiography, really, which is now available at all the cleaner bookshops.

No ostentatious drum banging or anything like that, rather more a mission of goodwill.

We started extending goodwill at Paddington, to get into the swing of it, as it were, greeting the ticket collector politely, and bowing to the Pullman attendant who found us our seats. Madame provided a nice touch here by complimenting him on the cleanliness of his train.

Upon finding our publisher already aboard, in place of the cascade of bitterness, accusation, derision and complaint which forms so much of the normal communication between publishers and authors, we even said good-morning to him, too, and he replied in like terms quite civilly.

After lunch we thanked the dining-car attendant for a really superb meal and shortly afterwards arrived in the beautiful city of Cardiff, in bright, warm sunshine, which is, of course, the normal climate of the lovely Principality. There we were met by Cardiff's most distinguished and intelligent bookseller, who was good enough to drive us to the headquarters of TWW, where I was to give a short television interview.

We commiserated with everyone we met at TWW on the dastardly treatment that had been handed out to them by the ITA and promised that on our return to London we would do all in our power to publicise their cause.

Cardiff's most distinguished bookseller then drove us out to his charming house in the country, where we met his exceedingly attractive wife. There we changed into our best and smartest clothes and then our generous host drove us back into the city and into the majestic purlieus of Cardiff Castle, where he was giving a party for us in the noble Banqueting Hall.

We were a little early, so that we were delighted to find that two young university students were more than willing to take us on a conducted tour of the Tower, and to outline in detail its many Turkish, Persian, Egyptian and Lebanese splendours, as created by the personal vision of the second, or possibly the third, Marquis of Bute.

It was then time for the reception. A lavish spread had been laid out, attended by two waitresses of charm and agility, who slotted five excellent dry sherrys into us before we really had time to take our bearings.

Then the guests began to arrive and Madame and I and our publisher, occupying three different spheres of influence, began chatting and laughing with Mr. and Mrs. Jones, and Mr. and Mrs. Jones, and various librarians, and Mr. Bevin and Mrs. Bevan, and the Principal of Cardiff University and his wife, and the ex-Principal and *his* wife, and Mr. and Mrs. Thomas, and

Mr. Thomas, and Miss Jones and Mr. Jones, and what had begun as a calculated mission of goodwill turned into a very, very gay party.

I even got a little beside myself and gave a Mr. and Mrs. Williams the benefit of a narrative of some considerable length, and then moved on to do it again for another Mr. and Mrs. Williams, and was just beginning to do it for a third time for a Mr. and Mrs. Jones only to find that they were the Mr. and Mrs. Williams for whom I'd done it in the first place. We got home very late to our host's charming house in the country, but were up at dawn to catch the 8 a.m. train to London.

We were approaching the outskirts of Southall when I noticed a curiously gloating look on Madame's face. I enquired into its origin.

"It was a lovely party," she said, "but after so much goodwill I'm now looking round for someone to bite. Starting," she said, "with the engine-driver, if he's as much as one minute late. Just by way of contrast, you understand," she added. I understood so well that I spent the afternoon, prudently, alone in a cinema.

SIGN THE SHOPPING BAGS HERE

"The best we ever did," he said, even the far-off memory of this great event bringing a gleam to his eye, "was Douglas Bader. Seven hundred copies, and he had to take a couple of hundred home with him. No time to sign."

"Oh, yes?"

I uncapped my fountain-pen and as usual it had overflowed. Although I was prepared for it, and had proceeded cautiously with the uncapping, I still got a lot of ink on the palm of my right hand.

"And now," he said, "we're hoping to get Sir Francis Chichester. That's really going to be something."

I tried to remove some of the ink on the underside of my right trouser-leg. One good thing had happened, at least. I was wearing a dark suit.

The manager fingered one of my own books. "Of course," he said, "this is a little bit slender for thirty bob."

Two ladies in hats, looking well-heeled, had paused in the middle distance, both of them looking at me with a kind of indignant curiosity. One of them whispered something to the other, seeming to shed a brief ray of light into a singularly dark and noisome corner. At any rate, the second one nodded curtly, registering the unpleasant news. Their indignant curiosity became an unmistakable glare of outrage, but at least they were still there.

I found a smile, and presented it to them with a courteous inclination of the head. It had an instantaneous effect. Apparent terror replaced the look of outrage. They hurried away without a backward glance.

"I think," said my publisher, standing behind me, "it might be better if you didn't meet their eye."

For the next five minutes or so both of us looked steadily at the top of the desk. It had been imported from the furniture department of the store, and still carried its price tag : £59 16s. 6d. I worked it out that I would have to autograph, and sell, rather more than 4,500 copies before I could buy the desk, on which perhaps to write another one. About 3,800 more than Douglas Bader. A considerable target at which to aim. To say nothing of Sir Francis Chichester, still to come.

After another couple of minutes of looking at the top of the desk I came to the conclusion that there was nothing whatever I could do in the way of aiming at anything, sitting there in the middle of this West End store, surrounded by hundreds of pictures of my face on the jacket, and another one on the back. With the addition of my own face, live, looking at the top of the desk, it all added up to an army of me sufficiently intimidating to put the whole Israeli Air Force to flight.

I said to my publisher, "Perhaps if we went away for a bit. Give them a chance to handle the goods without us here, ravenous for our thirty bobs."

He advised me to stick it out. "We'll get the lunch-time rush soon," he said.

We got one young man with a brown paper parcel. He unwrapped it carefullly. "I bought it in Hatchards," he said, "but I should be very much obliged if you could sign it for me."

I did so. The manager of the book department watched this performance with comparative indifference. As the young man went away, reparcelling his book, the manager said, "It happens sometimes." It was just another minor irritation in an autographing session which, unless it was Bader or Chichester, was bound to be alive with them.

Then we did get quite a little rush, though a modest one. It was halted by a volatile lady with a small child, who cried, "I'm not going to buy your book, but I've always wanted to meet you." She introduced me to the child, who didn't speak, but the damage had been done. Half-a-dozen people, who'd been hanging round the outskirts, came forward and asked for autographs, offering paper-bags containing their shopping, for me to sign.

Just before the end of the session an assistant-manager had a word of cheer. "You haven't done *too* badly," he said. "I believe Rebecca West once went all the way to Glasgow, and signed one."

My final score was 25 more than Miss West, and 675 less than Douglas Bader: leaving an open field for Sir Francis.

Bon voyage, mon vieux matelot.

FLICKER AWAY, PHILLIDA WISP

A surprising number of people know my secretary, Phillida Wisp.

Scarcely a day passes that people do not ring to say, "May I speak to Mr. Campbell's secretary, please?"

I have to tell them, "I'm sorry, I'm afraid she's not here at the moment, but this is him—he—I—me speaking. What can I do for you?"

Then they sound put out, even vexed. "Oh," they say, "I don't want to bother you. I just wanted to have a word with your secretary."

It sounds as though the contact with her employer has been too abrupt for them, the intimacy too immediate. Sometimes they ring off, without further ado, leaving me with the uncomfortable feeling that it's Phillida they wish to speak to, about a private matter with which I have no concern.

Other people write to say, "My small daughter, who is seven, would very much like to have a signed photograph of you. I know you're very busy so just get your secretary to look for a nice one and send it to the above address."

Phillida is never there when these requests arrive, and they tend to put a total stopper on my working day. I've got to do the whole thing myself, ringing around to various newspapers and magazines to say that I believe they had a photograph of me, taken some time in 1959 or, perhaps, 1960, by a photographer whose name I unfortunately do not remember, and could I possibly have a copy of same for which, naturally, I shall be only too glad to pay whatever they think is fitting.

They are the soul of courtesy, the newspapers and magazines.

They tell me they will try their level best to find the desired photograph and will forward it to my secretary as soon as possible, if they could just have the name.

"P. Campbell."

They laugh, with just a hint of impatience. "No, no—your secretary's name."

"Miss Wisp."

There is a short silence and then they thank me very much. I always suppose they are a little surprised by the unusual surname of Wisp.

One of the difficulties of employing Phillida is, of course, that she's only part time, and is literally never there when just for once she's got some practical job to do, so that I've got to deal with her work as well as my own. These frequent absences of hers drive me, I'm sorry to say, to ruse and subterfuge. After all, one does not wish to present to the world the image of an employer so lacking in authority that his secretary is constantly out on the toot, even at 10 o'clock in the morning.

Therefore, when someone rings and asks to speak to my secretary I delegate the task of answering to anyone who may happen to be in the house at the time. It might be the window-cleaner, the charlady, the messenger boy from the wine merchants, or just a friend. These persons, more often than not, have but a superficial grasp of my affairs and prove so much of an irritant to the caller that I have to step in and take the message myself.

There follows, inevitably, a long and, for me, pointless discussion about the increasing incompetence of secretarial help, which is terminated only by the caller giving me the name and address of an agency that he—or she—can personally recommend. They urge me to get in touch with the agency without further delay or—better still—seeing that I must be very, very busy, they will ring the agency on my behalf themselves. I block this kind offer as quickly as I can, and then they make me write down the telephone number and read it back to them, to make sure I've got it right.

Having Phillida Wisp has always been much more trouble than she's been worth. It is, therefore, with open arms that I welcome the new Selective Employment Tax, which mercifully will come into force within the next few days. It gives me a perfectly reasonable excuse for letting Phillida go. Yet, even here, she continues to dog my life with complications. Is she, within the meaning of the act, "a woman not contracted out of the graduated part of the National Insurance Scheme"? Is she to be treated as "over 60 and retired?" Or does Phillida come into the category of "certain married women and widows holding 'Special' cards"?

Under the circumstances, I feel that Phillida holds a "Special" card—the circumstances being that I have never had a secretary in my life and certainly hope never to be lumbered with one in the future.

Goodbye, Phillida Wisp. You go with my blessing, and a glowing reference to your next employer.

THE WORKMAN TEARS HIS TOOLS

It's as though Rubens had run out of burnt umber, as if Epstein were suffering from a deficiency of clay.

There is no typing paper in the house, or at least not in the quarto size. There is an unopened box of gleaming white foolscap but to use this would be like some such miniaturist as Fragonard trying to cover a canvas big enough to contain a Turner hurricane.

The foolscap could, of course, be reduced to quarto size by careful amputation. Fold up 3 ins. at the end, crease and tear along the line. Take another sheet of foolscap, fold, crease and tear. Then, to speed the process, take twelve sheets of foolscap, fold, crease and have such a struggle to tear that one finishes up with twelve jagged sheets, all of different length. Take a pair of scissors and try to trim these lengths so that suddenly the whole work desk is covered with strips of white paper and twelve sheets well below the accustomed and therefore inspiring quarto size. Carefully cut these sheets in half and staple them together along the top to from a handy pad for jottings and half the morning is already gone, expended in profligate style upon acting the goat.

Despite the fact that rain is cascading down in spring-like weather I do not hesitate. Into the car and down to the stationery shop, parking it fearlessly outside, beneath a No Waiting sign. Shoot in, snatch up a box of quarto, slap down the money and in no time at all I'm back at the work desk, vibrant with the virtue of decisive action and ready to weave, like S. J. Perelman, some merchandisable threads.

The new box of white quarto typing paper is green. The new box looks exactly the same as the one that contains white quarto paper, but this consignment is green. It actually says GREEN on the end of it, now that I have time to look.

I weave a merchandisable thread or two across the top of a page of green quarto, but it doesn't look right. Like some films,

I'm better in black and white than Technicolor. Green paper wants its own style.

"As I strolled through my London yesterday in the first balmy zephyrs of spring I saw the bowl of Heaven a-shimmering in the Serpentine and the daffodils dancing a queenly minuet in St. James Park . . ."

An emergency! Get back to white typing paper quickly before everything goes, with a soft gurgle, down the pipe.

This time there is a weatherproofed policeman standing in the cascading rain beside the No Waiting sign. I intercede with him through the car window, because I'm wearing only a woollen shirt in addition, of course, to trousers. No dice. He says I can see the sign and the sign means what it says. Ten minutes later I find a miraculously open space in a side street, leave the car and sprint through the rain to the stationery shop, sheltering the box of green quarto under my shirt.

There is a female shopper in the shop, trying to decide with the help of the sole assistant, a demented looking girl with a fringe hanging down *inside* her glasses, between an Easter chick and an Easter bunny as a suitable tribute to her niece, aged nine, who is very fond of animals but, on the other hand, the chicken is so sweet . . .

After several platefuls of this unspeakable slush I intervene, speaking very quickly, to explain that I am much pressed for time, desirous of changing green quarto for white, the green purchased only that very morning from this very shop—The demented girl halts the flood with severity. "Do you mind—I'm serving this lady here."

An aeon later I leave the stationery shop with a box of white quarto under my shirt, sprinting back through the rain to the car, which has gone. In its place is a vast open space, revealing a notice which says NO PARKING—SERVICE EXIT. The service exit is closed by two large wooden doors, upon which I pound unavailingly in the rain, seeking to learn what revenge the proprietors of this threadbare enterprise have wreaked upon my car, on finding it standing outside their mean and contemptible premises. There is no answer. I speed round the corner to the telephone box to report the loss of my car to the police, who have probably got it themselves.

The telephone box is filled, almost in its entirety, by an Irish building operative with the receiver pressed between his ear and his shoulder, laboriously taking down instructions from Costain himself, by the look of it, on the back of a cigarette packet. Three years later I have taken his place and am speaking to the police, when I see my car on the other side of the street, whence it has been pushed by the service exit mob. Swiftly, I sever my connection with the police and shortly afterwards am back at my work desk without, however, the new box of white quarto, which I have left in the telephone box. When I get back there it's gone.

Meticulously, I measure 3 ins. from the end of a sheet of foolscap, fold it back, crease it and tear carefully, one sheet at a time, doing the job properly . . .

FACING THE FRAUD SQUAD

One could have got ten years in Parkhurst, as director of a fraudulent company, in exactly the same way.

One might have met, socially, this genial member of the board and after a lot of laugh-laugh chat-chat found that one had been co-opted to sit on it too. "No need for you to *do* anything, old man. Just drop in from time to time, we'll give you a damn good lunch and a nice box of cigars to take away. All we really want is your name."

A month later all the other members of the board are in Liechtenstein or Buenos Aires on one-way tickets. Only the chairman, talking rather too vehemently, remains and he's gone by the following Monday, leaving the most recently co-opted member of the board to open the door to the Fraud Squad, and to explain.

It was precisely in this way that I have become the Guest Speaker at the Booksellers Association Conference, and will be rising to my feet to open the door, as it were, to the Fraud Squad at the Inter-continental Hotel in Dublin tomorrow night.

Hah-hah-hah! Hee-hee!

It was smoothly done. My publisher begged me to attend this banquet on the grounds that it would be "good for business". Apparently to ensure that it would be good for business, he promised me that I would be denied the opportunity to speak "even three words".

A fortnight later he wrote to say, "It would be marvellous if you could just let the booksellers have a couple of sentences when the serious speeches are over. Jolly them up a bit. You know?"

I have to admit that the prospect was not too distasteful. After an hour of listening to speeches about printing costs and distribution difficulties, coupled with expressions of grateful thanks to our capable and energetic secretary without whose herculean labours this Conference would never have di-diddley-dahed or even di-

diddley-bonged, the booksellers would surely be sitting ducks for something a little lighter and a little shorter, however irrelevant or disordered it might be.

It was almost possible to hear the tinkling of the chandeliers, as they were agitated by the roars of laughter and applause. Good, indeed, for business. I said I might just be able to oblige, and would leave my contribution to the inspiration of the moment.

Almost immediately on the notepaper of the Booksellers Association, a lady called Mary E. Curtis, Secretary, wrote to say how delighted she was to learn that I had consented to become Guest Speaker at the Association's banquet. "Of course," she added, "your publishers will have told you what kind of things we would like you to say."

I rang my publishers instantly, to find that one of them was in Africa and the other incommunicado, with lemon juice, at a health farm some considerable distance away.

Liechtenstein and Buenos Aires, and the fall guy chained hand and foot to the hot seat.

Hah-hah!

In the field of public speaking there is, of course, a tendency towards false modesty. "After the brilliant wit of the last speaker I can only crave your indulgence for my own inadequacy. . . ."

There is also a tendency to simulate terror before the event. "I've been practising for the last three nights in the bathroom mirror and I can't even remember my own name. . . ." And then they go on to speak competently for twenty minutes, because these boys have done it before.

I, on the other hand, have never before spoken in public in my life. A certain amount of gabbling on television, but that's a small, warm, enclosed world, with only a few members of a tiny audience visible beyond the lights. Nothing like six hundred booksellers in a banqueting hall, waiting to be instructed and amused, and feeling their oats.

As the gates of Parkhurst are oiled, however, for my reception I feel neither falsely modest nor in a state of dread. I feel only a sense of mild and not unpleasant expectation—the hopefully smiling member, newly co-opted to the board. As yet no word has been put to paper, no thought allowed to intrude itself upon my mind. I am entirely innocent——

Strewth! I'm not! I've done it before! I've got some form. I'd forgotten. That fearful golf club dinner when—insanely—I agreed to propose the health of the Guests. I spilt a pint of beer over the list of their names. I couldn't read it. I tried to sing the "Rose of

Tralee". And forgot the words. And when the bitter, shameful shambles was over someone said, "Poor old Arthur was jolly hurt—you forgot to mention his name."

Innocent—as hell.

Liechtenstein, here I come.

A WOMAN, STRADDLED ON THE GRASS!

A couple of French persons, for about half an hour, caught glimpses of us through the cypress hedge doing something perhaps a little queer in the garden the other day.

There was a perfectly rational—well, fairly rational—explanation of our activities. Would you like to guess what they were, using for guidance the probable course of the conversation, freely translated, that passed between the eye-witnesses?

He begins. "But, regard, Louise, the English are walking out on to their grass, carrying miscellaneous equipment. How strangely the foreigners behave in winter."

She replies : "How foolish it is of them, too, to spend so much time, money and water upon the growing of grass, when they could be enjoying a good harvest of potatoes, green beans, lettuce, beetroot, cauliflower, even cabbage on the same spot. Evidently, they do not love to eat well, like we French."

"Evidently. But regard again. She is carrying a mattress, of the type that one would normally use on the beach, in fine weather."

"But today, even in full sunshine, it is as cold as the North Pole. It is so true to say that the English are quite, quite mad."

"More mad than you think, dear. For is *he* not carrying a fishing-rod, to catch perhaps the trouts on the grass of his lawn. But look there! She is lying down on the mattress, and he is making supple motions with the rod. It is a good pleasure for us to have passed by today, to observe such a thing. It is to wonder that the English have the temerity to enter the Communal Market, when they believe that French trouts can be entrapped upon . . . Alas!"

"What is it that passes itself now, Hercule? My sight is impeded by the cypresses."

"So much the better, my poor Louise. She is lying prone upon the mattress and he is advancing himself upon her with his fishing rod at the ready. Does he mean to hook her through the nose? Perhaps to destroy the sight of her eyes with the tip of the rod? He is adopting a very menacing mien. Oh, no no! Veil your eyes, my love. Something of totally disgusting is about to take place. He is placing his feet on either side of her lying-down body. He is aiming at the rod at the very pinnacle of her nose. Do not push, Louise!"

"I beg it of you, Hercule. I must see. I have heard so much of the northern people's permissive society that now, in the afternoon of my life, I must see it for myself, personally. Look there! He is making his first pass. He makes to stroke the skin of her visage but oh so gently with the end of the rod. It is altogether charming, is it not? What a folly. But evidently they are well in love. But alas, now he stops his pass. He is not satisfied. But I have understood that they are always more virile than this in the Road of the King, in the department of Chelsea."

"He breaks off his actions altogether! Look he leaves his love lying desolated on the grass, while he absents himself in the other direction."

"She lies there all alone, while crying. But what is that small black object with which she plays? I have a bad view. Is it perhaps a pistol? She has the intention of shooting him for the betrayal, when he returns. But look there. He re-enters."

"He carries in his hand two cans of petrol. It is his wicked plan to burn her to the ground. Run for the policeman! But no. It is evidently not his intention to burn. For look, he places the cans on either side of her lying-down body. He puts his feet on them. He mounts. Once again he makes supple motions with the rod. The action recommences itself. My faith, she has truly shot him . . ."

"That flash of light. What a crime of passion. But regard—he does not fall. Still he makes manœuvres with the instrument. She has missed. To preserve her honour she must pull again. She has! Still he holds himself upright. Either she is a very bad shot or he is a man of iron. . . ."

Actually, we can only hope she's a pretty good shot. Admittedly, the whole thing was a little out of the ordinary, but all that she was trying to do was to take a picture of me for the jacket of a new book about golf—the picture being taken from the viewpoint of the ball, with a flash or two to brighten the winter scene.

We're still waiting for the pics to be developed. In the meantime, our reputation is undoubtedly developing far more quickly in the village.

THIS IS YOUR *WIFE?*

It seemed like a reasonable proposition, one even over-generous in some of its aspects.

Two return tickets, Nice–London–Nice, three days and nights in the Savoy Hotel, use of limousine when required and some folding money in the reticule—all for doing a little Christmas chat with Ned Sherrin on the telly.

It was Madame who received the news by telephone, while I was out. She mentioned Thames Television as the sponsors of this enterprise, but I knew that must be wrong. "It's the B.B.C.," I explained, a little wearily. "Ned always does it for the B.B.C." I accepted her brief apology. "All the same," I said, "they're certainly lashing it out—for a bankrupt corporation. Three days in the Savoy! Why three?"

"Perhaps," she suggested humbly, "they want you there early, in case of fog or trouble at London Airport."

"You didn't ask who else was on the programme, I imagine." She bowed her head. "I forgot." She brightened a little. "Anyway," she said, "we'll be able to go to the wedding as well." I had to allow that it was a fortunate coincidence.

The scene shifts to the Savoy Hotel, some evenings later. Madame has had another phone call, again while I am out. A young man called Martin Something is calling with a car to take us to the studio. I begin to worry a little about what kind of nonsense Ned Sherrin has in store for us, and who the other performers might be.

Martin Something—is it Robertson or Robinson?—arrives, introduces himself to me. Then I introduce him to Madame. They shake hands politely. Robertson-Robinson tells me the other people on the show are Malcolm Muggeridge, Germaine Greer and—he hesitates—Dee Wells. "I believe," he says, a shade anxiously, "you once had rather an argument with her on television. I hope you don't . . ."

I quell all his doubts with a generous gesture. "Fine, lovely, great," I tell him. "All forgiven and forgotten. All that happened was this. . . ."

All down the long corridor of the hotel, with Madame bringing up the rear, I told him about the argument with Dee Wells, and continued to do so in the lift. I was approaching the end when we entered the foyer, and I saw through the glass doors a Rolls-Royce in the courtyard outside. I knew a conference had been going on all day in the hotel about the take-over bid, and presumed that the newsreels were there to take pictures of the tycoons departing.

A uniformed chauffeur was waiting beside the Rolls with his back to me. I hurried out of the swing doors, with the intention of nipping round the back of the Rolls to get out of the way of the newsreel boys when the chauffeur turned round and it was Eamonn Andrews and he handed me a large red book and he said, "Patrick Campbell—this is your life."

They had been working together on this enterprise for two long months, and I'd known nothing about it. She *and* my daughter had been at rehearsal that morning when I thought they were getting their hair done for Jonquil's wedding. And we were going to be able to go to the wedding because *she* had insisted that the show be recorded the day before. All this had been done by endless telephone calls to London in a house belonging to some friends of ours down the road, when *I* thought *she* was helping them with their Christmas decorations.

There was no need for me to introduce Martin to her because she and Martin had been in unbroken communication for weeks. But, at the studio, *she* had to introduce *me* to Mary and Leslie and God knows who because they were old friends of hers and I'd never heard of them.

Duplicity beyond belief. Not only was my daughter in on it but also my step-son. In fact it was he who suggested Dee Wells to Martin as an element to distract my attention. Deception beyond compare. They had found in Athlone me old friend Micky, who used to help with the engine of a boat I had on the Shannon *in 1937*, and even he hadn't tipped me the wink.

Conspiracy most foul, and perhaps at its foulest when I found that the first guest on the show was Ned Sherrin himself, with whom I thought I was going to have a Christmas chat, in the company of Malcolm Muggeridge, Germaine Greer and the controversial, outspoken Dee Wells.

I can see now, quite clearly, how Kim Philby got away with it for so long.

Acknowledgements

The author wishes to thank all those editors and publishers within whose pages most of these pieces originally appeared, especially The Editors of *The Sunday Times, The Sunday Dispatch, Lilliput, Holiday Magazine,* and *The Irish Times,* and *Hutchinson & Co Ltd.* and *Penguin Books Ltd.*
He would also like to thank Mr. Ulick O'Connor whose idea it was that this definitive anthology would be welcome.

Index to Essays by Title